The Unadjusted Gospel

Other Together for the Gospel Conference books:

Proclaiming a Cross-Centered Theology, 2009

Preaching the Cross, 2007

TOGETHER FOR THE GOSPEL

The (Unadjusted) Gospel

Mark Dever
J. Ligon Duncan III
R. Albert Mohler Jr.
C. J. Mahaney

Contributions by
Thabiti M. Anyabwile
John MacArthur
John Piper
R. C. Sproul

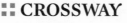

CROSSWAY
WHEATON, ILLINOIS

The Unadjusted Gospel

Copyright © 2014 by Together for the Gospel

Published by Crossway
        1300 Crescent Street
        Wheaton, Illinois 60187

Cover design: Wahl Design, Matt Wahl

First printing 2014

Printed in the United States of America

Trade paperback ISBN: 978-1-4335-3187-3
PDF ISBN: 978-1-4335-3188-0
Mobipocket ISBN: 978-1-4335-3189-7
ePub ISBN: 978-1-4335-3190-3

Library of Congress Cataloging-in-Publication Data

    The unadjusted gospel / Mark Dever, J. Ligon Duncan III, R. Albert Mohler Jr., and C. J. Mahaney ; contributions by Thabiti M. Anyabwile, John MacArthur, John Piper, and R. C. Sproul.
        pages cm. — (Together for the gospel)
    Includes bibliographical references and index.
    ISBN 978-1-4335-3187-3 (tp)
        1. Christian life. 2. Jesus Christ—Person and offices. I. Dever, Mark.
BV4501.3.U523 2014
248.4—dc23   2013036217

Crossway is a publishing ministry of Good News Publishers.

LB		23	22	21	20	19	18	17	16	15	14
15	14	13	12	11	10	9	8	7	6	5	4	3	2	1

Contents

"I would remind you, brothers, of *the gospel I preached to you*, which you received, in which you stand, and by which you are being saved . . ."

1 Corinthians 15:1–2

Introduction

Ligon Duncan

In the course of the church's history, there have been times when God has called a minister of the gospel to minister alone for a season. One might think of the missionary and his wife who set foot among an unreached people for the very first time and spend years before seeing a convert. Praise God for the fortitude and perseverance of such saints.

More commonly, God in his grace has seen fit to have his ministers live and minister together for the gospel. And how heartening and sustaining this fellowship of ministers is! Indeed, does it not prepare us for those times when, by God's strange providences, we are called to minister alone?

The Together for the Gospel Conference, first hosted in 2006 in Louisville, Kentucky, grew out of my friendship with three other ministers of the gospel: Mark Dever, C. J. Mahaney, and Al Mohler. They remain dear friends and partners in the gospel to this day. All four of us are delighted to present you these chapters drawn from the third conference of Together for the Gospel, which was held in 2010, called "The Unadjusted Gospel."

Four Observations and Two Hopes

From the very beginning the apostles warned that teachers would enter our churches with *this* or *that* version of an adjusted gospel. Not that such teachers would bear all the blame—their adjustments would find a ready market among the itching ears that demanded them.

Yet God in his grace has granted that most of us minister together for the gospel so that we might encourage one another to stand for an unadjusted gospel. It is this goal that brought the conference together in 2010 and that I have been privileged to watch in an increasing number of ministers today, especially in the younger generation represented at the

9

various Together for the Gospel conferences and other gospel-centered conferences like it.

Let me point to four things in particular that I have observed and that I pray will continue to flourish. First, I have been grateful to see a *commitment to truth* among a growing generation of ministers. More and more young pastors recognize that truth, doctrine, and theology matter. Their ministerial lives testify to this.

Ironically, you see this even among points of disagreement. People often ask what I think about Mark Dever's "teasing" me about "the sin of infant of baptism." I smile inside whenever I get this query. Mark is absolutely, deadly serious about being biblical in his practice of baptism. This is *not* teasing that you are seeing. You haven't been there at night when he's gone after me! And even though Mark thinks (he would say "knows") I'm wrong, I love him for it. And I do so not in spite of our difference on baptism but (at least in part) because of it. I love him because he cares about the truth, and he loves me enough to challenge me about it, and because he also loves me enough to forbear with me in what he considers a not insignificant error.

It seems that I have begun to see more of this posture among young ministers in our day. Some still mistakenly decide that secondary matters are unimportant matters, especially if they pertain to ecclesiology. But the unity that results from this type of calculus is, "We stand together because our differences don't matter that much." It is a shallow and shortsighted unity. One of the things I love about the generation of ministers represented at Together for the Gospel is that they know better. Everyone at the T4G conferences, I think, has been encouraged to look out and know that the crowd represents a variety of fellowships and denominational settings across which there is typically minimal interaction: fundamentalists, Sovereign Grace, Presbyterians (of various ilk, mainline and otherwise), Acts29, Methodists, Mennonites, Christian and Missionary Alliance, Bible church independents, Southern Baptists, Anglicans, Congregationalists, and more. In spite of our differences on secondary matters, many of us have discovered a unity not because the truth doesn't matter or because we have deemed important things secondary, but because we share profound things in common and love one another. So even though we disagree about important things, we rejoice in one another and in the shared theological commitments we hold.

Second, I also deeply appreciate the growing *commitment to confessionalism* among this rising generation of ministers, that is, commitment to public, deep, clear, churchly theological statements and standards. Whether it is the Westminster Confession of Faith, the Abstract of Principles, the New Hampshire Confession, the Three Forms of Unity, the Thirty-Nine Articles, the Baptist Faith and Message, or the Sovereign Grace Ministries Statement of Faith, more and more brother pastors have personally and ecclesially resisted the theological reductionism so typical of parts of evangelicalism in our time. People have sometimes said that to be truly "together for the gospel" you should care only about the gospel, while other theological commitments (such as inerrancy or a historical Adam or complementarianism) shouldn't matter. Well, the many brothers whom I have had the privilege to rub shoulders with in 2006, 2008, and 2010 understand the fatal flaw of that kind of theological reductionism and indifferentism. In the mid-twentieth century, some evangelicals suggested unity around mission instead of doctrine. The saying went, "Doctrine divides, mission unites." This enterprise failed because you can't have true unity in mission if you don't have unity in the message. Others pitted the gospel against theology and argued for a doctrinal minimalism. More and more pastors are seeing through that and so model within their own fellowships a kind of unity based on deep truth. The gospel is theology and is set in a profound theological context. Theological reductionism cannot create or sustain unity. It only marginalizes and compromises truth, and ultimately it destroys unity and undermines the gospel. There is an exhilarating gospel movement afoot today. For it to continue, it must be unashamedly and emphatically doctrinal. This is one reason we produced the T4G Affirmations and Denials.

In connection with this, there is a third thing that I see in more and more ministers and for which I praise God. They understand *the connection between theology and ministry*, truth and practice, doctrine and church life. There are many in evangelicalism today who see no connection between theology and methodology (or who do not ground their method adequately in their theology). The motto seems to be, "Fixed in our theology but flexible in our methodology." Now, flexibility is all good and fine, but is there any connection between what we believe and how we minister, between the gospel and our methodology, between truth and discipleship? If so, you wouldn't know it from this slogan. Christian ministry is informed by Christian doctrine and is therefore not infinitely flexible. The late James Boice, who served as president of the International Council on Biblical Inerrancy and founded the Alliance of Confessing Evangelicals, often said this about the connection between theology and methodology: "What you win them by, you win them to." His point was that the way we go about making a disciple will determine the kind of disciple we make. Our methods teach a theology, whether or not we realize it . So two questions are always appropriate to ask about our methods: (1) What are our methods teaching our people, and (2) Are our methods biblical; that is, are they derived from the Scriptures and sufficiently related to the gospel?

Connected to this, finally, is the *commitment to the primacy of the local church and the ordinary means of grace* that I observe in more and more ministers today. This is one reason we have held the T4G conference only every other year and why we have been deliberately minimalist organizationally. The conference is meant to encourage the local church, not compete with it. True and lasting change comes through the weekly diet of the preached Word.

I could easily go on, but these are important things that I have observed in the lives, views, and ministries of a growing generation of ministers.

Looking forward, then, what do we hope to see come of all this? In some ways the answer is, "More of the same!" We praise God for what he's already given. But here are two things that many of us hope and pray for:

> 1) We long to see the old evangelical alliances renewed around the gospel and to see a strong coalition of Bible-saturated, truth-driven, God-entranced, prayer-soaked, aggressively evangelistic, Christ-treasuring, Christ-exalting, Spirit-filled, sovereign-grace-loving, missions-advancing, hell-robbing, strong-thinking, real-need-exposing, soul-winning,

mind-engaging, vagueness-rejecting, wartime-lifestyle-pursuing, risk-taking, justice-advancing, Scripture-expounding, cross-cherishing, homosexuality-opposing, abortion-denouncing, racism-resisting, heaven-desiring, imputation-of-an-alien-righteousness-proclaiming, justification-by-faith-alone-apart-from-doing preaching, inerrancy-affirming, error-exposing, complementarian, joyful, humble, loving, courageous, happy pastors working together for the gospel. (Thanks to John Piper for so many of these words and thoughts).

2) We also want to see those pastors leading strong evangelical churches that *both* aim to be biblically faithfully in their doctrinal distinctives *and* band together for the gospel on a basis that is robustly doctrinal, historic, orthodox, Reformational, world-opposing-while-at-the-same-time-world-loving, Bible-preaching, scriptural-theology-inculcating, real-conversion-prizing, deep-biblical-evangelism-practicing, New Testament church-membership-implementing, church-discipline-applying, healthy and growing disciple-making, and biblical church leadership teaching and obeying—for the display of God's glory in the churches.

May the Lord continue to raise up such a ministerial fraternity—not on the basis of doctrinal minimalism but on shared conviction of the truth and gospel forbearance in the areas we differ; not to the detriment of our distinctives in faith and church practice but to their enhancement. And may the Lord raise up churches that display the glory and power of God's saving grace, outposts of heaven, suburbs of eternity. For the church is God's strategy, and there is no plan B.

If the T4G conferences can play a small part in encouraging these things, we will feel the effort worthwhile.

The Book

The contents of this book are, as noted, the refined presentations of T4G 2010 in Louisville. The overall theme of the conference was the unadjusted gospel, and though not all the talks directly addressed that theme, many did.

In the first chapter Mark Dever makes the case that the church is the gospel made visible. This is one reason we cannot afford to be indifferent or unbiblical in our ecclesiology. The life of the church is a gospel issue. Unhealthy churches undermine gospel proclamation. So Mark sets out to show how the local church displays the great truths of the *unadjusted* gospel about God, humanity, Christ, and the necessary response. This chapter is classic Mark and very edifying.

In chapter 2 R. C. Sproul reflects on fifty years of ministry and on the theological developments and problems that he has seen over the last half-century. His chapter is called "The Defense and Confirmation of the Gospel" and explores two important ways that the gospel has been "adjusted" in evangelicalism. First, he brilliantly surveys the problem of syncretism. Then he looks at compromises of the gospel itself, exemplified in the "Evangelicals and Catholics Together" statement on justification. No one is better suited or more qualified to speak to these things than R. C.

Al Mohler addresses trajectories toward an adjusted gospel, in chapter 3. Noting that the gospel is most often "adjusted" by those purporting to rescue it from obsolescence and imbue it with new relevance, Al asks: "How does the gospel come to be adjusted? How is it that, given the impulse to save Christianity for relevance in a modern age, some decide to make huge doctrinal adjustments? How do we trace the motivations and the patterns?" He argues that we must take a sober look at past trajectories toward adjusted gospels in an attempt to avoid similar catastrophes in the future. Then he catalogues and discusses eight different trajectories toward an adjusted gospel. I found this address riveting.

Thabiti Anyabwile's address is found in chapter 4, "Fine-Sounding Arguments: How Wrongly 'Engaging the Culture' Adjusts the Gospel." One doesn't have to listen to conversations for long in our theological neck of the woods before hearing someone speak of cultural engagement. Thabiti provocatively argues that the very language "engaging the culture," "winning the culture," or "changing the culture," ambiguous as it is, signifies that mission drift is already underway. Thabiti puts on his Van Til, as they say, and teaches us a little about "antithesis," and calls us to be gospel men.

The next chapter is John MacArthur's "Sowing Seed and Sleeping Well." In it John, reflecting on a phrase in Mark 4:27, addresses the issue of God's sovereignty and our responsibility in the matter of evangelism. He explains how knowing that God is the one who converts allows us to spend ourselves in gospel work and yet rest in confidence that God is the one who ultimately draws his people to himself. I loved how this message encouraged me to be confident in the might of the Word and to rely on the gospel as the power of God unto salvation.

John Piper's "Did Jesus Preach the Gospel of Evangelicalism?" is chapter 6. It is the best address I have ever heard on the topic. Don't be fooled by the title. His purpose is not to critique or question evangelicalism's presentation of the gospel but rather to ask, "Did Jesus preach Paul's gospel?"—the gospel of justification by grace alone, through faith alone, on the basis of Christ's blood and righteousness alone, for the glory of God alone. He tackles the question, because there is a history of scholars alleging a dichotomy between Jesus's and Paul's messages. Piper offers a riveting exegetical demonstration that Jesus's gospel is also Paul's. Indeed, Piper's explanation of Luke 18:9–14 was alone worth coming to Louisville. And his "Implications" section is theologically rich and pastorally profound. Get ready to enjoy and re-read.

In chapter 7 I ask, "Did the Fathers know the gospel?" In other words, was the gospel lost or obscured in the post-apostolic era, and did the early church fathers understand and proclaim the gospel? My chapter is not a polemic against Roman Catholicism but a commendation of the early church fathers to conservative evangelicals. I argue that we need to read the Fathers respectfully, but carefully, under the authority of Scripture. I further suggest that the gospel was not lost in the days of the church fathers but that neither did the church fathers articulate the gospel (and especially imputation) clearly, sufficiently, and specifically enough to settle current controversies about the substance of the gospel.

Finally, C. J. Mahaney gives us a real treasure in chapter 8, "Ordinary Pastors." This message deeply affected me. Few people encourage pastors like C. J., and few seem to have such a deft ability to apply this kind of material to shepherds of souls in a ministerial conference. C. J.

expounded 2 Timothy 4:1–5, giving us a biblical definition of ministry in order to clarify our goals, purify our hearts, and liberate our souls in gospel service. He leads us to God's Word in order to help protect us from the temptation to compare ourselves with others, to realign our motivations for ministry, to shield us from discouragement, and to sustain us in joyful service to God's people. It is outstanding.

Read with joy and then serve with gladness.

1

The Church Is the Gospel Made Visible

Mark Dever

How does your church make the gospel visible?

Imagine a church in which faith in Christ is affirmed but the lives of everyone in the church are otherwise, well, normal. Some people in the church are more "religious." Some are less. But all of them are happy together. The cross is regularly, though vaguely, affirmed. In fact, all the talk about God and Christ is indistinct and muted. Sin is not really discussed. And prejudices are not confronted. Do you think this church would commend the gospel?

In fact, such a church reminds me of one English bishop's response to a question about the mission of the church. Richard John Neuhaus wrote of this bishop, "He seemed a little taken aback by the question, but finally allowed that he supposed the mission, so to speak, was something like 'keeping alive aspects of the Christian heritage for those who are interested in that sort of thing.'"[1]

In a similar vein, I remember the strong words of Frank Thielman's father, Cal Thielman, who was a wonderful Presbyterian pastor and preacher for many years in Montreat, North Carolina. While driving him to his hotel during a stay in New England, I pointed out an historic church building. He asked me about the theology taught at that church. I said, "It's quite liberal. They don't really believe the Bible is true." Mr. Thielman frowned, shook his head, and snorted, "I wish God would just burn it down!"

I wonder how many churches would actually help spread the gospel *by closing down*. And how many more churches simply don't matter much.

Has your life been full of spiritually unhelpful churches? Has church been a place of testing more than resting, of trial more than triumph, of employment more than enjoyment? Would you and other members in your church say that spiritual growth has come from publishers and college fellowships, from musicians and authors, from friends and family, from websites and Internet preachers—but not really from your church itself?

In fact, a local church exists to make the unadjusted gospel visible. And the purpose of this chapter is to consider how the local church then displays the great truths of the unadjusted gospel about God, humanity, Christ, and the necessary response. These four words give you a summary of the gospel.

- *God* is holy and loving.
- *Humans* have been created good and in his image. Yet we have sinned against him and now deserve his judgment.
- *Jesus Christ,* God's one and only Son, has mercifully come to rescue us from the guilt and punishment of sin. He lived a life of perfect trust in his Heavenly Father, died in the place of sinners, and rose from the dead in victory over sin and death.
- He calls us now to *respond* by repenting of sin and putting our trust in him, and so being reconciled to God now and forever.

This is the gospel. Nothing I say means to diminish the verbal nature of the gospel and the sufficiency of God's Word. A healthy church reinforces and encourages evangelism; it doesn't replace it.

But we must also realize that an unhealthy church undermines our careful proclamation. The two are related. Even as the church is created by the gospel, so the church also reflects and helps define what we mean by the words we preach.

God

First, let's consider God and how his nature and character are to be displayed in the church.

Holiness. Distinct lives point to a distinct God. The lives of our congregation members should be marked by the fruit of God's Spirit—"love, joy, peace, patience, kindness, goodness, faithfulness, gentleness and self-control" (Gal. 5:22–23).[2] Sometimes these qualities will be welcomed and admired. Other times they will be rejected. As Paul said of his own ministry, "For we are to God the aroma of Christ among those who are being saved and those who are perishing. To the one we are the smell of death; to the other, the fragrance of life" (2 Cor. 2:15–16). Our distinct lives help to clarify what God himself is like.

Think of the command, "Be holy because I, the LORD your God, am holy" (Lev. 19:2). Peter quotes this very verse to some young Christians in Turkey in the middle of the first century. "Just as he who called you is holy, so be holy in all you do; for it is written: 'Be holy, because I am holy'" (1 Pet. 1:15–16; cf. 1 Cor. 6:9–11, 19–20). Brother pastor, is your church marked by such holiness? Or is your church so much like the world that those around you have no questions to ask you?

Is the awesomeness of God reflected in our public gatherings? Is God presented in our individual lives and church gatherings as one who is unique, holy, set apart, and distinct? In our day, we treat casualness as the height of intimacy with God. But it was not so in the Bible. Consider the responses that people in the Bible have to God. Job repents in dust and ashes (Job 42). Isaiah confesses his sinfulness (Isa. 6:5). Ezekiel falls face down (Ezek. 1:28). As Jeremiah put it, "No one is like you, O LORD; you are great, and your name is mighty in power" (Jer. 10:6). Our God is majestic and holy and awesome. And we show something of God's holiness in the reverence of our public assemblies and in our personal obedience.

Satan wants us to think of holiness as bondage, when it's really freedom. Your church and mine, by reflecting God's character, become lights that shine in a very dark world. One holy person can draw people's attention. But a holy community creates a picture of humanity that people have only dreamed of.

Love. Our churches should be distinct from the world in part through our love for God and others. Local churches should be marked by concern for others. They should be communities in which, as Paul says, "nobody should seek his own good, but the good of others" (1 Cor. 10:24). Would you notice a community like that? Is that what our non-Christian friends and neighbors see when they watch the life of our churches? Without such love, we are just like any other club.

Authority. Another important distinction from the world around us is in our understanding and use of authority. I stumbled across this idea when preaching through 2 Samuel, and I came to David's last words:

> The God of Israel spoke, the Rock of Israel said to me: "When one rules over men in righteousness, when he rules in the fear of God, he is like the light of morning at sunrise on a cloudless morning, like the brightness after rain that brings the grass from the earth." (23:3–4)

The Holy Spirit used these verses—and pastoring a congregation full of people who probably work in government!—to cause me to reflect on how our use of authority is meant to reflect God's. When Satan tempted our first parents, he was teaching them that authority and love cannot go together. He was telling them that "love" will always let people do whatever they want and that true love won't deny us something so desirable.

Of course, we know that that's false. When we regard God as Jesus did—as perfectly trustworthy—we live as God intends people to live. And his authority simply works. The right use of authority is fruitful; it blesses those underneath that authority. And it is glorious—like the light of morning at sunrise. Authority well used reflects the character of God in a special way.

So when we live in communities where we experience firm, gentle, patiently correcting, attentively guiding care for one another, then something deep inside of us is stirred. We begin to hope for a more humane life than we had previously thought possible. There is a God who both loves us and corrects us. And we want to know this God. A community functioning like this provokes people to become aware of their native thirst and hunger for such good authority.

On the other hand, without local churches like that, authority might be abused as it often is in the world, which destroys. Or it can be absent altogether, which enervates. Authority abused in the home, office, government, or church tells an especially destructive and evil lie about God. And our churches should show the world something different, something better. Our churches should be places in which trust might not be fully earned, but by God's grace it is extended. Such trust should be given to fellow Christians and especially to those called to lead our congregation. And this trust should be honored. A local church like that, where holy, loving, and healthy authority is exercised, helps to illustrate and explain something of God and his character to others in our world.

Human Beings

A healthy local church also helps to clarify the truth about human beings—what we are and what we were made to be.

Image of God. The local church should be a congregation in which all people are valued because they are made in God's image, not because of their job, status, wealth, education, or similarity to us. Therefore, churches should be characterized by friendships and relationships that cross natural boundaries.

When they do, and when they don't reflect a solitary slice of the community or one kind of person, they reflect the fullness and variety of God's creation. As Paul said, "From one man he made every nation of men, that they should inhabit the whole earth" (Acts 17:26a). A church community that lives out what it preaches about the value of each member points back to what is preached—that we were all created in God's image. A local church is not only for people of one social class or ethnicity, because God himself is the Father of all people. Our conscience, our moral sense, and our ability to relate to others show that he has made each one in his image. Our churches help to display that reality.

Depraved. But our churches should also teach and model an understanding of human depravity. I'm sad to say that we certainly model depravity when we sin. But our congregations should be places where we both teach about and confess our sin to one another. And we help one another fight it.

The church should *not* be an assembly of the self-righteous but an assembly of people who admit that they are not righteous apart from God's grace.

Is your church a community in which no one is encouraged in moral self-satisfaction but in which humility is honored? Humility should be honored because, as Christians, we know that humility is appropriate for sinners such as us. The Bible teaches that we "all have sinned and fall short of the glory of God" (Rom. 3:23). Our churches should clearly teach this important truth, even if it is culturally unpopular.

Brother pastor, in your presentations of the gospel, use God's law to awaken the conscience of the sinner. And preach about sin to the saints, as well. For instance, the fact that redeemed folks continue to struggle with sin points to one argument for church membership. Church membership offers accountability to Christians. By identifying with a particular church, members tell the pastors and other members of that church that they intend to be committed in attendance, giving, prayer, and service. They *increase others' expectations of them* in these areas, and they make it known that *they are the responsibility of this local church.*

Church membership is more related to the gospel than many pastors think. A careful practice of church membership makes our witness to non-Christians clearer. It makes it more difficult for weaker sheep to stray from the fold. It gives shape and focus to the discipleship of more mature Christians. And it aids church leaders in knowing exactly who they are responsible for. In all of this, God will be glorified.

When we step into this community of the local church, it makes us *morally visible* to ourselves. It is the context in which sinners may first see themselves *as sinners.* We do not cultivate Christian lives to hide, cover over, or deny our sinfulness. A Christian church, in that sense, may be the most honest, least flattering, frank congregation of people someone has ever come into and yet, at the same time, be marked by love, encouragement, and sensitivity, because we are a congregation of people who believe that not only is the visitor a sinner but that *we* are *all* sinners.

Years ago, when I was preparing to leave England and move back to the United States, I met a relative whom I had never met before. After some chitchat, she asked me what I was going to do. I answer a question about my occupation in one of two ways—tactful or direct. I decided to go for direct: "I'm going to be a Baptist preacher."

"Oh!" she said, dropping her eyes down to her coffee and stirring it, obviously uncomfortable with the turn the conversation had just taken. "I don't have much use for church."

I waited a moment and then said, "Do you mind if I ask you why?"

She replied, "They're just pits of vipers—all the gossip and backbiting!"

I then asked, "And do you think the world outside is really any better?"

She said, "Well, I guess not, but at least they know they're vipers!"

Again, I waited a moment and then observed, "You might be surprised how much I agree with you. You're right about the world—it is a pit of vipers. And I think you're right about the church, too! I know that the church is a pit of vipers. But I think where I would disagree is that I don't think that the world realizes that they are a pit of vipers. But Christians do. Now there are churches that don't realize that they are a pit of vipers, and I wouldn't touch those churches with a ten-foot pole! But any church I go to will know that it is a pit of vipers. That's why we are there. And you know what? There is always room for one more to slither on in!"

When our churches confess that humans are made in the image of God *and* that humans are fallen and depraved, we offer a compelling and accurate description of human nature. It captures the good and the bad. The simple ability to understand ourselves and our world in such realistic terms will both bring sanity and commend the gospel. It will discourage our churches from being glibly triumphalistic or morbidly pessimistic. And we pastors must lead the way in trying to cultivate the appropriate humility within ourselves, as we confess our sins to God and to our brothers and sisters.

Without a community built to teach, understand, and live in the light of these twin truths, our real problem will be left undiagnosed. It is our understanding of human sin, combined with an understanding of God's goodness and righteousness, that sets up the human problem—how can we sinners be accepted by such a holy, loving, and good God?

Christ

That brings us to a third aspect of the gospel that the church makes visible—the Savior Jesus Christ.

Person. In one sense, it is difficult to speak of making the unique Son of God visible. He *was* visible, but now he is interceding for us before the throne of God, and he will visibly return in power and great glory to judge the world. In a very profound sense, he is not here.

Precisely what marks out this current stage of redemptive history is that Jesus is present with us through his Spirit, his Word, and his people. He is invisible to us at this juncture, between his ascension and his return. But the local church should be a community in which the unique person of Jesus Christ—fully God and fully man—is to be *metaphorically* visible in the sense that we bear his name, his teaching, his gospel purposes, his glory, and his fame. The church worships Christ.

We can certainly take up the New Testament language of the church as the body of Christ. And we know that we who are filled with his Spirit and purchased by his blood are his temple (Acts 20:28; 1 Cor. 3:16).

So how do we make Christ visible in our local churches? We do so by teaching that he is fully God and fully man, who become incarnate for us and for our salvation. And we do so by imitating him in our lives. We show who Jesus is by worshiping him and being devoted to him on Sunday and every day.

Without a community that teaches this message, the truth about Jesus Christ would be unknown. Without a church in whom God's Spirit works, people would never go to tell and live out this message, and the message would never be told. Without local churches like this, Christ would be left without a witness in this world.

Work. At the very heart of our local congregation, however, is the commitment to understand and present not only *who* Jesus Christ is but also *what* Jesus Christ did. In the same way, our lives together should be provocative. We should form communities in which loving forgiveness is regularly granted. We should be collections of people marked not by self-righteousness but by a knowledge of our own sin, by humility, and by an understanding of our need for grace and therefore by a gracious and merciful attitude.

Your church and mine should be marked by outgoing love. Our churches should demonstrate the love of God. "But surely we know and love God," someone might say, "because our hearts are moved, and tears roll down our cheeks when we sing this hymn or that chorus." No, says John. "We know that we have passed from death to life, because we love our brothers. Anyone who does not love remains in death. . . . This is how we know what love is: Jesus Christ laid down his life for us. And we ought to lay down our lives for our brothers" (1 John 3:14, 16).

God is love, and he will be *known* as such. And if we are his children, we will love, too, not just on the basis of being created in the image of God, as we were thinking about a few moments ago, but also on the basis of being bought by the blood of the Lamb. What about those in your congregation who are different from you—of a different nationality, a different ethnicity, or a different political view?

Brother pastor, we must teach our people to prize and cherish those differences. Help them to recognize that those differences are God-given opportunities for a church to express and display love in ways that are inexplicable to the world. Remember what John heard the creatures and elders singing before the Lamb in heaven: "With your blood you purchased men for God from every tribe and language and people and nation" (Rev. 5:9).

In our world today, generation seems to be one of the biggest divides, but our churches should offer a different kind of picture. I remember how excited an older lady in our congregation became when she recounted the story of how a young man in our church brought his small group of young men to spend their Friday night with her in the rest home after she had a stroke. She said the other folks in the rest home asked her who she was—was she some kind of celebrity? She said no; it was simply what her church was like.

We have seen non-Christian friends converted simply by watching the relationships in our congregation as the gospel begins to come alive to them.

I have sometimes said to young theology lovers in our congregation, "If you love to read Wayne Grudem and John Piper but won't inconvenience yourself to go pick up an older person and give him a ride to church, I don't know if you're a Christian." It is the nature of loving real people that such love can become difficult and inconvenient. It's what happens when we covenant together with a flock of imperfect sheep. On the other hand, the lack of commitment fostered by a lack of formal membership tempts our flesh and presents an opportunity for self-deception. The inconveniences of love are minimized, and therefore the worth of our love offers less compelling evidence of its divine nature. Membership functions to instruct us in the very nature of Christian love and to encourage its expression.

How can we point to Christ's sacrifice of himself for us if we are not members of Christ's body who sacrifice ourselves for one another?

It is as we sacrifice ourselves for one another that racism ends in the church: "Now in Christ Jesus you who once were far away have been brought near through the blood of Christ" (Eph. 2:13).

It is as we sacrifice ourselves for one another that favoring the wealthy ends in the church: "My brothers, as believers in the Lord Jesus Christ, do not show favoritism" (James 2:1). He who was rich beyond all splendor all for our sakes became poor.

Christ's example of sacrifice also leads us to forgive: "Forgive as the Lord forgave you" (Col. 3:13).

Our evangelism must be more than advertising. Instead, our churches must be characterized by an unusual degree of mutual care, even going to the level of regularly inconveniencing ourselves to love others: "By this all men will know that you are my disciples, if you love one another" (John 13:35). Our love for one another becomes a description of Christ's love for us.

Christ's sacrifice also warns us against a wrong form of denominationalism. Think of Jesus's prayer "for those who will believe in me . . . that all of them may be one" (John 17:20–21). You know, don't you, that there can be a right and a wrong denominationalism? Given our disagreements over some points of the Bible, denominations are good, not bad, because they allow each church to follow Jesus according to conscience, and they keep strife between Christians of different convictions at bay. But if those denominations become the ultimate focus of our loyalty, then they are terrible idols. Keep clear fences but keep them low, and shake hands over them often.

One thing a faithful pastor must also do is lead his flock to unity even against those members who believe the right thing but value their belief in an unbalanced way and would divide the flock over it.

Christians should divide from other Christians reluctantly and only over those matters in which agreement is necessary to function as a congregation. So in my own church's statement of faith, you will find statements only on those matters that we think are essential for salvation *and* that are essential for living peacefully and productively together in one congregation, united and happy.

In fact, all this is captured by two facts about our church's outdoor sign, which reads: "Capitol Hill Baptist Church." (1) The word "Baptist" is there, because a decision about baptism is necessary for functioning together as a church. (2) Yet the word "Baptist" is the smallest word, because we want to signify that non-Baptist churches can still be true Christian churches.

Our congregation's love and holiness should point back to the supreme expression of God's own love and holiness on the cross of Christ. It is the death of God's Son that allows the Father to forgive with both justice and mercy, thus perfectly fulfilling both his holiness and his love. That is why Paul can say that God presented Christ as a *sacrifice of atonement*, as a *propitiation* (Rom. 3:25). In Christ's death on the cross, God offered the solution to the problem of the fall. He solved the ancient riddle of how he as a holy and good God could show mercy. Do you remember how it was stated in Exodus 34, at the end of the Golden Calf debacle?

> Then the LORD came down in the cloud and stood there with [Moses] and proclaimed his name, the LORD. And he passed in front of Moses, proclaiming, "The LORD, the LORD, the compassionate and gracious God, slow to anger, abounding in love and faithfulness, maintaining love to thousands, and forgiving wickedness, rebellion and sin. Yet he does not leave the guilty unpunished." (Ex. 34:5–7)

This really is the riddle of the Old Testament, indeed of the ages. How could God both "forgive wickedness, rebellion and sin" and yet "not leave the guilty unpunished"?

With the coming of Christ, we learn the way. God *has* saved us, and in a way that *is* consistent with his character. At the cross of Christ he demonstrated his justice—he *is* good and therefore will take vengeance. No sin will go unpunished. And yet, at the same time, at the cross he showed himself to be full of mercy. Therefore Paul could say that God is the "just and the justifier of those who have faith in Jesus" (Rom. 3:26).

How is God's character here reflected in our churches? Without the local church actually *being* a community like this, the cross, even if it is taught, seems unrelated to life. Unless our churches live as we have described them—cross-centered and cross-relishing, working for Christ's sacrifice for us to be the center of our relationship with God and with each other—our relationship with God will be taken for granted, and our relationships with each other will become casual and selfish. Without this Christlike love, our lives raise no questions, excite no expectations, and hold out no hope.

Response

That brings me to the last aspect of the gospel that our churches illustrate: the right response to Christ.

Repentance. Our congregations should teach and model repentance. A community in which people humbly admit their faults and then work to change is a remarkable community. How appropriate that baptism—a confession of our uncleanness, of our needing to be washed—stands as the sign of admission to this community. This is why we can say that our church is only for sinners, and among them only for repenting sinners.

For example, Christians must repent of selfishness by helping other people follow Jesus. Helping others follow is a basic part of following Jesus ourselves. The letters of James and 1 John clearly teach that the Christian life may be personal, but it is not private. Just think of what John says about those who claim to love God but not their brothers. Repentance necessarily involves us in the lives of others, which means that the local church is where our repentance should become visible.

We should not try to run the race of the spiritual life alone. I remember asking a godly friend once why he came to church only in time for the sermon. He responded that he didn't get anything out of the rest of the service. I asked him if he had ever thought of joining the church. He looked at me like I had three heads and then said, "I know what I'm here to do—evangelize and disciple! If I linked arms with all those people, they'd just slow me down."

I thought for a minute and then asked him, "Do you think that if you joined arms with all those people, they might slow you down, but you might help to speed them up, and God might be more concerned about the corporate whole than simply about you?"

The fact that we are sinners called to repent sometimes means we need other people to help us repent. Sometimes it even takes the corrective discipline of the whole congregation to help us repent. In our congregations, we love each other by holding each other accountable. All of us will have times when our flesh wants to go a different way from what God has revealed in Scripture. And submitting to the loving discipline and accountability of a local church is part of how we love God, who is holy and calls us to be holy. He does not want us to bear his name in vain.

What a tremendous privilege and great responsibility it is to make gospel repentance visible! It means that repentance must typify our churches. Admitting our sins and repenting of them continually depicts the gospel and makes it credible.

And, brother pastor, it is especially important for you to build relationships and set up structures in which you can receive godly encouragement and correction. How are you and I modeling repentance in our lives?

Faith. A local church is a community in which invisible realities control our behavior. It is where belief in God's promises are the foundation of the hopes that we live for. It is where God's Word is central to our lives. Your church and mine are communities that should treasure the preaching of God's Word, because it is our GPS system. God's Word directs us like a GPS directs our cars on the road. (Though, unlike the GPS, he never makes any errors!) We trust God's promises. We live in hope. And just as certainly as God has always created his people by his Word, so we can be certain of the centrality of God's Word in our lives and churches.

People say that we are in a visual age today, but we have always been in a visual age. We were made that way. There is an immediacy to our sense of sight. We long to see. But consider how God reveals himself to us. When our first parents sinned, they were cast out of the garden. They lost sight of God. Then, in God's amazing grace, God spoke a Word of promise to them. When they were out of the sight of the eye, God came to them by the Word addressed to their ears. We are not in the age of the *eye* but of the *ear*.

Ever since the fall, we have been in the age of the ear, and the centrality of the Word in our churches points to this salvation reality. God's Holy Spirit creates his people by his Word: "Faith comes from hearing the message" (Rom. 10:17).

We can, in a sense, create a people by other means. And this is the great temptation of pastors. We can create a people around a certain ethnicity. We can create a people around a fully graded choir program. We can find people who will get excited about a building project or a denominational identity. We can create a people around a series of house groups, where each feels loved and cared for. We can create a people around a community service project. We can create a people around dress codes, around opportunities for socializing for young mothers, or around singles doing Christian cruising. We can create a people around men's groups. We can even create a people around the personality of a preacher. And God can surely use all these things. But we can only see the true church of God if it has been created by the Word of God—by those who crave it and feed off of it for their souls.

Of course, a day will come when faith gives way to sight, and sermons will be no more. And let me tell you, there is nobody who looks forward to that more than I do—when we don't need faith anymore because we can see the Lord. That is the climax of the Bible: "They will see his face" (Rev. 22:4). At that point this old cane of faith can be cast aside, as we can run and see him with our eyes. But we are not there right now. We are still laboring under the results of the sins of our first parents and our own sins. Yet because of God's grace this is not a time of total despair. He gives us his Word, and he gives us faith. We are in a day of faith. So, like our first parents before us and like Noah and Abraham, the Israelites, and the ancient apostles, we rely on God's Word.

Most fundamentally, our local church is a community of people shaped by our belief in Jesus Christ and his promise to save all who will trust in him. Sermons are, therefore, central to our churches because it is in God's Word that we have these promises held out.

This sacrifice and our anticipation of salvation now and ultimately are signified by the Lord's Supper. It offers us a dress rehearsal of the marriage supper of the Lamb, when we will be forever and finally reconciled to God and brought into his unmediated presence.

Our community makes sense only in light of these truths, and these truths are illustrated and displayed by our church's life. We live differently because of believing in God's truths. Paul even argues that we give differently because of God's promises (2 Corinthians 9). Consider, for instance, the example of the early Christians: "You sympathized with those in prison and joyfully accepted the confiscation of your property, because you knew that you yourselves had better and lasting possessions" (Heb. 10:34). Our giving—our sacrifices—for each other makes sense only in light of these coming realities.

A local church, then, is a congregation of people who trust God. And it is not just our understanding of all his purposes that we trust, because those are sometimes hidden from us. We trust his character. We are a community of people shaped by our common understanding of and expectations for the future. Our fears about the future, of course, are rooted in those places where *our* will differs from God's will. But as a whole, a local congregation consists of people whose future is beginning to take shape even now. And we move together trusting God.

We are to be a community of people like Jay Smith in London. Jay preaches in Hyde Park at Speakers' Corner to passing Muslims. After the subway bombings a few years ago, he asked the assembled crowd what they thought of the bombing. Many said that those who had committed those crimes were heroes. Jay replied to one crowd in which I was standing, "My wife understands that I will probably *be killed* for what I am doing."

So why would Jay risk his life that way? Jay risks it because he knows that it is good to announce the gospel, and he lives in the sure and certain hope of the resurrection of the body, and, therefore, nothing he will need for eternity is within the power of mere mortals to take away.

Churches are whole communities of people who live by this same hope for the future.

Without such a community, a call to trust in Christ alone for salvation begins to seem abstract and empty. Again and again, people simply won't know what we mean when we call them to trust in Christ or to believe in him. Our local churches illustrate and make believable repentance for sins and trust in Christ.

Conclusion

Brother pastor, do you see something more of how the church is Jesus's evangelism plan?

Many Protestants have begun to think that because the church is not essential to the gospel, it is not important to the gospel. This is an unbiblical, false, and dangerous conclusion. Our churches are the proof of the gospel. In the gatherings of the church, the Christian Scriptures are read. In the ordinances of the church, the work of Christ is depicted. In the life of the church, the character of God himself should be evident. A church seriously compromised in character seems to make the gospel itself irrelevant.

The church is important because it is tied to the good news itself. The church is to be the appearance of the gospel. It is what the gospel looks like when played out in the lives of people. Take away the local church, and you take away the visible manifestation of the gospel in the world. Christians in churches, then, are called to practice "display evangelism," so that the world will witness the reign of God begun in a community of people made in his image and reborn by his Spirit. Christians—not just as individuals but as God's people bound together in churches—are the clearest picture the world sees of who God is and what his will is for them.

Brother pastor, you may be very careful in explaining the gospel, and rightly so. But you should also be careful for the church that Christ gave this gospel to. Recapturing seminaries and even whole denominations for the gospel is good work, but its fruit will not last long if we don't get on with the work of cleaning up thousands upon thousands of local congregations that are bearing a poor witness to Christ. Don't undermine in the pew what you preach in the pulpit. Don't think that you help the cause of Christ by denouncing abortion from your pulpit when you let the doctors who perform them remain as members in good standing in your church. Sermons about love ring hollow in the church that will not confront stinginess, self-centeredness, or gossip. Pray that God will use our imperfect but really changing congregations for his glory. May John Newton's prayer for himself be our prayer to God for our churches: "I am not what I ought to be. I am not what I wish to be. I am not what I hope to be. Yet I can truly say, I am not what I once was. *By the grace of God* I am what I am."

In the church the content of the gospel should be taught and the character of the gospel should be displayed. Paul writes, "His intent was that now, through the church, the manifold wisdom of God should be made known to the rulers and authorities in the heavenly realms, according to his eternal purpose which he accomplished in Christ Jesus our Lord" (Eph. 3:10–11). The church is the pattern for, the foreshadowing of, God's work. And it is also the means he uses to bring about his glory in our families and neighborhoods and also in the world and even beyond— throughout the rulers and authorities in the heavenly realms.

Have you realized that all *that* has been going on in your local church? What gospel is your church making visible?

2

The Defense and Confirmation of the Gospel

R. C. Sproul

As I reflect on fifty years of ministry and on the theological developments and problems that I have seen over that half-century, I can think of more problems that I have witnessed and more concerns that I have for the church of our day than I can possibly cover in this brief chapter. So I'm going to restrict my comments to two of the most important concerns that I see and how they have developed over the past fifty years.

In my boyhood days, there was a popular song by Johnny Mercer that reached the top of the charts. The lyrics to this song went like this:

> You've got to accentuate the positive,
> Eliminate the negative
> Latch on to the affirmative,
> Don't mess with Mr. In-Between.[1]

In this brief overview, I want to deal first with the danger of messing with "Mr. In-Between." Then I want to look at the danger of messing with the gospel itself.

Messing with Mr. In-Between

Let me begin by directing your attention to the New Testament, to the apostle Paul's second letter to the Corinthians, where we read:

> We have spoken freely to you, Corinthians; our heart is wide open. You are not restricted by us, but you are restricted in your own affections. In return (I speak as to children) widen your hearts also.

Do not be unequally yoked with unbelievers. For what partnership has righteousness with lawlessness? Or what fellowship has light with darkness? What accord has Christ with Belial? Or what portion does a believer share with an unbeliever? What agreement has the temple of God with idols? For we are the temple of the living God; as God said,

> "I will make my dwelling among them and walk among them,
> and I will be their God,
> and they shall be my people.
> Therefore go out from their midst,
> and be separate from them, says the Lord,
> and touch no unclean thing;
> then I will welcome you,
> and I will be a father to you,
> and you shall be sons and daughters to me,
> says the Lord Almighty."

Since we have these promises, beloved, let us cleanse ourselves from every defilement of body and spirit, bringing holiness to completion in the fear of God. (6:11–7:1)

I'm afraid that this text often is used as a justification for radical apartheid, separation to what we would call the "secondary level," where people retreat from any kind of interaction with the world or with other groups of believers. But I don't think that it was the apostle's intent to give a credo for radical separatism. I think Paul was addressing one of the principal problems that has plagued the church since the days of Abel.

That brings me back to "Mr. In-Between." In the Old Testament, one of the critical problems that the people of God faced in every generation was syncretism. This was the attempt to blend elements of pagan religion with elements of the religion of Israel. Ideas were borrowed from the cults of Baal, Ashtoreth, or Dagon, then blended with Judaism. Such attempts always ended in disaster, because syncretism is a type of synthesis, and synthesis is what I call "Mr. In-Between."

To understand what has taken place in the past fifty years, we have to go back a little earlier to the watershed moment of Immanuel Kant's critique of the traditional arguments for the existence of God and the attempt of theoretical thought to reach beyond the realm of this world into the realm of transcendence, the realm of the supernatural. Kant's critique, written in the eighteenth century, was an attempt to demonstrate that, from a viewpoint of theoretical thought, it is impossible to move from this world to the realm of transcendence. That skepticism and agnosticism gave way to the nineteenth century's embrace of radical naturalism. Naturalism taught that the natural realm is all that exists. There is no supernatural realm. It's not that we cannot *know* the supernatural realm but that there *is* no supernatural realm.

The first synthesis that took place at that time was the attempt to merge naturalism and historic Christianity. That yielded what is called "nineteenth-century liberalism."

With that watershed experience with Kant, the history of theoretical thought took a significant turn. Up until the time of Kant, theoretical thought was directed toward either questions of metaphysics or questions of epistemology. But once skepticism about reaching the truth of metaphysics set in, the attention of nineteenth-century thought centered on this world, and thinkers began to focus on giving a philosophy of history. There were two important men who sought to develop a philosophy of history. One was Karl Marx, whose philosophy is known as "dialectical materialism." But Marx's philosophy piggybacked on a more comprehensive philosophy of history that was introduced by the man whom I believe was the leading philosopher of the nineteenth century, Friedrich Hegel.

Hegel's philosophy of history could be called "dialectical idealism." For Hegel, the whole movement of history can be explained by the dialectical conflict of ideas, not of economic forces, as Marx saw it. It was the conflict between thesis and antithesis. Hegel said that for every thesis set forth, inevitably an antithesis is proposed, and these two are then locked in conflict. This conflict can be resolved only if a synthesis can be achieved between the thesis and antithesis. So it is necessary to take an element from the thesis and an element from the antithesis and blend them to get what Hegel called a "synthesis." But as soon as that synthesis is achieved, it essentially becomes a thesis, and then someone challenges it with its antithesis, and there is a new conflict that can be resolved only by a new synthesis. So history moves up a ladder of thesis, antithesis, and synthesis.

I labor this point because the history of heresy, I believe, follows this course of action. Decades ago, Francis Schaeffer gave a serious warning when he said the church had lost its sense of antithesis. If that was true thirty years ago, it's true with a vengeance today. The relativism of our culture allows anyone to have a thesis just as long as he does not reject the antithesis.

Nineteenth-century liberalism was the first destructive synthesis that tried to marry naturalism with historic Christianity. That attempt to de-supernaturalize the Christian faith by denying the miracles of Jesus, the virgin birth, the resurrection, the return of Christ, and all the other supernatural aspects of Christianity was a fool's errand, because Christianity essentially is antithetical to naturalism. They cannot live together.

At the end of the nineteenth century, with the church facing this crisis, a new movement emerged in Europe, principally in Switzerland and in Germany, with the rise of so-called dialectical theology, which is more popularly known as "neoorthodoxy." The leading patrons of this movement were Karl Barth, Emil Brunner, and, in the early days, Rudolf Bultmann. The agenda of these men was to overcome the barrenness of nineteenth-century liberalism that had reduced Christianity to the things of this world and to restore a place for a transcendent God who speaks to us through the revelation that is contained or at least mediated through the Bible. Barth and others called the church back to a biblical faith and away from the rational speculation that followed Hegelian philosophy.

Neoorthodoxy found its patron saint in the nineteenth-century philosopher Søren Kierkegaard, who also reacted strongly against Hegel and his form of rationalism, and cried for a new way of understanding truth. For Kierkegaard, truth is not a rational concept, a cognitive idea, but is, rather, subjectivity. It cannot be captured in creeds and formulas. Creeds and formulas are for spectators to life, those who are not passionately, existentially thrown into the midst of all of the problems of pain and suffering, which is where the Christian church is supposed to be. Kierkegaard said the problem with our age is that it is paltry; it lacks passion. He said he preferred to read the pages of the Old Testament because the people there lie, steal, and commit adultery; in other words, they're real. They are existentially engaged in life and in the ambiguities that surround faith in God.

So a new view emerged from dialectical theology as Barth and others called for a return to sacred Scripture in the life of the church. But we must not mistake this for a return to orthodoxy. At the same time that Barth and Brunner repudiated nineteenth-century liberalism, they also repudiated the orthodox view of the Bible. There was no room in their theology for an objectively inspired, infallible, inerrant Bible. Barth considered the doctrine of inerrancy to be an example of what he called "biblical Docetism," a deification of the writings of human beings without taking seriously the most human element of the authors of Scripture, which is error itself. He was fond of citing the famous maxim *errare humanum est*, "To err is human." Barth said that what we have in Scripture is the *verbum Dei*, that is, "the Word of God," but not the *verba Dei*, "the words of God." The Bible itself is not objective divine revelation, and revelation certainly cannot be reduced to propositions. Rather, the Bible is a vehicle for the Holy Spirit to speak in and through to people as they engage with it. Barth and Brunner said that rather than being revelation, the Bible is a pointer or witness to revelation. The Bible becomes the Word of God for us when the Holy Spirit works through its words to awaken faith more or less existentially in our hearts.

This idea gave rise to attempts within evangelical Christianity to flee from the classic standards of inerrancy and infallibility. There have been countless arguments that inerrancy was the invention of seventeenth-century Protestant scholastics. It is said that inerrancy was unknown in earlier church history, and that it certainly was not a doctrine fostered by the magisterial Reformers such as Martin Luther and John Calvin. It is true that the word *inerrancy* cannot be found in the writings of Luther or Calvin. Luther said that the Scriptures never err. As they say, "A rose by any other name would smell as sweet." If the doctrine of inerrancy was not taught by Luther and Calvin, I'm prepared to dine on my hat. Even though the doctrine was not called "inerrancy" in the sixteenth century, the battle for authority under the banner of *sola Scriptura* certainly included that concept.

Of the neoorthodox theologians who sought to make this synthesis between Christianity and existentialism, Bultmann became the most radical. He finally concluded that we cannot make sense of the Bible if we read it as modern people. He believed that we cannot use such things as electricity, telecommunications, and modern antibiotics while still believing in a world filled with angels, demons, and miracles. The point of the Bible, Bultmann said, is not what happened in history. To get anything out of the Bible, we have to hear the Word of God not on the horizontal plane of redemptive history but on a vertical axis, where God speaks to us directly and immediately from above, provoking in our souls that moment of decision by which we enter into a life of faith. This idea was rightly called not only "neo-liberalism" but also "neo-Gnosticism."

The idea here is that the Word of God cannot be reduced to propositions, to truths that can be contained in our creeds and confessions. The title of a little book that Brunner wrote says it all: *Wahrheit als Begegnung*, which means "Truth as Encounter." Brunner saw truth not as a series of sentences, assertions, or affirmations, but as an event—specifically, as an encounter with a person. This idea has become very popular in our day.

Other attempts to achieve a synthesis between existential philosophy and historic Christianity were tried in this country, for example, by Paul Tillich in his systematic theology. Similarly, Russian philosopher Nikolai Berdyaev attempted to synthesize existential philosophy and Eastern Orthodoxy, just as Martin Buber sought a synthesis of existentialism and contemporary Judaism.

Skipping ahead, there was a synthesis that took hold in Europe in the 1960s before it made its way across the ocean and helped turn the culture of the United States upside down. This was the advent of so-called liberation theology, which was a conscious attempt to create a synthesis between historic Christianity and Marxist philosophy. Again, this was a fool's errand. How can one who knows anything about the philosophy of Marx and about historic Christianity not see that a synthesis of the two is simply not possible? But movements sprang up all over the world espousing "liberation"—free speech, free sex, free abortions, and all the rest—with an underlying Marxist philosophy.

There followed a new synthesis between analytical philosophy and Christianity. As existentialism gave way to logical positivism, and logical positivism in the realm of philosophy to analytical thought, the question was raised, "How can we embrace the insights of analytical philosophy and still be Christians?" The question then became, "Is any of our language about God meaningful, or is it all meaningless?" Since God cannot be verified with the senses, we have no scientific references for God. Therefore, are our statements about God intelligible, or are they merely expressions of human emotion? With that came the "God-talk controversy," which went to the extreme of theothanatology, the "death of God theology," which was born amid the doubts about the adequacy of human language to say anything meaningful about God. Again, it was another synthesis with a pagan philosophy that did much damage to the church.

Other such syntheses have arisen more recently. I think, for example, of open theism, which involved a synthesis between process philosophy and historical Christianity, as well as a humanistic understanding of the free will of man. Clark Pinnock self-consciously made the statement that he was trying to design a theology that would move away from classical theism to what he called "free-will theism," making room for mutations, changes, and learning within God himself. When I was doing my doctoral work in Europe in the mid-1960s amid the rise of Bultmann, my professor, G. C. Berkouwer, made the comment, "Theology can sink no lower." But he hadn't seen the death-of-God movement or open theism; if he had, I don't think he would have made that hasty rush to judgment.

Likewise, Peter Jones has done a remarkable service for the church today by pointing out all the attempts to synthesize Gnosticism and new-age thinking.

All of these movements mess with "Mr. In-Between." None of them is satisfied to declare from one generation to the next that which we have received from the apostles, the unvarnished Word of God that does not need to be made more palatable by gilding it with the brass of pagan philosophy.

Messing with the Gospel

Of course, I think the greatest crisis I have witnessed in my lifetime is over the gospel itself. When I graduated from seminary, there were two things I was sure of with respect to American evangelicalism. I was convinced that the two rock-solid premises that bound together evangelicals in all of their diversity were the doctrines of *sola Scriptura* on the one hand and *sola fide* on the other. I certainly did not anticipate the crisis that we had to address through the International Council on Biblical Inerrancy when we saw evangelical institutions abandoning *sola Scriptura*. But if that was unforeseen, what really amazed me was the crisis that developed over our understanding of the gospel. Whatever else united evangelicals from every conceivable background and denomination, it was the wholesale commitment to *sola fide*, justification by faith alone. Or so I thought.

The first crack that I saw in my lifetime was the outbreak of the lordship-salvation controversy, which, for the most part, was an intramural debate within the family of dispensational evangelicals, who argued over whether one can embrace Jesus as Savior without at the same time embracing him as Lord. This controversy, frankly, astonished me; I never thought something like that would take place. But there was fallout from that, and more issues regarding the gospel were soon raised.

To me, the most surprising movement within evangelicalism was the initiative that led to the document called "Evangelicals and Catholics Together," published in 1994. ECT was initially understood as an attempt for evangelicals to join with Roman Catholic signatories in an effort to address serious common-grace matters that were the focal points of controversies tearing at the very fabric of our culture and society—issues such as abortion, the sanctity of marriage, the philosophy of relativism that had taken over the public school system, and others. This document was an attempt at co-belligerency between leading evangelicals and Roman Catholic scholars to address issues that are important to all of us. The only problem was that in a small section of that document the authors declared to the world that they had a unity of faith in the gospel. I thought that declaration vitiated the very real value of the rest of the document with respect to the cultural issues. When I saw that statement, I asked myself: "How have we come to have a unity of faith in the gospel? What happened? Did Rome repudiate the Council of Trent? Did evangelicals come to Rome and say, 'Mea culpa,' and abandon their insistence on the doctrine of justification by faith alone?"

That particular initiative had a tremendously negative impact on evangelical unity, although, in truth, it didn't hurt or destroy evangelical unity; it just exposed that what we thought was unity was not really there. In conversation with evangelical signatories of that document, I made this observation: "You say that you have a unity of faith in the gospel with people who embrace the Council of Trent, which condemns the gospel as we understand it. I know I don't have a unity of faith in the gospel with those people. So my question is this: Do I have a unity of faith in the gospel with *you*?"

Well, this was no small issue, so a second document, "The Gift of Salvation," was presented in 1997 in an attempt to address the question of whether we really agreed on justification by faith alone after all these years. That document almost addressed that issue, and the signers affirmed in it common areas of conviction. But at the end they said that the language of imputation would have to be left on the table for later consideration. Again I had to speak out, and I said that if we don't have imputation, we don't have *sola fide*. And if we don't have *sola fide*, we don't have the gospel.

Is all this merely the ragings of abstract theologians? In the sixteenth century, when the church was torn apart by the Protestant Reformation, there were serious attempts to heal the breach and to bring union and peace back to Christendom. One of the most important meetings took place at Regensburg, Germany, when the leaders of the Protestant movement and the leaders of Rome came close to resolving the difficulty. What caused it to fall apart? The cause was imputation. Here is the issue: Is the ground of our justification a righteousness that, as Trent says, inheres or is inherent, within us, or is the ground of our justification a righteousness that is apart from us, what Martin Luther said is *extra nos,* an alien righteousness, namely, the righteousness of Jesus for us?

Now, here's where "Mr. In-Between" comes in and insists we can agree on this. It's both, he says. But I'm afraid there is no *tertium quid*. The ground of our salvation is either a righteousness that is in us or a righteousness that we receive by imputation. This is a true either/or issue. And that has been sorely obscured.

To get a handle on that, I want to go back in time to 1958. During that year, the tenure of Pope Pius XII ended with his death. It had been a long pontificate, and he had been a very influential pope, so the choice of his successor was very difficult. The white smoke did not appear immediately from the chimney of the Vatican, as the College of Cardinals had to deliberate seriously to find a candidate that they all could agree on. In the providence of God, the Roman Catholic Church basically turned to a compromise candidate whom the cardinals saw as an interim pope until a greater unity could be reached. They chose the seventy-seven-year-old Angelo Giuseppe Roncalli, who then took the name John XXIII.

This elder statesman shocked not just the church but the whole world by doing something that was completely unexpected. He called for a new ecumenical council, a council for the whole Roman Church. It was to be like Vatican Council I, which had been the first council after the Council of Trent in the sixteenth century. Many people had believed that Vatican Council I would be the last ecumenical council of the church for the simple reason that it was at Vatican I in 1870 that the infallibility doctrine was defined under the leadership of Pius IX. With that, the leaders of the Roman Catholic Church declared that the pope is infallible, and, therefore, there would be no need to hold another ecumenical council; the church would be able to settle any theological controversies or disputes that might come along in the future by appealing to the decisions of the holy father. That is why it was so shocking when John XXIII called for a new council, Vatican Council II, which I think has perhaps been more misunderstood by Protestants than any ecumenical council in history.

John XXIII's personality made an imprint on Vatican II. He was avuncular in his demeanor and pastoral in his behavior. He would visit the prisons in Rome and show up at the hospitals. He had a genuinely irenic spirit about him and was marked by his compassion. John's dream was the reunion of Christendom. In his encyclicals, his letters, and his speeches, the common theme was the parable of the good shepherd, and he said that it was not God's intent that there should be a Roman Catholic sheepfold, a Lutheran sheepfold, an Anglican sheepfold, a Presbyterian sheepfold, and so on, but rather one sheepfold with one shepherd, who, of course, would be the vicar of Christ on earth, the bishop of Rome. Because his was a kinder and gentler spirit, he referred to those outside of Rome, particularly those in the Eastern Orthodox Church and those in the Protestant community, as "separated brethren." That was a long way from Vatican I, which referred to Protestants as schismatics and heretics.

John decreed at the beginning of Vatican II that theological issues such as justification were not to be discussed. Vatican II was to be concerned only with ecclesiology. Even the disputes that were going on at that time between the Greek church and the Latin church over the role of Mary in the history of redemption were not to be addressed under soteriology but only under the rubric of ecclesiology. He was trying to do away with non-doctrinal things, such as eating meat on Friday and the recitation of the Mass in Latin, so as to make the Roman Church more approachable, more inclusive, and thereby to bring the sheep back into the sheepfold. It was in this context that he made his famous statement, saying he wanted to open the windows of the church and let the fresh air of the Spirit blow through.

John's strategy has been in place now for more than fifty years, and it's been extremely successful. However, in that same period of time, not one article of the Council of Trent has been repealed. As a matter of fact, as recently as 1994, with the release of the newest Catechism of the Catholic Church, Roman views on justification, the treasury of merits, purgatory, and all the other accretions that blur the New Testament gospel were reaffirmed and reasserted. So in one sense, ECT, to me, represents the ultimate attempt at synthesis that obscures the gospel itself.

Improving the Gospel

There is one final point I want to make. I also see the great danger in our day of all the attempts we've seen within evangelicalism to improve the gospel. The message has changed. Now the gospel is the idea that God loves you unconditionally, that God loves you and has a wonderful plan for your life, or that God can give you purpose for your life. Those ideas may all be true (although I don't think they are), and they may be good news, but they're not the gospel.

I love to gather for the gospel, and I love the zeal at meetings such as Together for the Gospel, but I regret that such meetings always seem to end up being abbreviated by certain letters, such as T4G. I wish we could change that. I wish we could say T4TG, Together for *the* Gospel. I like the idea of keeping that definite article there because the gospel has a definite content according to the New Testament.

What is the gospel? The gospel is about Jesus—who he is and what he does. If we look at the apostolic sermons in the book of Acts, we see a theme over and over again. It is the declaration of this one whose coming had been predicted by the Old Testament prophets, who was born from the seed of David, who lived a life of perfect obedience, who died on the cross as an atoning sacrifice for our sins, who was raised for our justification, who ascended into heaven and is seated at right hand of the Father, who is the King of kings and Lord of lords, and who will come back at the end of the age. Those are the nonnegotiable elements of the gospel.

But the gospel also includes a subjective element, as the apostle Paul develops particularly in Romans, Ephesians, and Galatians, where he asks how the good news of what Jesus did becomes ours. The answer that the apostle gives is that it is received by faith alone. We must not tamper with that. If we say that it is by faith plus, by grace plus, or by Jesus plus, we are preaching another gospel, which, as the apostle says, is not another gospel.

The church is called to stand in the awful discomfort of antithesis. Who likes conflict? Paul himself, when he writes to the Galatians, says, "Am I now seeking the approval of man, or of God? Or am I trying to please man? If I were still trying to please man, I would not be a servant of Christ" (1:10). I think the greatest challenge for believers today is our personal fidelity to the gospel. I hear ministers say, "I've been ordained to the gospel ministry, and I preach the gospel all the time." In many cases, they have *never* preached the gospel, because they don't even know what it is. It's the person and work of Christ and his benefits appropriated by faith alone. Don't try to improve it, for these two reasons: first, it's not your gospel; it's God's gospel. He owns it. He revealed it. He gave it to his church. Second, you can't improve it. Any changes you make to it will be only deprovements.

I challenge you, brothers and sisters, to be faithful in season and out without compromise, without a synthetic gospel but with the real one, the biblical one, the saving one.

3

How Does It Happen? Trajectories toward an Adjusted Gospel

R. Albert Mohler Jr.

The news coming out of Poland was stunning. A plane carrying the Polish president and first lady, along with the top military and governmental leaders of Poland, had crashed outside Smolensk in Western Russia. Ninety-seven people were dead. Russian Prime Minister Vladimir Putin announced that he would personally lead the investigation to determine the cause of the crash.[1]

We are all too familiar with this kind of news. Airliners rarely crash, but when they do, it is nearly always a catastrophic event. Here in the United States, investigations like this are conducted by the National Transportation Safety Board (NTSB). They study the location of the crash and gather all of the wreckage. They find the airplane's black box, the instrument that records crucial flight information and even the words spoken by the flight crew. Then, in a giant hangar, they reconstruct the airliner in order to discover where the fatal fault and crucial failure took place. They measure tension points, stress, and metallurgy in order to determine the exact location of the breakdown.

It is fascinating to see just how determined we are to find the cause of a crash. It is not only because our minds need an answer. We also want to apply what can be learned from a catastrophe in order that subsequent disasters might be averted.

By contrast, the church has often been altogether careless when it comes to theological disaster. We should employ the same kind of scrupulous investigation, measuring the stress points and going back to the place of doctrinal disaster in order to determine how and why these things happened. We need to measure the structures of thought and locate where there is a break or weakness. In so doing, we may determine the reason for the breakdown and prevent subsequent disasters.

The problem all around us is the reality of adjusted gospels, ranging from the seductively revised to the blatantly false. We understand that this problem has been around since the beginning of the church because the New Testament provides ample warnings about the reality of false gospels. In Galatians 1:6–9, Paul writes:

> I am astonished that you are so quickly deserting him who called you in the grace of Christ and are turning to a different gospel—not that there is another one, but there are some who trouble you and want to distort the gospel of Christ. But even if we or an angel from heaven should preach to you a gospel contrary to the one we preached to you, let him be accursed. As we have said before, so now I say again: If anyone is preaching to you a gospel contrary to the one you received, let him be accursed.

Paul makes clear that there is not only *a* gospel; there is *the* gospel. This one gospel rightly tells of the salvation that comes through Jesus Christ, rightly detailing and describing what God did for us in Christ even while we were yet sinners. There is one gospel that leads to salvation.

Then, in 1 Timothy 6:3–5, Paul writes a warning to Timothy, his son in the faith:

> If anyone teaches a different doctrine and does not agree with the sound words of our Lord Jesus Christ and the teaching that accords with godliness, he is puffed up with conceit and understands nothing. He has an unhealthy craving for controversy and for quarrels about words, which produce envy, dissension, slander, evil suspicions, and constant friction among people who are depraved in mind and deprived of the truth, imagining that godliness is a means of gain.

These words were not penned by a public relations agent. Just as Paul uses the strong language of astonishment in his letter to the Galatians, he also writes candidly to Timothy, warning him against a suborthodox doctrine that does not comport with the sound words of our Lord Jesus Christ and the teaching that accords with godliness. Paul speaks of the motivation of false teachers, which is an unhealthy craving for controversy, and he points to the insidious divisions among Christ's people that result.

Again, in 2 Timothy 1:8–14, Paul writes about "sound words" that he admonished Timothy to guard and cherish:

> Therefore do not be ashamed of the testimony about our Lord, nor of me his prisoner, but share in suffering for the gospel by the power of God, who saved us and called us to a holy calling, not because of our works but because of his own purpose and grace, which he gave us in Christ Jesus before the ages began, and which now has been manifested through the appearing of our Savior Christ Jesus, who abolished death and brought life and immortality to light through the gospel, for which I was appointed a preacher and apostle and teacher, which is why I suffer as I do. But I am not ashamed, for I know whom I have believed, and I am convinced that he is able to guard until that Day what has been entrusted to me. Follow the pattern of the sound words that you have heard from me, in the faith and love that are in Christ Jesus. By the Holy Spirit who dwells within us, guard the good deposit entrusted to you.

Paul speaks of the apostolic command to guard what has been entrusted to us—to guard the good deposit.

Finally, Jude provides us with a similar and powerful charge, found in verse 3 of his letter:

> Beloved, although I was very eager to write to you about our common salvation, I found it necessary to write appealing to you to contend for the faith that was once for all delivered to the saints.

Jude's words remind us that there is such a thing as the Christian faith. In a postmodern age of relativity, it is perhaps even more important that we come back to proclaim what the New Testament itself emphatically repeats. There is a pattern of sound words. There is a treasure, a deposit entrusted to us, and a faith once for all delivered to the saints. The New

Testament is very clear about the reality of the one true gospel, even as it warns the church about the treachery of false gospels. This must be a primary concern of the faithful church, because to love Christ is to cherish and contend for Christ's gospel—the gospel unadjusted.

Throughout the history of the Christian church, there has been a long and lamentable history of adjustment. The early church faced a constant pull toward the false gospel of works righteousness. The church also fought adjustments to Christology, denials of the Trinity, and the false gospels of Pelagius, Gnosticism, medieval nominalism, sacramentalism, and sacerdotalism. The Reformation of the sixteenth century brought about a recovery of the gospel, carried and moved along through the faithful preaching of the Word of God.

In the previous few centuries, the church has wrestled with the challenges of the Enlightenment, Deism, and the rise of modern critical thought. No longer would the primary operation of the human mind be viewed as coming to terms with an objective external reality. Rather, the knower became the holder of authority and knowledge. This challenge to authority was a direct assault on revelation and was an intentional revising of the faith once for all delivered to the saints.

Underlying the vast project of modern theology and the emerging liberal theology was the assumption that the world had changed in such a way that what was true before was no longer true, or what was thought to be true before was no longer thought to be true. Living in the "age of Enlightenment," theologians and philosophers sought liberation from previous patterns and authoritative structures of thought. In particular, they sought freedom from having to find confidence in a divinely inspired Scripture. Then theologians of the post-Enlightenment period of the late eighteenth and nineteenth centuries began to speak openly of a mandate to revise the faith. They claimed that to rescue meaning for Christianity in this new intellectual age, the church must make major adjustments to the Christian faith—and thus, major adjustments to the gospel.

One cannot speak of this period of thought and of the changed mind of humanity without speaking of its seminal figures of thought. Charles

Darwin provided a new view of humanity and the cosmos. Karl Marx constructed a new view of human society, economics, and politics. For Marx, the doctrine of the fall was no longer about human sinfulness and rebellion against God but instead was about the economic repression of the proletariat by the economic elites who were aided and abetted by the bourgeoisie. Friedrich Nietzsche declared that God is dead and that we have killed him. Nietzsche thought that Christianity is the quintessential statement of weakness, worshiping a Christ who would die on a cross; Nietzsche said this was too pathetic for modern reverence, much less modern trust. Then along came Sigmund Freud, who said that the basic problems of humanity are psychological and psychiatric, all a matter of our subconscious. What is wrong with us is not our fault, Freud stated, because it is something that happened to us.

Added to all these intellectual challenges, the world also witnessed incredible scientific advances, new ideas, political revolutions, the toppling of monarchies and empires, and the ethos of liberation from the past. The whole world seemed to have changed, and the claim was made that the gospel must either change or perish. Bishop John Shelby Spong, arriving rather late on the scene, wrote a book with the title *Why Christianity Must Change or Die*.[2] The title embodies the central claim of the modern project—Christianity must change or be buried. Of course, the problem is that if Bishop Spong's theology is what Christianity is, then Christianity is already dead.

It is imperative to understand that theological disaster usually comes from the hands of those who would claim to save Christianity rather than to bury it. The basic apologetic impulse behind modern liberal theology is that Christianity needs to be saved. It is argued that if Christians continue to preach and parade all these claims of divine revelation, supernatural events, miracles, virgin births, and all the rest, Christianity will be buried in a pile of debris from an ancient past. The world has changed, and people will not grant credibility to such a Christianity. Christianity must be rescued from itself, so the argument goes. Those who have led this project sought to arrange the survival of some vestigial form of Christianity, stripped of its supernatural claims and substitutionary Savior. What remains is something they can call "spirituality," along with the claim that this will actually aide human progress, build human community, and solve problems.

Paul Tillich, one of the most influential leaders of the project of twentieth-century liberal theology, claimed that all theology is apologetic theology. Every single theological statement worth making, Tillich said, is an attempt to salvage some kind of meaning.[3] When the ardent atheist Sidney Hook read and reviewed Tillich's *Systematic Theology*, he said, in effect, "I am an atheist. Paul Tillich is an atheist. The difference is, I know I am an atheist. I am not sure he yet knows he is an atheist, but Dr. Tillich, take it from an atheist—you are an atheist."[4]

As part of the Nathaniel Taylor Lecture Series at Yale in 1986, Basil Mitchell told a parable that helps explain the modern theological predicament.[5] Mitchell said that the church is like a raft on a smooth, slow-moving, placid river. This raft is heavily laden with cargo, which represents doctrine that the church has taken on through its centuries of development. Eventually, however, the raft arrives at the waters of the modern world, not a placid, smooth, slow-moving, languid river. The modern world is a set of rapids, each more dangerous than the one before, and they pose a grave danger to the raft. Like this raft, heavily laden with cargo and headed into the rapids, the church has to make a very quick decision. Either it will go to the shore and do its very best to cling to the shore in order to maintain as much cargo as possible (Mitchell called that option "fundamentalism"), or it will ride the rapids and start jettisoning the cargo. According to Mitchell, if the church "unloads cargo"—doctrine by doctrine, truth claim by truth claim, and miracle by miracle—then it can ride through the rapids and survive.

To understand the logic of that parable is to understand the project of modern theology. The message to the church is this: do not hug the shore because you cannot do that and remain intellectually credible. Ride the rapids. But understand that you will not make it through the rapids without capsizing if you try to carry all the doctrinal and theological cargo of creed. Just decide what you are going to jettison, and the raft can be saved.

Eight Trajectories toward an Adjusted Gospel

How does the gospel come to be adjusted? How is it that given the impulse to save Christianity for relevance in a modern age, some decide to make huge doctrinal adjustments? How do we trace the motivations and the patterns? Thinking like the National Transportation Safety Board, we had better come to understand just how such a disaster takes place. Agreeing with the apostle Paul in his admonitions to Timothy and the Galatian church, we must take a sober look at past trajectories toward adjusted gospels in an attempt to avoid similar catastrophes in the future.

The Modern Trajectory

The first trajectory is the modern trajectory. In *Kerygma and Myth*, Rudolf Bultmann wrote, "It is impossible to use electric lights and the wireless, and to avail ourselves of modern medical and surgical discoveries, and at the same time to believe in the New Testament world of demons and spirits."[6] This is a quintessential statement of the modern mind as it evaluates the supernatural and, in particular, the New Testament. Rudolf Bultmann serves as our paradigmatic figure, our great illustration of the modern trajectory, as he says, in effect, "I am a modern man; I think like a modern man. I use electricity, and no man who uses electricity believes that Jesus walked on water. You walk into a room, flick on lights, and there is light. You listen to the radio. You go to the emergency room. Therefore, you do not *really* believe in a virgin birth, do you?"

Bultmann famously suggested that for the church to survive, Christianity must undertake the project he called the "demythologization" of Scripture. He said that the New Testament is full of myth. Primitive people in their primitive time and culture used their primitive language in creating their primitive myths—all in an attempt to produce an explanation of reality. Bultmann argued that modern humanity knows better now, so we must demythologize these myths. Once we scrape away all of the supernaturalism and get to the real human dynamic of the Scripture, we will find a connection between the existential concerns of primitive and modern persons.

The problem of modern knowledge is immense, and it does not serve us well to deny the problem or to minimize the challenge. We should be armed with the knowledge that all around us is an entire universe of thought that is inherently anti-supernatural, and it is most anti-supernatural where it gets closest to the issues that are the deep concerns of our heart and in the marrow of our bones.

Further, there is also the modern problem of history. Gotthold Ephraim Lessing spoke of history's ugly ditch, or the reality that we really cannot know what went on before.[7] That is, there is no way to use the scientific method to recapitulate history and measure whether an event actually happened one way or another, whether this person actually said something or not. The best that historians can do is to measure the accumulated evidence and gain a probabilistic understanding of what might have happened. The logical conclusion is that we had better not establish our meaning for life on something as remote and unknowable as history.

In the wake of the Enlightenment, the idea of revelation—that a supernatural God would communicate in actual words to humanity—was so far outside the worldview of the modern mind that those who shaped modern thought simply dismissed revelation as even a possibility. They viewed the Bible as an ancient book, still significant because of its historical influence, but a book that should be read in light of modern ideas and understandings.

Harry Emerson Fosdick, the famous liberal preacher of the early twentieth century, in *The Modern Use of the Bible* argued that preachers should locate something in Scripture that will have a point of psychological connection to the modern mind. The last thing we need to do, Fosdick argued, is to suggest that we actually believe in these supernatural events, because then the preacher and the church will lose all credibility.[8]

John Updike encapsulates this best in his novel *In the Beauty of the Lilies*. He writes of the Reverend Clarence Arthur Wilmot of the Fourth Presbyterian Church, who "felt the last particles of his faith leave him."[9] Set in the early twentieth century, Updike writes, "Clarence's mind was like a many-legged, wingless insect that had long and tediously been struggling to climb up the walls of a slick-walled porcelain basin; and now a sudden impatient wash of water swept it down into the drain."[10] Wilmot had been struggling against modernity, hoping to maintain his belief in the doctrines of the faith and in the creed to which he had once given assent. But he had lost the battle. In his own words, the minister says, "It was a ghastly moment, a silent sounding of bottomlessness."[11] Interestingly, the precipitating factor was a loss of confidence in the possibility of divine revelation. Reverend Wilmot came to believe that the Bible is not the Word of God. He decided that the Bible is not inerrant, infallible, or even inspired in any verbal or propositional sense. Instead, the Bible is an archaeological record, "the work of men—of Jews in dirty sheepskins, rotten-toothed desert tribesmen with eyes rolled heavenward."[12]

John Updike probably understood the intellectual leap like no other modern American novelist. He knew exactly what he was talking about in depicting the crisis of the Christian faith within the modern world. If we do not understand what Updike is saying here, then we miss something of the scandal of the gospel we bear, because whether we like his words or not, he accurately describes biblical Christianity.

We who *do* believe must face this clearly. If we are to stand together for the gospel, then let us be honest with ourselves and with the world in admitting that we do believe that God, the one true and living God, spoke his words through rotten-toothed, desert tribesmen. What is more, we are obligated to receive the Bible as God's own Word today, and we are under divine mandate to preach it. Indeed, those men wore sheepskins and wandered around the wilderness. Yet we are going to stand up in the twenty-first century and say, "Hear now the Word of God." If you do not feel that scandal, then you do not get it. But if you do feel it, and it feels right, then nothing is going to be a problem for you. If you know that the Bible is the Word of God, then you will not be like the bug trying to crawl up the porcelain wall of the sink, only to be washed away by modern thought. You will prepare, preach, and step back and see what God will do with his Word.

The modern trajectory inevitably leads to a total breakdown of theology and doctrine because once a person buys into the logic of anti-supernaturalism, there is no place to stop. It is well described as "universal acid," a term coined by Daniel Dennett.[13] Dennett said that as a little boy, he used to imagine an acid so strong that nothing would contain it. This acid would dissolve its own container, then the room that contained the container, then the building that contained the room that contained the container, and then the city, state, and the nation. Before long, this universal acid would destroy everything.

Anti-supernaturalism is a universal acid. If theologians exclude the possibility of a self-revealing God, then they have no reason to stop at one doctrine. Any decision to stop with one, or several, doctrines is merely exercising some arbitrary operation of the will and is not the consistent operation of a theological mind. Furthermore, eventually there are no more doctrines to deny. This is one of the most delicious predicaments of modern Protestantism. They started with anti-supernaturalism and then ran through the entire theological catalog. Bishop Spong denied every doctrine there is to deny, wrote a book on it, and went on morning talk shows to promote his nonbeliefs. There are no more doctrines left for him to deny, so he is retired now. If one follows the logic of the modern trajectory to its conclusion, eventually he will not need a church, a pulpit, or a preacher. Therefore, if one wants to salvage a theological or ministerial job, he is going to have to find a new trajectory.

The Postmodern Trajectory

Second, the postmodern trajectory came along at just the right time, turning the modernist vision into just one more ancient tale. Postmodernism says that there were ancient, medieval, and modern myths, each of which was understandable within the context of its time and the contours of its age. In our age, postmodernism argues that we do not have to debate over the question of truth, because truth is not an objective reality. While modernists thought that everything had to be true or false—and either accepted or denied supernaturalism—postmodernists say that something may be true only within a certain cultural-linguistic system.

Postmodernists say we should stop trying to answer the historical questions. They argue that even if one thinks something did not really happen—i.e., miracles, divine revelation, or the bodily resurrection of Christ—one can still find retrievable meaning in that system. In doing so, postmodernism turned modernism into one more form of rejected metanarrative. Postmodern philosophy of language casts doubt even on modernism's statements about doubt. Eventually, if language is indeterminate, then saying something did not happen is just as indeterminate as saying something did happen. Along came the postmodernist, grinning like the Cheshire cat and saying, "So what if it did not happen?"

In his book *The Nature of Doctrine*, George Lindbeck suggests that there are three different understandings of doctrine.[14] First, the cognitive understanding of doctrine sees doctrine as making a statement of fact. Second, the liberal understanding sees doctrine as an experiential expression. In gaining an understanding of liberal theology, Lindbeck says that one does not learn anything about theology, but one does learn a lot about liberals, because their theology is an expression of who they are. Third, Lindbeck eliminates both the cognitive and liberal understandings of doctrine in favor of the new postmodern understanding, in which doctrine is simply meaning within a cultural-linguistic system. Doctrine becomes a component of language. Doctrines do not make truth claims, Lindbeck argues. They just serve to regulate the way we talk. Every culture consists of a cultural and linguistic system, and from this system emerges meaning. The postmodernist would say, "I do not even have to answer the question of the historical truth of the Bible; because it is simply true for us. It is our book. This is our meaning."

Postmodernists can sing the ancient hymns with zeal, even as they acknowledge that they are not making statements of personal creed. They sing, "Immortal, invisible God only wise; in light inaccessible, hid from our eyes," without believing these statements as truth or reality. Behind this is an understanding of the relativity of truth, seeing the reader as the location of meaning and truth rather than the text. The Bible becomes a library of narratives and conversation, and people simply connect where they can.

The postmodern trajectory is very seductive. Many evangelicals hear postmodernists and assume they are saying something they are not. Postmodernists can preach as if they believe the text is true, and they can do wonderful things with narrative and the literary interpretation of Scripture. They can preach on a passage in such a way that when you hear it, you think it is powerful and meaningful. Indeed, you may even learn some literary dimensions of the text. But the postmodern preacher does not believe it matters whether the historical event described in the text actually happened. For such a preacher, even if you assume the event did not happen, the text can still be meaningful. The difference between the postmodernist and the modernist is that the latter feels obliged to let everyone know that he does not believe it happened, whereas the former is content to let everyone have it their own way—with a wink, a smile, and a glib use of the word "*whatever*."

The Moral Trajectory

The third trajectory is the moral trajectory. In the nineteenth and twentieth centuries, it became increasingly common to see the orthodox Christian gospel held up as immoral or submoral, beneath the standards of modern morality. Friedrich Nietzsche wrote that any man who senses the need to be saved is too pathetic to deserve to be saved. Christianity is immoral, Nietzsche argued, because it breeds weakness, and the only good to be desired is strength and power.[15]

The moral trajectory of theological disaster claims that the modern moral conscience is superior to the moral conscience of the ancient world, including the morality contained in the Scriptures. C. S. Lewis coined the term "chronological snobbery" as a description of the modern moral conscience.[16]

In describing his own theological pilgrimage, William Ellery Channing, one of the leading Unitarian liberals in American theological history, wrote about "the shock given to my moral nature" by the teachings of the Bible in orthodox Christianity.[17] As Channing grew into young manhood and began to read biblical texts for himself, he was appalled by them. He was horrified by the Bible, struck by what he saw as the immorality of the Scripture. Channing was responding to human depravity, blood atonement, divine propitiation, hell, wrath, and a God who acts in history with judgment. Washington Gladden, another liberal of that day and one of the fathers of the social gospel, had this to say about hell and divine judgment: "To teach such a doctrine as this about God is to inflict upon religion a terrible injury and to subvert the very foundations of morality."[18]

The moral trajectory assumes that we are morally superior to the morality of both the Bible and the figures in the Bible—the prophets, patriarchs, apostles, and even Jesus himself. One contemporary example of the moral trajectory is the increasingly large body of literature that describes substitutionary atonement as a form of "divine child abuse."[19] It is argued that if a father requires pain to be inflicted on his own child in order to forgive the sins of others, such an action would be child abuse. Modern morality sees Scripture as presenting God as a selfish monster who seeks his own glory. They are horrified by what they see as a picture of a self-aggrandizing, monarchial deity.

Another example of the moral trajectory is the new "fairness doctrine" concerning God. God has to be fair, so the argument goes, and this means we should apply contemporary human standards of fairness to God. Fair is a moral category that works well with two preschool boys in a playpen or sandbox or when dividing the pieces of a pie. In such cases, everyone wants things to be fair. The notion of fairness, however, is not applicable to a sovereign God who is holy and perfect and who acts in accordance with his perfection. Perfect is infinitely superior to fair, and perfect cannot be interrogated by fair. It is not fair, they will argue, that some are not saved or that any might be in hell. If we are actually going to understand anything even close to fair, however, it is not fair that *anyone* would be saved or in heaven.

Even in some evangelical circles, this moral complaint about God is growing more intense. Brian McLaren, in his book *A New Kind of Christianity*, speaks of the Bible as a community library into which we walk rather than as a constitutional collection of documents to which we are accountable.[20] According to McLaren, we can find an evolving morality even within God himself. McLaren finds many biblical depictions of God to be horrifying to modern morality, and he speaks of the Bible as moving from less to more mature views of God: "Scripture faithfully reveals the evolution of our ancestors' best attempts to communicate their successive best understandings of God."[21] That is the most McLaren can say about Scripture. But in trying to salvage the Bible and Christianity from its immorality and in saying that Scripture simply "reveals the evolution of our ancestors' best attempts to communicate their successive best understandings of God,"[22] there is not even a hint of revelation left in McLaren's understanding of Scripture. McLaren is light-years to the left of Fosdick when he writes the following footnote: "For this reason, I would grimly prefer atheism to be true than for the Greco-Roman Theos narrative to be true."[23] By the phrase "Greco-Roman Theos narrative," McLaren is referring to the gospel as we understand it to be clearly presented in Scripture. Such dangerous statements are exemplary of the moral trajectory.

The Aesthetic Trajectory

The fourth trajectory is the aesthetic trajectory. God is beautiful, and beauty is his creation for his glory. Because humanity was made in God's image, we are gifted with an aesthetic sense. We are aesthetic creatures, and the Christian worldview alone explains how the good, the beautiful, and the true find unity in God. The transcendental unites in the glory of the one true God and in the beauty of the incarnate Christ. Accordingly, beauty is an apologetic for the reality of God, even as Genesis 3 reminds us of our incompetence and incapacity to render any independent and adequate aesthetic judgment concerning truth. We are completely dependent upon God's revealed Word for a reset of our sense of beauty. After the fall, we are too easily seduced by the merely pretty; we are bought off by the superficial and the gaudy. According to the Scripture, the cross is beautiful, but it is not pretty. It is most beautiful when it is seen in light of what the world considers most ugly. Therein is the beauty of the suffering servant from whom the world turned its face.

The aesthetic trajectory toward an adjusted gospel is seen in the following statement made by feminist theologian Delores Williams: "I do not think we need a theory of atonement at all. I do not think we need folks hanging from crosses and blood dripping and weird stuff."[24] Though it may seem that such thinking resides far from evangelicalism, many evangelicals are tempted to make aesthetic judgments about doctrine and truth.

Peter De Vries, in his novel *The Mackerel Plaza*, wrote about the Reverend Peter Mackerel of the People's Liberal Church.[25] Mackerel describes the church as "the first split-level church in America." The pulpit is a free-form design by Naguchi, and it "consists of a slab of marble set on four legs of four delicately differing fruit woods, to symbolize the four gospels, and their failure to harmonize." Behind the pulpit "dangles a large multi-colored mobile, its interdenominational parts swaying, as one might fancy, in perpetual reminder of the Pauline stricture against those 'blown by every wind of doctrine.'" De Vries writes: "Thus People's Liberal Church is a church designed to meet the needs of today, and to serve the whole man. This includes the worship of a God free of outmoded theological definitions and palatable to a mind come of age in the era or relativity." Mackerel preached, "It is the final proof of God's omnipotence that he need not exist in order to save us."

The plot of this novel begins with the Reverend Mackerel calling the zoning commission of his town because someone has erected a garish billboard outside the window of his study. The billboard simply has two words on it: "Jesus saves." He calls the zoning commission and says, "It's vulgar. And the lettering is that new phosphorescent stuff—green and orange. No, this is a blight on the landscape and I protest." The official on the phone responds, "I know what you mean now that you mention it, you're not the first to complain. The Presbyterians are appalled. The Episcopalians are sick. All the better element there, with property values at stake." At the mention, Pastor Mackerel cuts her off and says, "Oh, property values! Please get that out of your mind, miss. Do you think I own the parsonage I live in? I'm talking about spiritual values. Spiritual and aesthetic ones. How do you expect me to write a sermon with that thing staring me in the face? How do you expect me to turn out anything fit for civilized consumption?"

We feel the biting caricature of a novelist in presenting a pastor who would think, act, and talk in such a way, and we know better than to think or talk that way ourselves. Yet he who considers himself theologically conservative and biblically faithful will never preach certain texts of Scripture because he recoils from the message and doctrinal truths contained in them. There are many who consider themselves fully orthodox who nevertheless refuse to teach from particular passages because they do not want people to consider them prudish, ugly, and unbeautiful. Once a preacher buys into that logic, he has succumbed to the aesthetic trajectory toward an adjusted gospel.

The Therapeutic Trajectory

The fifth trajectory is the therapeutic trajectory. We live in the age of Sigmund Freud, Carl Jung, Carl Rogers, Mr. Rogers, and Oprah. We live in an age of sovereign self, as Philip Rieff wrote in his book *The Triumph of the Therapeutic*.[26] We may not know much about ourselves, but we do know that we are sick, we have a syndrome, and we need therapy. The therapeutic worldview transforms sin into various syndromes and complexes. We are presented as victims, codependent and enabling. The answer is to mediate and medicate. All issues revolve around the sovereign self and the self's need to be happy or at least at peace.

A recent magazine article titled "Do You Have a Case of Recovery Envy?" suggested that people are now signing up for recovery programs for problems and addictions that they admit they do not have.[27] Apparently, you are not cool if you are not in therapy. Of course, if you are not in therapy, then you are simply in denial, so go talk to someone who can mediate and medicate. The bottom line is that we prefer to think of ourselves as sick rather than as evil; we prefer to be ill and afflicted rather than sinful and sinister. Within the therapeutic trajectory, the Bible is transformed into a message or technique of self-help, and theology is reduced to therapeutic meaning, relevance, and application.

In terms of American thought, the therapeutic trajectory can be traced back to William James, who, in *The Variety of Religious Experience*, wrote of two types of religion—sick-souled and well-souled.[28] Adherents of sick-souled religion come to a crisis requiring a conversion because they believe they have a need they cannot fulfill and must look for an external rescue. James certainly understood the gospel he was rejecting.

On the other hand, James said that the adherents of well-souled religion never come to such an abysmal conclusion about themselves. They never experience the crisis, and they never have to look for an external rescue. Theologian Horace Bushnell turned James's philosophy into a theology to be preached, but one does not have to be a Harvard professor to communicate this. All a pastor needs to do is preach a sermon about the "Be-Happy Attitudes." The therapeutic trajectory points to a self-defined problem and self-designated solution, with a self-actualizing eschatology. The problem, however, is that although the gospel saves and makes well, it is not therapy and cannot be reduced or accommodated to a therapeutic worldview.

The Pragmatic Trajectory

The sixth trajectory is the pragmatic trajectory. Pragmatism may be the most ingrained American temptation. Only in America do we have the rise of pragmatism as a major philosophical movement. Pragmatism is a sophisticated philosophy that has to do with everything from justice to meaning and truth, but it denies the propositional or objective understanding of truth. Truth is made an instrument, a tool to be used to the effect we desire. Pragmatists suggest that all solutions must be pragmatic, and they point to a pragmatic salvation. This temptation has always been there. Even in Genesis 3, pragmatism raises its head when Adam and Eve fashion aprons of fig leaves in order to cover their nakedness. Pragmatism says, "We have a problem. Let us solve it."

Many pastors would refute the modern trajectory, postmodern relativism, or theological liberalism, only to follow a pattern of ministry grounded in pragmatism. Pragmatism is among the most powerful background realities of modern ministry. It explains the managerial revolution that has shaped church life and ministry. It affirms efficiency, managerial expertise, results, statistics, numbers, and routinization as the highest priorities for the minister. No one has documented this so faithfully and so insightfully as David Wells in his classic work *No Place for Truth*, wherein he writes:

The pastoral ministry is thus being professionalized. It is being anchored firmly in the middle class, and the attitudes of those who are themselves professionals or who constantly deal with them are increasingly defining who the minister is. Once again, it is the old market mechanism at work—ministers defining themselves as a product for which there is a market. And so they feel they must present themselves as having a desired competence, and that competence, as it turns out, is largely managerial.[29]

The dominance of the pragmatic trajectory becomes obvious when you discover how pastors spend their time or how laypersons insist their pastors should spend their time. The pragmatic trajectory comes so easily because the gratification can come so quickly. Just a little managerial expertise can, it would seem, produce results that theology and doctrine alone cannot manufacture. Al Capone said that while a few good words may convince, a few good words and a revolver are even more convincing. Similarly, the pragmatic trajectory says that truth and doctrine have their place, but in order to get maximum results, there are ways a minister should routinize his methodologies. Charles Finney is a classic example of a theological pragmatist, orchestrating his efforts for what he felt were the needed results of his preaching. Of course, one must redefine the result in nontheological terms, because once a minister leans into the instrumental tools of pragmatism and leans away from doctrine, all that he will end up with is a pragmatic ledger sheet. While there may be an immediate payoff, one will simply end up producing crowds that are not churches.

The Emotional Trajectory

Seventh, there is the emotional trajectory. Even as we are rational, aesthetic, and moral beings, we are also emotional beings, a fact the Bible acknowledges. Upon hearing of the death of Lazarus, Jesus wept (John 11:35). Paul spoke repeatedly and passionately of his love and concern for the churches, and he used the most exquisitely emotional language (2 Cor. 1:1–11; Phil 1:1–11). As Jonathan Edwards would say, the gospel produces a profile of Christian affection. But though our emotions and affections may be at the heart of the modern sense of the self and the experiment of modern liberal theology, they are a devastatingly inadequate guide to truth.

Friedrich Schleiermacher, the father of modern liberal theology, wrote *On Religion: Speeches to Its Cultured Despisers* with an ambitious plan in mind.[30] In his own nineteenth-century context, Schleiermacher sought to convince the anti-supernaturalist, the "cultured despisers of religion," that the Christian faith still had meaning. He defined faith as "the feeling of absolute dependence," and though he meant more than mere emotion, Schleiermacher's "faith" was largely a matter of intuition, self-knowledge, and emotion.

But what happens to doctrine when one takes on an emotional framework of thought? When you enter this emotional trajectory, you lean *into* what appears to give you an emotional reward, and you lean *away* from those things that appear to come with an emotional cost. The resulting effects on the gospel are easy to see. Just read Schleiermacher's systematic theology, *The Christian Faith*, and you will find hundreds of pages without any reference to the Trinity. Then, at the end of the book, there is an appendix on the Trinity, and Schleiermacher, without any embarrassment, says, in effect, "I have relegated the Trinity to an appendix because it does not comport with my emotions. I feel no need for it."[31]

Many pastors preach what they think their people feel they need to hear. Unfortunately, a preacher's emotional state serves as a lousy determination of doctrine. A preacher should not trust himself for a minute to believe, teach, and preach only what feels right. Imagine the response if a pastor asked a congregant, "How do you feel about original sin?" Or, "What is your emotional response to total depravity, hell, or the Bible's teachings on sexual morality?" Preachers should not care how the listener feels about biblical truth. Well, they should care how people feel about them, even as they explain and exhort that one's feelings have nothing to do with whether something is true or not. The feelings of the congregation have no bearing on a preacher's obligation to teach and preach the whole counsel of the Word of God and to make clear that it is true. We must pray that our affections and emotions will be aligned in accordance with the Word of God, so that we will love every single word of Scripture as truth. Even so, Scripture is true regardless of how one feels about it.

The Materialist Trajectory

The eighth trajectory is the materialist trajectory. We are perpetually tempted to believe that what we can see with our eyes and hold in our hands is more real than that which we cannot see or hold. The material world has an immediate attraction precisely because of its immediate gratifications and fulfillments. Although the blessings of earthly prosperity are not foreign to the world of the Scripture, the Bible depicts wealth with brutal honesty, revealing its traps, temptations, and transitory nature. God warned Israel that the greatest temptation would come as they inhabited cities they did not build, drank from cisterns they did not dig, and enjoyed vineyards they did not plant (Deut. 6:11). The New Testament puts wealth into a gospel perspective, teaching that it is not an automatic sign of God's blessing and preference (Matt. 19:16–30; Luke 16:1931). Instead, in the gospel, we are promised the riches of Christ, and we are told to desire and be satisfied in those riches. We are told that where our treasure is, there our heart is also (Matt. 6:19–24). Eternity will reveal that far more Christians have lived and died in abject poverty than have lived in wealth or material comfort.

By contrast, the prosperity gospel follows a false logic of the materialist trajectory that makes God to be a liar because it does not produce prosperity. This false gospel presents a false hope and an empty promise, and it depicts God as apparently incompetent. It robs sinners of the salvation they may know through Christ and the infinite, eternal riches that would be theirs in him and in him alone.

A major news story of 2010 came from Los Angeles, as the Crystal Cathedral faced a $55 million budget deficit and was being pursued by its creditors and local vendors. When officials from the Crystal Cathedral met with creditors to ask for time, there was no mention of possibility thinking.[32] There is grief in this, not because a false gospel was demonstrated for its falsity but because the false hopes of so many people were invested in that gospel. How many people, by the millions, have driven by that facility and wondered if there is a god. Now, that god is presented to be false, empty, and untrue. This is a matter of grief and sobriety.

We are all tempted to trust in what we can see and hold, but faith is "the assurance of things hoped for, the conviction of things unseen" (Heb. 11:1). We are all tempted, as Eric Voegelin wrote, to "immanentize the eschaton," or, as one contemporary author writes, to long for "your best life now." Ironically, this life is "our best life now" for unbelievers only. The unbelievers who read that book indeed already have their best life now, insofar as they do not know Christ and come to the end of their life in that spiritual condition.

The temptation to seek immediate gratification is closer than we like to think. Many preachers who would never fall prey to the crude and obviously false hope of the prosperity gospel nevertheless do their best to "immanentize the eschaton" by satisfying themselves and their churches through material and programmatic fulfillment.

Conclusion

Following one trajectory or the other, how is it that we get to this theological disaster? If we assembled a doctrine and theology board, analogous to the NTSB, and reconstructed the crash, what we would find are multiple stress points that can lead to theological disaster.

First, there is no shortage of pilot error when it comes to preaching. There is a great danger of succumbing to what might be called "doctrinal fatigue." When we have to keep teaching and preaching, often against the tide, over and over again, brick upon brick, truth upon truth, text upon text, and doctrine upon doctrine, fatigue can set in. Doctrinal fatigue, if left unchecked, is disastrous for a minister and the church he serves.

A second way to move into theological disaster is through embarrassment. The apostle Paul wrote, "I am not ashamed of the gospel, for it is the power of God for salvation to everyone who believes" (Rom. 1:19). Yet if we are not careful to have our footing in the gospel, and if we are not absolutely secure that the Bible is the Word of God, then we will find ourselves awash with embarrassment before the world. It is as though we can read their thoughts: "Do you really believe this? Do you really believe this little infant is a sinner? Do you really believe eternal salvation comes only through Jesus Christ?" You may be talking to an international student at a university who, upon suddenly coming to understand the logic of the gospel, responds, "Are you really telling me that all my ancestors are in hell?" When faced with such a question, will you answer with embarrassment? If so, then take warning. This kind of embarrassment becomes an entry drug for theological disaster.

Nearly thirty years ago, James Davidson Hunter at the University of Virginia wrote about cognitive bargaining.[33] He said the coming generation of evangelicals needs to be very careful. Given all the pressures of the secular world around it, especially coming from the intellectual elites and their anti-supernaturalism and secularism, the great danger is going to be that evangelicals will start bargaining and bartering away the faith. The church is in the rapids and has to make a decision. Will it keep one doctrine but redefine or jettison another? If so, the church will eventually lose the faith once for all delivered to the saints.

In John 6, Jesus declared himself to be the bread of life (vv. 35, 48). He said, "Truly, truly, I say to you, unless you eat the flesh of the Son of Man and drink his blood, you have no life in you. Whoever feeds on my flesh and drinks my blood has eternal life, and I will raise him up on the last day" (vv. 53–54). Then, after he spoke these words, "many of his disciples turned back and no longer walked with him" (v. 66). Jesus asked the twelve disciples, "'Do you want to go away as well?' Simon Peter answered, 'Lord, to whom shall we go? You have the words of eternal life, and we have believed, and have come to know, that you are the Holy One of God'" (vv. 67–69).

Do you want to go away as well? This is a haunting question, is it not? We are on Basil Mitchell's raft, and we must decide what we are going to do. The problem with the parable, however, is Mitchell's assumption that it is our responsibility to take ownership of the raft. The raft is not ours. We are on the raft, and by God's grace, we have been given some responsibility to take part in the steering of it, but the raft itself is Christ's vessel. We have no right to jettison cargo. Our job is not to try to avoid the rapids—that is impossible. Our task is to understand that the Christ who saved us is the Lord of his church, that the gospel is his truth, and that he will vindicate his truth. It is not our task to convince the secular world of the credibility of the gospel. Yes, we enter into that conversation and seek to remove misunderstandings, but the Holy Spirit alone can make the gospel credible.

The haunting question is this: "Do you want to go away as well?" We have seen different trajectories, all resulting in an adjusted gospel—a false gospel that cannot save. It is not enough that we are here because of the gospel, and it is not enough that we are in the gospel. We must be together for the gospel, and that means the unadjusted gospel.

4

Fine-Sounding Arguments: How Wrongly "Engaging the Culture" Adjusts the Gospel

Thabiti Anyabwile

"Engage the culture. " "Win the culture. " "Change the culture. " "Transform culture. " "Create culture." There is a lot of talk about the notion of "culture" and the Christian responsibility or interaction with it. It's an important topic, and it's a massive topic. But it's also one fraught with complexities, ambiguities, complications, and pitfalls.

Three Introductory Questions

First, how would you define *culture*? We all use the term, but what meaning would you assign it? One college text I remember had an appendix that listed seventy-three different definitions of *culture*. So what it is becomes an important question. Most of us would define culture as "the belief and practices that define a particular people." But recently Andy Crouch took a much more tangible route to defining culture; he basically equated culture with "the things we make of the world." For him, culture is things, not ideas or worldviews but tangible products and goods.[1]

Right from the outset, we see part of the difficulty. What's the "it" we're trying to engage, change, win, or create? What do we mean by "the culture," and can we legitimately speak of "*the* culture"?

Second, at what level ought we to "change the culture"? Are we to aim at the pop-culture level, creating the Christian Britney Spears? Is that even possible? Is it desirable? Should we look to win ethnic culture by addressing the ways of being of particular people groups in one direction or another? Are we to engage the political culture, advocating and advancing particular policies and governing strategies that affect some level of government? Or do we look to change "high culture," the beliefs and ideals, structuring the philosophy of a society or people? Or all of the above? When we talk of "engaging the culture," what we mean depends not only on our definition of culture but also on the level of concern. What we're talking about depends in part on what level we're discussing.

Third, what does it mean exactly to "engage," win, change, or create culture? How do we define the objective? If we win, how do we know we've won?

A couple of recent writers have helpfully pointed out that this thing called "culture" resists easy definition.[2] Moreover, we can't predict with any certainty how any action we take will, in fact, change the culture. Nor can we predict the outcomes of the changes we make.

It turns out that changing the culture is a lot like trying to predict and plot the scatter pattern of individual drops of water from a sprinkler. That's a staggeringly complex task.

What are we engaging? On what level are we engaging it? And what are the terms and objectives of our engagement? These are not small questions in an evangelical world that seems very gung ho about engaging, winning, changing, and creating "the culture."

So perhaps we should stop and ask: Are these even the correct questions? Is it the responsibility of pastors and churches to "engage the culture"? Assuming we can define the what, the how, and the outcome of such an engagement, is it actually what we're called to do?

A Word to Fellow Pastors

I intend the bulk of this chapter to be a word especially to pastors about our role, about what the Lord has called us to do. I know there are people in the world uniquely gifted and called by God to play a role in shaping, directing, changing, challenging, co-opting, using, and resisting "the culture" on various levels. These are the Al Mohlers, the Marvin Olaskys, and the Ravi Zachariases of the world.

I know it's really bad form for an author to project his inadequacies onto his hearers, but I'm going to do it anyway. I'm going to guess that most of you are like me. You are not Al Mohler, Marvin Olasky, or Ravi Zacharias. Those guys have an equipment package—let's face it. I don't have it. Neither do most of you. Most of us are ordinary pastors trying to be faithful in our callings to shepherd the sheep of God. Therefore we—of all men—must think carefully and biblically about all these exhortations to "engage the culture" and whether such engagement is (a) commanded, and (b) being done in a healthy way.

To do that, I'd like us to consider the apostle Paul's letter to the Colossians. Here is the basic contention of this chapter: if we set out to "engage the culture" uncritically, we will likely see in sometimes subtle, profound, and disastrous ways the gospel being adjusted in that process of engagement. To put it another way: the idea of "engaging the culture" may be so immediately plausible to us (to use Paul's language here), that we may miss the deeper, more important strategy of *embodying* the gospel itself. From the apostle's philosophy flow four P's of pastoral ministry:

1) Pastoral *purpose*. What gets the apostle up in the morning? What gets his juices flowing? What ambition animates him?
2) Pastoral *philosophy*. What philosophy drives that purpose? What view of things, what wisdom, is animating his purpose?
3) Religious/cultural *practice*. What practices flow from that philosophy? There are distinctive ways of being that flow from Paul's philosophy.
4) *Perspective*. There is a perspective, an outlook.

1) Pastoral Purpose

The first thing to notice is Paul's pastoral purpose found in Colossians 1:24–2:5, most especially in verses 25 and 28. There is something that consumed the apostle. He gave his life to one great ambition:

> I became a minister according to the stewardship from God that was given to me for you, to make the word of God fully known. . . . Him we proclaim, warning everyone and teaching everyone with all wisdom, that we may present everyone mature in Christ. (vv. 25–28)

Paul is a minister to make the Word of God fully known, and he is making the Word of God fully known to present every Christian mature in Christ. He says he proclaims Christ, he proclaims the Word about Christ, he proclaims the gospel, and he instructs with both warning and teaching to pursue this one ultimate aim, namely, to present his hearers—the churches—mature, perfect, complete, and whole in Christ.

He wants to present the entire Christian church as a pure virgin, a chaste bride, to Christ. That's his all-consuming passion. Everything Paul does aims at this purpose. In verse 24 Paul says he joyfully *suffers* for this one purpose. In verses 25–28, Paul faithfully *preaches* for this one purpose. He is a steward, a minister, making the Word of God fully known so that he may accomplish this aim. In 2:1 Paul works hard—*toils*—for this one purpose. Paul is not lazy. He refers to "how great a struggle [he has] for the Colossians and for those at Laodicea," and really for all the churches. His care for the churches came upon him daily. And in 2:5 Paul *rejoices* to see progress being made toward this purpose.

It's as though Paul is doing all he can to take the church by the ears and with the Word of God push it up into Christ, to stuff them into the mystery, the glory, the full assurance of understanding and knowledge of God's mystery—which is Christ. That's his pastoral purpose, his apostolic ambition. Brothers, is this the burden of our ministries? Do we have such a singular purpose and ambition in our pastoral labors? Is that what we're consumed with? Is this why we drive to the office, open the books, set counseling appointments, prepare sermons, and pray? Are we aware that what God is doing with us is causing his people to be perfected in Christ?

Before we come to "engaging the culture," we first need to be gripped by the overwhelming glory and beauty of this task. How do we take that to the sixty-three-year-old grandmother caring for three grandkids, to the seventeen-year-old college hopeful trying to get good grades, to the thirty-five-year-old single woman desperately wanting marriage, to the forty-two-year-old business man professing Christ but too busy for family and church, and to the couple experiencing marital difficulty? How do we grab onto their ears by the Word and press them up into Christ. That's our calling. That's our task. That's Paul's purpose, and it's ours.

The Fine-Sounding Arguments That Lead Astray

But in the midst of this Paul points out the first danger, one snare that threatens this purpose. It's found in 2:4. Everything Paul has written to this point is "in order that no one may delude [them] with plausible arguments," or "deceive [them] by fine-sounding arguments" (NIV). Paul is concerned that the apparent plausibility of some ideas in the church may lure people from the riches in Christ.

It's possible for a particular view of the church, a particular view of the pastoral ministry, to sound correct and be wrong, leading us from the best things in Christ. It's possible for a kind of teaching or idea to enter the church and displace the goal we should be focused on. There can be a kind of mission drift where we falter away from the *main* things and focus on other good but lesser things. When that happens, oftentimes it adjusts the gospel by suggesting to us that the gospel is about something *else*, something *other* than presenting the church fully mature in Christ. Perhaps it's about redeeming the culture or societal structures.

A lot of goal displacement occurs in our pastoral labors under the banner of "the kingdom of God." Lots of things are inserted in our view as things we ought to do, things that are really good and right. We hear someone say, "Surely it's good to win/engage/transform the culture, right? That's what the kingdom is bringing, right? We ought to do those things, *right?*"

Consider these words written a generation ago: "The Kingdom of God is more than individual salvation." The author continues: "Surely theology will not become less Christian by widening the scope of salvation, by taking more seriously the burden of social evil, and by learning to believe in the Kingdom of God."[3] Sounds plausible, right? The author says this about his idea:

> [It] is the old message of salvation, but enlarged and intensified. The individualistic gospel has taught us to see the sinfulness of every human heart and has inspired us with faith in the willingness and power of God to save every soul that comes to him. But it has not given us an adequate understanding of the sinfulness of the social order and its share in the sins of all individuals within it. It has not evoked faith

in the will and power of God to redeem the permanent institutions of human society from their inherited guilt of oppression and extortion. Both our sense of sin and our faith in salvation have fallen short of the realities under the ["individualistic gospel's"] teaching.[4]

That author is Walter Rauschenbusch, one of the major proponents of the social gospel.

You can hear similar sounding things in so much of the conversation about the kingdom of God. We hear people saying, "Yes, it is about the gospel and individual salvation, but it is intensified and enlarged. It addresses social structures and so many other things." That fine-sounding, plausible argument enters our thinking, and we nod along like the Colossians, saying to ourselves, "Yes, yes. This makes sense." But the apostle Paul writes to the Colossians and to us to say, "Wait a minute! The kingdom of God is focused on this irreducible minimum. The gospel addresses this irreducible minimum, that individuals must repent and believe the message."

We all know what happened with the social gospel—it redefined the gospel as all about institutions and not at all about individual salvation. History continues to teach us that when we "intensify" and "enlarge" the gospel, so many things are driven right into the church that take us off the gospel and off our pastoral purpose.

Preventing the Danger of Mission Drift

How do we prevent that danger of mission drift, the loss of the gospel through adjusting the gospel by "enlarging" and "intensifying" it? We must be ruthless about rooting our pastoral purpose and the mission of the church in the Word of God itself, in the gospel itself.

So just to make the question plain: Is it the purpose of the church to "win the culture" or "engage the culture" or "change the culture"? Is that your pastoral purpose when you show up Monday morning at the church office?

I want to suggest to you that the very language—"engaging the culture," "winning the culture," "changing the culture"—as ambiguous as it is—signifies that mission drift is already underway. We are gospel men.

We are *proclaimers* of this gospel. We are *appliers* of this gospel. We are *representatives* of this gospel. We are *stewards* of this gospel. And the one thing we must do—and never depart from—is this gospel, its proclamation and preaching.

The Apostle Paul and Social Issues

Let's consider the apostle Paul in his social context. We tend to think that we live in a more complex world than the biblical world. He lived during a time where there were massive social and cultural issues at play. There is widespread idolatry. The emperor thinks he is God. Israel lives under Roman occupation. Women count only as second-class citizens in the culture. The society commonly practices slavery.

Let's take this last issue, slavery, as an example. How does Paul deal with the cultural problem of slavery in his day? Paul's nearly complete silence is deafening, and we're tempted to make some hard judgments against the apostle. Either Paul is a blind ignoramus unaware of the issue or, worse, Paul is aware but callously unconcerned about the issue.

But when we read the body of his letters and the New Testament, we see Paul operating on a more sophisticated, even more subtle, but ultimately more profound and powerful strategy to address the culture. And he does not address "the culture" per se.

First, Paul writes to address *the church*, not the culture. He writes his letters to God's elect, not the electorate, the voters, or the citizenry at large. His strategy centers on God's redeemed, not the unredeemed.

Second, with God's people as his audience, the apostle defines slavery as contrary to the sound doctrine of the gospel (1 Tim. 1:8–10). In doing so, he helps the church understand how it's to be different from the unlawful, the disobedient, the ungodly, sinners, the unholy and profane. He wants God's people to understand this issue as contrary to the gospel because only God's people can think in those two categories—consistent with the gospel/inconsistent with the gospel.

Third, when Paul addresses God's people this way, he pushes the gospel toward its radical implications. That's what he does in Philemon. If you look for a letter of protest or an abolitionist tract, you won't find it.

If you look for an appeal to government for a kinder, gentler policy, you won't see it in the Scripture. But Paul addresses this brother personally and calls him to embody the love of the gospel in setting Onesimus free. He appeals on the basis of love, calling Philemon to let the gospel love dynamic change how he treats a slave.

In all of this, Paul makes the embodiment of the gospel in the church the explosive charge he places at the load-bearing walls of the cultural practice of slavery. By making the church a clear cultural alternative, he undermines the prevailing cultural norm. He engages the culture by engaging the church.

Paul's singular purpose is to present every Christian mature in Christ. So what he engages is the church, the believer, with the gospel itself, and by doing so creates an alternative to the world.

2) Cultural Philosophy

This leads us to Paul's philosophy expressed in Colossians 2:6–7: "Therefore, as you received Christ Jesus the Lord, so walk in him, rooted and built up in him and established in the faith, just as you were taught, abounding in thanksgiving."

Since the Colossians have responded to the gospel by receiving Christ—in whom are hidden all the treasures of wisdom and knowledge—they should now walk in Christ; they should walk in that treasure of wisdom and knowledge. They should do this "just as [they] were taught."

They are captives of Christ (v. 8), for he is Lord. So, they should establish their values, their way of thinking, their conduct in Christ.

But how? How to walk in Christ as his captive? Paul says they were taught how. What was that teaching?

The Gospel Our Philosophy

The short answer is the gospel. The gospel of Jesus Christ is Paul's philosophy. He teaches the Colossians to live, to think, and to act in the good of the gospel. They must think and live in light of who Jesus is and what Jesus has done.

It's because of who Jesus is that Paul exhorts us to be enslaved to Jesus.

In Jesus "the whole fullness of deity dwells bodily" (v. 9). And Jesus stands as "the head of all rule and authority" (v. 10b). That's high Christology. That's not "Jesus is your boyfriend" or "your homey" philosophy. He's not your feel-good mate. Jesus is God—*fully*. And he rules over all other powers—*period*. He is the sovereign Lord of all creation. I love the Abraham Kuyper quote: "There is not an inch in the whole area of human existence of which Christ, the sovereign of all does not cry, 'It is Mine.'"[5]

And Paul rehearses for the Colossians what Jesus has accomplished in them and for them. He reminds them of the great benefits that have come to them by their union with Christ through faith.

"You have been filled *in Him*" (v. 10a). The fullness of God dwells in Jesus bodily, and we have been filled in him. We need nothing more. We need no new philosophies and no new ideas. Christ is all and in all.

They have a spiritual cutting away of the dead skin of sin. "*In him* also you were circumcised with a circumcision made without hands, by putting off the body of the flesh, by the circumcision of Christ" (v. 11).

Then Paul switches to a different way of talking about the gospel: baptism. "Having been buried *with him* in baptism" (v. 12a). Christ has died our death. And we have been buried with him. We identify with him not only in his death but also in his resurrection: "You were also raised *with him* through faith in the powerful working of God" (v. 12b).

He reminds the Colossians of their regeneration, their new life in Christ. "And you, who were dead in your trespasses and the uncircumcision of your flesh, God made alive *together with him*" (v. 13).

Finally, the apostle turns the diamond again to describe the gospel from the vantage point of forgiveness. All your sins have been forgiven in him: "Having forgiven us all our trespasses" (v. 13c).

In verse 14, Paul tells us which instrument the Lord used to accomplish this great salvation. It was through his cross. He canceled the record of our debt, the legal sanctions that we owed—namely death and wrath—by "nailing it to the cross."

In making the gospel his philosophy, Paul teaches his people to wake up in the morning and to live the day hearing the pounding of the nails in the cross and rejoicing that their sins have been nailed there with Christ.

He teaches them to recognize that in Christ they have received fullness, and in Christ they have received life—real life, eternal life, abundant life, indestructible life. All of the treasures of God are in Christ. Now they should think that way and live that way. Paul writes to the Colossians to teach them to always have this message of the cross in their thinking, as their philosophy.

The Danger: Forgetting the Antithesis

As Paul teaches them the gospel as the Christian philosophy, he identifies a second danger. The Colossians—and the church today—may be captive to human philosophy not according to Christ. Paul writes, "See to it that no one takes you captive by philosophy and empty deceit, according to human tradition, according to the elemental spirits [principles] of the world, and not according to Christ" (v. 8).

The warning here parallels the warning in verse 4. We might put Paul's concern in question form. When it comes to our philosophy of Christian life and ministry, even our philosophy of cultural engagement, are we captured by Christ or captured by worldly philosophy and tradition? Is it the world's ideas we hear and obey most, or is it Christ?

He uses the imagery of captivity. Picture a raiding party overcoming a village and hauling the people off in shackles and chains. Who captures us? The world or the Lord?

Both Dr. Sproul and Dr. Mohler gave us a rich litany of worldly philosophical movements that have crept into the church and taken people captive. [6] The list is too numerous to recount. But the end is the same: human tradition makes the Word of God of no effect (Matt. 15:6). Or, as Paul says in 1 Corinthians 1:17, depending on human wisdom empties the cross of its power.

So, when Paul writes verse 8, with one grand stroke of the quill he wipes away all worldly philosophy and principles as any kind of basis for Christian living and philosophy. He sets the gospel *over* and *against* everything springing from human traditions and the principles of the world. The world and Christ are in irreconcilable opposition or antithesis. There simply is no way to blend Christ with the principles of the world.

So we must ask ourselves if our approach to cultural engagement or winning the culture takes very seriously the dangers inherent in the world or the unsuitability of the world's philosophy for Christian living. I think there is a tendency to underestimate the lethal potency and sophisticated subtlety of the world. The world is not a safe place; the world is not like colorful, soft Play-Doh. We can't just mold it and shape it in whatever fun colors we like. The world enslaves. It shapes back.

This is where the warnings about the unpredictable nature of culture prove so useful. We must be ever mindful that we're attempting to manipulate something that manipulates back. Henry R. Van Til reflects on this danger well:

> Now it ought to be observed that one of the most subtle tactics in the arsenal of Satan is the attempt to soft pedal the antithesis, to lull the people of God to sleep so that they become at ease in Zion, and are complacent with respect to the world. Satan is ever trying to camouflage his real intention; he tries to make the world look innocuous to the people of God; he would have the people of God labour under the impression that there is a neutral zone in this world, a spiritual no-man's-land, in which they may hobnob with the enemy with impunity.[7]

In other words, there exists a deep antithesis between the kingdom and Christ on the one hand and the world and culture on the other. If we imagine that something called "secular" is the same as "safe and neutral," already we're being deceived by fine-sounding arguments. The word *secular* is not safe neutral ground. It is a ground that manipulates the gospel.

Think how often the Bible tells us of this antithesis. Already Paul has mentioned it in Colossians 1:13: "He has delivered us from the domain of darkness and transferred us to the kingdom of his beloved Son, in whom we have redemption and the forgiveness of sins." The gospel moves us from one domain into a completely different domain. Or think of the Lord's words in John 18:36 where Jesus says very simply, "My kingdom is not of this world."

Ephesians 2:1–2 tells us that this world represents the old pattern of life that led to our spiritual deaths: "You were dead in the trespasses and sins in which you once walked, following the course of this world." And the world continues its warfare with God. James 4:4 asks, "Do you not know that friendship with the world is enmity with God? Therefore whoever wishes to be a friend of the world makes himself an enemy of God." Moreover, 1 John 2:15–16 *instructs*, "Do not love the world or the things in the world. If anyone loves the world, the love of the Father is not in him. For all that is in the world—the desires of the flesh and the desires of the eyes and pride in possessions—is not from the Father but is from the world."

This is why Romans 12:2 commands, "Do not be conformed to this world, but be transformed by the renewal of your mind, that by testing you may discern what is the will of God, what is good and acceptable and perfect." The transformation of no longer conforming to this world enables the demonstration of God's good and perfect will.

Again, Van Til summarizes the issue quite well: "A Christian unaware of the problem of leading a Christian life in a non-Christian society is progressively being de-Christianized by all sorts of unconscious pressures that operate upon him through the media of culture."[8] Many people no longer recognize this. Paul's concern and our concern ought to be that our people may not realize this. Our people may not be thinking about the world and the culture with the ethical connotations the Scripture assigns to the world. Thus, they're vulnerable to being carried away captive to other philosophies and points of view.

How Forgetting the Antithesis Adjusts the Gospel

If our engagement with the world is uncritical, and we come to depend upon its philosophies and traditions, those philosophies and traditions will be Trojan horses brought into the camp while God's people are unaware. When we least expect it, the Trojan soldiers of worldly philosophy and tradition will raid and pillage the gospel city. Then either (1) we'll adjust the gospel by making it consistent with worldly philosophical aims and traditions, or (2) we'll stop talking about the gospel altogether.

That's why Christians who swallow the world's materialism end up with a bankrupt prosperity gospel, as we read from Dr. Mohler. The prosperity gospel accommodates the gospel to the materialistic impulse of the world. Many people who hold to the prosperity gospel are attempting in their own way to engage the world, in a sense. They're attempting to display to the world what they think are God's promises of prosperity so that the world would see the prosperity of God's people and be attracted. But the prosperity gospel is a tragic example of being swept away by a worldly materialism masquerading as the gospel.

Almost without fail, discussions of engaging the culture and winning the culture include some rationale for using the culture or the world in ways that undermine the gospel. For if we adopt the world's philosophies, we switch ground. We are to be rooted and built up in Christ (Col. 2:6–7), but by forgetting the antithesis we plant ourselves in the world.

That's problematic because all human cultures are fundamentally apostate. Augustine's famous description in the *City of God* demonstrates this well:

> Two cities have been formed by two loves: the earthly by the love of self, even to the contempt of God; the heavenly by the love of God, even to the contempt of self. The former, in a word, glories in itself, the latter in the Lord. For the one seeks glory from men; but the greatest glory of the other is God, the witness of the conscience. The one lifts up its head in its own glory; the other says to its God, "Thou are my glory, and the lifter of mine head." . . . The wise men of the one city, living according to man, have sought for profit to their own bodies or soul, or both, and those who have known God "glorified him not as God." . . . But in the other city there is no human wisdom, but only godliness, which offers due worship to the true God, and looks for its reward in the society of the saints, of holy angels, as well as holy men, "that God may be all in all."

There are two people in two cities, the city of God and the city of man. They live for two different glories and according to two different philosophies. But ours is the city of God and the wisdom or philosophy of God, the gospel of Jesus Christ. This has implications for our religious and cultural practice as well.

3) Cultural Practice

We're not surprised that a worldly philosophy and outlook on life lead to a worldly approach to knowing God and to cultural observances. So Paul addresses the Colossians' cultural and religious practice in Colossians 2:16–23.

Paul gives two warnings summarized by verses 16 and 18: "Therefore let no one pass judgment on you in questions of food and drink, or with regard to a festival or a new moon or a Sabbath"; and, "Let no one disqualify you, insisting on asceticism and worship of angels, going on in detail about visions, puffed up without reason by his sensuous mind."

The Danger: Justification by Other Means

Let no one judge you. Let no one disqualify you. Those are the twin dangers—that we would begin to evaluate ourselves not in light of the gospel but in light of the judgments of others, which are made not on the basis of the gospel but on the basis of self-made religion, asceticism, forms of self-righteousness, attempting growth that is not gospel growth. Can you see how worldly philosophy enters Christian thinking and the grounds of justification shift from grace alone through faith alone in the completed work of Christ alone to justification by cultural observance (v. 16), justification by religious intellect (v. 18), and justification by asceticism (vv. 20–22)?

The people making these judgments were apparently inside the church at Colossae. When the apostle says "let no one" judge or disqualify you, I think he means those outside the church as well. When he goes on to address food, drink, and religious days, he may have in mind a Judaizing influence with its emphasis on Jewish religious and cultural practices, but I think his words apply more broadly to culture and its influence in the church.

The problem is that these man-made religious and cultural practices have "an appearance of wisdom," but they are futile. They do not subdue the flesh (v. 23). Only the gospel does that. When we lose the gospel, we slowly slide toward justification by works. You collapse the categories of justification and sanctification. Religious preferences rather than the work of Christ take center stage.

When that happens, Paul says in verse 19, then we've lost our head. To take the world's cultural practices for our own is to lose our head, our attachment with Christ. We lose the substance by embracing the shadow. That is death, not growth. Christ and the gospel must inform our religious and cultural practice.

The Solution: See the Church as Embodying a Distinctive Christian Culture Given by God in Christ and the Gospel

But this raises an interesting problem. If it's true that Paul's approach to engaging the culture is (1) to engage the church, (2) to conform the church to the likeness of Christ, (3) to have the church adopt Christ as its distinctive philosophy and wisdom, and (4) to then live out of that philosophy in a distinctive practice, we're faced with the interesting question of how our various cultures relate to that pursuit. How then do we—coming from various cultural backgrounds—in one church live out a Christian life that is not dependent on those various cultural backgrounds originating in the world?

If every human culture is fundamentally apostate, and we're all saved from differing cultural backgrounds into this one new humanity (Eph. 2:14), into the church, I think this implies that part of what it means for us to push our people up into Christ is for our people to be like snakes shedding the old sin of cultural expectations, views, and ways of being.

For whenever we talk about "people groups" or ethnic groups, those people always have a culture, ways of being that are uniquely their own. So Filipinos have Filipino culture or ways of being. The same is true of Zulus in South Africa, the Riau Malay of Malaysia, and so on. Every people group is in part defined by their culture.

So the question is: What does it then mean for God to make us "his people," a "new humanity," a new spiritual ethnicity? Does it not necessarily mean that God gives us a culture, a distinctive way of being, a distinctive practice? I think this can, in part, be seen by the very way God calls his people to himself.

God's Culture Making and the Call of Abraham

In Genesis 12, after the tower of Babel demonstrates the staggering apostasy of human culture, God calls Abraham out of a pagan land and promises, essentially, "I'm going to make you a new nation." Do you realize that the first "Jew" was indeed a Gentile? God takes a pagan man from a pagan land and says, "I'm going to make you my people. You'll have descendants as numerous as the sea."

Notice that as God begins to multiply Abraham through his descendants, he also begins to separate them from pagan lands into the Promised Land (Exodus—Deuteronomy). In that land, the Lord gives Israel his law to live by, which defines their cultural, religious, and civic life. Over the long centuries of being God's people, Israel steadily acquires a culture.

Centuries later we arrive at Ephesians 2:14, where the Jewish apostle Paul refers to the law and its regulations as "the dividing wall of hostility." The people of God were called to embody the culture and practices of God such that they were set over and apart from all other peoples of the earth.

Did that process of acculturation stop with Israel?

God's Culture Making and the New Testament Church

Consider the challenge running through the book of Acts. In Acts 2, at Pentecost, the apostles speak in tongues, and Jewish worshipers from multiple nations hear the apostles speaking in their native tongue. In that supernatural moment, people from various nationalities and backgrounds are assembled as the church.

When we come to Acts 6, we read of a seriously threatening ethnic tension: Greek-speaking and Hebrew-speaking Jews suffer disparity in the daily distribution to widows. A little later the early church faces "the Gentile question." (It's interesting how the majority refers to the minorities coming into their experience as "a question." In the US, we once had "the Negro question.") In Acts 10, Peter arrives at Cornelius's house to preach the gospel when God the Holy Spirit falls on the Gentiles just as He did with Jews at Pentecost. In Acts 11, Peter's Jewish homeboys confront him, saying, "Man, what you doing at the Gentiles' house?" (There was now "a

Gentile question"). Peter replies, "Look man, I preached the gospel, and the Spirit fell on them like he fell on us. They said, 'Cool,' so I was cool with it." Grudgingly, scratching their chins and nodding, the other Jewish leaders slowly said, "Okay, okay. All right." They couldn't say anything to refute Peter's inclusion of the Gentiles, because Peter pulled the Holy Spirit card on them.

Then we arrive at Acts 15, the Jerusalem Council. The joining together of Jew and Gentile in the church and the cultural fissures and eruptions happening as different people were put together raised the question: What does gospel life look like with this mix of people and cultures? What is the gospel, and how do we embody it across our diversity? How do we put Jew and Gentile together?

It's startling to read Acts 15 and to hear the verdict, because in that scene you have people from Jewish backgrounds who for centuries were regarded as "God's chosen people" wrestling with the question of how to include people who had been outside the covenants since Abraham. And they conclude: "Let us not put any other burden on them other than what the gospel demands" (see vv. 28–29). In other words, they didn't say, "Let them become a little more Jewish like us. Let them be circumcised. Let them identify with who we are culturally."

I think there was a process happening in that council whereby not only Gentiles but also Jews were being shed of natural, human, cultural, philosophical skin that we all have and were being molded into a new people, a new culture, with a new practice consistent now with the gospel. Notice Paul's words in Colossians 2:17: all the other things—cultural and religious observances—were a "shadow," but the "substance," the body, was Christ. Christ has come, and now our practice is Christ. We live *out* the life that he is living *in* us.

This reminds us that there is a unique threat to the gospel. It's the threat of being complacent, relaxing into an unquestioning posture regarding who we are culturally and naturally. It's a threat that says, "Let me just gather with people like me." It's a threat that says, "Well, you know, culturally I prefer this style of music, so this is where I'm going to hang out." It's a threat that suggests to the world that Ephesians 2:14 is false. But Christ really has become our peace. He himself is our peace. He has abolished the dividing wall of hostility in his body on the tree. In his body he has made the two one. The gospel is the only conquering force over hostility and enmity—first with God and then with each other. So any attempt to acculturate the gospel—to make it fit into our own cultural wineskins as we engage the culture—is an adjustment of the gospel and less than the gospel.

Multiethnic, Not Multicultural

When we use the word *church*, I implore us to hear, think, and see certainly not the building or merely the Sunday morning gathering but people. And not just people, but by definition, nations. The church is a multiethnic reality. Biblically, the church is inescapably multiethnic. But it is not multicultural. It is multiethnic, but it is monocultural. And it's not any of our native cultures. It is a new way of being that God creates through Christ in the gospel. It is a gospel culture. And that's the practice that Paul wants the Colossians to embody.

We ought not be like players on the National Football League all-star team. Every year the NFL completes an all-star selection process in which the best players from around the league are chosen to play for their respective division's team. The players in each division wear a jersey of the same color. The National conference may wear blue while the American conference dons white. Yet those wearing the same color jersey do not really belong to the same team. During the game, each player wears the helmet of his in-season team, the team that pays his contract. During the all-star game the players do not run hard, hit hard, or risk injury because they are not out there playing for their real team.

So often Christians behave and think like players on the all-star team. We wear jerseys that say "Christ" but helmets that say "ethnic culture." Our ethnic teams are the actual teams we play for and the side we're on. After we finish our little intramural games across cultural backgrounds, we return to play for our real ethnic squads. Too many of us won't run hard or play hard or risk for those not on our ethnic rosters.

We need to reverse this thinking and attitude, and it's the gospel that enables us to do so as the gospel becomes our distinctive culture as the people of God.

4) Pastoral Perspective

We should consider our final *P*: Perspective. Paul describes his pastoral perspective in Colossians 3:1–4:

> If then you have been raised with Christ, seek the things that are above, where Christ is, seated at the right hand of God. Set your minds on things that are above, not on things that are on earth. For you have died, and your life is hidden with Christ in God. When Christ who is your life appears, then you also will appear with him in glory.

There is the danger that in our engagement with the culture, we can become earthly minded. We've all heard the saying, "Don't be so heavenly minded that you're no earthly good." There are other modern-day equivalents such as: "The church needs to be relevant." And sometimes, "The church must meet people's needs" (meaning earthly, physical needs). But that simply doesn't fit what Paul says here. The only way to be of any earthly good is to be increasingly heavenly minded. So Paul ends where he began.

Look Up and Look Out

Paul calls us instead to "seek the things that are above, where Christ is seated at the right hand of God. Set your mind on things that are above, not things that are on earth" (vv. 1–2). Paul grounds this exhortation in our resurrection and ascension with Christ: "If [we] have been raised with Christ," he says in verse 1, and in verse 3: if we "have died, and [our] lives are hidden with Christ in God . . ."

What has happened to Christ has happened to us through our union with Christ through faith. Since we're in heaven with Christ, what we seek has changed. We look up at Christ where he is seated in the heavenly realm. We look out to his coming.

When Christ who is our life appears, then we also will appear with him in glory. We are to be glory-seeking people. That's our perspective. We long and work and pray for the highest glory—the glory of God in Christ, which we will share when he comes! So the apostle really ends where he started: pushing us up into Christ. It's all Christ from beginning to end. Christ is our purpose. Christ is our philosophy. Christ is our practice. And Christ is our perspective. Let us be given over completely to Christ.

Paul lists the results of engaging the culture with an earthly mind in verses 5–11. In a word, the result is earthly living. We will hardly escape looking like the world in all its depravity. So we need desperately to raise our gaze from "the culture" and behold the Son seated in the place of honor beside his Father. As we look *for* him and look *at* him, we'll look *like* him (1 John 3:2–3). Since our lives are hidden in Christ, then we ought to be *looking for* and *leaning toward* and *longing after* the person and place where our lives exist. Our minds are to be on things above.

5

Sowing Seed and Sleeping Well

John MacArthur

Mark 4 records that great turning point in Jesus's ministry when he began using parables in all his public teaching. The chapter begins with an extensive, and very familiar, parable about the sower and the four soils (vv. 3–9). Our Lord later privately explained the meaning of that parable to the twelve disciples (vv. 10–20). In Mark's account, Jesus's exposition of that first parable is followed immediately by a series of shorter, more pointed parables about the kingdom (vv. 21–32).

Included in that second wave of short parables is this one, also about sowing seed (vv. 26–29):

> And [Jesus] said, "The kingdom of God is as if a man should scatter seed on the ground. He sleeps and rises night and day, and the seed sprouts and grows; he knows not how. The earth produces by itself, first the blade, then the ear, then the full grain in the ear. But when the grain is ripe, at once he puts in the sickle, because the harvest has come."

That brief passage contains a simple detail you might miss in a casual reading. But I want to underline it, because it gives us wonderful insight regarding the relationship between God's sovereignty and our responsibility in the matter of evangelism.

Notice the two words at the beginning of verse 27: "He sleeps." That two-word phrase is the hinge on which this entire parable swings. It makes a profound word picture, teaching us about God's sovereignty, the power of the gospel, the growth of the kingdom, and the responsibility of the human instrument in the spread of Christ's kingdom. Notice that the sower sows, and then he sleeps. He doesn't engineer, control, or regulate the growth that subsequently occurs. In the words of verse 28, "The earth produces *by itself,* first the blade, then the ear, then the full grain in the ear." The seed germinates and growth continues while the sower sleeps.

I've been blessed with the ability to sleep very well, even after crossing multiple time zones. I'm certain I would not sleep as well if I subscribed to the theology that seems to dominate the evangelical community today. If I believed that the salvation of souls ultimately depended on me—my presentation, my methodology, my cleverness, my ability to contextualize, my skill at gaining people's attention and admiration, or whatever—I could not sleep very well.

I understand the horrors of eternal hell. I understand the wrath of God. I understand eternal judgment. I understand what's at stake. It's a passion for me to reach people with the gospel. And I suppose with that kind of conviction dominating my heart, if I had to live within the framework of any man-centered or works-oriented theology, I would have a hard time sleeping because of the urgency of the issues at hand.

But my confidence is in the Lord and in his power, not in me. *The gospel* (not the coolness or cleverness of the one who proclaims it) is the power of God unto salvation. I can enjoy rest, refreshment, recreation, and occasional diversions from my labors because the Lord's work doesn't rise or fall on my personal skill and strategy. My responsibilities are extremely limited. I'm nothing more than a sower of seed. The seed is the Word of God, and the life and power are in the seed, not in the sower.

Recently a blogger who thinks my style is stodgy and my language is not cool enough to be truly "missional" wrote this: "MacArthur cannot reach the people that the missional Christian movement meets and reaches out to. So were he and his followers successful in delegitimizing it the number who would leave or never join the faith would hopefully only be in the tens of millions over the next century."

The fellow's specific complaint is that I'm not crass enough or explicit enough in dealing with sexual topics. He is convinced the relevance of the gospel hinges on our ability to adapt it to postmodern preferences, and he says we will be culpable if we refuse that brand of contextualization. He asks, "How many souls should be lost due to an unwillingness to be missional?" Then with a certainty that belies his wish to accommodate postmodern values, he declares that "tens of millions" of people are going to hell in the coming century because of my outmoded style. (Actually, ten million is just his best-case scenario. He can only hope I will inflict no worse damage than that.)

In his final paragraph, he says, "But MacArthur is Reformed so essentially he can be as ineffectual as he wants in outreach, since his works have no part in people being saved." That's a spin on my ministry I really hadn't encountered before. Somehow Reformed theology—my conviction that God is sovereign—makes me responsible for tens of millions of people ending up in hell. That strikes me as a rather radical expression of neo-Finneyist Pelagianism. Charles Finney, of course, was a nineteenth-century revivalist who denied the doctrines of original sin and total depravity. He insisted that sinners have sufficient free-will power to reform themselves and renew their own hearts. All the evangelist needs to do, he believed, is find effective ways to persuade people to follow Christ. Pragmatism became his ruling principle. And he left an impact on American evangelicalism that went to seed and is still creating mass confusion among evangelicals today.

Untold numbers of people who would call themselves evangelicals seem convinced that the success of the gospel is dependent upon human ingenuity, the church's ability to adapt its message to the culture, and the persuasive powers of whoever does the preaching. Practically every major trend in the evangelical movement for the past half-century or longer has had those ideas at its core. It is the reason contemporary churches are obsessed with entertainment, pop culture, and style—but cannot endure sound doctrine (2 Tim. 4:3).

Those who believe the effectiveness of the gospel depends on the messenger will inevitably make adjustments to the message, because the true gospel erects a major stumbling block in the way of the sinner (Rom. 9:33; 1 Pet. 2:8). Moreover, if I felt for one minute that people were going to hell because I failed to season the message to suit their personal tastes, or because I wasn't clever enough to persuade them to believe, I would have a very hard time sleeping. That's a mighty heavy burden to bear.

But that's not what we believe, is it? Surely one of the reasons you are here is that you are not easily motivated by the emotional rhetoric of bad theology. You are motivated by the Word of God. We share a common commitment to the gospel, and one vital aspect of that commitment is our unshakable belief that the gospel "is the power of God for salvation to everyone who believes" (Rom. 1:16). "Faith comes from hearing, and hearing through the word of Christ" (10:17). God's Word is like fire and like a hammer that breaks the rock into pieces (Jer. 23:29). No amount of human cleverness, religious ingenuity, or postmodern contextualization can add any power whatsoever to the unadulterated gospel. Our only duty is to proclaim it clearly, teach it accurately, and affirm it with real conviction.

So we come to the fourth chapter of Mark. This is a short collection of seminal parables about the kingdom of God and specifically about how the kingdom takes root, grows, and flourishes in a hostile, fallen world. Naturally, then, most of these parables deal with issues germane to evangelism. This chapter is largely paralleled in the thirteenth chapter of Matthew and the eighth chapter of Luke. At the beginning of the chapter, just by way of a brief introduction, it tells us that the Lord began to teach again by the sea, and such a very large crowd gathered to him that he got into a boat on the lake and sat down. The crowd was gathered by the sea. They were standing on the land; he was teaching them from the boat, and he taught many things in parables.

This became a daily scenario for Jesus during the year or more of his Galilean ministry. There were massive crowds—surging waves of humanity so persistent that on numerous occasions the Lord and his apostles couldn't even break for a meal. They couldn't shake free long enough to catch their breath. The crowds often numbered in the thousands. When Scripture describes the feeding of the five thousand, the number includes only adult men (Matt. 14:21). Add women and children, and it might have been a crowd of fifteen thousand to twenty-five thousand people. They would crush together around Jesus and press in so close to him that frequently he had to get in a boat, go offshore, and teach from that boat on the water just to put some space between himself and the crowd.

They were attracted by his power over demons, disease, and death. They were enthralled with his miracle-working power, which was undisputed even by his bitterest enemies. No one ever tried to explain away the miracles. His healings and other signs were incontrovertible in every way: too numerous, too well-attested, too open to scrutiny to be faked.

But very few of that multitude were true believers. In fact, so few were authentic believers that Luke 13:23 records that someone asked, "Lord, will those who are saved be few?" By that point in Jesus's public ministry, the whole messianic enterprise simply wasn't going the way everyone expected it to go. That's completely understandable, assuming the followers of Jesus were familiar with the Old Testament. Isaiah 9:6–7, that familiar prophecy of the Messiah's birth, says, "Of the increase of his government and of peace there will be no end." All Israel expected him to come and take dominion over the whole world. The Old Testament was full of prophecies that described Messiah ruling even the Gentile nations with a rod of iron. Their concept of the Messiah was a conquering hero who would dominate everything in his wake.

Jesus had been the focus of grassroots messianic hope from Galilee to Jerusalem for many months by this time. The events of Mark 4 occurred probably little more than a year before Jesus went to the cross, so Jesus's public ministry was nearly two years old. He had been the talk of all Galilee for months. And while there was clearly a widespread fascination on the part of those multitudes, most were still (at best) only superficial followers. They were mesmerized by the spectacle, hungry for more miracles, and intrigued with his power, but (in the words of John 2:24) "Jesus on his part did not entrust himself to them, because he knew all people."

What was wrong? Why was it this way? Where was the national repentance? Where was Israel's redemption? Where was the fulfillment of all the Old Testament promises about the messianic kingdom?

The fleshly response would be to say, "We need a different strategy; this one is simply not working." That's how flesh always responds to evangelistic disappointment and low numbers. It's still that way even today.

The response might be something like this: "Well, it's got to be our fault. We're not doing this the right way. We're out of touch somehow with the felt needs of the people." That's hard to sell, since Jesus had virtually banished illness from Israel, dispossessed countless people of indwelling demons, and stopped funeral processions dead in their tracks by raising the dead person to life.

Still, we think, *the fault must be ours. Maybe there are other ways to do this. Maybe we're out of touch with the trends, the sensitivities, the style, or the psychology of our time. Maybe we've got to find another way. We recognize that people are motivated psychologically. They're motivated materially. They're motivated emotionally. They're motivated by self-interest. Maybe we need to appeal to that.*

That kind of fleshly thinking is behind practically every contemporary evangelical adjustment to the gospel. We think that by some means *we* must overcome the sinner's resistance. So we try to do that by creating a message that the sinner doesn't resist as much. We package it in a style that is familiar to the sinner and with which he is somewhat comfortable. And, by the way, the message needs to be friendly, and it helps if it's also funny.

So the church has suffered from a parade of entrepreneurial types who offer to change the results by changing the message. And I think that kind of thinking must have even been in the back of the minds of the disciples: *Are we really going about this the right way? When does the fulfillment of messianic promise come to pass? Can we speed it up with a better strategy?*

So here we are in Mark 4. It is a year before the Great Commission. And the Lord gives us really a whole chapter of encouragement and evangelistic instruction in the form of parables. These parables are foundational to a right understanding of biblical evangelism. So it is critical for us to understand this chapter.

I want to begin with a look at the parable found in Mark 4:26–29. All the other parables in this chapter appear also in Matthew and Luke. This one is found only in Mark. These are all parables about the kingdom of God, and when Jesus used that term, he meant the sphere of salvation over which he reigns—the domain of his lordship over believers.

What is the kingdom like? It's like seed that sprouts and grows, and the farmer does not know how it happens. The farmer is the agricultural expert, by the way. But no farmer—not even a modern farmer with a degree in botany—fully understands the mechanism by which seed germinates and grows. In fact, the most erudite horticulturists, biologists, and agricultural wizards cannot explain the forces of life. Much less can anyone produce man-made seed capable of life and growth.

The wonder of the gospel is this: you sow the gospel, you go to sleep, and it grows. We have no control over how it happens. We don't even understand *how* it happens, any more than the farmer knows how seed that lies dead and dormant in the ground can produce abundant life.

But our duty as heralds of the gospel is simply to sow faithfully and then sleep while the crop mysteriously grows. The power of life doesn't come through the farmer—even the *best* farmer.

This is precisely what the apostle Paul taught: "I planted, Apollos watered, but *God* gave the growth" (1 Cor. 3:6). The same idea is also bound up in the familiar statement of John 1:13: The redeemed "were born, not of blood nor of the will of the flesh nor of the will of man, but of God." Spiritual birth, new life, the creation of seed that grows—God does these things; we cannot.

In John 3, in that familiar conversation between Jesus and Nicodemus, we encounter the same truth. Nicodemus certainly understands that Jesus is speaking in a metaphor. Jewish rabbis taught like that all the time. Nicodemus must have known Jesus was talking about spiritual birth, not the delivery of a physical baby. When in verse 4 Nicodemus asks, "How can a man be born when he is old? Can he enter a second time into his mother's womb and be born?" Nicodemus himself was talking in metaphoric language. He was saying, in effect, "I can't do that. I was not in charge of my first birth. How can I be *re*born?"

Jesus replies by saying, "Truly, truly, I say to you, unless one is born of water and the Spirit, he cannot enter the kingdom of God. That which is born of the flesh is flesh, and that which is born of the Spirit is spirit. Do not marvel that I said to you, 'You must be born again'" (vv. 5–7). Borrowing language from Ezekiel 36:25–26, Jesus rebukes

Nicodemus for his lack of understanding of the Old Testament doctrine of regeneration.

Then Jesus says, "The wind blows where it wishes, and you hear its sound, but you do not know where it comes from or where it goes. So it is with everyone who is born of the Spirit" (v. 8).

Nicodemus was asking how he could be born again. Jesus didn't say, "Here are four steps"; "Bow your head and close your eyes"; or "Pray this prayer." He essentially affirmed what Nicodemus had said: in effect, that rebirth is beyond the power and ken of the sinner. The Spirit does his work. He blows in like the wind, transforming, regenerating a heart. It is a divine miracle.

The wind blows, and you can't see or control it. The seed grows, but not by any doing of the farmer. The farmer doesn't even have any idea how it happens. He has no control over when it happens. He's not in charge of the power.

I want to show you an illustration of this. In Luke's narrative of the crucifixion, we have the account of the thief on the cross. Luke 23:39 says, "One of the criminals who were hanged railed at him, saying, 'Are you not the Christ? Save yourself and us!'" That was sheer sarcasm, mockery, scorn.

From a human viewpoint, that thief's skepticism certainly seems reasonable. Jesus claimed to be from God; he had been hailed as the Messiah; the whole city had shouted *Hosanna!* Now he was hanging on a cross, four great nails holding him there by the mutual consent of the Jewish leaders, the people of Jerusalem, Herod, and the Roman governor. He was suffering an execution reserved for the rankest of criminals and the basest of scoundrels. There was absolutely nothing convincing about his current position and posture that would cause anyone to give credence to his claim. Sarcasm might seem reasonable. *Are you kidding? You're supposed to be the Messiah?*

Since crucifixion was a punishment reserved for political insurrection, these "robbers" (Matt. 27:38) were not petty thieves. Matthew uses the Greek word *lestes*, meaning "brigands." These men were the first-century equivalent of what we refer to as *terrorists*. The thieves were most likely members of the virulently anti-Roman party known as the Zealots. They thus would have been Jewish, perhaps raised in a synagogue. They would therefore not only have known all the prophecies regarding Messiah; as Zealots they would have placed particular stress on the imagery of a conquering, indomitable Messiah. Certainly if the crucifixion of Christ is a stumbling block to the Jews, it is an insurmountable barrier to the Zealots.

And here was Jesus the very weakest point of his humanity—the victim of all victims, from every reasonable human viewpoint. So the initial mockery of the robbers was a perfectly understandable response.

"But," as one thief relentlessly continued mocking, "the other rebuked him, saying, 'Do you not fear God, since you are under the same sentence of condemnation?'" (Luke 23:40).

Where did that come from? This is a brigand, a criminal—a malefactor worthy of execution. And then this clear confession of classic Reformed and Protestant soteriology starts to come out of him: "We indeed [are suffering] justly, for we are receiving the due reward of our deeds; but this man has done nothing wrong" (v. 41). He affirms his own sinfulness, the justice of his punishment, and the sinlessness of Christ.

Bear in mind that Jesus was at that moment naked and bleeding, hanging on a cross, being scorned, mocked, ridiculed, and covered with shame. There was nothing whatsoever impressive about him. In the words of Isaiah, "He had no form or majesty that we should look at him, and no beauty that we should desire him" (Isa. 53:2). But this one thief, suddenly saw and understood the sinlessness of Christ.

Then he said, "Jesus, remember me when you come into your kingdom" (v. 42). In other words, he understood and affirmed the sovereignty of Christ, that he was a king. He reached out to Christ as savior, asking him to remember him. It was a plea for grace, reminiscent of the tax collector in Luke 18 who could do nothing but plead for mercy. The soundness of the man's theology is stunning.

And in that instant the thief on the cross was saved. Jesus said, "Truly, I say to you, today you will be with me in Paradise" (v. 43).

What happened? The only explanation for faith at that moment in the heart of that dying thief was the power of God on his soul. You think that somehow your cleverness is the source of someone's conversion? The Lord Jesus was at his weakest, most vulnerable. He looked totally defeated, hanging on that cross. But in that moment he brought life to a dead heart, light to a blinded soul, liberty to a condemned captive, and clear understanding to a sin-darkened mind. Faith instantly came to full fruition, and later that very same day that thief was in Paradise with Christ.

There is no human explanation for that. In my mind, it is the greatest conversion moment in the New Testament. But it reminds us that salvation is always *God's* work (Eph. 2:1-10)—an unexplained and inscrutable miracle.

The parable in Mark 4 contains an interesting expression worth noting carefully. Verse 28 says, "The earth produces by itself, first the blade, then the ear, then the full grain in the ear." The Greek term is *automatos,* meaning "spontaneously." Of course that is the term from which the English word *automatic* is derived. The word appears in only one other verse in the New Testament: Acts 12:10, which records how when Peter was released from prison by an angel, "the iron gate leading into the city . . . opened for them *of its own accord.*" Of course, that means God opened the gate. And when Mark 4:28 says the crop comes to life automatically, God's power is what causes the growth.

We may be the means by which God disseminates the gospel, but we are not the power. Do we understand that? We are messengers and agents in the proclamation of God's truth, but we are not the ones who make the gospel efficacious. We have no role but to sow the seed and go to sleep and let the work of God be done. And it *will* be done in the most amazing ways.

The success of the gospel does not depend on our power, our manipulation, or our entrepreneurial skills. Spiritual life—the regeneration of a spiritually dead soul—is from a human perspective spontaneous. And from a heavenly perspective, it is miraculous.

Of course, as in the realm of agriculture, the sowing of gospel seed requires that a few essential elements must be in place for the seed to produce fruit. Several of the parables in Mark 4 feature these essential elements. So let's broaden our perspective a bit and pay careful attention to some of the other parables in Mark 4. These are familiar principles, so I will merely highlight a few points, and we'll list them with simple key words. These are attitudes that ought to characterize our proclamation of the gospel.

Humility

First is *humility*. Keep in mind the central point: *the power of God unto salvation lies in the message, not in the messenger or the means.* All our enhancements and clever methodologies can obscure the gospel or diminish our effectiveness as evangelists, but we cannot make the gospel more powerful or more effective than it already is. We don't want to live under such an arrogant delusion.

That point is strongly hinted at in the familiar parable of the sower and the soils, when Jesus describes the seed that fell on good ground: "Other seeds fell into good soil and produced grain, growing up and increasing and yielding thirtyfold and sixtyfold and a hundredfold" (Mark 4:8). He was using superlative language and describing a scenario unheard of by the simple farming methods of that culture. *Thirty-, sixty-, and a hundredfold?* Well, that had to be good news to the small group of faithful disciples and true believers. Remember that they were discouraged and confused by the fact that there were so very few who were saved (Luke 13:23). Our Lord was suggesting that a superabundant harvest was coming.

Remember that when our Lord explained these parables, he spoke only to his closest followers in private (Mark 4:10, 34). "He said to them, "To you has been given the secret of the kingdom of God, but for those outside everything is in parables, so that 'they may indeed see but not perceive, and may indeed hear but not understand, lest they should turn and be forgiven'" (vv. 11–12).

So he begins the private explanation of his first parable with this: "The sower sows the word" (v. 14). The simplicity of that statement is worth noting. There are no adjectives to describe the sower. It's not about him. He's nobody special. He's totally anonymous: "the sower." That's just someone—anyone—who throws seed. There are no qualifications and no special skill required for the task.

The sower is not the issue here. It doesn't matter in the least whether he is using a beat-up, tattered burlap seed bag, or a designer seed bag. We don't need to hear what he looks like, how smart he is, or whether his academic credentials are impressive. Those things are all perfectly irrelevant to the question of what causes the seed to grow. The sower's only role is merely instrumental.

The seed, of course, represents the Word of God. That corresponds exactly to Romans 10:17, of course, which says faith comes by hearing the Word concerning Christ. This is not perishable seed but imperishable, "the living and abiding word of God" (1 Pet. 1:23).

While the fruit produced—including everything from initial salvation to mature fruit of the Spirit (Gal. 5:22–23)—is divinely wrought, the work of God, and (in the language of our text) *automatos*, it nevertheless does not occur apart from the message of Christ—the gospel.

Furthermore, the seed must be the true gospel and not a synthetic substitute or a partial message with the hard parts deliberately omitted. The true gospel is not about divine healing. It is not about all-you-can-eat food-multiplication miracles. It's not about prosperity, self-esteem, or social justice. And the gospel announcement is not only that Jesus is the Messiah. The heart of the gospel is the cross and the resurrection (1 Cor. 15:3-4). It is about sin, forgiveness, atonement, and justification. It begins with the sinner's guilt and culminates in a call to yield to the lordship of Christ.

Is the gospel offensive? You bet it's offensive. It is a stumbling block to the Jews and foolishness to the Gentiles (1 Cor. 1:23). But that doesn't change anything. Notice that the apostle Paul was not oblivious to what his audience wanted. "Jews demand signs and Greeks seek wisdom," he wrote in 1 Corinthians 1:22. Almost every twenty-first-century church-growth expert would insist that we must tone down the message for Jewish hearers and frame it in more sophisticated philosophical terms when we are trying to reach Greeks. Contextualize. We must address the felt needs of our audience.

Not Paul. "We preach Christ crucified, a stumbling block to Jews and folly to Gentiles" (v. 23). The Jews demanded signs; Paul gave them a stumbling block. The Greeks sought wisdom; Paul gave them folly. His approach was the polar opposite of the typical evangelical today. Why? Because to those who are called, both Jews and Greeks, the gospel of Christ is the power of God and the wisdom of God (v. 24). And in the end verse 30 says, "because of [God] you are in Christ Jesus." God is sovereign. Salvation is *his* work. And the gospel is not our message to adjust. "Let the one who boasts, boast in the Lord" (v. 31).

Therefore, Paul tells the Corinthians, "I, when I came to you, brothers, did not come proclaiming to you the testimony of God with lofty speech or wisdom. For I decided to know nothing among you except Jesus Christ and him crucified. And I was with you in weakness and in fear and much trembling, and my speech and my message were not in plausible words of wisdom, but in demonstration of the Spirit and of power, so that your faith might not rest in the wisdom of men but in the power of God" (1 Cor. 2:1–5). Paul understood the duty of the seed sower perfectly. You preach Christ crucified and risen—even if it's rejected; even if it looks like it's stupidity and shame. You preach Christ because to those who are the called, on whom the Spirit blows, in whom life is generated divinely, automatically, this is the power of God unto salvation.

Turn back now to Mark 4:3–20 and look again at that first of Jesus's parables. He was not teaching a lesson about how to be a better farmer. The parable is not about the sower or his technique. It's not even about the seed. The sower in Jesus's parable is using good, authentic seed—representing the true gospel. But the soils are the real point of the parable. When Jesus explains the parable in verses 15–20, it's all about the different kinds of soil.

What does the soil represent? In the parallel passage of Matthew 13:19, Jesus speaks of "what has been sown in his heart." So the soils represent various states of the human heart—some hardened, some shallow, some choked with thorns, and some prepared for the seed to take root. You and I can sow seed. But we can't change people's hearts. That is God's work.

We can't genuinely reach people for Christ by trying to make him seem more attractive to secular minds. We aren't truly proclaiming the gospel if we portray Christianity as a means to self-fulfillment or a way to gain earthly prosperity and personal benefits. We have no authority to set aside the hard truths of Scripture and substitute entertainment in place of the true seed as a means of attracting bigger crowds. It is not enough to generate good feelings about Jesus in the minds of unchurched people.

The world is full of hard hearts, superficial hearts, distracted hearts, double-minded hearts—carnal hearts. That is the context in which we minister, and Scripture recognizes this. In fact, the Bible portrays the natural state of fallen humanity as spiritually dead, totally unreceptive. You and I cannot give life to the dead. We can't enlighten darkened minds. We can't give sight to the blind. Only God can do that.

So we approach this ministry humbly. We know we're not the power; we're simply the human means. We sow seed. It is the Lord's work to take out the stony heart and give a heart of flesh. It's the Lord's work to put his Spirit in the heart (Ezek. 36:25–27). It's the Lord's work to write his law on the hearts of the redeemed (Jer. 31:33–34). We just sow seed, and after that, while the Lord does his miraculous work of redemption, we sleep.

Obedience

A second attitude that ought to characterize our evangelism is *obedience*. Look now at the parable found in Mark 4:21–23: "Is a lamp brought in to be put under a basket, or under a bed, and not on a stand? For nothing is hidden except to be made manifest; nor is anything secret except to come to light. If anyone has ears to hear, let him hear."

We are *humble* because we know we are not the power in salvation. We are *obedient* because we know we possess the light. That's the point of this parable.

We've been highlighting God's sovereignty in salvation, but we must bear in mind that divine sovereignty does not eliminate human responsibility. Someone might think, *Well, if God does all the work in salvation, then I don't have any role to play.* That's not the case, and that is why this parable is here. You don't cover up a shining light. You don't put your lamp under a basket or under your bed; you put it out where it can do its work.

Again, we are humble because we know we are not the power to change the heart. But we are obedient because we know we are the necessary means ordained by our sovereign God by which the light comes to those in darkness. "How are they to believe in him of whom they have never heard? And how are they to hear without someone preaching?" (Rom. 10:14). "Go into all the world and proclaim the gospel to the whole creation" (Mark 16:15). "Go therefore and make disciples of all nations" (Matt. 28:19). "Be my witnesses in Jerusalem and in all Judea and Samaria, and to the end of the earth" (Acts 1:8).

Jesus was saying to his disciples, "Look, it's axiomatic. Lamps are made to spread light. You don't light one to cover it up with a basket. You don't take a flat-pallet bed and put it on top of a lamp to hide the glow of the lamp. You put lamps on lamp stands, on the wall, or on top of a table. Better yet, put it behind a lens in a lighthouse and set it on a hill. "You are the light of the world. A city set on a hill cannot be hidden" (see Matt. 5:14). These are all simple, foundational biblical concepts. "Let your light shine before others, so that they may see your good works and give glory to your Father who is in heaven" (v. 16).

So while on the one hand it is not within our power to change hearts, it is nevertheless our responsibility to be obedient by letting the true light shine. Again, this is a mandate to proclaim the gospel in its pure, unadulterated form. It would be disobedience to this principle for us to try to dim or soften the light so that it won't seem harsh or too intense for eyes that are just emerging from darkness. It is not our prerogative to make that kind of adjustment to the gospel.

Be obedient. Scatter the seed. Shine the light. Spread the word about the gospel of Christ. Don't substitute a different message. Don't tamper with the seed. Don't try to tone down the true light. And don't give up the task.

Diligence

That calls to mind a third attitude highlighted in the parables of Mark 4: *diligence*. We undertake the task of evangelism humbly; we do it obediently; and we stay at the task diligently.

You have no doubt heard people argue that if we openly acknowledge

God's sovereignty in the salvation of sinners, that will take all the motivation out of evangelism. That's a common criticism of Reformed theology and its emphasis on the sovereignty of God.

But look at Mark 4:24–25: "Pay attention to what you hear: with the measure you use, it will be measured to you, and still more will be added to you. For to the one who has, more will be given, and from the one who has not, even what he has will be taken away." That is another axiomatic analogy. You reap what you sow (Gal. 6:7). "Whoever sows sparingly will also reap sparingly, and whoever sows bountifully will also reap bountifully" (2 Cor. 9:6).

Now, let me just stop there and say this: we are not the source of anyone's salvation, but we are the means by which the gospel is disseminated into this fallen world. We must be humble when we consider how God saves sinners, and we must be obedient when we observe the means by which the seed is scattered. It is our duty to let the light shine. We must be diligent to broadcast the seed.

How diligent should we be? Here's the motivation: "With the measure you use, it will be measured to you, and still more will be added to you" (Mark 4:24). Here we come right back to this astonishing promise, this truism, the axiom that ought to spur us to diligence: usefulness in the work of the gospel is proportionate to the seed sown and leads directly to eternal reward. Sow sparingly, reap sparingly. Sow bountifully, reap bountifully.

So you sow the seed; you sow it diligently because you know that your usefulness is proportionate to your sowing. And that leads to divine blessing. That leads to eternal reward. That's how you purchase friends for eternity. "To the one who has, more will be given, and from the one who has not, even what he has will be taken away" (v. 25).

Now there are plenty of false evangelists, phony Christians, and professional hypocrites who think they're going to get a reward. They're going to say, "Lord, Lord, did we not prophesy in your name, and cast out demons in your name, and do many mighty works in your name?" (Matt. 7:22). Jesus will say to them, "I never knew you; depart from me" (v. 23).

But the true believers who sowed authentic gospel seed will receive "still more" (Mark 4:24). More of what? More of everything, more of all the grace and goodness and kindness of God. In the words of Matthew 13:12, "He will have an abundance"—an overflowing abundance of blessing in life and eternity. That is certainly a motive for diligence.

Confidence

One more word—*confidence.* We sow and we sleep *humbly,* because we're not in charge of the results. We shine the light *obediently* because it is our privilege to be instruments in the process. We stay at the task *diligently* because our usefulness is proportionate to our faithfulness. Finally, we sow the seed *confidently* because God's Word is always effectual—infinitely more effectual than today's pragmatic styles of strategizing, scheming, psychologizing, and softening the hard edges of truth.

I love the final parable of Mark 4. Jesus asks, "With what can we compare the kingdom of God, or what parable shall we use for it? It is like a grain of mustard seed, which, when sown on the ground, is the smallest of all the seeds on earth" (vv. 30–31).

Now, if you were a discouraged disciple at that point, you might have said, "That's right. We have a diminishing group of beleaguered followers, fading from the public eye. That's our kingdom. Perhaps we need to revamp our whole approach."

No. Here's how we need to think about it: "It is like a grain of mustard seed. . . . When it is sown it grows up and becomes larger than all the garden plants and puts out large branches, so that the birds of the air can make nests in its shade" (vv. 31–32). Mustard seeds are tiny, and they do become large and leafy. But what Jesus describes—a tree large enough to provide nesting room for birds—is disproportionately and abnormally large. This is something extraordinary and unexpected—preternatural growth. Again, this can only be the work of God.

We can sow confidently because we know that God has determined an exponential outcome. Isn't that marvelous? What's going to be the final fruit of the seed we disseminate? What should we expect with this little tiny seed and these few disciples? Think of this: at one point in Jesus's earthly ministry, Christ's entire kingdom was in a boat in a storm. They all might have drowned right there. In human terms, what could they possibly expect?

But like a mustard seed, the kingdom that began as a tiny seed saw explosive growth. From small beginnings with a handful of fishermen and social outcasts, something no one could ever imagine happened. In less than half a century, people would be saying about this little kingdom: "These men . . . have turned the world upside down" (Acts 17:6).

And by the way, I love the fact that dropped in at the end of this parable is a reference to Ezekiel 17:23: "On the mountain height of Israel will I plant it, that it may bear branches and produce fruit and become a noble cedar. And under it will dwell every kind of bird; in the shade of its branches birds of every sort will nest." The birds, then, represent the nations of the world. You have similar imagery in Daniel 4:10–14. That passage describes Nebuchadnezzar's view of his kingdom as a tree that provided food for all nations. "The beasts of the field found shade under it, and the birds of the heavens lived in its branches" (v. 12). Again, the birds were symbolic of all the nations that had been assimilated into his empire.

So Jesus was telling his disciples that the very thing they thought *should* happen—the fulfillment of many Old Testament prophecies—*would* happen, in God's time and by his sovereign power. The gospel would spread across the world. Multitudes from every tribe, tongue, and nation would believe. And the kingdom would culminate in the return of Christ to establish his glorious millennial reign over the whole earth.

That is how Christ's kingdom grows. Our role in the process is instrumental only. We are sowers of the seed that God uses to bring fruit out of barren soil. We merely throw seed, and we need to sow humbly, obediently, diligently, and confidently. Having done that, we can leave the final result to the Lord and sleep peacefully, knowing that his Word is always effectual.

God himself has said: "As the rain and the snow come down from heaven and do not return there but water the earth, making it bring forth and sprout, giving seed to the sower and bread to the eater, so shall my word be that goes out from my mouth; it shall not return to me empty, but it shall accomplish that which I purpose, and shall succeed in the thing for which I sent it. For you shall go out in joy and be led forth in peace" (Isa. 55:10–12).

"Those who sow in tears shall reap with shouts of joy! He who goes out weeping, bearing the seed for sowing, shall come home with shouts of joy, bringing his sheaves with him" (Ps. 126:5–6). May we go forth humbly, work obediently, sow diligently, and sleep confidently, knowing that the Lord will accomplish all that he has ordained.

6

Did Jesus Preach the Gospel of Evangelicalism?

John Piper

The aim of my chapter title is not to criticize the gospel of evangelicalism but to assume that it is biblical and true, and then to ask whether Jesus preached it. If I had it to do over again, I would use the title "Did Jesus Preach Paul's Gospel?"—the gospel of justification by grace alone, through faith alone, on the basis of Christ's blood and righteousness alone, for the glory of God alone.

What I am driven by in this chapter, and in much of my thinking since my days in graduate school in Germany, is the conviction that Jesus and Paul preached the same gospel. There is a three-hundred-year history among critical scholars of claiming that Jesus's message and work was one thing, and what the early church made of it was another. Jesus brought the kingdom; it aborted; and the apostles substituted an institution, the church. And dozens of variations along this line.

Did Paul Get Jesus Right?

So the problem I am wrestling with is not whether evangelicalism gets Paul's gospel right, but whether Paul got Jesus's gospel right. I have a sense that among the reasons that some are losing a grip on the gospel today is not only the suspicion that we are forcing it into traditional doctrinal categories rather than biblical ones but also that, in our default to Pauline categories, we are selling Jesus short. In other words, for some—perhaps many—there is the suspicion (or even conviction) that justification by faith alone is part of Paul's gospel but not part of Jesus's gospel.

And in feeling that way, our commitment to the doctrine is weakened, and we are thus less passionate to preach it and defend it as essential to the gospel. And we may even think that Jesus's call to sacrificial kingdom obedience is more radical and more transforming than the gospel of justification by faith alone.

So I am starting where R. C. Sproul left off in his chapter.[1] I consider this chapter as an exegetical extension and defense of what he said: "If you don't have imputation, you don't have *sola fide* (faith alone), and if you don't have *sola fide*, you don't have the gospel." And my goal is to argue that Jesus preached the gospel of justification by faith alone apart from works of the law, understood as the imputation of his righteousness through faith alone.

A Word about Method

First, a word about method. One of my goals in this chapter is to fire you up for serious lifelong meditation on the four Gospels as they stand. I am so jealous that you not get sidetracked into peeling away the so-called layers of tradition to find the so-called historical Jesus. I want you to feel the truth and depth and wonder that awaits your lifelong labor of love in pondering the inexhaustible portraits of Jesus given us by Matthew, Mark, Luke, and John.

After spending twelve years of my life in the heady atmosphere of academic biblical studies, here is the conviction I came away with—and it has been confirmed every year of my life for thirty years. I commend it to you. It's the basis of the exposition I am about to give.

If you interpret faithfully the deeds and the words of Jesus as he is portrayed in the four Gospels, your portrait of Jesus will be historically and theologically more in accord with who he really was and what he really did than all the varied portraits of all the critical scholars who attempt to reconstruct a Jesus of history behind the Gospels.

Or to state it even more positively: If, by means of historical and grammatical effort, accompanied with the Spirit's illumination of what is really there, you understand the accounts of the four Gospels as they stand, you will know the Jesus who really was and what he taught.

Joy Awaits

If you believe that, what a lifelong challenge and treasure lies before you! To meditate day and night on the four Gospels with a view to knowing your Lord Jesus with ever-deepening understanding, and ever-deepening love, and ever-deepening fellowship. I really believe that the ultimate reason God gave us four portraits of Jesus in the four Gospels is so that we would more fully and accurately see and savor the glories of the Savior that we meet personally in the gospel, and that we would enjoy fellowship with him in this life, as we know him personally from what he did and said in his days on earth.

So those are my assumptions and goals. Let's go to Luke 18:9–14. How shall we read this paragraph? We will read it in the light of the big picture of the gospel and in the light of surrounding paragraphs that shed light on it. First, the big picture.

The Big Picture in Luke's Gospel

Every verse of all four Gospels is meant by the authors to be read in the shadow of the cross. When we start reading one of the Gospels, we already know how it ends—the death and resurrection of Jesus as a substitute for our sins (Matt. 26:28; Mark 10:45)—and we should have that ending in mind with every verse that we read. And this is exactly what each of the Gospels intends.

For example, Luke begins his story with the great word from the angel to the shepherds: "Fear not, for behold, I bring you good news of a great joy that will be for all the people. For unto you is born this day in the city of David a Savior, who is Christ the Lord" (Luke 2:10). And Luke does not leave us wondering how Jesus would be a savior.

He connects the suffering and death of Jesus to the new covenant of forgiveness—"This cup that is poured out for you is the new covenant in my blood" (Luke 22:20). And the new covenant promises forgiveness for sins: "I will forgive their iniquity, and I will remember their sin no more" (Jer. 31:34). So, according to Luke's portrait of Jesus, the blood of Jesus is being shed for the forgiveness of sins.

Jesus's Most Explicit Reference to Isaiah 53

In Luke, Jesus makes his most explicit claim to be the suffering servant of Isaiah 53. And, amazingly, he does it in a way that calls attention to Jesus's work of justification through a righteous one, not only to the forgiveness of sins. In the garden the night before he died, Jesus said, "I tell you that this Scripture must be fulfilled in me: 'And he was numbered with the transgressors.' For what is written about me has its fulfillment'" (Luke 22:37).

Those words, "he was numbered with the transgressors," are a quotation of Isaiah 53:12. The verse immediately preceding in Isaiah 53 (v. 11) speaks of many being counted righteous (justified) by the righteous one. "Out of the anguish of his soul he shall see and be satisfied; by his knowledge shall *the righteous one,* my servant, make many to *be accounted righteous*, and he shall bear their iniquities." So in the Gospel of Luke, the way Jesus saves is by shedding his blood for the forgiveness of sins and by being a righteous one and counting many righteous.

Luke 18:9–14

Now let's look at one of the places where Jesus speaks explicitly of justification, Luke 18:9–14:

> He also told this parable to some who trusted in themselves that they were righteous, and treated others with contempt: "Two men went up into the temple to pray, one a Pharisee and the other a tax collector. The Pharisee, standing by himself, prayed thus: 'God, I thank you that I am not like other men, extortioners, unjust, adulterers, or even like this tax collector. I fast twice a week; I give tithes of all that I get.' But the tax collector, standing far off, would not even lift up his eyes to heaven, but beat his breast, saying, 'God, be merciful to me, a sinner!' I tell you, this man went down to his house justified, rather than the other. For everyone who exalts himself will be humbled, but the one who humbles himself will be exalted."

You can tell by the way the parable comes to a climax in verse 14 ("this man went down to his house justified") that the parable is about how to be justified and how not to be justified. Of course, the parable doesn't tell the whole story of justification, because Jesus had not finished his justifying work on the cross yet when he told this parable. He had not died for our sins and been raised for our justification. So what we are seeing is not the whole story of how we are justified before God but one of the key dynamics in how it happens.

Three Aspects of the Pharisee's Righteousness

There are three things we need to see about these people in verse 9 who "trusted in themselves that they are righteous." They are represented by the Pharisee in the parable. First, his righteousness is moral. Second, his righteousness is religious or ceremonial. Third, he believes his righteousness is the gift of God.

1) *Moral*

First, his righteousness is moral. Verses 10–11:

> Two men went up into the temple to pray, one a Pharisee [that's the one who trusts in himself that he is righteous] and the other a tax collector [who had a terrible reputation for cheating the people]. The Pharisee, standing by himself, prayed thus: "God, I thank you that I am not like other men, extortioners, unjust, adulterers, or even like this tax collector."

Notice how he presents his righteousness: "I am not like others, extortioners [that is, robbers, thieves, cheaters], unjust, adulterers." In other words, "I am financially honest, just in all my dealings, and sexually faithful to my wife." That is what I mean by "moral righteousness." He was a morally upright man, at least outwardly. This is what Jesus meant when he said that the Pharisee trusted in himself that he was righteous: he was a morally upright man, he kept the commandments (like the rich young ruler, ten verses later in Luke 18:21). This was his confidence before God.

2) *Religious*

Second, this Pharisee's righteousness was religious or ceremonial. Verse 12: "I fast twice a week; I give tithes of all that I get." These are what you might call "religious" or "ceremonial" acts: fasting and tithing. They relate to spiritual disciplines before God and not so much to how you treat other people. This too was part of his righteousness. He was a morally upright and religiously devout man. This was his confidence before God.

3) A Gift from God

Third, he believed that this righteousness was the gift of God. Verse 11: "The Pharisee, standing by himself, prayed thus: 'God, *I thank you* that I am not like other men.'" He gives God the credit for making him upright and devout like he is. "I thank you that I am morally upright and religiously devout." In other words, this man is not what theologians call a Pelagian—a person who believes he can make himself righteous without God's help. He may not even be a semi-Pelagian—a person who believes that God's help is needed but the human will is decisive and can successfully resist God's help. But none of that is mentioned here. It's not the point or the problem.

The problem is not whether the man himself has produced the righteousness he has or whether God has produced it. The problem is: *he trusts in it*. This is his confidence. Verse 9: "[Jesus] also told this parable to some who *trusted in themselves* that they were righteous." Now, make sure you see what this is saying. It is not saying that he is trusting in himself to make himself righteous. No. *He says explicitly he is thanking God for that. He is not trusting in himself to make himself righteous. He is trusting in himself that he is righteous with the righteousness that he believes God has worked in him.* That is what he is trusting.

Not an Overt Legalist

As far as we know, this Pharisee was a total advocate of the sovereignty of God. As far as we know, he would have said, "Not I but the grace of God in me has worked this righteousness." He says, "I thank you, God, that I have this righteousness." *That* was not his mistake. His mistake was that he trusted in this apparently God-produced righteousness for justification.

When it came to justification—for that is the issue, as verse 14 shows—this man was trusting in the wrong thing. He was looking at the wrong basis for his righteousness before God. He was looking at the wrong ground for his righteousness before God. He was looking at the wrong person and the wrong righteousness. *He was looking to his own righteousness—and it was his, not because he created it, but because he acted it.* It was not an alien righteousness. It was inherent in him. It was in his will and in his heart and in his actions. It was his, and it was put there, he believed, by God. That is what he was trusting in.

He is not presented as a legalist—one who tries to earn his salvation. That is not the issue. One thing is the issue: This man was morally upright. He was religiously devout. He believed God had made him so. He gave thanks for it. And that is what he looked to and trusted in for his justifying righteousness before God—for his justification. And he was dead wrong to do so.

Confirmation in Luke 17:10

To confirm that we are on the right track here, glance back to Luke 17:10 where Jesus says, "So you also, when you have *done all that you were commanded*, say, 'We are unworthy servants; we have only done what was our duty.'" This is simply astonishing. It is as though Jesus had the Pharisee of Luke 18:11 in view in Luke 17:10. The man lists his moral and religious achievements. Jesus doesn't focus on whether in fact he has done "all that he was commanded," because, in one sense, according to Luke 17:10, it doesn't matter. A person who has done "all that God commanded" is still an "unworthy servant"—meaning, he has no claim on God's justification at all. That is just not how justification comes. No amount of law keeping can provide it—not even the very best.

Terrifying Words: "Rather Than the Other"

We see this in the way the parable ends in Luke 18:13–14: "But the tax collector, standing far off, would not even lift up his eyes to heaven, but beat his breast, saying, 'God, be merciful to me, a sinner!' I tell you, this man went down to his house *justified*, rather than the other."

What becomes of the Pharisee? Don't miss the terrifying four words in the middle of verse 14 for this Pharisee: "I tell you, this man [the tax collector] went down to his house justified, *rather than the other*." The Pharisee, the righteous one, the devout one, the one thanking God for his righteousness, was not justified. He was condemned.

What Justified the Tax Collector

And what about the tax collector? What did he do? He looked away from himself to God. He trusted in nothing in himself. He trusted in God's mercy. And Jesus said, "God declared him righteous and acceptable." That's what *justified* means (see Luke 7:29).

From this side of the cross, we know more about how God counts sinners, who are not righteous in themselves, as righteous. "[God] made [Christ] to be sin who knew no sin so that in him we might become the righteousness of God" (2 Cor. 5:21). By trusting Christ alone, we are united to him. And because we are "in him," what he is counts for us—his righteousness, his morality, his devoutness (see Rom. 3:28; 4:4–6; 5:18–19; 10:3–4; 1 Cor. 1:30; Gal. 2:16; Phil. 3:9).

A Clue in the Context

But is there a clue *in the context of Luke 18* that Jesus himself is the ground of the justification in verse 14? We've already seen, in the big picture of Luke, that Jesus saw himself as the suffering servant who is the righteous one that makes many to be accounted righteous (Luke 22:37=Isaiah 53:12). But look just briefly at the story of the rich young ruler in Luke 18:18–21:

> And a ruler asked him, "Good Teacher, what must I do to inherit eternal life?" And Jesus said to him, "Why do you call me good? No one is good except God alone. You know the commandments: 'Do not commit adultery, Do not murder, Do not steal, Do not bear false witness, Honor your father and mother.'" And he said, "*All these I have kept from my youth*."

Does that sound like anything we have heard before? Notice, the issue is not primarily whether he was right when he says, "All these I have kept from my youth." Jesus has already shown in Luke 17:10 that a person who keeps all the commandments is still an unworthy servant if he depends on them for justification.

Only One Thing Missing

And Jesus has shown in Luke 18:11–12 that the Pharisee's moral righteousness, and religious righteousness, and his claim to depend on God for it all—none of it counts for righteousness before God. He must despair of what is in himself and look away.

So, when it comes to justification, it doesn't matter whether the rich ruler is right when he says, "All these I have kept from my youth." What matters is what he is depending on. What he is trusting in. So Jesus says to him in Luke 18:22, "*One thing* you still lack. Sell all that you have and distribute to the poor, and you will have treasure in heaven; and come, follow me."

This is amazing. He says he only lacks "one thing." Presumably, if he had that one thing, then he would be perfect. In fact, that's the way Matthew records Jesus words: "If you would *be perfect* (Greek, *ei theleis teleios einai*), go, sell what you possess and give to the poor, and you will have treasure in heaven; and come, follow me" (Matt. 19:21). So he is *not* perfect. Not in God's eyes. He needs something else. No matter how much law keeping he has mustered, he needs something. The one thing is still missing.

One Thing or Three?

What is this "one thing"? It sounds like three things. Verse 22: (1) Sell what you possess, (2) give it to the poor, (3) follow me. How are these three demands really one? These demands may be summed up like this: "Your attachment to your possessions needs to be replaced by an attachment to me." It's as though the man stood there with his hands full of money, and Jesus said, "You lack one thing; reach out and take my hands." To do this, the man must open his fingers and let the money fall. The "one thing" he needs is not what falls out of his hands but what he takes into his hands.

The poor are always the beneficiaries when this transaction happens—when a person treasures Jesus above money. That's why Jesus mentions the poor. *But the main point is what is happening between this man and Jesus.* You lack one thing. You lack *me.* Stop treasuring money and start treasuring me. You want to inherit eternal life. You want to enter the kingdom of heaven. You want to be justified. Only by your attachment to me will you inherit eternal life, enter the kingdom, be justified. If you would be perfect—which is the only way into God's kingdom—follow me. Be connected to me. Depend on all that I am for you.

Jesus: God's Righteous One

So my answer is yes, there is a clue in the context about the basis of our justification. No matter how obedient we are to the commandments (17:10; 18:11–12; 18:21), we will always lack one thing, unless we look away from ourselves to the mercy of God in the person of Jesus. He is God's righteous one by whom many will be counted righteous.

Now we turn to some concluding implications and applications.

Implication #1: Jesus's Gospel Is Also Paul's

Jesus taught the Pauline doctrine of justification by faith alone on the basis of an imputed righteousness, not an inherent righteousness that God works in us. In fact, when we listen to Paul in Philippians 3:4–9, we are tempted to think he was the Pharisee in Jesus's parable in Luke 18:9–14.

> If anyone else thinks he has reason for confidence in the flesh, I have more: circumcised on the eighth day, of the people of Israel, of the tribe of Benjamin, a Hebrew of Hebrews; as to the law, a Pharisee; as to zeal, a persecutor of the church; as to righteousness under the law, blameless. But whatever gain I had, I counted as loss for the sake of Christ. Indeed, I count everything as loss because of the surpassing worth of knowing Christ Jesus my Lord. For his sake I have suffered the loss of all things and count them as rubbish, in order that I may gain Christ and be found in him, not having a righteousness of my

own that comes from the law, but that which comes through faith in Christ, the righteousness from God that depends on faith.

This is not just Paul's gospel. It is Jesus's gospel as well.

Implication #2: Nothing We Do Is the Basis for God's Acceptance

No matter how righteous you are, or how moral you are, or how religious you are, or whether God has produced all that in you, or you have produced that in yourself, do not trust in anything that is in you, or that you do, as the basis of your justification before God. That is not how you are accepted. That is not how you come into God's eternal favor. That is not how you will be justified now or in the last day. Trust in Christ—his blood and righteousness—as the sole basis of your justification.

Implication #3: Our Standing with God Is Based on Jesus, Not Us

Take heart in your struggle with indwelling sin, and remember that your standing as a cherished child of God is based not in yourself but in Christ alone. When you feel like a failure as a father or a husband or a pastor or a friend, where will you look if not to Christ for your righteousness? When Satan accuses us that we have never done a perfectly motivated deed in our life—not one—and then reminds us of God's standards of perfection, how will we thrust Satan down but by this truth, this reality?

Implication #4: Transformation Is the Fruit, Not the Root, of Justification

Never forget, therefore, that all moral transformation that pleases God is the fruit, not the root, of justification. The Pharisee, it says in Luke 18:9, looked on others with contempt. Not even a believer in sovereign grace who trusts in inherent righteousness will escape lovelessness. William Wilberforce, who derived decades of persevering political labors of love from his joyful justified standing with God, argued in his book *A Practical View of Christianity* that all the immoral behavior of the nominal Christians of his age resulted from the mistaken conception entertained of the fundamental principles of Christianity. They consider not that Christianity is scheme "for justifying the ungodly" [Romans 4:5], by Christ's dying for them "when yet sinners" [Romans 5:6–8], a scheme "for reconciling us to God—when enemies" [Romans 5:10]; and *for making the fruits of holiness the effects, not the cause, of our being justified and reconciled.*[2]

This error is common right now in our day. People, in order to create greater moral seriousness (especially with the radical commands of Jesus), are making morality part of the ground of justification. This backfires because it destroys the joyful confidence that alone can bear the fruit of Christ-exalting love. It takes away the one and only ground and source of the very transformation they long for.

Implication #5: All Our Goodness Is Evidence and Confirmation, Not Grounds

Never forget that all your good attitudes, all your good intentions, and all your good works will serve at the judgment not as the ground of your acceptance but only as the public fruit and evidence and confirmation that you were indeed born again, and that you did have faith, and that you were united to Christ, who is your sole justifying righteousness.

Settle it once and for all that the dozens of places in the Bible that make your good behavior the condition of your final salvation are a condition only as the fruit and confirmation of justification, not the ground of it. If you do not settle this, you will live in continual turmoil wondering what all those texts mean that say to Christians: "The unrighteous will not inherit the kingdom of heaven" (1 Cor. 6:9). Don't submit to that torment. Settle it. All the good that God requires of the justified is the fruit of justification by faith alone, never the ground of justification. Let the battle of your life be there. The battle to believe. Not the battle to perform.

Implication #6: The Gospel Is for Every Person and Every People

The gospel of Christ's righteousness imputed to us as the basis of our acceptance with God through faith alone is universally needed and universally valid in every culture and should be spoken to every person and every people group on the planet.

The first Adam failed to trust and obey, and we all fell in him—every human! The second Adam trusted and obeyed perfectly so that *any* and all who are in him are accepted because of him.

> For as by the one man's disobedience the many were made sinners, so by the one man's obedience the many will be made righteous. (Rom. 5:19)

The fall was universal for all in Adam. The reconciliation is universal for all in Christ. Take it everywhere.

Implication #7: Jesus Gets the Full Glory

Give Christ all his glory in the work of salvation, not just half of it. Half is the work of pardoning sin by becoming our wrath-absorbing punishment. But the other half is the work of providing our perfection by fulfilling everything that God required of us and then imputing it to us.

Don't rob the Lord of half his glory in bringing you to God. Christ is our pardon. Christ is our perfection. Therefore, knowing that Jesus and Paul preached the same gospel, let's join Paul from the heart in saying,

> I count everything as loss because of the surpassing worth of knowing Christ Jesus my Lord. For his sake I have suffered the loss of all things and count them as rubbish, in order that I may gain Christ and be found in him, not having a righteousness of my own that comes from the law, but that which comes through faith in Christ, the righteousness from God that depends on faith. (Phil. 3:8–9)

In the end, we sing:

> Hallelujah! All I have is Christ.
> Hallelujah! Jesus is my life.

7

Did the Fathers Know the Gospel?

J. Ligon Duncan III

Our forefathers often said that God has two books: the book of Scripture and the book of Providence. By the "book of Providence" they simply meant observing the study of God's ways with us as they unfold in history. Of course, the book of Providence can only be properly understood when interpreted by the book of Scripture, which is our final authority. What follows is an exercise in reading the book of Providence. However, many brothers have had their faith in what the Scriptures teach unsettled by their encounter with the book of Providence. This is often the case when it comes to the early church fathers, and so some guidance for us, some help there, is a good thing.[1]

1) Apology for History

On September 3, 1992, I was awakened by a phone call from my youngest brother, Mel, saying that my father had died in the middle of the night. Because it was early in the morning in Jackson, it took a while before I could arrange a flight to fly back to Greenville. The earliest flight I could get left Jackson after lunch. I was already scheduled to teach a class on the history of philosophy and Christian thought at Reformed Theological Seminary, and I decided, "I think I'll just go in and teach that class before I go out to the airport and catch the plane." It so happened that the class that morning was going to be on the subject of historiography. And as I stood up before the class I had these two realities in my mind: my father had just died, and I was getting ready to teach a class on historiography.

So I asked the students, "What possible justification could there be for looking at a subject such as historiography in a moment like this? There are a lot of answers to that question. One answer is, when we study church history, we are studying the history of God's providence with our people. These are our people. These are our for-bearers. These are people who rested and trusted in Jesus Christ, many of whom died because they loved him. And if we do not pay attention to the stories of God's dealings with them, we are not paying attention to the story of our own people. Furthermore, we miss great edification when we do not attend to the lessons that are to be learned from the story of God's dealings with his church.

Many of us are familiar with C. S. Lewis's famous introduction to Athanasius's book on the incarnation. Athanasius is one of those people who taught us that what you believe about the person of Christ is absolutely essential to the work of Christ, that Christology is absolutely essential to soteriology, and if you demean what the Bible says about who Christ is, you rob his capacity to do what the Bible says he had to do in order for us to be saved. When C. S. Lewis wrote an introduction to the modern English translation of Athanasius's classic work on the incarnation, he gave an apology, a defense of our reading the old classic works, even from the patristic period that includes Athanasius on the incarnation. It is such a classic that it's been reprinted in many places. Here's what Lewis says:

> There is a strange idea abroad that in every subject the ancient books should be read only by the professionals, and the amateur should content himself with modern books. . . . Now, this seems to me topsy-turvy. . . . I would advise [the amateur] to read the old. . . . A new book is still on its trial and the amateur is not in a position to judge it. . . . It is a good rule, after reading a new book, never to allow yourself another new one until you have read an old one in between. If that is too much for you, you should at least read one old one to every three new ones.
>
> Every age has its own outlook. It is especially good at seeing certain truths and especially liable to make certain mistakes. We all, therefore, need the books that will correct the characteristic mistakes of our own period. And that means the old books. . . .

We may be sure that the characteristic blindness of the twentieth century—the blindness about which our posterity will ask, "But how could they have thought that?"—lies where we have never suspected it. . . . None of us can fully escape this blindness, but we shall certainly increase it, and weaken our guard against it, if we read only modern books. . . . The only palliative is to keep the clean sea breeze of the centuries blowing through our minds, and this can be done only by reading old books.[2]

So for all these reasons, it is worthwhile to give attention to the church fathers, but evangelicals in general do not know patristics. *Patristics* is a word with Greek origins for the study of the early church fathers; another term, with Latin origins, is *petrology*. Typically, the patristic era is said to cover about the first eight centuries of the church's history, but I'm going to confine myself to the earliest church history, prior to the Council of Nicaea in 325, because of our particular concern today. I want you to see what the earliest church fathers say and emphasize.

2) Studying the Fathers

Roman Catholics, Eastern Orthodox, Anglicans, and Restorationists— that is, those who believe in a repristination of primitive Christianity, that we should go back to the golden age of the very earliest post–New Testament church for the revival of Christianity in our own time—all give great attention to the church fathers in their writing and theology. But Protestants, conservative, evangelical Protestants in particular, have rarely given the attention to the study of patristics that is comparably found in these other traditions. Historically that has not been the case. The sixteenth-century fathers of the Reformation, the magisterial Reformers, were masters in the study of the church fathers. From Luther to Calvin to Bucer and on, they knew the church fathers.

When we study the Fathers today, two views tend to emerge. One view says that the Fathers' teaching reveals that the Reformers' theology of grace was wrong, as well as how they formulated the gospel, and that they were wrong in how they formulated the core doctrines of our faith. The argument is that since the church fathers lived relatively near the time of Jesus and the apostles, their understanding of Christianity and of the New Testament must be determinative and even authoritative for our understanding of the New Testament, able to correct the supposedly wrong Protestant interpretation of the gospel and of justification. That's one view amongst those who study the church fathers.

Another view is that the gospel itself was lost from the time of the end of the New Testament to the sixteenth century, at which time it was rediscovered by the magisterial Reformers. Those who hold this view claim that the New Testament's theology of grace was lost as early as the apostolic fathers and did not reappear until the day of the magisterial Reformation.

Neither of those readings of the Fathers is accurate, sufficient, or helpful. How, then, should we read the Fathers? We should read the Fathers respectfully but carefully under the authority of Scripture. Hughes Old, in his amazing volume *Worship: Reformed according to Scripture*, says this about worship and the tradition of the church on worship and the Bible: "In the last analysis, we are not as much concerned with what tradition tells us about worship as with what tradition tells us about what Scripture has to say about worship."[3] Old is charting a proper biblical attitude toward tradition.

Our greatest concern in studying the church fathers is not to read what they said about a particular doctrine and then decide that what they said is authoritative, infallible, and true, but to learn what they said about a particular doctrine in order to know how they read the Scriptures. The Scriptures are our final authority, and the church fathers help test our reading of Scripture. Sometimes they were right, and sometimes they were wrong, but either way they help us to better read the Bible and to sit under its authority. We must not go back and say, "What did they say about this doctrine? Whatever they said about this doctrine must be infallibly true." No, we say, "What did they say about this doctrine? What they say about it will help me see if I am completely out to lunch as to how I'm reading the Bible. They may be wrong, and I may be right. I may be wrong, and they may be right, but I'll read the Scriptures in conversation with these early expositors of God's Word."

So we read the Fathers respectfully but carefully under the authority of

Scripture. This is exactly what the magisterial Reformers did in the days of the Reformation.

John Calvin was an incredible patristic scholar. In 1536, when he was twenty-seven years old, he went along to a disputation between Protestants and Roman Catholics in Lausanne, and during that disputation the Protestant representatives were faring badly against their Roman Catholic opponents in the area of church fathers. The Roman Catholic representative was citing the church fathers against the views of the Reformers, and the representatives of the Protestant side were not coming back with rebuttals. And there was young John Calvin, who had been a Christian for only a few years. His first edition of the *Institutes* was just coming out, a small book at the time, but he knew the Fathers. He rose to his feet and began to cite from memory almost verbatim from numerous church fathers in rebuttal to his Roman Catholic opponents. Everyone knew right then that he would be a brother to contend with in the days ahead. Bruce Gordon says this about Calvin's approach:

> The model set up by Calvin in his dedication of a conversation between the Reformers extended to his treatment of the church fathers, who were central to his attempt to understand Paul's writings. "Hence the tradition of the Fathers must be examined and it is a mark of prudent discretion to observe what they contain and whence they proceed. If we discover that they have no other tendency than to the pure worship of God, we may embrace them; but if they draw us away from the pure and simple worship of God, if they infect true and sincere religion by their own mixtures, we must utterly reject them."

> They were humans, they disagreed with one another, and could get it wrong. Indeed, Calvin felt no compunction about rejecting their views. In the biblical commentaries Augustine and Chrysostom not infrequently are declared to be dead wrong. Nevertheless, for Calvin, as for the other Protestant reformers, the church fathers were so highly regarded that they were constantly quoted and referenced. In his writings he rarely named any contemporary authors, even those from whom he borrowed heavily, such as Bucer or Melanchthon. Likewise, the medieval scholastics, although certainly present in his arguments, almost never appear by name. Early-modern authors including

Calvin did not footnote sources; they felt no obligations to state from where they took their arguments or against whom they were speaking. Contemporary writers did not merit such attention, and, besides, the learned public reading the text would usually be able to identify those sources. With the church fathers it was an entirely different matter. They were both named and quoted as a mark of respect.

Calvin's use of the church fathers was grounded in the firm belief that the consensus of their views supported his theology. He did not, however, simply trawl through their works seeking evidence for his own position; he read them carefully and widely and was guided by their views. They were, in his words, witnesses from a "primitive and purer Church," though everything they said had to be subjected to the rule of Scripture.[4]

Here's how Calvin himself puts this in the *Institutes*, speaking of his dialogue with the Roman Catholics:

Morever, they unjustly set the Fathers, the ancient fathers against us, (I mean the ancient writers of a better age of the church) as if in them they had supporters for their own impiety. If the contest were to be determined by patristic authority, the tide of victory—to put it very modestly—would turn to our side. Now, these Fathers have written many wise and excellent things. Still, what commonly happens to men has befallen them too, in some instances. For these so-called pious children of theirs, with all their sharpness of wit and judgment in spirit, worship only the faults and errors of the Fathers. The good things that these Fathers have written they either do not notice, or misrepresent or pervert. You might say that their only care is to gather dung amid gold. Then, with a frightful to-do they overwhelm us as despisers and adversaries of the Fathers! But we do not despise them; in fact, if it were to our present purpose, I could with no trouble at all prove that the greater part of what we are saying today meets their approval. Yet we are so versed in their writings as to remember that always all things are ours (1 Cor. 3:21–22), to serve us, not to lord it over us (Luke 22:24–25), and that we all belong to the one Christ (1 Cor. 3:23), whom we must obey in all things without exception (cf. Col. 3:20). He who does not observe this distinction will have nothing certain in religion, inasmuch as these holy men were ignorant of many things, often disagreed among themselves, and sometimes even contradicted themselves.[5]

Interestingly, the contemporary Roman Catholic patristic scholar Filoramo makes the same observation. Filoramo summarizes the Fathers' formulation of eschatology as a complex process of continuity and change over a long period of time, with the thought of any one Father exhibiting several oscillations.[6]

So, for instance, Irenaeus is often cited as one of the proponents in the early church of chiliasm or millenarianism, but in the first three books of his great work *Against Heresies*, he seems to be what we call today an "amillenialist." It's only in the final two books that he sounds like a chiliast. Charles Hill, a great New Testament and patristic scholar, has argued that Irenaeus's views changed as he was writing *Against Heresies,* and the change in his views was designed to help him address the Gnostic controversy. So if you say that the Fathers are authoritative, here's your problem: the Fathers contradict one another and sometimes contradict themselves.

So the conservative, evangelical Protestant way of reading the Fathers is not only more faithful to that reality but also consistent with two or three things that we should never forget. The first concerns the doctrine of total depravity. We are all prone to get it wrong. There's only one infallible rule for faith and practice. Second, this way of reading the church fathers is more consistent with the New Testament. Both Jesus and Paul say that error comes not from outside the church but from within it. Wolves will come. So a reading of the church fathers that recognizes that they sometimes got it wrong is more consistent with what Jesus and Paul in the New Testament tell us to expect. Furthermore, it allows us to go to the church fathers and avoid trying to press them into our preconceived mode—that they were Tridentine Roman Catholics fifteen hundred years before Tridentine Roman Catholicism existed, or that they were in lock step with Luther and Calvin at every point fifteen hundred years before Luther and Calvin were born. So we should read the Fathers respectfully but carefully under the authority of Scripture.

We should also bear this in mind: the Fathers were best in polemics. We do not like polemics today; at least, we don't like it for very long. It feels too negative. When godly men start criticizing other Christians after just a short period of time, we get the heebie-jeebies, and there's a psychology to that unique to this generation. When you read the Fathers in areas that were not disputed, contested matters of church doctrine in their own time, let me give you this word of advice: watch out, because they are all over the map. But when you read the Fathers in any area that was a matter of dispute and debate in their time, they almost always got it right and gloriously so. Heresy served the church to get the Bible's proper understanding rightly articulated to the people of God through the church fathers. You find this repeatedly. So the church fathers will serve you best in the areas where the truth of the Scripture was under assault in their own time; but where it was not under assault, you'd better watch out, because sometimes they assumed the gospel, muddled the truth, and contradicted one another.

Furthermore, in reading the church fathers you have to remember the pressure of their own age on them. The church fathers, especially the earliest church fathers from the first four or five centuries of the church, lived in a time when stoic and Manichean and other types of determinism were dominant in the philosophical world of the day. In other words, an impersonal fatalism was dominating large swathes of philosophy in their time. In reaction to that fatalism, that impersonal determinism, what do you think they stressed? They stressed free will. They meant absolutely nothing like what Arminius meant sixteen centuries later, or even what high-medieval Roman Catholicism meant, and they are rightly reacting against something that is unbiblical, because determinism is unbiblical; fatalism is unbiblical. But they did so in reaction to their context in a way that often compromised their clear expounding of the sovereignty of God in his purposes of grace. What they were reacting against needed to be reacted against, but they allowed the culture to dominate their response to the culture rather than the Scripture to dominate their response to the culture in those areas.

There's a lesson for us there. We don't just react to our culture; we work out of Scripture in response to our culture. If you simply react to the culture by embracing it or rejecting it, then the culture is setting the terms of the discussion. It is better to respond to the culture by saying, "I'm going to the Word of God, and the Word of God is going to give me my marching orders." Some people don't like their parents' authority, so they do the opposite of whatever their parents tell them to do. Guess who's controlling them? Their parents, because whether they do everything their parents want them to do or nothing, the parents are controlling them. Scripture, not culture, is lord over our conscience, and the Fathers give us some hard lessons in that regard. So that's how we should read the Fathers—respectfully but carefully and under the authority of Scripture.

3) Help from the Fathers

How do the Fathers and the study of the Fathers help us? Let me rifle through a few areas. First, they help us in the status of the Old Testament. Christians, for one hundred years after the days of the apostles, continued to work fundamentally out of the Hebrew Scriptures as they preached the gospel, because the New Testament Scriptures had not been widely circulated in the form of the collection that we have now. You just don't understand the privilege we have in holding this book altogether. Do you realize it was sixteen centuries before many people could hold the Bible together, and even then one had to go to the church to hold one, and it was chained to a pillar. So the Bible of the earliest Christianity was the Hebrew Bible, but that did not keep them from preaching salvation by grace alone through faith alone in Christ alone. Look at what Paul says to Timothy: "From childhood you have known the sacred writings" (2 Tim. 3:15 NASB). What sacred writings? The New Testament canon did not exist yet, so Paul was talking about the Hebrew Bible. "Timothy, from childhood you've known the Hebrew Bible, which is able to give you the wisdom that leads to salvation through faith which is in Christ Jesus. Your Hebrew Bible can teach you salvation by grace alone though faith alone in Christ alone," Paul is saying. "Your Old Testament can give you the wisdom that leads to salvation, which is through faith in Jesus Christ.

Timothy, you've known it since you were a boy sitting on your mother's knee and your grandmother's knee."

In the early days of the church, the Gnostics arose with a dizzying variety of theological viewpoints. Gnosticism is not just one thing any more than Hinduism is just one thing. There are gazillions of Hinduisms, and there were gazillions of Gnosticisms, but one thing that Gnostics and Marcionites largely shared in common was a rejection of the Old Testament. Marcion, in order to try to expunge the Old Testament from Christianity, got rid of Matthew, Mark, John, and parts of the Pauline epistles. He edited them all, wrote introductions, and then took scissors to the Gospel of Luke and tried to get out every reference to Judaism. In that context, with people being influenced by that kind of teaching, how do you argue for the divine authority of Holy Scripture in the Old Testament? Well, you pull out J. I. Packer. But Packer hadn't been born yet! So, what do you do?

In earliest Christianity as Christians argued in the context of Judaism for the messiahship of Jesus Christ, they had used collections of Old Testament texts applied to Jesus Christ in order to show that Jesus was the Messiah promised, the one predicted by the writings of the Old Testament. These collections were called the *Demonstratio Evangelica*, the proofs of the gospel. And so church fathers such as Irenaeus and Tertullian said, "Look, if someone is saying the God of the Old Testament is not the God and Father of our Lord Jesus Christ and that the writings of the Old Testament are not the writings that come from prophets inspired by the one true God revealed in Jesus Christ, then why do we find those passages as proof of who Jesus is?" In other words, they turned the old argument that had been used in the context of Jewish evangelism around. It's not just that the Old Testament proves that Jesus is the Messiah; it's that the appeal to the Old Testament by Jesus and the apostles that he is the Messiah proves that the Old Testament is inspired by the God and Father of our Lord Jesus Christ and by his Spirit. They turned the argument around, and the Fathers gloriously and convincingly made that case in the first century of the church's life after the days of the apostles.

The Fathers help us in the doctrine of the authority of Scripture. If you are having a debate with somebody who denies the inspiration, authority, infallibility, and inerrancy of Scripture, the Fathers are your friends. You stand with them against every skeptic that has ever lived. But they also help you in the area of the canon. I find that evangelicals are most unsettled when they begin to study the history of the canon of Scripture, the authoritative books of the Bible. It is argued that the church created the canon, determing what is Scripture and what is not. This is a famous Catholic argument against Protestantism, that the church created the Bible, and therefore the church is authoritative in how the Bible is to be understood. Well, that contradicts Scripture, because in Scripture the Word of God always creates the people of God. The people of God never create the Word of God. The people of God are created in Genesis 12 with the call of Abraham out of Ur of the Chaldeans. Thabiti Anyabwile wrote in his chapter that the first Jew was a Gentile, but it is worse than that—the first Hebrew was an Iraqi! Abraham was a pagan idolater from Iraq, but the Word of God made him the people of God. The Word of God was not created by Abraham; the Word of God created Abraham as a part of the people of faith, and that goes all the way through Scripture.

So when it comes to the canon, you say, "But doesn't it seem arbitrary that the church is determining what books are in and what books are out?" The church didn't determine that. The church recognized what was the true Word of God on two grounds: the marks of apostolicity and inspiration. That is, the church asked, "Was this written by an apostle appointed by the Lord Jesus Christ or someone in his circle; in other words, does it have the mark of apostolicity?" The church also asked, "Does this book bear the marks of inspiration?" In other words, "Does this book comport with the truth taught in our Hebrew Bible?" The church always had a canon—the Hebrew Bible. The question was what books were going to be recognized as authoritative new-covenant revelation. Inspiration was a mark. That may sound arbitrary to you, but it is really quite simple. The great competitors to the truly inspired Scriptures in the New Testament in the early days of post-apostolic Christianity were the Gnostic writings. The Gnostics denied the goodness of creation, and they denied that the true God had created material things. The Fathers looked at a book and said, "How does this book square up against the first verse in the Bible, 'In the beginning, God created the heavens and the earth'?" And if the book denied the goodness of material creation, it could not be considered inspired because it was in contradiction of the very first verse of the Bible. They didn't create or determine the canon; they recognized what was inspired Scripture according to the qualities of Scripture itself.

The church fathers help us even in the issue of the dating of the canon. In the nineteenth century, liberal scholars commonly argued that large portions of the New Testament were not written until years after the apostolic age, sometimes way into the late second century. A great scholar named J. B. Lightfoot came along and asked, "How can we address the issue of when the New Testament writings were completed?" He said, "We need to find some fixed point in history that we can date definitively, and then we need to see if the writings of the New Testament are being quoted authoritatively at that date, and then we'll know that the New Testament writings came before that time." Where would we find these? The apostolic fathers were all written from about AD 95 to about AD 115, so whatever they're quoting had to come before then, and before then was the days of the apostles. John lived until about AD 90. Lightfoot went through the apostolic fathers and saw them citing the New Testament as authoritative, and he said, "Here's the terminus—the New Testament is before that."

In the 1960s, John Robinson, a very famous liberal scholar, argued that all the New Testament had been written prior to AD 70, but it was because of the study of the Fathers that that conclusion came about.

Or what about the issue of the incarnation? In the popular Dan Brown version of the history of early Christianity, the early church believed that Jesus was human and invented the idea of his divinity at the Council of Nicaea in AD 325. Therefore, in Brown's view, the earliest church believed that Jesus was a man and that he was given the status of deity only three hundred years after his death, by a council that had been led after accretion in the evolutionary development of Christianity. The problem is that all the primary resources say it's exactly the opposite. The early church, even the Gnostics, had no problem with the idea of the deity of Christ.

There were almost three centuries before someone had the chutzpa to deny the deity of Christ, and when he did, he was so roundly crushed by Athanasius and the Nicaeans that it was fifteen hundred years before anyone had the guts to raise that question again.

The early church struggled with the humanity of Christ. They knew he was the Son of God, but was he really flesh and blood? Even our Muslim friends are confused in this area. So many people in the early church were Docetic, and they said that Jesus appeared to be a man but wasn't fully human. That teaching undermines the gospel, because if Jesus did not die in our flesh and blood and was not raised in our flesh and blood, we are without hope. The church fathers manfully resisted this kind of false teaching, and I can think of no better example than Tertullian.

Tertullian, in response to Marcion's denial of the incarnation of Jesus Christ, said:

> But answer is now required, murderer of the truth: Was not God truly crucified? Did He not, as truly crucified, die? Was He not truly raised again, seeing of course He truly died? Was it by fraud that Paul determined to know nothing among us save Jesus crucified, was it by fraud that he represented Him as buried, by fraud did he insist that He was raised up again? Fraudulent in that case is also our faith. In the whole of what we hope for from Christ will be phantasm, you utter scoundrel, who pronounce innocent the assassins of God. For of them Christ suffered nothing, if He in reality suffered nothing. Spare the one and only hope of the whole world: why tear down the indispensible dishonor of the faith? Whatever is beneath God's dignity is for my advantage. I am saved if I am not ashamed of my Lord. "Whoever is ashamed of Me," He says, "I will also be ashamed." I find no other grounds for shame, such as may prove that in contempt of dishonor I am nobly shameless and advantageously a fool. The Son of God was crucified: I am not ashamed—because it is shameful. The Son of God died. It is immediately credible—because it is silly. He was buried, and rose again; it is certain because it is impossible. But how can these acts be true of Him, if He Himself was not true, if He had not truly in Himself that which could be crucified, which could die, which could be buried and raised up again—this flesh, in fact, suffused with blood,

scaffolded of bones, threaded with sinews, intertwined with veins, competent to be born and to die, human unquestionably, as born of a human mother? And in Christ this flesh will be mortal precisely because Christ is Man, and Son of Man. Else why is Christ called man?[7]

The way the Fathers got at issues such as that put them in a fight, and they got it right. If you read the *Epistle of Diognetus*, you will find an exposition of the understanding of Paul. This was written in the early second century of the church.

The Fathers also help us against modern problems such as liberalism. They even help us in a gospel motivation to live the Christian life. Let me give you one example. You cannot battle the affections of the flesh with the command; the command is no match for the affections of the flesh. You can only battle the affections of the flesh with the affections of the Spirit, with the affections of the gospel. That's why Thomas Chalmers, the great Scottish pastor, said, "We need the expulsive power of an alien affection in us if we are going to be able to battle against the desires of the flesh." This post-sixteenth-century, Reformed, conservative, evangelical Protestant understanding was not the first time it had been put forth. As Augustine states:

> There can be no hope for me except in Your great mercy. Give me the grace to do as You command and command me to do what You will. You command me to control my bodily desires. Truly it is by continence that we are made as one and regained the unity of self which we lost by falling apart in the search for a variety of pleasures. For a man loves You so much less if besides You he also loves something else which he does not love for Your sake. O love ever burning, never quenched. Oh charity my God set me on fire with Your love. You command me to be continent, chaste. You command me to be pure. Give me the grace to do as You command and command me to do what You will.[8]

Those are gospel affections in the war against the flesh. The command can't help you. The gospel, grace, the Spirit, and the affections that are created by the gospel—can help you in that war against the flesh. The Fathers can help us in so many ways.

4) The Fathers and the Gospel

Did the church fathers clearly articulate the gospel and doctrine as they could have, particularly for the well-being of the church? No. Are the Fathers authoritative in how we are to read Paul and Jesus? No. Are they helpful? Yes. Listen to what the apostolic Fathers and the early church said about some of the key points of the doctrine of salvation, such as the atonement. Writing in the 90s, Clement of Rome stated: "Because of the love He had for us, Jesus Christ our Lord gave His blood for us by the will of God. He gave His flesh for our flesh and His soul for our souls." Here is Diognetus:

> The Father Himself placed upon Christ the burden of our iniquities and He gave His own Son as a ransom for us, the holy One for the transgressors, the blameless One for the wicked. For what other thing was capable of covering our sins than His righteousness? O sweet exchange! O unsearchable operation! O benefits surpassing all expectation that the wickedness of many should be hid in the single righteous one and that the righteousness of the one should justify many transgressors.[9]

Diognetus wrote that in the early second century. He'd obviously never read N. T. Wright.

Melito of Sardis preached an Easter sermon from Exodus 12, the Passover, and he said:

> On Behalf of Isaac the righteous one, a ram appeared for slaughter, so that Isaac might be released from bonds. That ram slain, ransomed Isaac; so also the Lord, slain, saved us, and bound, released us, and sacrificed, ransomed us.[10]

Irenaeus tells us he can remember the day when he sat in Smyrna under a man whom he simply calls "a certain elder," which was probably Papius. That elder said, "I remember sitting where you were sitting when John taught me. That John, the man who laid his head on Jesus' breast." Irenaeus studied under a man who studied under John, and here's what he says:

> To do away with the disobedience of man that had taken place at the beginning by means of a tree, He became obedient unto death, even the death of the cross. He thereby rectified that disobedience that had

occurred by reason of a tree through the obedience that was upon the tree that is the cross. In the first Adam, we had offended God Himself for Adam did not perform God's commandment. However in the second Adam we are reconciled to God, being made obedient even unto death for we were debtors to no one else but to Him whose commandment we had transgressed at the beginning. By transgressing God's commandment we became His enemies. Therefore in the last time, the Lord has restored us into friendship through making us righteous? No. Through His incarnation He has become the mediator between God and men propitiating indeed for us, the Father against whom we had sinned. He has cancelled our disobedience. By His own obedience He has conferred upon us the gift of communion with and subjection to our Maker.[11]

Read what the church fathers say about conversion. The church fathers didn't invent the idea of conversion; they got it from their Hebrew Bibles. The Jewish people of the first century knew all about conversion. This is what Justin Martyr says about conversion, in particular, how he was converted:

When I was delighting in the doctrines of Plato I heard Christians being slandered and yet I saw that they were fearless in death and unafraid of all other things that are considered fearful and I realized that it was impossible that they could be living in wickedness and pleasure. For what sensual and intemperate person could welcome death which would deprive him of his enjoyment? Such a person would prefer to continue always in the present life.

It was the lives of Christians that arrested his attention, although that did not convert him. He was converted when a Christian shared the gospel with him. He recalls:

When this Christian had spoken these and many other things he went away exhorting me to attend upon them. I have not seen him since, but immediately a flame was kindled in my soul and I was possessed by a love of the prophets, of the Scriptures, and of those men who are friends of Christ.

He was converted.

8

Ordinary Pastors

C. J. Mahaney

Some pastors are extraordinary gifts to the church—Al Mohler, Mark Dever, Ligon Duncan, R. C. Sproul, John MacArthur, John Piper, and Thabiti Anyabwile among them. It is a privilege to listen to and learn from these men. When I think about these men, I often think of the PGA tour motto: "These guys are good." These guys are smart. These guys are unusually gifted. (Although that certainly isn't how they see themselves.)

Chances are, if you're a pastor, you think of yourself as somewhat ordinary.

If you are like me, you feel very ordinary indeed. Every so often I get the privilege of having lunch with Al, Mark, and Lig. At those meals the conversation is fast and furious, and I get dizzy trying to keep up with them. The discussion sweeps from century to century, dropping into a particular year, then zooming out again, a whirlwind tour of history, philosophy, literature, theology, politics—everything except sports. They kindly assume I understand what they are talking about. I can assure you that most of the time I don't.

These guys are smart. I am not. I am comforted, though, and here's why: most of the smart guys I know have no athletic ability whatsoever. I've got an extraordinary jump shot, but I am an ordinary pastor.

I want to introduce you to another ordinary pastor. His name was Tom. Tom's life began in 1911 and ended in 1992. During those eighty-one years, Tom was a faithful and loving husband, a kind and wise father, and the faithful pastor of a small church in Canada. I doubt you have heard of Tom Carson. If you have, it's only because he had a remarkable son:

Don Carson, the brilliant biblical scholar and prolific writer. Dr. Carson has written or edited more than sixty books, including one about his dad: *Memoirs of an Ordinary Pastor: The Life and Reflections of Tom Carson*.[1] In his introduction, Don Carson explains the purpose for this memoir:

> Some pastors, mightily endowed by God, are remarkable gifts to the church. They love their people, they handle Scripture well, they see many conversions, their ministries span generations, they understand their culture yet refuse to be domesticated by it, they are theologically robust and personally disciplined. I do not need to provide you with a list of names: you know some of these people, and you have been encouraged and challenged by them, as I have. Some of them, of course, carry enormous burdens that watching Christians do not readily see. Nevertheless, when we ourselves are not being tempted by the green-eyed monster, we thank God for such Christian leaders from the past and pray for the current ones.
>
> Most of us, however, serve in more modest patches . . .
>
> Most of us—let us be frank—are ordinary pastors.
>
> Dad was one of them. This little book is a modest attempt to let the voice and ministry of one ordinary pastor be heard, for such servants have much to teach us.[2]

Let's be frank: most of us are ordinary pastors. We mean well. We work hard. But our sermons are average at best. Thousands of people all over the world are not downloading our sermons on iTunes. No, it's just average stuff, with maybe an occasional good sermon in the mix (or so we think until we talk with a few church members and realize, yeah, maybe not). Most ordinary pastors will not write a best-selling book. Most ordinary pastors will not write a book at all.

Occasionally I'll be flipping through channels and catch Al Mohler being interviewed on TV. I don't get interviewed on TV. My closest brush with celebrity status is when people stop me in airports because I bear a striking resemblance to Captain Picard (Patrick Stewart). This happens all the time. If you are an ordinary pastor, you are not going to be recognized like a celebrity, unless by mistake.

Most of us are ordinary pastors. We are truly called, and we are genuinely gifted by God for our task, but we are not unusually gifted.

We are, however, predictably tempted.

Ordinary and Discouraged

At a conference like Together for the Gospel, ordinary pastors are particularly vulnerable to the temptation to compare themselves unfavorably with other pastors. Perhaps you are familiar with this temptation. I certainly am.

At conferences like this, we listen to extraordinary sermons, purchase extraordinary books, and remember that members of our churches are more enthusiastic about these guys' sermons than about our own. We begin to wonder if we are really making a difference in anyone's life. Eventually, a man who once was not only amazed by the grace of God in his salvation but also amazed that he was called to pastoral ministry, slowly loses the wonder and joy of his pastoral calling. The inevitable result is discouragement of soul.

Too often, ordinary pastors are discouraged pastors.

Tom Carson was an ordinary pastor and often a discouraged one. His son Don Carson devotes an entire chapter to this (chapter 6, "Discouragement, Despair, and a Vow"). In that chapter we get a glimpse of Tom Carson's private journals, entries such as this one:

Sunday, Mar. 5, 1961

Rose 6:50 a.m. Prayer and study. Preached (poorly) from 2 Cor. 2. Twenty-four present. . . . Rested. Studied. Evening 19 present. Preached from Rom 1:1–17 (poorly).[3]

Tom Carson wasn't writing this for anyone else. He had no idea this journal entry would one day be published. And he was obviously discouraged. His son Don writes, "The reasons for such discouragement are many, but some of them, at least, overlap with Tom's self-doubt, guilty conscience, sense of failure, long hours, and growing frustration with apparent fruitlessness."[4] Perhaps this describes you. At some point in our lives, we can all relate to Tom Carson.

Pastoral Ministry Defined

I want to interrupt our tendency to unfavorable comparison, unattainable aspirations, and the resulting discouragement of soul. I want to ask a question: Why are we discouraged?

Often we are vulnerable to discouragement because we have forgotten what pastoral ministry truly is. We measure ourselves against unattainable standards, and inevitably we do not measure up.

So if you find yourself discouraged, you're not alone. I'm familiar with this state of soul. And the most effective way I can encourage you is to remind you of the definition of genuine pastoral ministry as revealed in Scripture.

In 2 Timothy 4:1–5, we find a biblical definition of ministry that will clarify our goals, purify our hearts, and liberate our souls. This passage can protect us from the temptation to compare ourselves with others. It can realign our motivations for ministry. It can protect ordinary pastors from discouragement. And it can sustain us through many years of joyful service to God's people. Paul writes to Timothy (and to all of us):

> I charge you in the presence of God and of Christ Jesus, who is to judge the living and the dead, and by his appearing and his kingdom: preach the word; be ready in season and out of season; reprove, rebuke, and exhort, with complete patience and teaching. For the time is coming when people will not endure sound teaching, but having itching ears they will accumulate for themselves teachers to suit their own passions, and will turn away from listening to the truth and wander off into myths. As for you, always be sober-minded, endure suffering, do the work of an evangelist, fulfill your ministry.

Pastors, this is your definition of ministry.

But it is more than a definition—it is a charge! Paul, who is facing imminent execution, says to Timothy, "*I charge you* in the presence of God and of Christ Jesus" (v. 1). When reading it, we should imagine Paul's voice appropriately raised, infused with seriousness and urgency. In these words, Paul places Timothy—who, in comparison to the apostle Paul, is an ordinary pastor—under a divinely inspired obligation.

And this divinely inspired letter is not just personal correspondence between Paul and Timothy. "These words," John Stott writes, "are Paul's legacy to the church. . . . It is impossible to read them without being profoundly stirred."[5] These words are Paul's charge—and God's—to every extraordinary pastor and every ordinary one.

We all have differing gifts, influence, and even fruitfulness. Let's be honest: I can't match the gifting and influence of John Piper or Al Mohler. And neither can you. But regardless of our varying gifts, we all have the same charge: pastoral faithfulness.

Pastoral ministry that is pleasing to God is not ultimately about gifting, influence, or even fruitfulness. It is not about how many books you have written, which conferences invite you to speak, or how many of your sermons are downloaded on iTunes. It is not even about whether your church membership numbers grow or shrink. Pastoral ministry that is pleasing to God is about faithfulness to the charge of 2 Timothy 4. You and I are called to be faithful to this charge.

On the following pages we'll look at the three areas in which Paul calls us to faithfulness: faithfulness to the message (where we'll spend most of our time in this chapter), faithfulness to the ministry, and faithfulness to the Savior. As we examine this passage, let's allow Paul's pastoral charge to address our motivation for ministry, shape our aspirations, and protect us from discouragement.

Be Faithful to the Message

Paul's first charge is this: "Preach the word" (v. 2). As pastors, we are called to be faithful to preach—and not to preach just anything; the content of our preaching is "the word."

Timothy would recognize this as yet another reference to Scripture in general (3:16–17) and the gospel in particular (1 Tim. 1:15; 2 Tim. 2:8). Paul does not need to further specify or clarify for Timothy. The "deposit," "sound teaching," "the truth," or "the faith"—these are all references to the gospel: the "trustworthy" saying, "that Christ Jesus came into the world to save sinners" (1 Tim. 1:15).

The charge is be faithful to preach the gospel. The content of our teaching, of each sermon, should be informed by this specific charge. We must never assume that those in our churches have sufficient knowledge of the gospel or have exhausted their need for the gospel. We must never address a topic isolated from the gospel. We must never exhort anyone to obedience apart from the gospel. And we must never preach more passionately about any topic other than the gospel.

You and I have been entrusted with the old, old story. We must not alter, adjust, or add to that story. Instead, we must faithfully proclaim it.

Preach the Word

You will be tempted to stray from this story. If you haven't been tempted already, you will be before long. Straying from this story is sometimes an effective way to gain applause, or win personal approval, or satisfy those Paul describes in 2 Timothy 4:3–4: "For the time is coming when people will not endure sound teaching, but having itching ears they will accumulate for themselves teachers to suit their own passions, and will turn away from listening to the truth and wander off into myths."

But regardless of the temptations, you must be faithful to preach the Word!

Here's something I've discovered: faithful proclamation of the message requires an unwavering commitment to unoriginality. In his book *Pastoral Theology*, Thomas Oden writes this at the outset: "I hope this work will be as unoriginal as possible. This is the first time I have attempted to write an entire text with an absolutely clear commitment to unoriginality."[6] Pastors, every sermon we preach must reflect the same thing: an absolutely clear commitment to unoriginality.

You see, if you don't resolve to be unoriginal, you'll be enamored by all that is new, trendy, popular, and supposedly original. If you don't resolve to be unoriginal, you'll be easily distracted by matters of secondary importance. Church structure and administration will trump gospel preaching. Your intelligence, rhetorical skill, or personality will take precedence over your faithfulness to the message of the gospel. If you don't resolve to be unoriginal, you will lose sight of what matters the most.

Dr. Harry Reeder is the senior minister of Briarwood Presbyterian

Church in Birmingham, Alabama. He helps us to appreciate what matters most with the following story:

> When I was sixteen, my father bought me a car at an auction for $75. It was a pink '57 Ford, which Dad insisted was "coral." I couldn't drive a pink car to school! I then heard words that in a not-to-distant future my children would hear, "Son, a poor ride is better than a proud walk." It was said so convincingly I knew it was probably in the Bible. Then my Dad opened the hood, and to my surprise, underneath was a 390 engine with two four-barrel carburetors. The car had been a South Carolina State Interceptor (a highway patrol car). Nothing had more power under the hood. Space and conviction prevent me from detailing the surprises that Corvettes and Roadsters would get after they looked laughingly at my pink '57 Ford while sitting side by side at stoplights. It didn't look like much, but there was power under the hood.
>
> Young Christian [and I would add: ordinary pastor], the world despises the gospel in its simplicity and disdains the vessels entrusted to carry and proclaim it. But there is power under the hood. Live the gospel, believe and preach the whole gospel—the gospel blessings that declare who you are in Christ, the gospel imperatives that call you to your new life for Christ. This gospel transforms the hearts, minds, and wills of sinners. Thankfully, it continues to transform mine. Preach it to yourself, to each other, and to the lost, and know the joys of the gospel-driven life.[7]

This is what matters—the message of the Savior who died for sinners like you and me.

Faithful gospel preaching is unoriginal, and whatever is unoriginal will be despised by the world. But unoriginal gospel preaching is powerful.

Fellow ordinary pastor, you might not look like much. The church property and building might not look like much. Your church might not run as smoothly as a Fortune 500 company or project the ambience of a Starbucks. You might not have a cutting-edge website as sleek as an Apple computer ad. But if you are preaching the gospel and building the church upon the gospel, then there is power under the hood. Your church is being edified, and the lost will be evangelized.

So, my friends, let's maintain "an absolutely clear commitment to unoriginality." Let's be faithful to the charge to preach the gospel.

And here's the thing: this is good news for ordinary pastors. You and I are ordinary, but by God's grace we can do this! Spurgeon once said, "Whitefield and Wesley might preach the gospel better than I do, but they could not preach a better gospel."[8] Ligon Duncan and Mark Dever can preach the gospel better than I can, but they cannot preach a better gospel.

Ordinary pastor, resolve to be faithful to this charge.

Be Ready in Season and out of Season

Faithfulness to "preach the word" requires that you persevere in prosperity and adversity. Paul writes, "Preach the word; be ready in season and out of season" (v. 2). It's not clear whether "in season and out of season" is directed to Timothy and his varying temptations to timidity and fear, or to his audience, who could be either receptive or antagonistic. The smart guys who serve us with their commentaries differ on this. I'm persuaded by those who think it's a reference to the audience, because verses 3 and 4 describe hearers who "will not endure sound teaching."

Faithful preaching of the gospel isn't broadly appealing, and when the message isn't appealing, you can be tempted to compromise. John Stott writes, "Whenever the biblical faith becomes unpopular, ministers are sorely tempted to mute those elements which give the most offence."[9]

But whatever the demographics and disposition of your locale, and regardless of numerical growth or lack thereof, your charge is to be faithful to preach the gospel in season and out of season. You must preach this Word, whether your hearers are receptive, indifferent, or even antagonistic.

Reprove, Rebuke, and Exhort

But there is more. Being faithful to the message requires more than exegetical precision and homiletical skill. Faithfulness to the message requires pastoral wisdom and discernment: "Reprove, rebuke, and exhort" (v. 2).

We aren't proclaiming a message in a vacuum. We are preaching the gospel to specific congregations, to people with names and faces. In these words—"reprove, rebuke, and exhort"—these people are in view. Each Sunday we preach to a group of hearers with varying perspectives, temptations, and levels of maturity. And pastoral discernment is required so we don't rebuke someone we should exhort, or exhort someone we should reprove.

To *reprove* is to confront or to expose. As Timothy was to confront false teaching, we are to confront false ideas. To *rebuke* is to humbly and boldly address those who are not listening or responding to God's Word, who have hard, proud hearts. To *exhort* is to encourage those who are teachable, attentive, and responsive, to explain to them how to live in light of the gospel. And any of these people could be in your church every Sunday.

Familiarity with the text is required but not sufficient. We must also be familiar with our church. A pastor must spend time with those he serves. He must get to know them so he can wisely, appropriately, compassionately, and skillfully address them from the text, both through his preaching and in private conversation. Someone once said, "The pastor doesn't get his message from his people, but he does get his message with his people." There is wisdom in that. Don't think you can craft effective sermons while isolated from those you serve.

Faithfulness to the message requires pastoral wisdom and discernment, which you gain by taking the time to know your people. The more you know them, the more skillfully and effectively you can reprove, rebuke, and exhort your church.

With Complete Patience

I am brought up short every time I read the phrase "with complete patience and teaching" (v. 2). Every time. Pastoral ministry requires not just patience but *complete* patience." "Complete patience" emphasizes the extent to which this quality must be present in our preaching and in our entire ministry. And it is essential, not optional.

Yes, we must be theologically accurate and exegetically precise. But if we fail to be patient with those we are addressing, we aren't being faithful to fulfill this charge.

I'd argue that pastoral patience is more difficult than theological precision. For most of us, it's easier to prepare and preach a sermon than to be patient with people. I think this is the most difficult challenge in this passage: "with complete patience."

Every day of your pastoral ministry, you will face temptations to be impatient with people or opportunities to cultivate patience with people. There is that guy you have counseled for months, possibly years, who just doesn't seem to get it. He is sincere, but consistent growth in godliness seems to be lacking from his life. Counseling session after counseling session doesn't seem to yield any noticeable change.

It is also hard to be patient with the people who are consistently critical about a minor point in your sermon, or who always notify you about what you failed to address. One time after I finished preaching, a guy approached me and said one thing: "You mispronounced a word." That's all he said—without any greeting or small talk. Now, I grew up reading *MAD* magazine, so I have all kind of snappy answers for what I think are stupid statements. That guy had no idea how evident the power of the Holy Spirit was in my life when I restrained myself from responding.

I was reading an article by a pastor who regularly received anonymous critical letters from someone who signed each note, "The Thorn." Attached to the first note was an explanation that since the apostle Paul had a thorn in the flesh, this writer felt that his pastor should have one too. So he had appointed himself "The Thorn." This pastor wanted to find out who The Thorn was and send him an anonymous letter signed, "The Hedge Trimmer."

Or there's the person who just wants to talk with you after the sermon and update you on his life—an update that is unrelated to your sermon. He just wants to talk, and it's as if he didn't even hear your sermon. You've finished preaching, you're stepping down from the pulpit, you're tired, and you can see him waiting for you.

I could give you a list of temptations. Your temptation probably involves whomever you are thinking about right now.

If you don't cultivate patience with those you serve and lead, your irritation and frustration will eventually surface. It will become evident in the tone and content of your sermons, your counseling, and your conversation after a Sunday meeting. And when you no longer have faith that God is working in your people, and instead you find yourself frustrated with your people, your soul will become weary.

In an article in *Fast Company* magazine, bestselling authors Dan Heath and Chip Heath reported on a surprising study of kids who dropped out of high school. Some Johns Hopkins University researchers discovered that they could predict which students wouldn't graduate—as early as eighth grade. According to the article, "The school district could identify more than half of the students who would be likely to drop out before they even set foot in high school."[10] I read that and immediately thought: *What if you could identify the early warning signs of a weary and discouraged pastor?*

Well, you can. One of the early warning signs is increasing frustration with people—the absence of complete patience.

So how does a pastor cultivate complete patience with those entrusted to his care over a period of many years? Here are a few suggestions.

Remember God's patience with you

When I am impatient with others, I have temporarily lost sight of God's patience with me. At the root of my impatience is self-righteousness and pride. Daily remembering God's patience with me protects my soul from sinful impatience with others. I love this reminder from J. I. Packer:

Appreciate the patience of God

> Think how he has borne with you, and still bears with you, when so much in your life is unworthy of him and you have so richly deserved his rejection. Learn to marvel at his patience, and seek grace to imitate it in your dealings with others; and try not to try his patience any more.[11]

"Think how he has borne with you, and still bears with you, when so much in your life is unworthy of him"—when you're fifty-six, you appreciate a statement like this more than when you were twenty-five. I appreciated God's patience then; I just appreciate it more now. He has patiently borne with me for thirty-one more years. My wife, my children, and the men I serve with in ministry know how true it is: there is so much of my life that is unworthy of him.

"Learn to marvel at his patience," Packer says. You have got to marvel before you imitate. Have you marveled at it recently? If you haven't, that is an early warning sign. Learn to marvel at his patience, and seek grace to imitate that patience in your dealings with others.

"And try not to try his patience anymore." I love that little parting appeal from Dr. Packer. Immediately I think, "Okay, I will try. I am not sure how that is going to go, but I will try."

Aren't you grateful that, as Psalm 103 proclaims, God does not treat us as our sins deserve? As you contemplate God's patience with you, your soul will be humbled, and you will begin to treat others with complete patience.

Remember that sanctification is slow

Sanctification is a process—an extremely slow process—for us all. Comprehending truth, applying truth, mortifying indwelling sin, cultivating the fruit of the Spirit—it's a process that usually takes place by small increments over a lifetime. Normally, people don't grow dramatically as the result of a single sermon or sermon series. And neither do you. Look at it this way: for ordinary pastors, the slow process of sanctification is a form of job security.

Too often I expect those I serve to comprehend and apply God's Word quickly, when it has taken me many years. I easily forget how much time my theological journey has taken. I am glad John Newton didn't forget. As a wise and a patient pastor, he recognized this truth. He wrote,

> I have been thirty years forming my own views; and, in the course of this time, some of my hills have sunk, and some of my valleys have risen: but, how unreasonable would it be to expect all this should take place in another person; and that, in the course of a year or two.[12]

So let me ask you: Ordinary pastor, what are your expectations of those you serve? Are you patient with them? Or do you expect them to comprehend quickly what took you years to grasp? Understanding truth takes place slowly and gradually. And applying it takes place slowly and gradually. That is why our preaching must be accompanied with "complete patience."

So what are your expectations of those you serve? Let me recommend a few realistic expectations.

First, I think you should be amazed that those who heard you preach last Sunday come back—and even at times bring guests. No one should be more amazed than the ordinary pastor when people return. Why should I be amazed? Because I preached last Sunday! "If some men were sentenced to hear their own sermons," Spurgeon said, "it would be a righteous judgment upon them, and they would soon cry out with Cain, 'My punishment is greater than I can bear.'"[13] Keep that in mind when you think about your church. We should be grateful they come back.

Second, we should be grateful they stay awake while we are preaching! Here's something I find great encouragement in: Jonathan Edwards had to address people who were falling asleep in his church. J. I. Packer describes it this way:

> In a sermon weightily titled "When the Spirit of God Has Been Remarkably Poured out on a People, a Thorough Reformation of Those Things That Were Before Amiss Amongst Them Ought to Be the Effect of It," Edwards speaks against sleeping in church and urges that "persons would avoid laying down their bodies in their seats in the midst of public worship."[14]

I cannot imagine the sight. Edwards looks out during public worship, and there is nothing subtle about it: people are stretched out. Edwards did not deserve this. I deserved Northampton, Edwards's church. Edwards deserved Covenant Life Church, my church. I can find more than sufficient reason for gratitude in the fact that those in my church—most of them, anyway—stay awake while I am preaching.

If I have realistic expectations of my church, it will be easy to be patient even when they (like me) grow slowly.

Trust God's timetable

You may have noticed that the most common biblical metaphors for ministry are drawn from the world of agriculture: sowing, watering, harvesting. Agriculture is slow. God is patient. Most of the time, he works out his purposes gradually. He is comfortable with seasons, years, and generations. For me, a month is a long time. My time frame is days, minutes, seconds. I don't like to be patient.

My pastoral ministry can be more informed by the world of technology than by the world of agriculture. I turn on my iPhone, and I want a signal *now*. If I count one-Mississippi, two-Mississippi, three-Mississippi and there's no signal, I want to know what is taking so long! But if I look up from my iPhone and bring that attitude to a conversation with a church member, someone for whom Jesus died, I am being unfaithful to the pastoral charge. My pastoral ministry cannot be informed by the world of technology; it must be informed by the world of agriculture.

God won't be rushed.

So how about you? Does the way God normally works shape your view of your church? Are you completely patient? Here's a recommendation: don't assume you are sufficiently patient. Ask around. Ask your wife, ask your children, ask your staff, ask your elders. Say to them, "I want to have an unhurried time when we can evaluate my soul in this area. I don't want just my preaching evaluated; I want my heart evaluated. Am I pastoring you with complete patience?"

When I am impatient with others, I have usually lost sight of God's patience with me. I have forgotten that sanctification is a process. I need to be reminded of God's timetable.

So what is Paul's charge—God's charge—to ordinary pastors like you and me? Preach the gospel faithfully, in season and out of season, with pastoral discernment and complete patience.

Be Faithful to Your Ministry

But Paul is not finished. He begins to summarize the pastoral call, and he paints the picture this way: "As for you, always be sober-minded, endure suffering, do the work of an evangelist, fulfill your ministry" (2 Tim.

4:5). The pastor's legacy should be a simple one: he was sober-minded, endured suffering, did the work of an evangelist, and fulfilled his ministry.

He is *sober-minded*, not like those described in verses 3 and 4 who are vulnerable to fads and trends. He is not seduced by novelty or religious innovation.

He also *endures suffering*. He understands that suffering isn't rare; it's the norm. He is not going to avoid it. If you are a faithful pastor, it's going to happen: you'll be the target of criticism from within the church and slander from without. You'll be opposed by the world when you preach the gospel. And you won't be exempt from the personal suffering that's part of living in a fallen world—suffering that God will use to accomplish his purposes in your life. God wants you to be confident that he is at work through your suffering, so that you can endure it with a solid, not superficial, joy.

The pastor is to *do the work of an evangelist*. Even though Timothy is serving in an area where evangelism and church planting are taking place, Paul wants evangelism to remain a passion in his life. This is all too easy for pastors to neglect in their preaching and personal life.

These imperatives combine to make one point: *fulfill your ministry*. Be faithful. Discharge the full range of your responsibilities. Persevere until the task is complete. Regardless of opposition or apathy, regardless of apparent success or lack thereof, regardless of church size, regardless of suffering—fulfill your ministry.

For the duration of our lives and ministries, we are called to relentless faithfulness. Today, be sober-minded, endure suffering, do the work of an evangelist, fulfill your ministry. Tomorrow, be sober-minded, endure suffering, do the work of an evangelist, fulfill your ministry. Do it today, and do it all again tomorrow, and do it all again the day after tomorrow. Keep doing the same things.

In an article that appeared in *The Briefing*, Tony Payne recounts this story:

> I once was sitting with the inestimable David Jackman in an airport, which is where we often seem to meet, and asked him what the big challenges were looking ahead for The Proclamation Trust. He paused

a moment and then said in his characteristically gentle and mellifluous tone, "You know, I think it's to keep on doing the same thing we've been doing for the past 15 years."

These were wise and very apt words for me at the time. I'd been at Matthias Media and The Briefing for about 15 years as well, and the natural thoughts running through my mind were, "Well, where do we head now? What's the next thing, the bold new direction, the brilliant strategic shift that will take us to a new level?"

David was reminding me that for all the benefits of dreaming, scheming, strategizing and improving what we're doing, one of the hardest and most crucial tasks for any ministry is to keep doing the same thing—the thing that our Master has commissioned and commanded us to do: to proclaim, to pray, to work with people.[15]

In a culture where innovation is paramount, and the calls to produce something new seduce not just the world but also the church, this is wisdom from above: Pastor, just keep doing the same thing. No innovation needed. This is what Paul is charging Timothy and what God is charging us to do: be faithful. Do the same thing. Don't be distracted by what's new. Fulfill your charge. And do it all again tomorrow.

Be Faithful to the Savior

At the outset of this passage, Paul informs Timothy that he gives this charge in the presence of God ("I charge you in the presence of God and of Christ Jesus") and in light of the final day of judgment ("who is to judge the living and the dead, and by his appearing and his kingdom"). Paul wants Timothy to be motivated by an eternal perspective.

During a recent NCAA college basketball tournament, I read the following excerpt from a press conference with Bob Huggins, coach of the West Virginia University basketball team:

Predictably, the first question Huggins was asked after his team's victory had to do with how he felt about being one step from the Final Four so many years after his first—and only—trip to college basketball's promised land.

"I never look back," he said, deadpan as always. "I've just never been that way."

Then he told a story. "When I was a kid growing up in West Virginia, I went to play one day," he said. "I got in a pickup truck in Midvale with a guy and I noticed that he didn't have a rearview mirror. I said to the guy, 'Hey, there's no rearview mirror.' He looked at me and said, 'Boy, we ain't goin' backwards.' That's the way I've lived my life."[16]

There is no rearview mirror in this passage either. Paul draws Timothy's attention to the future.

Paul had fulfilled this charge, and he eagerly anticipated his reward: "Henceforth there is laid up for me the crown of righteousness, which the Lord, the righteous judge, will award to me on that Day" (v. 8). Those are truly remarkable words. Paul is absolutely certain that he will receive a crown of righteousness.

Pastor, when you imagine the last day, what do you picture? When you contemplate a once-for-all evaluation of your life's work, do you feel sufficient? Or as you imagine that day, do your failures rise up and accuse you?

It's easy for us to imagine Paul being commended by the Savior. And it's easy for us to imagine the extraordinary pastors we know of being commended on the last day. But for us ordinary pastors, what easily comes to mind is a long list of failures, shortcomings, and sin. So often I don't expect to hear, "Well done"—I expect to hear "Nice try."

Ordinary pastor, here's what you can expect on the last day: a crown of righteousness. You—yes, you—can expect a commendation from the Savior.

Paul will undoubtedly receive commendation. But he writes, "There is laid up for me the crown of righteousness, which the Lord, the righteous judge, will award to me on that Day, *and not only to me but also to all who have loved his appearing.*" I am so glad he says, "not only to me, but also to all." If he had just said, "I will receive a reward," I would have understood that. Of course Paul will be commended by the Savior! But the good news for ordinary pastors is this: the reward is not unique to Paul. *All* who have been faithful to this charge will receive their reward. If we are faithful to preach the Word, faithful to fulfill our ministry, and faithful to the Savior, we too can look forward to receiving the Savior's commendation on the last day.

How can this be? How is it possible that I—who have sinned and so often fallen short—will receive this crown? So much in my life is unworthy of him.

This is where the shadow of the cross falls across this passage. This reward is only possible because of the cross, where sins are forgiven and the service of ordinary pastors is sanctified.

Stop for a moment and think about that day. On that last day there will be a parade of ordinary men, whose names you have never heard, who will hear the following from the Savior: "Well done, good and faithful pastor."

And this parade will include men like Tom Carson. At the conclusion to the biography of his father, Don Carson writes these words:

> Tom Carson never rose very far in denominational structures, but hundreds of people in the Outaouais and beyond testify how much he loved them. He never wrote a book, but he loved the Book. He was never wealthy or powerful, but he kept growing as a Christian: yesterday's grace was never enough. He was not a far-sighted visionary, but he looked forward to eternity. He was not a gifted administrator, but there is no text that says, "By this shall all men know that you are my disciples, if you are good administrators." His journals have many, many entries bathed in tears of contrition, but his children and grandchildren remember his laughter. Only rarely did he break through his pattern of reserve and speak deeply and intimately with his children, but he modeled Christian virtues to them. He much preferred to avoid controversy than to stir things up, but his own commitments to historic confessionalism were unyielding, and in ethics he was a man of principle. His own ecclesiastical circles were rather small and narrow, but his reading was correspondingly large and expansive. He was not very good at putting people down, except on his prayer lists.
>
> When he died, there were no crowds outside the hospital, no editorial comments in the papers, no announcements on television, no mention in Parliament, no attention paid by the nation. In his hospital room there was no one by his bedside. There was only the quiet hiss of oxygen, vainly venting because he had stopped breathing and would never need it again.

But on the other side all the trumpets sounded. Dad won entrance to the only throne room that matters, not because he was a good man or a great man—he was, after all, a most ordinary pastor—but because he was a forgiven man. And he heard the voice of him whom he longed to hear saying, "Well done, good and faithful servant; enter into the joy of your Lord." [17]

Pastor, if you find yourself weary and discouraged, meditate on that day. Ponder Paul's description of the day that is coming for all ordinary pastors who love Christ's appearing. God himself, with countless reasons to condemn us, will instead commend us—all because of the perfect life and substitutionary death of Jesus Christ.

That is extraordinary grace for ordinary pastors.

Notes

Chapter 1: The Church Is the Gospel Made Visible

1. Richard John Neuhaus, "A Candid Word about an Untold Story," *First Things* (April 2001): 73.
2. Scripture quotations in this chapter are taken from The Holy Bible, New International Version®, NIV®. Copyright © 1973, 1978, 1984 by Biblica, Inc.™ Used by permission. All rights reserved worldwide.

Chapter 2: The Defense and Confirmation of the Gospel

1. From the song "Ac-Cent-Tchu-Ate the Positive," originally recorded by Mercer with The Pied Pipers and Paul Weston's Orchestra, Capitol Records, 1944.

Chapter 3: Trajectories toward an Adjusted Gospel

1. Nicholas Kulish, Ellen Barry, and Michal Piotrowski, "Polish President Dies in Jet Crash in Russia," *New York Times*, April 10, 2010, http://www.nytimes.com/2010/04/11/world/europe/11poland.html?pagewanted=1and_r=1 (accessed April 10, 2010).
2. John Shelby Spong, *Why Christianity Must Change or Die: A Bishop Speaks to Believers in Exile* (San Francisco: HarperSanFrancisco, 1998).
3. Paul Tillich, *Systematic Theology*, vol. 1 (Chicago: University of Chicago Press, 1951).
4. Sidney Hook, "The Atheism of Paul Tillich," in *Religious Experience and Truth: A Symposium*, ed. Sidney Hook (London: Oliver & Boyd, 1961).
5. Diogenes Allen, *Christian Belief in a Postmodern World: The Full Wealth of Conviction* (Louisville, KY: Westminster, 1989), 6–9.
6. Rudolf Bultmann, "New Testament and Mythology," in *Kerygma and Myth: A Theological Debate*, ed. Hans Werner Bartsch, trans. Reginald H. Fuller (New York: Harper & Row, 1961), 5.
7. Gotthold Ephraim Lessing, "On the Proof of the Spirit and of Power," in *Lessing: Philosophical and Theological Writings*, ed. and trans. H. B. Nisbet, Cambridge Texts in the History of Philosophy (Cambridge, Cambridge University Press, 2005), 83–88.
8. Harry Emerson Fosdick, *The Modern Use of the Bible* (New York: Macmillan, 1924).
9. John Updike, *In the Beauty of the Lilies* (New York: Random House, 1996), 5.
10. Ibid., 5–6.
11. Ibid., 6.
12. Ibid., 15.
13. Daniel C. Dennett, *Darwin's Dangerous Idea: Evolution and the Meanings of Life* (New York: Simon & Schuster, 1995), 61–84.
14. George A. Lindbeck, *The Nature of Doctrine: Religion and Theology in a Postliberal Age* (Louisville, KY: Westminster, 1984).
15. Friedrich Nietzsche, *The Antichrist*, in *The Portable Nietzsche*, ed. and trans. Walter Kaufmann (1954; repr. New York: Penguin, 1982), 565–656.
16. C. S. Lewis, *Surprised by Joy: The Shape of My Early Life* (New York: Harcourt Brace Jovanovich, 1955), 206–7.

17. William Ellery Channing, *Memoir of William Ellery Channing, with Extracts from His Correspondence and Manuscripts*, vol. 1, 2nd ed. (Boston: Crosby & Nichols, 1848), 344.

18. Washington Gladden, *Recollections* (Boston and New York: Houghton Mifflin, 1909), 224.

19. R. Albert Mohler Jr., "Why They Hate It So: The Denial of Substitutionary Atonement in Recent Theology," in *Proclaiming a Cross-Centered Theology* (Wheaton: Crossway, 2009), 145–70.

20. Brian McLaren, *A New Kind of Christianity: Ten Questions That Are Transforming the Faith* (New York: HarperOne, 2010).

21. Ibid., 103.

22. Ibid.

23. Ibid., 272.

24. Phillip Jenkins, *Hidden Gospels: How the Search for Jesus Lost Its Way* (New York: Oxford University Press, 2001), 176.

25. Peter De Vries, *The Mackerel Plaza* (New York: Penguin, 1986), 7–8.

26. Philip Rieff, *The Triumph of the Therapeutic: Uses of Faith after Freud* (Chicago: University of Chicago Press, 1987).

27. Simon Dumenco, "Do You Have a Case of Recovery Envy?" Details, April 2010, http://www.details.com/culture-trends/critical-eye/201004/recovery-envy-rehab-obsessed-addiction (accessed April 10, 2010).

28. William James, *The Varieties of Religious Experience: A Study in Human Nature*, First Touchstone Edition (New York: Simon & Schuster, 1997).

29. David F. Wells, *No Place for Truth or Whatever Happened to Evangelical Theology?* (Grand Rapids, MI: Eerdmans, 1993), 236–37.

30. Friedrich Schleiermacher, *On Religion: Speeches to Its Cultured Despisers* (Cambridge: Cambridge University Press, 1996).

31. Friedrich Schleiermacher, *The Christian Faith* (Edinburgh: T&T Clark, 1928).

32. This story continued to be updated throughout 2010, culminating in October as the cathedral filed for bankruptcy: Nicole Santa Cruz, "Crystal Cathedral Files for Bankruptcy Protection," *Los Angeles Times*, October 19, 2010.

33. James Davidson Hunter, *American Evangelicalism: Conservative Religion and the Quandary of Modernity* (New Brunswick, NJ: Rutgers University Press, 1983).

Chapter 4: Fine-Sounding Arguments

1. Andy Crouch, *Culture Making: Recovering Our Creative Calling* (Downers Grove, IL: InterVarsity, 2008), 17–36.

2. See, e.g., Ibid.; D. A. Carson, *Christ and Culture Revisited* (Grand Rapids, MI: Eerdmans, 2008), 1–8.

3. Walter Rauschenbusch, *Toward a Theology of the Social Gospel* (1917; repr. Louisville, KY: Westminster, 1997), 22.

4. Ibid., 5.

5. Cited in Henry R. Van Til, *The Calvinistic Concept of Culture* (1959; repr. Grand Rapids, MI: Baker Academic), 117.

6. See their addresses in this volume: R. Albert Mohler Jr., "How Does It Happen? Trajectories toward an Adjusted Gospel"; R. C. Sproul, "The Defense and Confirmation of the Gospel."

7. Henry R. Van Til, *The Calvinistic Concept of Culture* (Grand Rapids, MI: Baker Academic, 1959), 181.

8. Ibid., 212.

Chapter 6: Did Jesus Preach the Gospel of Evangelicalism?

1. See chap. 2 in this volume.

2. William Wilberforce, *A Practical View of Christianity*, ed. Kevin Charles Belmonte (Peabody, MA: Hendrickson, 2006), 79.

Chapter 7: Did the Fathers Know the Gospel?

1. There is way too much material to cover in the space allotted in this volume. If this chapter piques your interest, there is an interview that I did with Tony Reinke of Sovereign Grace Ministries in which mention is made of many rich resources that are available to us in the church fathers. I commend that to you: Ligon Duncan and Tony Reinke, "Patristics for Busy Pastors: An Interview with Dr. Ligon Duncan," (April 9, 2008), http://www.sovereigngraceministries.org/blogs/cj-mahaney/post/patristics-for-busy-pastors-interview-with-dr-j-ligon-duncan-iii-patrology.aspx.

2. C. S. Lewis, "Introduction," in *On the Incarnation* (Crestwood, NY: St. Vladimir's Seminary Press, 1996), 3.

3. Hughes Oliphant Old, *Worship: Reformed according to Scripture*, rev. and exp. ed. (Louisville, KY: Westminster, 2002), 171.

4. Bruce Gordon, *Calvin* (New Haven, CT: Yale University Press, 2009), 106–7.

5. John Calvin, *Institutes of the Christian Religion,* trans. Ford Lewis Battles (Philadelphia: Westminster, 1960), Prefatory Address 4, 18–19.

6. G. Filoramo, "Eschatology," in the *Encyclopedia of the Early Church*, ed. Angelo Di Berardino, trans. Adrian Walford (New York: Oxford University Press, 1992), 284–86.

7. Ernest Evans, *Tertullian's Treatise on the Incarnation* (London: SPCK, 1956) 17–19.

8. Augustine, *Confessions* (New York: Penguin, 1961), 233.

9. *The Apostolic Fathers*, 2nd ed., ed. Michael Holmes, trans. J. B. Lightfoot and J. R. Hammer (Leicester, UK: Apollos, 1990) 302–3.

10. Melito of Sardis, *On Pascha and Fragments*, ed. and trans. Stuart George Hall (Oxford, UK: Oxford University Press, 1979), 77.

11. Irenaeus, *Against Heresies*, in *The Ante-Nicene Fathers*, vol. 1 (New York: Cosimo, 2007), 544.

Chapter 8: Ordinary Pastors

1. D. A. Carson, *Memoirs of an Ordinary Pastor: The Life and Reflections of Tom Carson* (Wheaton, IL: Crossway, 2008).

2. Ibid., 9.

3. Ibid., 82.

4. Ibid., 92.

5. John Stott, *The Message of 2 Timothy* (Leicester, UK: Inter-Varsity, 1973), 105.

6. Thomas C. Oden, *Pastoral Theology: Essentials of Ministry* (New York: HarperCollins, 1983), 7–8.

7. Harry Reeder, "The Gospel-Driven Life," September 2, 2010, Providence Presbytery of the Presbyterian Church in America, http://www.providencepresbytery.org/articles.php?aid=55, accessed November 12, 2010.

8. Charles H. Spurgeon, "The Exceeding Riches of Grace," in *Metropolitan Tabernacle Pulpit*, vol. 28 (1882; repr. Pasadena, TX: Pilgrim, 1973), 339.

9. Stott, *Message of 2 Timothy*, 112.

10. Dan Heath and Chip Heath, "Business Advice from Van Halen," March 1, 2010, FastCompany.com, http://www.fastcompany.com/magazine/143/made-to-stick-the -telltale-brown-mampm.html (accessed March 8, 2011).

11. J. I. Packer, *Knowing God*, 20th anniversary ed. (Downers Grove, IL: InterVarsity, 1993), 165–66.

12. Richard Cecil, *Memoirs of the Author: And General Remarks on His Life, Connections, and Character, in The Works of the Rev. John Newton*, 3rd ed. (1820; repr. Carlisle, PA: Banner of Truth, 1985), 1:101.

13. C. H. Spurgeon, "The Necessity of Ministerial Progress," in *Lectures to My Students*, vol. 2, *Lectures, Second Series* (1881; Pasadena, TX: Pilgrim, 1990), 28.

14. J. I. Packer, "The Glory of God and the Reviving of Religion: A Study in the Mind of Jonathan Edwards," in *A God-Entranced Vision of All Things: The Legacy of Jonathan Edwards*, ed. John Piper and Justin Taylor (Wheaton, IL: Crossway, 2004), 84n9.

15. Tony Payne, "The Same Thing or the New Thing," *The Sola Panel* (blog), May 5, 2008, http://solapanel.org/article/the_same_thing_or_the_new_thing/.

16. John Feinstein, "Bob Huggins Leads West Virginia to a Big Victory in the Sweet 16," *Washington Post*, March 26, 2010, http://www.washingtonpost.com/wp-dyn/content /article/2010/03/25/AR2010032504537.html.

17. Carson, *Memoirs of an Ordinary Pastor*, 147–48.

General Index

Scripture Index

A Call to Pursue Gospel-Saturated, Preaching-Centered Ministry

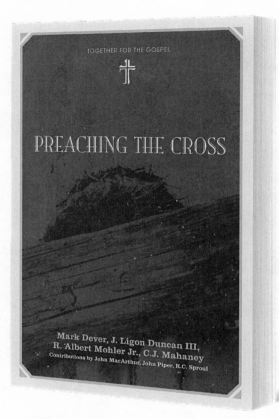

Proclaiming the gospel is without a doubt the most important task of pastoral ministry. And yet other seemingly more urgent activities often obscure it. From time to time all pastors and preachers need to be reminded of the primacy of the gospel.

Preaching the Cross is a call to expository gospel-centered preaching. Every contributor enthusiastically celebrates the centrality of the cross of Christ—keeping the main thing the main thing.

Includes contributions from Mark Dever, J. Ligon Ducan III, R. Albert Mohler Jr., C. J. Mahaney, John MacArthur, John Piper, and R. C. Sproul.

For more information, visit crossway.org.

Exploring the Church's Need for Faithful Proclamation

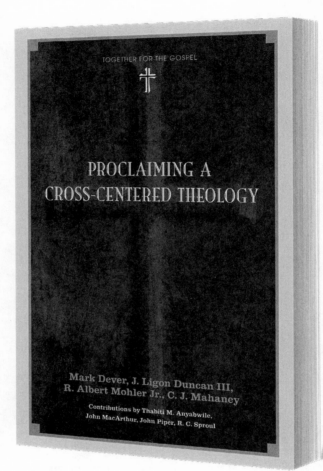

Developing and preaching a cross-centered theology is critical, for by Christ's atonement the church lives or dies. As leading voices in evangelical Christianity elaborate on the church's need for a fully biblical theology, they call every pastor and congregation to scripturally saturated thinking.

Includes contributions from Mark Dever, J. Ligon Duncan III, R. Albert Mohler Jr., C. J. Mahaney, Thabiti M. Anyabwile, John MacArthur, John Piper, and R. C. Sproul.

Joe Simpson

THIS GAME OF GHOSTS

THE
MOUNTAINEERS

To my God-daughter
Rosie Catherine Geraldine Hayman

Joe Simpson has asserted his right under the Copyright, Designs and
Patents Act, 1988, to be identified as the author of this work.

First published in the United Kingdom in 1993 by Jonathan Cape,
Random House, 20 Vauxhall Bridge Road, London, England SW1V 2SA.
This edition published 1994 by Vintage/Random House UK

A CIP catalogue record for this book is available from the British Library

**Published in the United States in 1994 (this edition published 1995) by
The Mountaineers, 1011 SW Klickitat Way, Seattle WA 98134**

Published simultaneously in Canada by
Douglas & McIntyre Ltd., 1615 Venables St., Vancouver BC V5L 2H1

ISBN 0-89886-460-7 (North America; paper)

Typeset by SX Composing Ltd., Rayleigh, Essex
Printing and bound in Great Britain by Cox & Wyman, Reading,
Berkshire

Cover photo by Ian Whitaker

CONTENTS

> I'll go with you, then,
> Since you must play this game of ghosts. At listening-posts
> We'll peer across dim craters: joke with jaded men
> Whose names we've long forgotten.

Siegfried Sassoon, 'To One Who Was with Me in the War'

INTRODUCTION
FEAR IS THE KEY

A SPASM OF PAIN erupted in my broken leg as it caught across the mule's flank. Simon and Richard gave another powerful shove and I was up in the high pommelled saddle, grabbing desperately at the mule's mane to stop myself toppling over the other side. I felt hands pushing my left foot into the leather box of a stirrup and pressed down hard to get myself upright in the saddle. I swayed unsteadily for a moment and waited with my eyes tight closed for the flushes of pain to subside.

'Are you okay?' Simon asked. I opened my eyes and peered down at his anxious face.

'Yes. It's going away now.' I glanced across at Richard, who grinned encouragingly. 'Simon, I don't think I can cope with this.'

'You have to. We can't risk infection.'

My right leg was protruding stiffly from the cushion of Karrimats draped across the saddle. I remembered what it had looked like when Simon had cut away my trousers. Bloated into a thick log of fatty swelling with purple streaks betraying the haemorrhaging where the knee and ankle had been shattered, it had felt strangely separate from me. I had been dragging it around in that state for so long that it seemed more like a piece of unwanted offensive baggage than part of my body.

The mule driver, Spinosa, took the reins and, clicking his tongue, urged the animal into a slow walk. I almost fell.

'Simon . . .' I pleaded, but he ignored me and slapped the mule on its flank.

1

'Richard, I can't . . .'

'It's all right, Joe, we'll be on each side. We'll take it easy. You'll be okay.'

We jolted off down the high Andean valley, leaving the deserted campsite and the lifeless Sarapoqoucha lake behind us. I glanced back as the mule stepped delicately across the icy stream running down the centre of the scree-strewn valley. Yerupaja soared majestically into the sky, Siula Grande lay somewhere behind it. A few cotton wool clouds clung to the summit ridge. In the foreground I saw the dam of compacted moraines down which I had crawled in the snow-swept night. The snow had melted in the morning sun. There was no trace of the slithering tracks I had made. It seemed so long ago now, so hard to believe it had ever happened.

Simon walked ahead of the mule. He turned for a last sight of the mountains we were leaving and caught my glance. For a moment there was an empty lost gaze in his blue eyes before he smiled gently, as if to say *don't worry, it's over now, it's time to leave,* and then he walked on without looking back again.

For hours the jarring, painful riding continued. I slipped between semi-consciousness and screaming wakefulness as the mule crashed my injured leg into trees, bushes, boulders and walls, despite the best efforts of Spinosa.

I couldn't understand why Simon was in such a hurry but I was too weak to argue. If I had seen myself, I would have known that it had nothing to do with a fear of infection. The sunken eyes and emaciated face would have been enough to tell me that my leg was the least of his worries. In four days of crawling alone down the mountain, dragging my unwanted limb behind me, I had lost over three stones in weight, almost 40 per cent of my usual body weight. Despite the sweet tea and porridge forced down my throat I was dangerously weak, enfeebled almost to the point of collapse, and Simon knew it. He had smelt the acetone on my breath, a side-effect of serious starvation. No amount of tea and porridge would help me. I needed glucose drips, tender loving care, hospital treatment, anything but being stuck in a remote high camp.

2

By comparison the state of my leg was insignificant. If it had been an open fracture, the stink of gangrene would already have poisoned the air. Fortunately it appeared only swollen and battered and sore, but not life threatening.

I watched it loll heavily in rhythm with the mule's stride and once again my eyes began to close. I was so tired, so deathly tired. I tried to think about everything that had happened, tried to make myself believe that it was all over, but it was useless. I couldn't lose the memory of Simon's eyes when he had seen me high on the north ridge with a broken leg and the sad pitiful look he had been unable to hide. The certainty that I was going to die had been so strong at that moment. I knew I could never forget those eyes, that odd air of detachment, the unnerving pity in the stare, as if from a witness to an execution.

I remembered the panic surging through me, a belief that he would leave me and that I would die alone. And then — after the endless agony of being lowered on the rope in freezing cold that sucked the last of the fight from me — the fall. When he had cut the rope it had been almost a relief — a silent swooping, weightless, fearless fall into darkness, only to find it wasn't all over. So much worse was to follow, more than I could ever have imagined.

As the mule stumbled I jerked awake and looked wildly around me, seeking Simon. He was there ahead of us, walking steadily, head down. He was there. It was so important that he was there. He was company and friendship, proof that I was alive, confirmation that the loneliness had been banished.

I kept glancing at Simon, at Richard and Spinosa, even at the mule, still bewildered by the sudden reunion with living things. So long alone and then so many people, so much more to do. It confused me. I could scarcely grasp how desperate I had been.

During the long hours of darkness and gloom in the crevasse I had been so convinced of a slow death that I had preferred a form of suicide to the untold days of madness while waiting to die of a broken leg. I could scarcely grasp how desperate I had been. Only twice had the true enormity of what it meant seeped into my mind. The first had been on the ice ledge deep in the crevasse, when suddenly I knew that either Simon had died or left me to die, and that there was no way out of the crevasse. That had been a time of hysteria, with one lucid moment in which I had made the hardest and the most frightening choice of my life. I doubted whether I would ever be faced with such a choice again.

With frostbitten hands I had abseiled deeper into the crevasse, leaving behind any means of reascending the rope. Deliberately I had dropped the rope without a knot so that, if I found no way of escape, then the inevitable slide off the end into the abyss would be a mercifully swift end.

Three and a half days later, after hopping, crawling and falling down the glacier, I had found myself swaying unsteadily atop a boulder in a dark snow-swept night somewhere in the vicinity of our base camp. Exhausted and delirious, I had crawled through the latrine area and become smeared with the high sharp faecal stench of our sewage. I kept sniffing my gloves and recoiling at the stink, trying to understand what it meant, until at last the slow realisation emerged. Simon and Richard would be asleep nearby. I had shouted hoarsely into the drifting snow and stared fixedly into the night. When no answer came, then something had snapped inside me. In that moment I knew my deep dread – that I would always be alone, that whatever I did I would die alone – had come true. My friends had gone. They had left me and I had no more strength, no will to carry on. That moment of despair had seemed endless. There was the black, silent, unresponsive night; there were the cold snowflakes on my face and warm tears on my cheeks; there I was, waiting for a voice, a light, realising I was too late.

Even as I registered the muffled voices and the flare of yellow torchlight, I was already tipping into a limbo world. Strong arms and Simon's shocked cursing drew me back from the edge, hauled me sobbing into a tent full of soft warm down and caring hands. Faces flickered across my sight in the muted candlelight and our nightmares came tumbling out in a rush of urgent voices. I knew I would never be like that again, never see such things again.

As the mule swayed down a long steep hillside of scrubby bushes and the spectacular icy peaks of the Cordilerra Huayhuash were finally blocked from view I vowed never to return. It was not the first time I had stared into the void and drawn back, but I would not do it again. I was finished with mountains. There was no sense to it. It was madness, utter madness. Yet a chink of light also remained. I could remember it from childhood. A recollection of horror first experienced and never forgotten. With those first memories of fear came a glimmer of light that always seemed to stay with me, whatever terrible things conspired to extinguish it for ever.

I had seen the cobra first. Sean stumbled head first into my back. I was lucky to keep my footing and not fall face first on to the snake.

'Cobra!' I hissed.

'What?'

'King cobra, there.' I pointed shakily at the long grass a few feet ahead of me. 'Don't move,' I added unnecessarily.

Sean attempted to make himself as small as possible, relieved to have me between him and the snake. I stood stock still. I was barefoot, wearing shorts and nothing else. Ma and Da had always insisted that we wore something on our feet, and for that reason we never did. There were things called 'hook worms', we were told, and they had a nasty habit of burrowing through the sole of your foot and worming their way up to your brain. Once there, they settled down for a few years, chewing until you died – brainless. A horror story we chose not to believe.

I glanced nervously at my filthy feet and tried not to wiggle my toes and disturb the grass. I wished I had borrowed Da's jungle combat boots. They were black rubber-soled affairs with high green canvas ankles laced together with impressive hooks and plenty of black leather thongs. Sean and I used them for missions into the jungle behind the banana tree at the back of my parents' house. The ankles reached to the back of my knees and my feet flapped about in them. Still, I believed the boots made me invincible, and with them on I would happily hurl myself from high branches on to unsuspecting creatures, confident that I couldn't possibly hurt myself.

If only I was wearing them now, I thought, I could stomp this cobra to death. What a trophy that would be! Even Sarah would be impressed. I was turning over the delightful idea of putting the slain cobra into her bed when Sean whispered, 'I think it's moved.'

'Wha . . . ??'

'No it hasn't. It's still there,' he said.

Why, oh why, didn't we use the boots?

'Shall we run for it?' Sean whispered.

'No,' I squeaked. 'They go too fast.'

'Do they? I didn't know snakes chased you.'

'Oh yes, loads of people get chased.' I had no idea if this were true. I just knew that, being nearest, I was the more likely to get bitten.

'Cookery snakes don't chase you.' Sean was intrigued by my new snake theory.

'They're not poisonous,' I snapped. 'Just stay still, shut your eyes and make sure it doesn't move.'

'But if I shut my eyes I won't see it move,' Sean whined.

'If you don't shut them it'll blind you. These ones can spit for miles.' At least that was true, but he did have a point. I squeezed my eyes tight shut and promptly lost my balance.

'I thought you said we should stay still?'

I flailed my arms and regained my balance, all the while staring bug-eyed at the motionless cobra. 'Sorry,' I mumbled.

With one eye shut, I squinted through the almost closed lashes of the other. Harsh tropical sunlight made the eye water and I lost sight of the snake.

'Have you got your stick?' I asked, and Sean said 'no' in a tremulous voice. *Oh, he's going to cry,* I thought. *Boys don't cry. Everyone knew that. That's the difference between being seven and him only six.*

'Shut up.' I heard a sniffle, then silence.

6

After an age standing motionless in the merciless sun, bare-chested and prey to thousands of hook worms, I could take no more. The idea that hook worms only got in if you stopped moving had better be wrong or we'd be brainless by the evening.

'Do you think it would hurt having your brain eaten?' I asked, and heard a faint whimper behind me.

'Can we go now?' Sean whined, wiping his nose noisily on his wrist. 'Mum said not to be long.'

'She won't mind if you tell her about the cobra.'

I wondered whether snakes breathe. Perhaps it was asleep. After all, it was very hot. If we crept away it might not wake up. But if it did it would be really angry, and I was closest.

'Halloo.' The call came from the road twenty feet away across the long grass to my left.

'It's Kabun,' Sean shouted joyfully.

Kabun, the Malay word for gardener, and all we ever called him, was grinning broadly at us as Sean waved him closer.

'Kabun, Kabun, come quickly!' Sean yelled. 'Look! It's a big snake, Kabun, a cobra.'

Kabun's smile disappeared as soon as he heard the word cobra. He laid his heavy black bicycle on the ground and, hitching up his yellow sarong, stepped cautiously towards us. He held out his long stick and scanned the grass in front of us. Unable to stay still, Sean was suddenly yipping with the excitement of it all, grabbing my arm and shaking it.

'Kabun will get it for us, Joe,' he yelled into my ear. 'He'll get it and we can put it in Nicola's satchel, or we could ask Kabun to make a belt with it, or a whip . . .'

'Shut up and stay still,' I said shrilly. 'He hasn't got it yet, so it can still get us.'

With a lightning fast lunge past my thigh, Kabun pinned the cobra firmly to the ground. Sean and I broke and ran, yipping and yelling and laughing all at once, free from imminent death and with the chance to torture our sisters at the same time. Life was too good.

A great guffaw of laughter came from the long grass and Kabun strode towards us with the dead cobra hung limply over the tip of his stick. He flapped it from side to side in our faces and we flinched away, scared that it might not be properly dead. They were the great enemy on our forays into the jungle; and only our jungle combat boots would save us from slow agony. Kabun reached forward and grabbed the cobra. Holding it out gleefully, he said something in Malay that we didn't understand. I touched it quickly and pulled my finger away. It made no attempt to bite me. In fact it looked rather odd.

'He skinned it for us,' Sean said excitedly and clapped his hands.

'No, no.' Kabun rolled his head from side to side with a huge white smile on his face. He then mimed the action of shuffling off his sarong.

'Oh no,' I said, 'I hope he won't tell Sarah and Nicola.'

'Tell them what?' Sean asked as he felt the snake skin, his eyes glistening with pleasure.

'Tell them that we stood here all this time in front of a skin. That's what Kabun thinks is so funny. There never was a snake. This is just the skin it had got rid of.'

'Do they do that?'

'Yes,' I replied glumly.

'Cor!' Sean examined the skin with greater wonder. 'And they can chase you as well. Crikey!'

When Kabun stopped laughing he dug into the saddlebag on his bike and gave us a lump of nutty crackle – peanuts encased in rock hard treacle. We thanked him and pushed our abandoned bicycles wearily back to Sean's house. He still held the sloughed off cobra skin in his hand. It flapped against the crossbar of his bike. The beautiful colours of the skin had been bleached by the ageing effect of the sun.

On the way we spotted a colourful snake in the middle of the road. We could barely tolerate the heat of the tarmac on our bare feet and I wondered how I would feel, lying like the snake on my stomach in the road.

'It's a cookery snake, isn't it?' Sean asked.

'I think so.'

Our notion of the different types of snake was sketchy to

say the least. This one was as thin and long as a leather bootlace and banded in multicoloured lozenges and diamond patterns, so that it appeared to shimmer in the heat haze rising from the road. It swirled its coloured length in a couple of sinuous movements, curling its body into a loop against its head and then pushing forward.

'Quick, quick!' Sean yelled, 'It's getting away. Stop it.'

'Why?'

'So we can capture it. It's much better than this one.' He had lost all interest in the cobra skin and threw it aside contemptuously. 'Quick, before it reaches the grass.'

'Well, what do we do?' I asked, a little afraid of the snake.

'Go on, stand in front of it. It will see you and turn around.'

'What if it doesn't see very well?'

'Course it does. Come on, it's getting away.'

I wheeled my bike in front of the snake which stopped immediately. It lifted its tiny spade-shaped head and flicked out its tongue, sensing danger. I made sure the bike was safely between me and the snake and held it with outstretched arms, feeling uncomfortably naked again in my bare feet. The snake coiled itself up and then changed direction, heading back to the middle of the road.

'What now?'

'You'll have to kill it,' Sean said with great authority.

'I don't want to kill it.'

'Cissy!' Sean snapped. 'I thought you weren't scared of snakes.'

'I'm not. Well, only cobras. They're really bad.'

'Well, kill it then.'

'How?' I was running out of excuses. 'It might bite me,' I ventured hopefully.

'It's not poisonous. You said so.'

'Well, I could be wrong. Anyway, I don't want to be bitten. It will hurt.'

'It's only small.' Sean manoeuvred his bike to keep the creature in the centre of the road. 'I know,' he said brightly, 'you can run over it on your bike. Then it can't bite you.'

I glanced across at Sean's house. 'What if your Mum sees us? She won't like it.'

'She won't see. Come on, run it over.'

Without really knowing why I pushed my bike away, mounted it and pedalled down the road.

'Don't do it fast,' Sean yelled, 'I want to see what happens.'

I turned the bike round and let it free-wheel slowly towards the snake which lay momentarily still on the hot ground. I can remember looking down through the front forks as the wheel crossed the centre of its glorious coloured back. In the next moment I clattered on to the road, grazing my knee and palms painfully. The snake had arched back the instant my tyre had touched it and had coiled itself round the wheel and spokes with lightening speed. As it span up towards me it jammed in the front brake blocks, stopping the bike abruptly.

'Quick!' Sean yelled, 'Quick, it's still alive, it's coming for you. Quick!'

My legs were still tangled between the crossbar and the saddle. I saw the snake uncoiling itself from the brake blocks. I saw raw flesh and blood where the metal had bitten into it. As luck would have it, the snake uncoiled in my direction. I thrashed my feet to clear them and succeeded in jamming my foot between the bicycle frame and the back wheel.

'Come on, come on!' Sean was waving his arms and jumping up and down, a mixture of horror and fascination on his face. I'd had enough of snakes and frights for one day. The high pitch of fear in Sean's voice set me off and I began to scream. Utter panic consumed me as I screamed and kicked my legs and tried to shuffle back from the snake, dragging the bike after me and the snake with it. Tears were running down my face and I didn't care about being older than Sean. I wanted it all to stop.

'Sean. What's going on?'

It was his mother's commanding voice. Sean stood looking sheepish and I screamed at her. With a horribly sharp thud she hit the poor tortured snake with the spade she had brought with her, beheading it with one quick slice. The snake's body went into violent spasms and its head fell from the blade as I screamed that it still wasn't dead. Mrs Thurgood grabbed my shoulder and pulled me to my feet.

Sean was despatched to the house with a slap on the thigh. The sharp stinging smack on my leg stopped my sobs with shocking abruptness. As I pedalled home, worrying about what my parents would do when they heard what I had done to the snake, I thought of the pathetic mangled remains left in the road, the torn white flesh and wine dark blood, and the bright colours fading quickly in the sun.

Remembering it now, it surprises me that we could be so cruel. Are all children cruel, or was it just part of our growing up in Malaya, where crocodiles and snakes were commonplace, and tigers lived in the Cameroon Highlands, and monkeys chattered in the mango trees and sometimes bit people? A snake was a snake – poisonous, dangerous, worthless. One had to get rid of them. Pain never came into it and the meaning of death and killing was completely beyond our innocence.

I've always felt bad about that snake. It was the first really bad thing I can remember doing. I mean bad in the sense of knowing intuitively that it was wrong. We had killed many creatures before – fish, and giant toads, poisonous caterpillars and barnacles. Often we had done it just to see if we could, to see what it was like, or to get rid of the creature because it gave us the willies and we didn't like it. Adults did the same thing in exactly the same careless manner, but they did it with weapons and armies and torture chambers, and they did it knowingly. For me, the killing of that beautiful snake was the start of a long process of education that told me what was right and what was wrong – in my heart, and not because others said so. It was also my first experience of real fear.

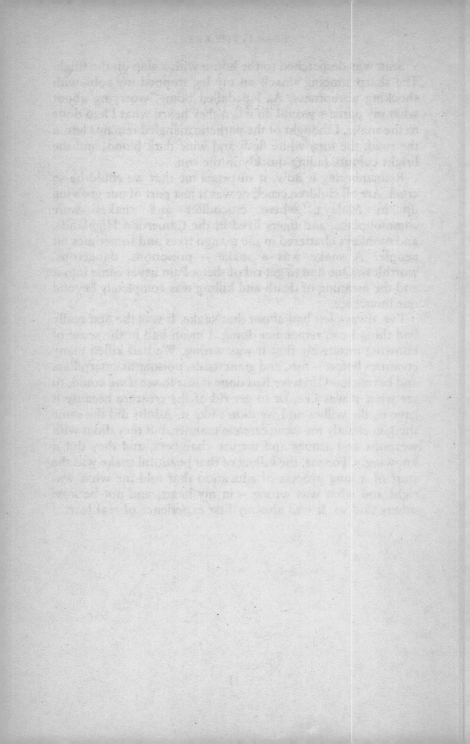

PART ONE

I

INNOCENCE ABROAD

I WAS LATE IN coming, thus causing some acrimonious disagreement between my mother and the doctors at the White Elephant Hospital in Kinrara. They insisted that she must have got her dates wrong until it became necessary to induce my birth. It was 13th August 1960. I do not know if it was also a Friday. My Father wasn't surprised by the stubborn manner of my arrival, one month overdue. It was a trait the whole family had inherited in large measure.

So, reluctantly, I became the fifth and youngest member of the Simpson family, immediately facing up to the challenge of Sarah, the next up in age, who became the bane of my early childhood. I was half Irish, quarter Scottish, and quarter English, though I prefer to deny the latter.

My mother came from Listowel, a small town on the banks of the river Feale in County Kerry, Southern Ireland. On Sundays the local farmers would ride into the town square and keep their ponies and donkeys tied to the railings of the Protestant church while they attended mass in the Catholic church, and as a youngster Ma took delight in borrowing the poor beasts for a little ride round. Her father, Joe McGuire, a respected doctor, ran a general practice and a chemist's shop in the town. It was a devout Roman Catholic family, and Ma saw to it that we were all brought up steeped in catechisms, first communions, and the attendant guilt that burdens every Catholic the world over, lapsed or otherwise.

My paternal grandfather, Grandad Jack, or Grandad Scotland as we called him, came from the village of Nairn, on

15

the shore of the Moray Firth, not far from Inverness and in sight of the Monadhliath Mountains. A little under a century after his birth I climbed on those mountains of his childhood.

To me Grandad Scotland was a heroic figure, a true Highlander who had joined the Black Watch regiment at the start of the First World War when he was only sixteen. At seventeen, he was wounded in the eye in the battle of the Somme while fighting as a Lewis gunner. The doctor treating him guessed that he was under age and sent him home. I suspect it was the compassion of a caring doctor for a young boy that got him Blighty and a discharge. The Blighty was the wound all soldiers dreamed of – serious enough to get home but not too serious, a bullet through the hand or foot, shrapnel in the legs, an eye wound, nothing too bad, just enough to get him out of the carnage of the trenches and home to Blighty. A few months after his discharge he became old enough to rejoin his regiment legally, and fought on through the rest of the war on the Western Front, surviving the slaughter and reaching the dizzy rank of lance corporal.

He told my Da that you could always tell which Highlanders had fought in the trenches by the thick callouses on the backs of their knees. The heavy weighted hem of the battle kilt, thumping muddy and wet against the back of their knees, left a permanent war scar.

Between the wars Grandad Scotland served as an officer of the civil service in Jubbulpore in central India. He was commissioned into the Auxiliary Forces, and my father (although he was born in Cheshire) spent much of his childhood in India, returning to boarding school in England, just as we were to do from Malaya, Gibraltar and Germany a generation later. I have an old sepia photograph of Da as a young boy, standing by a birdtable with my grandmother beside him. She is beautiful and dressed in elegant twenties-style clothing. It is an image I can never reconcile with the frail hypochondriac old woman I met on a few occasions in my later years. Draped across the birdtable is a young tiger cub that had been brought in by a bearer after its mother had been killed in the jungle. In the photograph my father is feeding the tiger cub with milk from a bottle. It is like a glimpse into a fantasy world that existed only in fanciful books.

I have always treasured the stories passed on to us by my Da and the photograph of Grandad Scotland in India, sitting with his full-grown pet leopard Felix in his lap. He was a great one for shooting in the days when big game hunting wasn't frowned upon. He'd shot bear, deer, pig, pea fowl, jungle fowl, and the great delicacy, giant porcupine, but he had never shot a tiger. I had listened in awe to the story of Grandad Scotland's friend Harry Brewer, who one day, while in the jungle with gun bearers and porters, had surprised a tigress with its recently killed prey, a Sambhur, the largest of the Indian deer. The tigress had grabbed the deer's neck in its jaws and slung it effortlessly across its shoulders. Unable to retreat towards Harry and reluctant to abandon its kill, the tigress had approached a wide stream that blocked its escape. Harry, unprepared for the appearance of the tigress, wasn't armed with a sufficiently powerful rifle, and requested the gun bearer to give him the shotgun loaded with a single lead ball. Before it could be put into his hands the tigress had hurled the three hundred pound deer clear across the stream, leapt after it, grabbed it up and vanished into the jungle.

I never met Grandad Scotland. He died of cancer a few years before I was born, yet he retains that reverential awe of my schooldays. Even today he seems more like a figure from a Hemingway story than a real grandfather. At the age of forty-two, after the outbreak of another world war in 1939, he was mobilised as a reserve officer in the Cameron Highlanders. Too old for active service, he was first stationed near the Kyle of Lochalsh on the north-west coast of Scotland, guarding naval installations. Then, bored with such mundane duties, he took himself off in 1943 to British Somaliland, where he joined the Somaliland Camel Corps as a captain. He had one last adventure in the closing days of the war when he was involved in the capture of a German U-boat on the shores of the Red Sea. A camel mounted Highlander leading his men into battle against modern technology – pure Boys Own Paper!

Wars and military service have run in the family until my generation broke the mould. My father joined the Black Watch at the age of eighteen on the outbreak of the Second World War. He was later commissioned in the Prince of Wales's 4th Own Gurkha Rifles, where the author John Masters was briefly his commanding officer, and served for three months on the North West Frontier, the land of the Khyber Pass and legendary Raj battles against fierce Pathans. Then it was across the Irrawaddy and the Chindwin rivers with the Chindits to fight behind the Japanese lines in the first campaign ever to rely entirely on air supply drops. His admiration and respect for the Gurkha troops with whom he fought in Burma left a deep impression on me, and marked my later trips to Nepal, where I met these proud and courageous people.

A broken neck, sustained whilst racing mules over rock-hard sun-baked ground, and a severe case of scrub typhus were the legacy of Da's war in Burma with the Forgotten Army. The typhus made all his hair fall out and the neck injury came back to plague him in later years.

But for the war, I doubt if Da would have opted for a military career. As it was, he stayed in India until Partition in 1947, when much of Europe remained economically and physically devastated. With Britain still under the hardship of rationing, it seemed logical to stay in the army, and so he joined the Royal Artillery and served with the regiment until his retirement in 1977. He was posted to Malaya where he trained Malaysian officers in staff work and jungle warfare at the time of struggle against encroaching communist forces in Borneo. North-east across the South China Sea lay Thailand, Cambodia, Laos and Vietnam. Exactly thirteen months before my birth Major Dale Buis and Sergeant Chester became the first Americans to die in the Vietnam struggle at a place called Bienhoa, near Ho Chi Minh city. Three months after my birth John F. Kennedy became President of the United States, and in September 1961 our family left Malaya and sailed to England for a three year spell based in Colchester. By the time we departed again on a two year posting to Gibraltar, Kennedy had faced off the Soviets over the missile crisis in Cuba at the most dangerous moment in the Cold War and a month later, on 22nd November 1963, he was assassinated in Dallas.

By November 1965 American troop strength in Vietnam had risen to a quarter of a million, and the G.I.s had just fought and won the first big conventional clash of the war, defeating North Vietnamese units in the Ia Drang valley. Operation Rolling Thunder, the sustained heavy bombing of North Vietnam had started and was to continue for another three years before President Johnson stopped all bombing of North Vietnam in August 1968. A greater tonnage of bombs was dropped in that conflict than in the whole of the First and Second World Wars and the Korean War put together – a record not exceeded until the aerial and artillery onslaught in the Gulf War of 1991. South East Asia was being decimated. Half a million foreign troops were in Vietnam by the time I left Malaya in July 1968. That year had begun with the Tet offensive before American marines were surrounded and besieged at Khe Sanh by a massive communist force in a battle reminiscent of the humiliating encirclement and defeat of French troops at Dien Bien Phu fifteen years earlier. Far worse was to follow before a humiliated United States finally withdrew the last of its soldiers from the country in 1973 – the year I was introduced to rock climbing.

Despite the army background and the proximity of war, my childhood was spent in a largely peaceful world, enlivened by a dangerously adventurous spirit inherited from largely Celtic parents. We lived in Port Dickson, a small settlement on the south-west coast of the South China Sea, overlooking the Straits of Malacca at the purplish hump of Sumatra that was visible on clear days.

David, Jane, Johnny, Sarah, and then the youngest, me – that was the hierarchy of brothers and sisters, a volatile mix of Irish and Scottish blood. Argumentative, passionate, and above all pig-headedly stubborn, we seem to have fought each other ferociously – though with love – throughout our lives. Because of Da's regular postings to different parts of the world, we quickly learned to be highly independent children. If our parents brought up a boisterous and strong-willed brood that did little to promote my father's military career, they also instilled in us a sense of freedom. From the age of eight we all travelled back and forth between schools in Britain and places as far away as Malaya, Gibraltar and Germany with a carefree nonchalance that I took for granted.

A pile of tangled brushwood blocked my view of the way ahead. The limestone was cool under my feet, despite a blazing hot Mediterranean sun. The streets of Gibraltar were spread out below me. Light flashed off the flat calm sea in the straits. I could just see the red tiles on the roof of our home, Gowland's Ramp, an eighteenth-century building whose back wall was carved out of the lower flanks of the Rock of Gibraltar. It had a unique water collection system, and I could just about make out the tanks on the roof.

Across the straits a faint smudge betrayed the coast of North Africa. On a clear night you could see the lights of Tangier and watch the twinkle of navigation lights as ships threaded their way through from the Mediterranean out into the empty reaches of the Atlantic. Two hundred miles south of Tangier lay the Atlas Mountains, stretching for 400 miles between the cities of Fes and Marakech, until the foothills dipped into the Sahara Desert.

The Rock of Gibraltar stood silent sentinel at the frontier between the two continents of Europe and Africa – 1,300 feet of limestone rearing up from the most southerly tip of Spain like a magnificent natural observation post.

A destroyer approached the harbour mouth. On the far side of the wide natural harbour I could see the small town of Algeciras perched on the edge of the Iberian peninsular. Geographically, Britain might seem to have little right to any claim over Gibraltar. Strategically, it was of vital maritime importance to keep control over the gateway from the Atlantic to the Mediterranean. Although primarily a naval base, Gibraltar was garrisoned in 1963 by the Royal Artillery

Regiment, and it was to there that my father was posted until our move back to Malaya two years later.

I was standing on a limestone outcrop quite unaware of what the view was or meant but concentrating on summoning up enough courage to leap over the pile of brushwood that lay before me. All that concerned me was to avoid landing in my shorts in the middle of it, or even just scraping against the branches, which would be painful. It never occurred to me to ask why I should be trying to jump over a pile of brushwood. Such questions don't occur to a five-year-old once the excitement of a challenge has been presented.

I pulled back far enough to give myself a long approach run and then set off, all fears gone and a wonderful tingling hollow in my stomach. My flip-flops slapped noisily on the rock as I sped towards the jump. Timing it to perfection, I hurled myself into the air and watched the woody barrier pass beneath me. Then suddenly I saw what I was about to land on – or rather what was not there to land on. The brushwood pile had obscured my view of the spot and I had assumed it to be exactly the same as my take-off zone. Now I saw that the wood had been piled on the edge of a vertical drop which plunged hundreds of feet on to steeply angled sharp-edged stone steps.

Well, not hundreds of feet perhaps, more like fifteen, but you have to account for scale, and it seemed an awful long way down to me at five years old and a little under three feet tall. I managed to get a flip-flop on to the very edge of the rocky abyss as I hurtled down from my prodigious leap but it only succeeded in toppling me sideways into the fall instead of feet first.

I have broken many bones in my time, lacerated myself, knocked my teeth out, and generally battered myself, but I have yet to succeed in fracturing my skull. It's not for want of trying, I assure you. I once spent twenty-four hours unconscious in Scarborough Hospital at the age of twelve after knocking myself out in a game of rugby. I had butted the biggest player on the pitch in an attempt to stop a certain try. The result was amnesia and a cracking headache, and he, poor lad, suffered a shattered knee. Still, it was a good try. Two matches later saw me unconscious again after running head first and with terrific force into one of the goal posts.

I am told that the brushwood leap in Gib was my earliest assault on a virgin skull. It connected with a sickening crack against the unyielding edge of one of the stone steps. I don't recall passing out but I do remember howling my head off as I sat in stunned surprise on the blood-spattered steps. The wails of anguish were soon heard and I was trawled off to the hospital by my anxious mother. Painful stitches and more howling finally saw me back home temporarily subdued.

A week later I was playing on my tricycle outside our house, happily enjoying the excuse to be absent from the Loretto Convent and avoiding the wrath of Mother Superior and the crack across the knuckles she administered with the thin edge of a wooden ruler at the first sign of misbehaviour. Instead I had spent most of the afternoon sitting in a wisteria tree with an adopted black cat called Jimmy. The wisteria stood in the middle of a small circular stone-flagged patio from which ran a steep flight of steps up to the house. Eventually, bored with Jimmy, I had climbed the stairs to play on my tricycle, one of those heavy old-fashioned affairs with large rear wheels and a tin boot set between them for storing essential adventure supplies. I wheeled contentedly in circles trying to pedal as fast as I could while leaning out to the side in the hope of lifting one of the wheels off the ground. I was rubbing a grazed knee after successfully turning the thing over when Sarah appeared. I righted the tricycle and watched her suspiciously as she dropped her satchel near the top of the steps.

'It's very steep, isn't it?' she said innocently enough.

I pedalled cautiously over to where she stood looking down at Jimmy in the wisteria tree.

'I counted ten steps?' I lied.

'Twenty nine, silly,' she snapped contemptuously.

I peered down the steps from my tricycle and felt the first tremors of apprehension. I back-pedalled and swung round in a wide circle away from them.

'I bet you couldn't ride down them on your trike,' Sarah said with just a hint of threat in her voice.

'I don't want to. My head still hurts.'

'You're just scared.'

'I am not. Ma said I had to be good today. I'm going to the hospital and she says the doctor will take my stitches out.'

'You're a cissy.'

She skipped round me shouting cissy in a taunting sing-song way. I pedalled over to the stairs and looked down. It looked a fearfully long way. I kept an eye on Sarah. I wouldn't put it past her to give the trike a helpful shove.

'It will tip over,' I announced, confident that this would be enough to get out of the dare.

'Not if you lean back it won't.'

I looked down at the long fall to the wisteria tree. It's strange how quickly your mind can persuade you to do exactly what you don't really want to do.

'Go on,' Sarah said, sensing my curiosity.

'Do you think it will be all right?' A building feeling of excitement had started in my stomach.

'Course it will.'

'I don't know . . . ' I said, lining the front wheel of the trike up to the centre of the top step and peering uncertainly over the handlebar. I sat back and set my feet on the pedals. As the rushing urge to do it swept over me I pushed down hard with my feet. Somehow it all builds up. You know you're going to do something but you have to wait for the tension to mount up, for all your private arguments to sort themselves out until, *bang* – you go.

I rattled down the steps at a horrifying speed. Leaning back seemed to be working. I gripped the handles tightly, watching the lifted front wheel skipping over the edge of the steps. There was a squeal of delight and encouragement from behind me as I crashed past the half way point. *I'm gonna do it, I'm gonna do it, I'm gonna do it* I muttered to myself through chattering teeth as I hung on the raging bucking bronco that my trike had become. I was dimly aware of enjoying myself and of being terrified at the same time. The tingling in my stomach had gone berserk as I watched the patio approach like the view of a runway from a landing aircraft. *Yes, yes, I'm gonna . . .*

The ferocious juddering stopped, and for a moment everything was peaceful and quiet as I hurtled through the air towards the wisteria tree. I cracked head first into the tree and bounced across the sun heated flagstones of the patio. My trike lay on its side, one wheel dented, the other spinning slowly to a halt. I explored my head with a tentative hand which came back bloody, and then threw back my head and howled.

The doctors sprayed an anaesthetic on to the wound and sewed the gash back together. It ran straight across the old wound. My mother looked worried and embarrassed. They took out the old stitches at the same time and I bawled loudly as I was driven home with a very sore head and a broken tricycle. I managed to relieve myself of the worst of my misery by telling my mother that Sarah had pushed me.

Everything about life in Gib at five now seems enlarged and dramatic. I remember the big black Barbary apes that lived freely on the rock and scared me. I remember the horrible yellow bruise and the teeth marks on Johnny's neck where a mother ape had bitten him when he went too close to her young. There were the shark warnings in the harbour after one had been spotted inside the netted swimming area and the panicky rush of swimmers making for the high rusty iron rung ladder that was fixed on to the harbour wall. I heard the warning siren once while I was floating happily in my rubber ring and crying with fright when no one pulled me out. I remember that horrible vulnerable feeling you get when you think something huge and nasty is about to bite off your legs.

There was a raft in the centre of the harbour, a big wooden thing lashed to sealed oil drums and tethered by a long hawser, draped with seaweed, that seemed to angle down in endless shadowy depths. The older kids would play a game of chicken when the shark warning went off. The boldest would swim for the raft rather than the ladder. There a game of rounders would be played with a tennis ball and a flipper as a bat. The batsman would try to hit the ball past some luckless fielder and into the water. After nervous scrutiny of the surrounding area the poor fielder would have to dive in and retrieve it. Of course sharks never really bit anyone, or so we thought, until a diver was badly mauled near the shark net. Only his wetsuit kept him alive and in one piece. After that the rounders on the raft stopped for a while.

There were trips to Morocco and the edge of the Sahara, or so Da told us, though it was probably just a large area of sand. I remember Da trying to catch an octopus and seeing the black dye jetted into the water around him as it made its escape. Jane got stung by a Portuguese man-o'-war, a huge ocean jellyfish with tentacles that could shoot out sixty feet and a vicious sting that some said could kill. There was the playground with the biggest slide in the whole world and a sand-pit, where we dug for lost threepenny bits, and the swings on which Sarah hurt herself while trying to loop-the-loop and made me laugh.

All too soon it was over and we moved back to Malaya before I was six. What a place in which to spend your childhood. I recall it more in colours and smells than any sequence of events. It flies back to haunt me like a friendly ghost when I recognise a particular atmosphere, and it makes me feel excited and at once safe.

We lived in a rambling old colonial-style house with great wide windows and balconies that looked out over the straits of Malacca. The beach and the reef were a short walk away down the steep hill. Sean and I spent most of our time as truants from the army school, playing on the beach or hunting beasties in the jungle behind our house.

In the garden there were banana trees that bore small green delicious fruit and a profusion of bougainvillaea and frangipani trees laden down with heavy white magnolia-like blossoms. The branches snapped easily and copious bitter stinging sap came out, coating everything. A magnificent mango tree stood in front of the house and bore such wonderful mangoes that local women came to buy the yearly supply. Another old mango tree stood near the driveway, a chattering noisy group of monkeys living in its shaded canopy. Sean and I tormented them by throwing stones into the branches and watching them screech and leap around in fury.

The back garden was bordered by our 'jungle'. It wasn't real jungle but a densely overgrown area of rubber and hardwood trees draped with vines and cluttered with fallen rotting boughs. One large specimen had been cleaved in two and blackened by lightning. It became a favourite vantage point, our own tropical den high in the burnt split trunk of the tree, from which we could survey our jungle battlefield – a battlefield swarming with giant toads, poisonous caterpillars, snakes, pig-eating pythons and the dreaded cobras.

Our fear of cobras was quite justified. A huge one, over eight feet in length, was caught and killed in the garden when I was a baby. One day Johnny was contentedly playing in the safety of a large baby pen when Jane spotted the snake advancing towards him. She ran into the kitchen to tell Ma that there was a large worm in the garden, but Ma was too busy to do more than humour the child. On Jane's third visit to the kitchen, wide-eyed from the sight of the cobra so close to Johnny, she said, 'Mummy, it is a very big worm.' Ma resigned herself to the interruption and went out to look. After that pandemonium reigned.

The army and fire service eventually ran the snake to ground in a drain and, using a steam hose, forced it out and killed it. It was found to have a full supply of poison. Later I saw the creature's fearsome body coiled in a huge jar of formaldehyde in the Negri Sembilan Hygiene Centre. The hooded head was too big for the jar and had to be cut off and preserved in a separate jar.

In the evenings, as the sun set across the straits, the night sky would come alive as the colony of fruit bats in the monkey tree roused itself to feed. During the day these large bats would hang upside-down like dried tobacco leaves and then fill the sky with black shadows as they flitted across the fading glow of the sun. Sometimes small black bats (vampires, as we thought of them) flew in through the open balcony windows and clattered around the room in disorientated panic. If Sarah was there, I would try to will a terrified bat to fly into her and get tangled in her hair. They never did. It was difficult to pin them down and gently release them outside without getting a nasty bite. I usually ran away.

Gecko lizards, 'chee char' we called them, infested the houses. They were friends rather than vermin, performing a vital role in keeping down the ever present insects. If you caught one by the tail, it would snap off, allowing the chee char to escape, unhurt, to grow another tail. The severed tails used to twitch frenetically and reminded me of the spasms of the dead chickens in the market. When the wide-bladed slow swinging fans that hung from the ceiling of every room were switched on, a dozing chee char would often be caught out on the smooth metal surface of a steadily accelerating blade. Unable to grip the shiny surface, the lizard would slip towards the end, dragged irresistibly out by the centrifugal force until, at last, it span off across the room. Often it lost its tail on landing before it scurried hastily up the nearest wall and clung vertically near the ceiling. There it would doze off again in the humid midday heat.

The twenty mile car journey from Port Dickson to Seremban market with my mother took a road that cut a long straight through thick jungle after following the coast through mangrove swamps. A huge python had been captured here after escaping from the local zoo. It was discovered asleep on the edge of the wooded road, having caught and eaten a small pig in a nearby village. The hugely distended bulge in the snake's middle gave it away as it lay dormant while digesting the huge meal. I told Sean of this added hazard to our combat-booted adventures. We could deal with poisonous snakes, or so we thought, but pig-eating pythons were altogether another matter. I reinforced my point by reminding Sean that, although I was a bit bigger than him, he was just about a perfect match in size with a small pig. He looked suddenly nervous.

The market fascinated me with its bustling atmosphere. While my mother shopped, I would go to my favourite haunts. The stall owners were friendly and laughed as they harangued their customers. At the chicken stall I would sit entranced, watching the Malay stall keeper selling his wares. The chickens were kept in large wicker baskets, the best specimens held singly in small cramped boxes, cocking their heads from side to side with a surprised expression as people rummaged through the stack. When a chicken was finally chosen the poor bird would be hauled out and hung with the feet in the owner's grasp as he engaged in a frenzied bout of haggling. Occasionally a wing would escape the man's grip and flap irritably as if the chicken wanted to add to the argument about price. To me, the birds seemed to take great interest in what was going on, tipping their heads from side to side and curiously examining the customer. It never occurred to me that their treatment might be cruel. That was how people bought chickens. I had no idea of cling film wrapped frozen food. The only ice I saw was in huge blocks, melting slowly into the filthy market ground from under layers of newspaper and hessian sacking, until the man got his saw and pick and cut a large chunk of ice for a customer.

When the haggling came to an end the owner pulled out a small knife and, bending the bird's neck between his fingers and thumb, deftly cut its throat. As the gush of blood erupted from the bird's neck it was popped into a circular wicker basket through a down-turned opening, not unlike the neck of a lobster pot. The miserable and now extremely surprised bird thrashed round the bloodstained basket in frenzied death throes. I was fascinated by the fine spray of blood vented through the gaps in the wicker. Some died quickly and calmed into a twitching bloodied mass after a few moments. There was more blood with the bigger birds.

Sometimes, when a bigger bird was chosen, it put up a more determined struggle and was rewarded for its trouble by being hauled from the basket before it had died. These were the ones that mesmerised me. Their wings flapped feebly, their beaks opening and closing in silent throatless squawks, with the awful wound open and bubbling thick blood as they were dropped into the de-feathering machine. Only once did I see signs of life in a bird when it was picked from the rotating steel drum that looked like an old tumble-drier with stiff rubber knobs set into the walls. As the owner plonked the bald bloody carcass on to a sheet of newspaper I saw the breast lift feebly and a wing twitch. It seemed to fix me with one baleful eye in a look of incredulous astonishment before the paper closed over the bird's head and it was rolled into a tight neat package.

If I grew bored with watching chickens die before Ma returned, I would wander through the market looking for the man who sold live green turtles. Unlike the chickens, the green turtles, tethered by their leathery necks to a post driven into the hard-baked earth, seemed unendurably piteous. They were tormented by the heat, the dust and the flies that flickered around their watering eyes. The turtle's long wrinkled necks were pulled painfully out from their carapaces and the rough rope cut wet bleeding weals into the thick skin. Sometimes Chinese and Malay children would sit on their backs or pull the ropes. I hated them for doing it but was too scared to complain.

Accustomed as I was to the casual cruelty meted out in the market, it was the turtles that first made me look at Malay and Chinese stall owners with a private impotent anger. I felt like shouting at the turtle man, stamping my foot and hitting him, but I never worked up the courage. I would leave near to tears, hoping that no one would buy turtles and that they would be set free on the coast that evening.

Once, in July, before the north-east monsoon, we travelled over to the east coast beaches at Kuantan, where leatherback turtles came to lay their eggs in a long exhausting moonlit night. These great creatures, as big as a small car, rose slowly from the sea like black humping boulders and made agonizing progress up the beach. When clear of the tide mark they laboriously dug deep pits with their flippers and then laid hundreds of eggs. The Chinese and Malays were there to rob the nests of the eggs as soon as the turtles had finished and turned their tear-streaked heads towards the long haul back to the sea and another year of peaceful meandering. I watched one man sitting astride the back of an exhausted turtle while his companion stole its soft white eggs the size of ping-pong balls.

In autumn the tail-end of the north-east monsoon would hit the east coast of Malaya, but we were sheltered by the spine of high jungle hills running down the Malaysian peninsular, and didn't experience a proper monsoon. There were none the less spectacular lightning storms after weeks of sticky humidity. We used to stand under the corner of the house where columns of warm rainwater plunged from the gutters and giggle as it pummelled us to our knees. The storm drains by the side of the road would soon fill and a torrent thundered down the hill. The drains were narrow, only eighteen inches wide, but deep, and we were small enough to jump in and career down the torrent as if it were a water slide. It was innocent but dangerous fun. A jammed branch would have trapped our small bodies and the weight of water plunged us under. It didn't occur to us and never happened.

Sometimes, in the typhoon season, huge seas would swell down the straits. Once, when my elder brothers and sisters had returned from boarding school for the holidays, we swam at night in the protected waters inside the reef. Huge raindrops exploded off the surface of the sea in silver curtains and a massive swell lurched us up and down as we trod water in a tight group. We could see the lights of the club gleaming on the beach. A game of touch tag began in the remnants of a hurricane sea. It was sheer fluke to surface beside the catcher and only a speedy dive and frantic strokes allowed a successful escape. At a command, everyone ducked underwater and hurriedly breast-stroked away. Due to the swell and the erratic currents running through the lagoon, a few strokes could take you a great distance. On surfacing we looked wildly round to see where the one who was 'it' had popped up.

For family holidays seven of us would drive north in a noble old diesel Mercedes and take the ferry to Pangkor island, where coral-whitened beaches, fishermen's shacks and a tiny lodge were the setting of a true paradise island. I watched Da catch barracuda on lines trailed behind a fisherman's chugging petrol engine boat. Wickedly dangerous-looking fish they were, their jaws crammed with needle-sharp teeth. They hunted in shoals, and were far more of a threat to swimmers than sharks. Once a small shark was hauled on to the beach and I watched it curiously, surprised to see how small it was. The barracudas were more frightening, and I dreamt of being chased through the outer reef by a pack of them that swung left and then right, questing for me with ugly fanged jaws as I swam with bursting lungs until I awoke thrashing in the mosquito-net around my cot.

A jumble of sea-rounded boulders stood on the edge of the shore, and we dived from them and played on them. Johnny had slipped barefoot down the razor-sharp coral surface of one of them before I was born and had stripped the skin from the soles of his feet. Seven years later, despite the warnings, I did exactly the same and can clearly remember the tears and the pain as I hobbled, bloody-footed, back across the sun-heated salt-stinging sand to find Ma.

There were also visits to the Cameroon Highlands. These high rain-forested hills, a hundred miles north of Kuala Lumpa, were beautiful and frightening to me. I was told that people had walked only a few yards into the jungle from the road never to be seen again. There were tigers lurking in the undergrowth and a unique aboriginal tribe lived deep in the forest. No doubt it was a scary tale to stop us wandering off, but I believed it whole-heartedly. We stayed at an old colonial lodge with lush green croquet lawns and a very English tea party atmosphere.

Crocodiles lived in the brackish waters where mangrove swamps marked the meeting of small rivers with the sea near Port Dickson. Once David, Jane and Johnny went on a crocodile hunt in dugout canoes with friends whose parents were rubber plantation owners. No crocs were shot, though they returned with a wealth of lurid crocodile stories. There was an apocryphal story of the riverbank fisherman who was grabbed by a hungry croc in a sudden violent lunge and dragged underwater. Crocodiles were said to be unable to chew, the bite of their ferocious jaws having no sideways sawing motion. Because of this they preferred their meat soft and rotten and easily torn apart. They tended to drown their victims and then take them to their lairs to putrefy. The lair would be dug from beneath the surface of the river into the muddy bank so that a chamber could be excavated above the water level. The only access was from the river itself. In this case the poor fisherman passed out, but didn't drown. He regained consciousness in the dark lair that stank of corruption. In blind terror he managed to dig his way to the surface before the host returned.

It seemed entirely plausible to me, at the age of seven, though I doubt the story's veracity. I always reminded myself never to stand close to a river bank in case a croc snatched me or I stood on the thin roof of its lair and plunged through on to a furious sharp-toothed handbag. My worst fears were realised one day when I was with Sean and his father in their dinghy. We were nearing the shallow mouth of one of these rivers when the outboard motor cut and his father said that he had dropped a vital pin which kept the engine going. We searched diligently for the pin in the knee-deep water while Sean's father held the dinghy to prevent it floating away. Unnoticed by Sean and me, he steadily edged away from us while our backs were turned.

'Crocodile!' he yelled with sudden panic in his voice. 'Come on, quick! Get into the boat.'

In blind panic I tried to run through the heavy drag of the water, consumed with dread, convinced that the croc had already snaked round between us and the dinghy. At any moment it would grab us in a welter of churning bloody spray – and then I fell, stumbling chest first into the water. I was up again, coughing, and running with knees up, pumping my arms, bawling in terror. The dinghy seemed to be no nearer. Then Sean was down, and I gained on him. I fell again, and scrambled up – screaming now, and hearing screams from Sean. When I reached the dinghy I was too exhausted to scramble over the high side. Sean's Dad was laughing until he realised that the joke had backfired and we were genuinely terrified.

It was soon forgotten as we plunged back into the ongoing battle with Sarah and Sean's sister, Nicola. They liked to play 'mothers and fathers' and to frogmarch the two of us out to a small island beyond the reef that could be reached when the tide was out. Once the tide returned, there was no escape. We could swim to the reef, but by then they would have us stripped naked and taken away our plimsolls. We would then be unable to cross the coral reef without lacerating our feet.

Revenge came unexpectedly when Sean and I were dressed as Red Indians and running along a wall beside the house. Suddenly my foot dislodged a stone and revealed a nest of scorpions. Sarah, a fearsome cowgirl in full pursuit, rushed barefoot into the nest of small black scorpions with their wicked yellow tipped stings. As she fell from the low wall, screaming, we pounced on her and dragged her off to be tied to the nearest tree. Our war dance of triumph was short-lived, however, for we were soon chased off by Nicola. All the same it was a rare and precious moment of victory.

2

SIBLING RIVALRY

SARAH AND I attended the nearby army school in Malaya. David, Jane and Johnny went to Catholic boarding schools in England and Scotland. After my father was posted to West Germany in 1968 we were all sent to schools in Britain, travelling back to Germany at the end of each term. My mother later confessed that it broke her heart to be separated from her children in this way. Perhaps it broke ours as well, although not for long. We had been brought up to be strongly independent, and if separation was a wrench at first, we quickly adjusted.

It never occurred to me to think that we were in any way privileged. Going to private schools far from home was simply a matter of expediency. To change schools every time my father was posted would have been very disruptive, and so my parents took advantage of the generous help that the Armed Forces gave for travel expenses and sent us boys to preparatory school, and then to public school at Ampleforth College. They could scarcely afford to put five children through such an expensive education, but somehow they managed. The advantage of living in Germany was that we could afford cheap skiing holidays in Austria and Italy.

The light was flat. A white late afternoon glare from a low winter sun that masked all the undulations in the ski slope. I saw a faint shadow, a grey shade rising from the whiteness. *A jump! Great!* I crouched into an unstable sitting position and aimed my skis directly at the faint line between shadow and snow.

It came as some surprise when my skis went straight through the small slope and clattered painfully into something hard beneath the powder. I catapulted forward with my skis crossed and then twisted painfully to the left as I bounced off the obstacle under the snow. My left knee wrenched round with an agonizing gristly tearing sensation, and then my boot ripped from its binding. I was screaming before I hit the ground. My face and glasses were plastered in compacted snow and I raised them blindly to the ski slope and howled in pain and shock.

Nothing happened. I wailed louder. Hot fiery liquid seemed to be flowing around my knee. I had never felt such pain. In the nine years I had so far managed to stay alive I had split my scalp, burnt myself, skinned the soles of my feet on coral, had been deservedly thrashed on many occasions (and on a few when it should have been Sarah) and in various ways tortured physically and mentally by my darling sister. All these troubles put together didn't amount to what I could feel burning up my thigh.

As blobs of snow fell from my glasses I spotted Johnny and Sarah in the distance, skiing towards me. I howled louder and tried to wave my arm. They turned away and glided down towards the ski tow. Frantically I searched the slopes for some sign of David. Wet clumps of snow fell from my cheeks released in tiny avalanches by a flood of hot tears.

'Joe. Are you all right?'

I turned to find David standing a few feet below me. Parallel tracks beneath him showed where he had side-stepped up to me.

'No! I've hurt my leg.' I blurted out through sobs.

He bent over and released my right leg from its binding and moved me into a less twisted position. I wailed as he tried to move my left leg.

'Come on. Try to stand up,' he said, lifting me by the arms and pulling me to my feet. As soon as my weight came on to my left leg there was a vicious spasm of pain in my knee and I cried out.

'I can't stand on it, David,' I whined. 'It's broken. I know it's broken.'

'Don't be silly.' He adopted the condescending and dismissive tone all my brothers and sisters used when talking to their youngest brother. 'You're not trying. Stop being a baby.'

'I'm not,' I wailed, bursting into tears and contradicting myself.

'And stop crying,' David snapped testily. He looked up the slope behind me, spotted Johnny and Sarah swinging down from the top of the tow lift and yelled for their attention.

'What's up?' Johnny asked as he stopped below the spot where I had collapsed, sobbing, on to the snow.

There was a swishing sound as Sarah came to a sudden halt above me and deliberately sprayed a wash of freezing snow over me.

'What's that?' she asked, pointing to a pile of exposed bricks. I looked at them sheepishly. The pile was roughly the size and shape of a small chimney stack. One side was hidden by a smooth sweep of snow, the other had been laid bare where I had cannoned into the covered bricks.

'I was trying to jump over it,' I said as I saw the look of utter scorn on their faces.

As they began chorusing their contempt and ridicule over me in the usual bombastic Simpson manner I started to cry again, which only made things worse.

For a moment confusion reigned. They were unsure whether I was injured or simply causing a fuss. A few experimental tugs on the leg accompanied by my caterwauling screams almost swayed them into believing me and produced a satisfied grin on Sarah's face.

'We'd better call the blood wagon,' Johnny suggested. Everyone brightened up. It meant they could happily abandon me and let the rescue people come up with their sledge-style stretcher while they got the last few runs in on the first day of our holidays.

'It's too late for that,' David said, 'and anyway it would cost a fortune.'

Sarah glared at me angrily. 'Well, what else can we do?'

'I'll carry him, and you two can take his skis and sticks down. We can ski right to the hotel.'

I looked anxiously at David. He was the eldest, eight years older than me and the natural leader of the family. I trusted him implicitly, but only because I hadn't yet experienced the scrapes into which he was later to lead us all. He lifted me easily from the snow and slung me across his shoulder. Johnny shouldered my skis and Sarah pushed off clutching both David's and my sticks.

'Be careful, David. Please don't fall,' I pleaded as he set off down the slope, snow-ploughing over the hidden bumps and ruts. My leg jolted painfully with each abrupt shift in direction.

By the time we reached the hotel the pain had subsided to a dull ache and I found I could put a fraction of my weight on to the leg. This resulted in a chorus of abuse about my being wet and wasting everyone's time. I could barely hobble down to the cosy dining-room for the evening meal, despite the codeine tablet and glass of red wine which had been generally regarded as the best treatment. Their main effect was to make me drowsy and unable to finish the mouth-watering food laid before us. I hobbled painfully to bed, leaving the raucous din of an inebriated family playing the inevitably argumentative game of five-card poker.

Next morning the knee was hugely swollen and the family spent some while practising as expert doctors and physiotherapists, ignoring anything I said and pronouncing 'water on the knee' as the only possible diagnosis, before they disappeared for an enjoyable day on the sunny pistes above the South Tyrolean village of Pragraten. I spent the time in the hotel poking the chubby knee and trying occasionally to put my weight on it.

That evening in the dining-room an Austrian man, who had noticed my discomfort, came over and asked if he could inspect the knee. He was a sports physiotherapist, for which I was grateful; I was tired of being examined by the Simpson experts. Badly torn ligaments was his diagnosis, and next morning I was taken off to the clinic and fitted with a thigh-to-toe plaster. This had the twin benefits of terminating all the pain and allowing me to bask in the sympathy of family and hotel staff alike.

When the holiday was over I was checked into the RAF hospital at Wildenwrath, close to my father's base in West Germany, and underwent an operation to set the ligaments correctly. Nine months later I began physiotherapy on the withered leg. It was my first injury and rescue on a mountain, my first operation in hospital, and my first experience of the painful but restoring work of physiotherapists – a sequence of events with which I was to become all too familiar.

In Malaya I had been firmly under Sarah's thumb, but as I passed my tenth birthday I began to resent the dominant pressure she exerted over me. Unfortunately I was not strong enough, brave enough, or sadistic enough to break free from the situation. Eighteen months older than me and my nearest sibling, Sarah was growing away from me as she approached adulthood and began to identify more closely with her elder brother Johnny. I slipped steadily into a vacuum of despair as I was forced to fight back against the stigma of being the youngest, the baby, the pest. Yet the more petulant I became in my efforts to stand up for myself, the more I seemed to be derided. In the end it came to fist fights with my brothers before I managed to establish a tenuous independence.

There was no deliberate malice involved. We were a vociferous, argumentative and confrontational family. To an outsider it might appear that we were irrevocably divided and deeply entrenched in a spiteful schism. It would be easy to miss the love that has always bound us together. Even today the highly charged emotional outbursts that attend our meetings would probably be confusing to strangers.

As a ten-year-old, my school holidays in Germany were spent largely in Sarah's company. Drawn reluctantly into her schemes, I always seemed to be the one who was blamed whenever they went wrong and punished. Sarah had a wonderfully deceptive and cajoling manner. I would resist her first approaches firmly, but gradually she would whittle down my protestations until she had persuaded me that her idea was the most exciting adventure imaginable.

There was a small German newsagents and sweet shop near our home and it had long been our practice to buy ice creams there on our mother's credit. Only when she discovered our game and told the shopkeeper not to serve us did the racket collapse, with Sarah's loud recriminations ringing in my ears. In her eyes it was my fault that Ma didn't actually have an account at the shop. Even an idiot would have known we would be found out. I tried to protest that I had pointed this out when Sarah had first mooted the idea, but a sharp crack across the ear soon shut me up.

With that source of free goodies closed down, Sarah decided that we had no choice but to turn to crime. I suggested that maybe we could ask Ma and Da for more pocket-money but received such a glare of withering contempt that I bit my lip and lapsed into silence.

The plan, she explained, was to wear wellington boots with our jeans tucked into them when we went to the shop. Once inside, it would be a simple matter to slip the long sticks of bubble gum down our trousers where they would collect in our boots. It was a scorching hot summer's day when she decided to put the scheme to the test. There had been no rain for weeks.

'Don't you think it will look a bit funny, wearing these?' I asked as I watched Sarah pulling on over-sized wellies. She glowered at me threateningly and I meekly pulled my trainers off and reached for my boots. There was a hollow feeling in the pit of my stomach as we approached the shop.

'I don't like this, Sal,' I whined plaintively. 'They'll catch us and put us in prison and Da will whack us.'

'Course they won't' was her haughty reply. 'Come on, pull yourself together.' She pushed the glass door open with a confident kick from her welly. It was then that I noticed that she had forgotten to tuck her jeans into the top of the boots.

'Sal, Sal . . . ' I grabbed her arm urgently.

'Come on, stop being a cissy,' she hissed, determined to scotch my desperate attempt to back out.

'No, Sal, you're . . .'

'Shut up!' She pulled her arm free. 'Everyone will notice.'
And with that she headed confidently towards the sweet rack.

I stared fixedly at the shop assistant who had her back to me
while she was serving a customer. She couldn't see Sarah
stuffing handfuls of bubble gum down her waist band. Sarah
directed a steely glare at me and mouthed 'come on' as she
moved casually away from the rack of sweets and feigned a
nonchalant passing interest in some nearby magazines. She
made urgent waving motions with her hand behind her back.

There was nothing for it. We would be caught and arrested,
but I was scared of Sarah – so scared that I approached the
sweet rack in a state of resignation and despair and began
grabbing handfuls of bubble gum and shoving them down my
trousers. I imagined it as a state not unlike that of a condemned
man being led, shackled and shaven, to the electric chair. A
numb weary passiveness. There seemed to be a huge glowing
sign above my head flashing the words 'THIEF' for all to see.
My ears burned and my back prickled with the contemptuous
stares of disgusted shoppers. Catholic guilt and memories of
my first communion and all those promises I had made when
studying my catechisms echoed through my mind. I half-
expected the immense power of the Almighty to blast me from
the shop, leaving only a pair of melting wellies smoking on the
shop floor. Sarah would be forgiven. She always was. I
suspected that even God was scared of her. I would be, if I were
him.

I looked up to see Sarah vigorously nodding her head in the
direction of the door. To my surprise no one had taken any
notice of me. I turned away hurriedly, wriggling my hips in an
attempt to work the bubble gum down my trouser legs. Sarah
overtook me and headed for the door. Two strides from safety
I saw a stick of bubble gum fall from the hem of her jeans. My
heart sank. With her next stride another stick of gum flew out
from her swinging leg and struck the glass door. For a moment
she froze. Just long enough for me to reach past her, pull open
the door and rush out into the sunlight. I heard a shout from
behind me, a harsh German command that shuddered through
me. I turned to find that the door had swung shut. There was

no one after me. I had done it. There was no sign of Sarah. I started laughing nervously. *They've caught her. That's it. She's in trouble now.*

I sat on a low concrete wall and chewed my gum while waiting to see Sarah being dragged unceremoniously from the shop and handed over to the frightening pistol-packing German police. There was a long pause, punctuated by some muffled angry shouting from inside the shop, and then the door swung slowly open. Sarah stepped out, blinking in the sunshine. She searched around until she spotted me on the wall and then lifted her arm and pointed at me. The shop assistant appeared in the doorway.

'That's him,' I heard Sarah say. I stopped chewing. The assistant was clutching a handful of bubble gum. A shopper looked at us with a expression of curiosity and disdain. I couldn't believe it. Sarah had betrayed me. *My own sister!*

We were hustled back into the shop. I had my boots pulled roughly from my feet while the assistant scolded me in a mixture of German and English. Sarah stood to one side, as if it had nothing to do with her, and grinned at me.

'Why did you tell?' I asked as we trudged home towards some serious trouble.

'I got caught.'

'So?'

'Well, we were in it together, weren't we?' she said blithely. 'One for all and all for one.'

'But now we're in double trouble. And we haven't got any gum.'

'You wouldn't let me take all the blame, would you?'

I gawped at her. 'Why not? I didn't want to do it anyway.'

'Well, you did, so that's that. If I was going to be caught, I thought that you should be as well. That's how it is, okay?'

I said nothing. I knew that when it came to the crunch with Ma and Da she would betray me further, until it was all my idea, and wonderful innocent little sister would win again.

The scolding we received from our parents ended with our pocket-money being suspended. Sarah spent several weeks acting the angel in an attempt to get it reinstated but failed. I tried to keep my head down and avoid Sarah for the rest of the holidays.

After a fortnight she cornered me, fixed me with a paralysing stare, and then smiled disarmingly. I knew the signs, and that they meant trouble.

'Let's go to the cinema,' she said with a beguiling casualness.

'What's on?' I asked.

'*Patton, Lust for Glory.*'

'That's a war film, isn't it?'

'Yup. Come on, the matinee starts soon.'

'Right . . . er, hang on, Sal. We haven't got any money.'

'So?' she said over her shoulder as she swung round and headed for the main road.

'Well, we can't get in.' I shouted as I ran after her.

'Course we can.'

'How? Oh no! No, we're not doing that again.'

'Stop being wet and get a move on,' she barked.

'But we'll get caught. I know we'll get caught.' I ran after her.

The last time we had sneaked into the cinema, after the ticket booth had closed and the usher had sat down, we had stumbled blindly in the sudden darkness, trying to find empty seats. The usher had turned on her red torch and advanced towards where I sat cowering beside Sarah. The beam of light must have illuminated my white guilty face before it flashed across to Sarah, who was concentrating unwaveringly on the film. She turned and directed a familiar haughty stare at the usher with just the right trace of irritation at being disturbed. The light had flashed back to me and I had smiled weakly, attempting the innocent ten-year-old cherub pose. It worked. Unfortunately for me, the rest of the film was an unnerving, skin-crawling anticipation of the return of the usher, the public scolding and my crestfallen embarassment.

We loitered by the glass swing doors of the cinema. From time to time Sarah glanced in to check the ticket booth, casing the joint with a practised eye. I stood biting my finger-nails, hoping that Sarah might change her mind. I hated that tight nervous tension, with the fear building up as every minute passed until my whole world seemed concentrated on an aching empty hole in my stomach.

By the time Sarah had grabbed my arm and hustled me through the doors I was virtually catatonic with fright. She dragged me towards the left-hand side entrance of the auditorium. I gave her a last imploring look before she pushed open the door a fraction and shoved me inside.

It was pitch black. My eyes couldn't adjust to the sudden change. I found myself on my knees and began crawling forward, squinting at the rows of seats in the hope of quickly finding one that was empty. At any moment I expected the torchlight to reveal me among the crisp packets and Kia Ora cartons. My forehead bumped painfully into the metal bracket of a chair leg and I yelped in surprise. Stretching out my hand, I felt that the swing seat was up. It was empty! I scuttled into it and tried to bury myself as low as possible. I had heard Sarah moving somewhere behind me but, glancing back, I couldn't see her.

I felt a hand on my leg, gave it a sharp kick, and heard her scuttle away. Suddenly there was uproar behind me. A man's deep voice was demanding to know what was going on. A torch flickered on and began questing towards the back of the cinema. I risked a look behind me to see the door swing open and a bright flush of light wash in. Framed in the doorway was a tall man in a suit firmly shoving Sarah outside.

The door swung to and darkness returned. General Patton appeared on the screen with his distinctive black polished helmet studded with four gold stars. This was going to be good.

Five minutes later the door swung open again.

'Joe. You've got to come out.' Sarah's voice once again struck the fear of God in me. I shrank into my seat. She didn't know where I had chosen to sit.

'Come on, Joe.' People began muttering and shuffling around to see what was going on. I concentrated on being small.

The torchlight flicked on and began searching down the aisle seats in a penetrating white beam. My head sank below the back of the seat. I began to appreciate what wartime bomber crews felt like when the searchlights groped for them in the black night sky.

'There he is.'

The note of triumph in Sarah's voice made me glance wildly about me. *What was she doing?* I wondered whether I could crawl quickly beneath the seats and find a new spot. As I began to slide off the soft seat cover the light blinded me and a bony hand grabbed pain- fully at my ear. I was frog-marched into the foyer where I blushed with shame.

Another scolding put an end to pocket-money for the rest of the holidays. Sarah at least had the grace to look sheepish at having betrayed me again. I was furious and determined on revenge. Unfortunately, although my anger momentarily let me overcome my fear of Sarah, it hadn't made me any stronger. It would be several years before I grew taller and stronger than her. So, I awaited some small opportunity that could be quickly exploited.

It arrived unexpectedly one evening when our parents were out playing bridge. I was reading in the sitting-room by the light of a small table lamp which I pulled nearer and succeeded in burning my fingers on the hot bulb. As I ran cold water over the burnt finger tips a cowardly and vicious plan began to form in my head. I dismissed it at first as being too nasty and then remembered the two betrayals.

'Sarah,' I called up the stairs.

'What?'

'Can you come down and check this lamp? It keeps flickering.'

'Do you know where the spare bulbs are?'

'No,' I replied. 'It's not the bulb.'

'All right, I'm coming.'

I heard her approach the landing and ducked back into the sitting-room, heart pounding with anticipation of the battle to come.

I switched off the lamp just as the door opened and Sarah walked in with an irritated look on her face.

'What is it?' she asked crossly.

'I dunno. It's just gone off again.'

As she moved towards the lamp I sidled round behind her and waited my chance.

'It's only the bulb,' she said.

'I think it's loose. Can't you see where it leans sideways?'

She bent over the lampshade, squinting down at the fitting. With a lightning fast move I reached out and pressed down on the back of her head. Taken by surprise, her head bobbed down, and I saw her nose disappear into the top of the shade. I was sure I heard a faint hiss as her nose squashed on to the hot glass of the bulb, but almost simultaneously there came a scream of pain and her head jerked back out of my grip. That was the signal for plan two to swing into action. I sprang back, turned and ran from the room, taking the stairs three at a time and slamming my bedroom door. I turned the key almost without drawing breath. I heard howls of pain and the sound of running water from the kitchen. I sucked my burnt finger tips and tried to suppress my giggles. The crying went on for some time until it began to upset me. I hadn't meant it to be that bad. Guilt began to well up, and also fear of what my parents might do when they returned. It wasn't a nice thing to do; it seemed mean and cowardly now.

I turned the key slowly, trying to make no sound. There was a click as I turned the knob and froze, with my foot blocking the door. Nothing. I risked a glance through the crack in the door. All was clear. I crept to the top of the stairs and listened.

'Sarah,' I whispered furtively. 'Sarah, are you okay? I didn't mean to hurt you. Sarah . . . I'm sorry. I'm really sorry. Are you going to tell Ma and Da?' There was silence. Where was she?

'Sarah, it was an accident. My hand slipped . . .'

A blood-curdling shriek momentarily paralysed me with shock. Then I saw Sarah hurtling towards me from the left. I hadn't heard her creep quietly upstairs to her bedroom and bide her time. Hearing my voice, she had sneaked out and launched a sudden attack, cutting me off from the sanctuary of my room.

Her first charge caught me off-balance as she shouldered into me, trying to knock me down the stairs. She attacked with unrestrained ferocity, scratching viciously at my face and tearing a tuft of hair from my scalp. As usual, I fought back like a cornered rat. She dug her knee into my groin with precise and expert accuracy. I doubled over, moaning at the cold flood of pain rushing across my stomach. She grabbed a handful of my hair and yanked my head back. I tried to resist but her strike at my groin had given her the advantage. She knelt across the small of my back with my left arm in a half- nelson, my right trapped beneath my body, and my head hitting the bannisters repeatedly. I decided it was time to start crying. My spectacles snapped and tumbled down the stairs. There was a yell of triumph from above when she realised I was as good as blind. As she swung my head painfully into the woodwork there was an angry shout.

'Sarah! Stop it at once.'

She banged my head firmly into the wood and I let out my most impressive howl.

'Sarah. Stop!'

When the hysterical recriminations and counter claims had at last been settled by my father, we were both sent to our rooms. I was delighted. My head hurt a bit and the scratches stung but they were easily forgotten with the memory of Sarah's blistered nose. If she hadn't attacked me, I would have faced the full wrath of my father, but as it was she had been caught trying to push my head through the bannister posts, and despite her tearful complaints that it was I who had started it, she was given the sternest telling off.

The blisters soon faded but her nose remained bright and shiny for months to come. I kept a wary distance from her for the rest of the long summer holidays, trying to guess what her response would be. In the last few weeks relations seemed to improve slightly. She became chatty and friendly, but I wasn't going to be taken in so easily.

On the nearby playing fields we had discovered a new game. The goal posts on the football field were strung with nets at the weekend and once the players had gone off home we would run up and launch ourselves as high as possible on to the sloping nets. They draped loosely down at a thirty degree angle from a thin wire stretched across the top between the angled rear struts giving the familiar flat topped wedge shape. They were just tight enough to catch our fall and tumble us harmlessly to the ground. I launched myself as high as possible, arms up and fingers splayed.

I didn't come down. There was an unbearable cutting pain in my left hand and I looked up to see that I was hanging by my thumb which had become trapped between the thin wire and the nylon mesh of the net. It felt as if my thumb was about to be severed. However hard I tried, I couldn't get any purchase on the net with my feet to take the weight. When Sarah tried to climb up the net it pulled even tighter around the first joint of my thumb and I start screaming in agony and despair.

'Get me down. Please get me down.'

I glanced at Sarah as she pointed at her red nose, grinned, and then walked away.

'Sarah. You can't leave me. Sarah, get some help.'

She never looked back. Ten minutes later a man heard my screams and lifted me up and then down. I trudged home massaging a purple thumb.

Within a year Sarah had made that sudden shift into adolescence which left me in the lonely world of the youngest child. She no longer deigned to associate with me. It was then that I realised how good our childhood together had been, and how lonely I was now that she was drifting away from me. I would have welcomed the chance to be dragged into one of her mad schemes; even a good battering would have been appreciated for old times' sake, but it was not to be. Our childhood was over. At least, the innocent, seemingly fearless childhood had gone, and it was replaced with something much more confusing which I never fully took on board – learning to be an adult.

3

INTERNATIONAL GRANNIES

I USED TO TRAVEL from Yorkshire to Germany accompanied by my brothers until they left the College. Afterwards I travelled alone. The teachers would put me on the King's Cross train at York and an International Granny would meet me at the other end and look after me until it was time to take the bus out to Luton or Gatwick airport. These grannies were employed by an agency set up to take care of minors when they passed through London.

I soon decided that it was tiresome to be shepherded around by these oldies. I knew how to confirm my air ticket at the airline office near King's Cross and getting the bus to the airport was simple enough. If I could avoid the granny and do this myself it would leave four or five hours in which to enjoy myself in the teeming capital.

On leaving the train I would attach myself to a suitable-looking adult without him or her knowing. I would walk close to them, with just enough obedient sibling glances to convince any onlooker that I was related.

You could spot the granny a mile off, holding up a large piece of card bearing my name. Studiously avoiding eye contact, I would walk confidently past the poor woman and out of the station. Usually, by this time, the adult I had selected would be looking uncomfortable and wondering why this child was following. If I felt my cover was about to be blown, I would ask innocently how to get to the tube station and then obediently follow directions.

Once clear of the station I would get my ticket confirmed

and then head back for the tube, keeping a wary eye out for perplexed looking grannies searching the station. By the age of twelve I was an adept granny avoider. There was a special delight and excitement in fooling the adults and escaping the tea and scones of an interminably boring afternoon. I never considered the plight of the poor grannies, assuming that they would be equally pleased to have a free paid afternoon.

One summer afternoon, on the way to Germany for the long summer holidays, I evaded the waiting granny in my usual manner and discovered that there was a full six hours before the airport bus departed. I returned to King's Cross station intent on taking the tube to Leicester Square, where an all-day cartoon programme was showing at the Odeon.

A visit to the toilet was a necessary risk, despite the lurking presence of an angry granny. I kept my eyes on her back while she talked earnestly to a British Rail guard at the end of the platform where my train had arrived. Once inside the Gents I would be safe – or so I thought.

I had just finished peeing against the cracked ceramic wall of the urinal when a strong hand gripped my shoulder and pulled me to one side. There had been no one else in the lavatory when I arrived and I hadn't heard anyone come in after me. I tried to twist away but the man's grip was too strong. His arm was around my shoulders as he pulled me against him. I don't remember what he said but can recall the smell of him, musky and sour. He wore a white kaftan shirt with intricate gold embroidery round the open collar. He was a huge man, and I was a four-foot-six twelve-year-old.

He pressed my face against his fat belly, pushing my head down towards his waist as he manoeuvred me backwards. I couldn't understand what he wanted. I was glad that the airline office had my ticket and passport, so I could still get home after he had robbed me. I was too frightened to say anything or cry out. He dragged me towards the row of cubicles lining one wall. He did not make any attempt to go through my pockets. I pressed my back against the cubicle door jamb and stuck a foot out to resist being pushed inside. I tried to squirm free but he squeezed harder, making it difficult to breathe as he pushed my head down. His penis looked enormous. It stuck up out of the open fly of his jeans as a thick black swollen staff. I shut my eyes as he pushed my face down on to it. I felt it prodding against my cheek and nearly lost my glasses. He said something in a deep husky voice that I couldn't understand.

It was only then that I realised this was no ordinary robbery. I had no idea what he wanted but sensed it was something I wouldn't like. I twisted violently from side to side. It felt as if my ears were about to rip off. His belt buckle gouged painfully into my temple as I kept twisting. I remembered how we had been taught to twist and turn to avoid being held in the loose mauls in rugby. Suddenly an arm was free and I lashed out, feeling something hot and fleshy against my fist. He grunted and slackened his stranglehold. With a lunge off the door jamb, I succeeded in half breaking free, but I wasn't quick enough to avoid his flailing fist from thumping into my chest.

The wind whooshed from my lungs and I sat down heavily. I glanced up to see the man's cowboy boot swinging towards me. I tried to avoid it but the sharp hard leather toe dug painfully into my upper thigh, making me shriek more in fear than from pain. I saw him grab himself as he turned and ran towards the exit, zipping up his fly as he went.

At first I couldn't stand up. My thigh muscle had gone dead from the kick and refused to work. My uniform shorts were wet from spilt urine on the floor. I got to my knees and managed to stagger up the stone steps to the platform. The granny was nowhere to be seen and suddenly I wished we were going for tea and scones and a boring afternoon.

I sat on the tube in a confused state. It had been so quick and I doubted my memory of what had taken place. It didn't make sense. *What had he wanted? Was his willy really sticking out?* I had heard a story at school of two brothers who had got into trouble with a farm worker near their house. He had grabbed one of them and tried to piss into his mouth – at least, that's what his younger brother had told us. We called the unfortunate boy 'piss breath', as kids do, but no one understood, and no one explained it to us.

My chest hurt where he had hit me but my leg soon recovered. I kept turning the experience over in my head, hoping that I would work out what had happened and why, but it was hopeless. I had no idea why someone would want to piss in my mouth; it didn't make sense – except that adults behaved very strangely. We all knew that.

By the time I left the tube station at Leicester Square I had put the incident behind me and was looking forward to the cartoon show. At least I still had the money for the ticket. I was beginning to glow with pleasure at the way I had fought him off, not let him rob me. Then I saw him, standing on the pavement, staring at me.

He's following you, he'll get you. I dived back down the stairs, racing through the exit ticket barrier and on down the escalator, hearing behind me a shout of protest from the ticket collector. A train screeched to a halt with a hiss of compressed air, doors opening, people streaming out and pushing impatiently past me. I leaped into a carriage and turned to stare fearfully at the platform, waiting for him to appear. At the next station I jumped out of the train just before the doors closed and rushed to the escalators. I ran up the moving stairway and down again to a different platform, where another train was pulling in. I dashed on to it before I knew where it was going. An hour later I found my way back to King's Cross and hurried to the nearby airline office. There I sat for four hours on an uncomfortable plastic chair, miserable and confused, until the airport bus arrived.

It had been the moment when I had lost that unquestioning trust of adults. They didn't simply behave oddly; they were dangerous as well. Although it was several years before I fully understood what the man had wanted me to do I knew at once that there were serious things out there in the real world. For the first time I had been deeply scared, and the first seeds of cynicism had germinated.

My parents were waiting for me as the plane landed at RAF Gutersloh. I left it until the next day before I told Ma what had happened, and was surprised by her horror. She didn't explain.

*

Two years later my father was posted to Northern Ireland and we moved into a cramped, almost derelict cottage while he and Johnny converted the two adjoining stables into a home.

It was a strange time. To me, there seemed to be a weird contrast between the hauntingly beautiful countryside with its friendly and hospitable people and the constant reports of IRA rocket attacks, bombs going off in Londonderry and Belfast, soldiers shot in Omagh, and regular sectarian murders. It was unnerving to find city centres fenced off and be searched at the entrance of every shop. Several people were killed when a bomb exploded in a butcher's shop that Ma had just left in nearby Coleraine. She rushed home in our Citroën 2CV, forgetting that she had left Sarah and me in the library. She drove two miles past our house in a panic before she remembered.

Although I visited only in the holidays, the sense of threat was always present. As a fourteen-year-old with an overactive imagination it was easy to let things get out of hand. My greatest fear was of assassination. For some reason, I became convinced that Da would be singled out; he was an army officer and our home seemed to me a vulnerable and easy target. Sometimes I would lie awake at night, wondering what I would do if an IRA gang burst into the house. I worked out all the places in which it was possible to stand or crouch without being seen or shot from the outside. I knew where the rifle was kept and I hid a handful of shells in my bedroom, just in case. I had some shotgun cartridges as well – those that were loaded with a heavy charge, not just birdshot. I never expressed this fear until many years later when Johnny, who spent all the time in Ireland, told me that he had done just as I had. We laughed at the ludicrous way we managed to exaggerate the threat and convince ourselves an attack was imminent.

One day, on Castlerock golf course, I had carried the clubs over to the first tee, and was waiting for Ma to come out of the clubhouse, when a man arrived and prepared to tee off. As he reached for a driver I saw him surreptitiously pull an automatic snub-nosed pistol from his waistband and slide it into the top of the golf bag. He had clearly tried to disguise it from me. I looked away quickly to prevent him from seeing I had noticed. I wanted to run to the club house and warn Ma. Then I thought about it. *It would be Da they would go for, not Ma. Maybe they followed our car in the hope that he would be playing as well?* By the time Ma arrived the gunman was just finishing his putts on the first green. I didn't tell her until the evening, and of course there was an obvious explanation. Far from being a terrorist, the man was an off duty member of the Security Forces, armed for his own protection. I felt foolish to have been so terrified by the sight of the pistol.

My father travelled to work each morning in a car provided by the army with Northern Ireland number plates that couldn't be traced to him. He also wore a large overcoat to cover any sign of his uniform. Unfortunately the disguised cars appeared to be all the same make, and one of only two colours, so anyone seen travelling in a heavy overcoat on a hot summer day in such a car was a dead ringer as a target.

In the holidays Da taught me how to use the shotgun and the .22 rifle and I prowled round dew-sodden fields that overlooked the river Bann in the early morning mist. When I returned to the house I always did so from a different direction, keeping out of sight until the last possible moment. I half-expected to see a group of men with Armalite rifles and in black slit-eyed balaclavas creeping up on the defenceless cottage.

Occasionally I shot a rabbit and once I wounded a hare that somersaulted in the air after it was shot. It ran for cover in a thorny ditch and screamed in a horrific piercing whine when the dog sniffed it out. Da reached in to grab it and chop his hand down to break its neck while I stood and watched and felt sick with remorse.

In the summer holidays of our last year in Northern Ireland my mother drove Sarah and her school friend and me out to the coast to see the Giant's Causeway. Across the North Channel of the Irish Sea a faint hazy smudge betrayed the islands of Islay and Kintyre. The causeway itself was an extraordinary promontory of basalt jutting out into the sea. The rock had formed into octagonal columns, identical in size, when first extruded by ancient volcanic activity. On our return we noticed a sign advertising a wildlife park near Bushmills.

I don't know why they allowed us in. The 2CV was a noisy car with an exposed soft roof and Ma's gear changes left much to be desired. Sarah and Louise chattered in the back while I sat beside Ma in the front clutching two milk bottles. We all remarked on how bored the animals looked. It was a hot, torpid sort of day and even the baboons seemed to prefer sleeping to their main enjoyment of tearing cars to pieces. By the time we reached the last section, the lion area, we had become so bored ourselves that we had opened the two front windows and were laughing at the groups of anaesthetised big cats.

The large male lion nearest to the car lurched to its feet when the two-stroke engine made a sudden screeching sound as Ma changed down into first.

'Ah well, at least that one's still alive,' Sarah remarked from the back. The lion loped towards the passenger side of the car. We were travelling at about ten miles an hour when I reached outside, unhooked the window catch and let the glass section drop shut.

'I think you'd better speed up, Ma,' I said as the lion increased its speed. 'It's getting a bit close.'

Ma accelerated but forgot to change gear. The engine howled in protest, and the lion broke into a determined canter. She got a quick view of it as it angled in from the side. The car faltered.

'Don't stall,' Sarah and Louise chorused from the back.

The car was barrelling across the safari park to the distant exit gates, rolling in the peculiar way that 2CVs do, with the engine noise reaching crescendo pitch. Suddenly it felt vulnerable and flimsy, with its thin tinny body and soft roof. Sarah and Louise started screaming when the lion drew level with us. I simply gawped in horror as it galloped alongside.

The beast's huge head was made all the more impressive by its thick dark mane. It drew level with my door and raced along less than a couple of feet from me, fixing me with a baleful stare from merciless golden eyes. I had read enough Wilbur Smith to know that the three hundred pounds of enraged muscle, fangs and claws wasn't about to listen to reason.

I clutched the milk bottles in both hands, wondering what to do if it sprang on us. It could easily leap on to the roof, in which case I might be able to fend it off with the bottles. *Perhaps I should break one? No, if it came through the roof I would leap out the door. Then it would be so preoccupied with Ma and the girls that I might be able to leg it.* I reached for the door handle as Ma, with her foot flat on the floor, headed for the gates.

'They're shutting the gates!' Sarah howled from the back. 'Open the gates, open the gates!' We all screamed at the two men who were hurriedly pulling the high chain link gates closed. The car seemed to be full of frantically waving arms and screams of anguish.

'Don't stop, Ma, for God's sake don't stop. It'll have us if we stop.'

Ma crouched over the wheel and aimed the 2CV remorselessly at the gates and the donkey rides and the picnic area on the other side. We were going through. *Oh my God, we're going through.*

I know now how cats mesmerise their prey with their eyes. Since the lion had drawn level with us I had been staring fixedly into those huge yellow eyes, the maned head completely filling the window of the car. There were flecks of gold in the dark stiff mane and its fangs seemed huge and stained a nicotine yellow. I was so transfixed by the stare that I felt as if I had been paralysed, injected with some lethal narcotic that froze every muscle. The lurching ride, the screams and the frantic waving arms seemed to be outside my world. All I had was this beast's awful demented eyes. I knew with absolute certainty that it would go for me first.

Suddenly a shot rang out, like a car backfiring. The lion flinched and swung away. A zebra-striped landrover flashed past us. Ma, at top speed in first gear, was not to be distracted. The surprised keepers had barely swung the gates open before we surged through, flashed past a startled group of toddlers on donkeys with a kangaroo lurch as second gear crunched into place, and on out of the park to the main road with the four of us still wailing hysterically.

During that summer of '74 my mother temporarily lost her voice. I thought nothing of it at the time, though I could sense a heightened tension in the house. A few days before I was due to return to school she took me to one side and told me that she had been diagnosed as having throat cancer. She was clearly frightened. She cried and hugged me, telling me not to worry, that everything would be fine. I felt embarrassed to see her crying and upset and thought that, if she was going to be fine, then why all the fuss? At school I was blissfully unaware that her long period of chemotherapy wasn't working.

Six months later the doctors discovered that there were more cancerous cells in her throat and decided that they would have to operate. My parents had decided that I was too young to be told the truth. The tracheotomy was performed in the superb Royal Marsden Hospital in London, and this effectively removed her ability to pass air through her vocal cords. She could no longer speak. She almost died after the operation and indeed had given up fighting when a catholic nurse reminded her that no good catholic could give up like that and that she must pray and fight to live.

Years later, when she told me, I felt angry and betrayed that they had kept it all from me. I felt as if I had been cheated. It would have come as a terrible abrupt shock if she had died. From that time on I resolved to tell my parents everything about my climbing, of the accidents and the risks, and of friends lost. I couldn't pull the wool over their eyes and tell them I was hill walking in the Alps as one friend did when in fact he was attempting the North Face of the Eiger. It was difficult enough to deal with the selfishness of serious mountaineering without betraying them as well.

Ma believes it was the power of prayer and her faith in God that pulled her through the crisis. Although I have great respect for her faith, I myself cannot believe in it any more. It seems to me more likely to be her tenacious determination that got her through. She learnt the desperately difficult method of speaking in an astonishingly fast time but she had lost the beautiful soft Southern Irish brogue in her voice. Within three months, and against medical advice, she started playing golf, learning a completely new swing that her damaged left shoulder would allow, becoming Lady Captain of her club and using only a five iron and a putter to win the majority of the prizes in that year. To me it was an incredible feat of determination and courage. Ten years later, during desperate days in the Peruvian Andes, I remembered how she had refused to give up.

I discovered rock climbing in that long hot summer of 1974. I had been an enthusiastic games player at school, becoming captain of the school's junior rugby team, but I was far too small to succeed at the game. At Ampleforth every match seemed to be an exercise in violence which I experienced mostly beneath sixteen large members of the two scrums. My legs were too short, and if I ever got the ball I couldn't run fast enough to get out of trouble. At cricket I was a passable wicket keeper but a useless bat. I excelled at swimming, something I had done all my life, and swam for the school, but after years of tedious repetitive training I realised that I was never going to beat my rival in the two hundred metres breast-stroke. I took up fencing. That was fun before my friend broke my big toe by stabbing it with a rigid épée sword. For one term I dallied with judo until I was squashed in a body slam by the fattest boy in the school. My eldest sister Jane offered to teach me ju-jitsu but put me off by poking two long-nailed fingers into my eyes, almost blinding me, and then jamming them up my nostrils and demanding surrender.

We were required to take up boxing, which at first seemed

57

a good idea. I was paired off with my best friend, the only boy among 750 at the school who was smaller than me. I spent three minutes punching him in the head, dancing nimbly round him as he struggled to recover, and catching him with more quick punches. At the bell I wandered happily back to the corner, thinking how easy it was, when a stupefying thump on the side of my head dropped me on to the floor. My friend, enraged at the beating I had given him, had rushed over from his corner to deliver his retribution. I was so stunned and disorientated by that one punch I refused to box any more. My friend never spoke to me again.

We were forced to join the Cadet Corps in the first year. It was an endless round of parade practice, rifle cleaning and mindless night exercises with faces blackened and thunder flashes exploding all over the place. It all culminated in an attack on Lion Wood Hill. The misfits and the pacifists (like myself) were each given five blank rounds and a .303 rifle and told they were Chinese whose objective was to capture the British troops at the top of the hill. The British comprised those boys who were keen on the Cadet Corps, officer material, and they had the advantage of being armed with all-purpose machine guns and a plentiful supply of ammunition.

The hill itself was surrounded with dense forests of stinging nettles that waved as we crawled through it and gave away our positions to those defenders who were deaf and hadn't heard our howls of agony. Needless to say, we were slaughtered many times over and forced to surrender. My one consolation was shooting a particularly obnoxious boy in the back at point blank range after I had given myself up. The wadding from the blank came out with such force that it knocked him down, bruising him. I was on rifle cleaning for a month, but it was worth it.

In an effort to avoid a second year of marching round on the drill ground I elected to join adventure training, which seemed to involve packing an enormous rucksack and hitch-hiking to the nearest pub that would serve under-age kids. This led me into the Venture Scouts and a visit to Peak Scar one Saturday afternoon. Three hours later I had found the sport that I was looking for.

In Germany that summer I read *The White Spider*, Heinrich Harrer's classic history of the attempts to climb the North Face of the Eiger. He himself had been a member of the first ascent team in 1938. The book held me spellbound, and horrified. The grim black and white photographs became a source of my worst nightmares. Max Sedlmayer and Karl Mehringer, who on the first attempt in 1936 froze to death at a spot since called 'Death Bivouac', stare out from the past among photos of men wearing dome-shaped felt hats, moleskin breeches and nailed boots, thick hawser-laid ropes tied round their waists as they perch on black beetling crags and rockfall-blackened ice fields. Reading of the successes and tragedies confused me. One moment I wanted to climb like that, the next I could imagine nothing more terrifying. The story of Adolf Mayr attempting the first solo ascent of the face in 1961 seemed an epitome of the glory and the absurd waste that climbing mixes strangely together.

Mayr reached a point high on the ramp, just below the notorious waterfall pitch, when he came upon the 'Silver Trench', a feature seen occasionally when the late afternoon sun gleams on the mirrored surface of a tongue of ice in the back of the deep shadowed ramp. It sounds a pretty glittering place, something pleasant that sparkled gaily from the lowering shadows of the immense north face. The lone climber (Adi to his friends) was a tiny point of life, of sheer nerve and courage, in this cold, shadowy vastness. To me he was a symbol of the incredible power that lies within every human life, a power that challenges the unknown, confronts the greatest of fears in the confident belief that it will overcome anything.

Adi was seen trying to cross this obstacle in long, hesitant, jerky strides and managing to recover after each failure. He was seen working on the *mal passe* with his axe, clearly attempting to improve the hold he was reaching for with his foot. Then, at twelve minutes past eight in the morning, he tried the risky long stride again. Suddenly his body flew out from the shadows to fall four thousand feet to the screes below and that brilliant point of life was extinguished. For me the significance lay not in the fact that he died but in what he had dared to attempt.

I read the account of an early attempt at a first ascent of the face by four young climbers which became a desperate retreat ending in disaster. The story of their battle to survive only to die almost within reach of rescue has become legendary. Toni Kurz, the last to die, was left hanging hopelessly in space. I saw a photograph of him hanging, slumped on his rope, with foot long icicles growing from the points of his crampons, frozen in his last living moment when he had whispered 'I'm finished' to his rescuers and died only yards from salvation. The manner of his death was the most poignant, most desperate and heroic that I had ever read.

When I finished reading *The White Spider* at fourteen I vowed to myself that I would never be a mountaineer. I would stick to rock climbing. Little did I realise that eleven years later in a peculiar twist of fate I would find myself in a similar position to Toni Kurz and remember him as I fell into darkness.

4

SAWMILLS AND GELIGNITE

A THIN VEIL OF smoke lay across the surface of the field. My footsteps crunched loudly on the freshly cut stubble. A weak early morning sun failed to burn off the sliding low mists. I seemed to be walking on footless legs. The woods on the edge of the field were silent. No breeze disturbed the branches. Somewhere off to my right I heard the rapid *crak-crak-crak* of a pheasant breaking cover. Two woodpigeons flew above me. The soft sound of their wing beats alerted me too late and as I swung the shotgun up to my shoulder they disappeared into the safety of the trees.

Across the field I could see the red-tiled roof of a farmhouse. Smoke rose straight up into the still air from the single chimney. A stark black elm tree pierced the horizon to the left of the farm. Its diseased leafless branches were home to a large colony of rooks, and I could hear their faint insistent caws as they lifted off in a black swarm. A white van passing on the road below had disturbed them. They circled the tree twice, cawing in affronted rage before settling back on to their large twig nests that dotted the bare branches like black tumours. I could see the roof of my parents' bungalow through the trees below. The north Yorkshire small village of Oswaldkirk, where they had chosen to retire, was silent. Plumes of smoke rose from a few houses as people blearily prepared for another working day.

I slipped the safety catch off the gun and held it high across my chest ready to fire the instant a rabbit broke from the stubble and raced for the green safety of the wild garlic carpeting the floor of the woods. It would be hard to get a clean shot through the low mists. I doubted whether I would even see the rabbit; only a flashing swirl in the grey smoky field. I checked my watch. Five thirty. I had half an hour to get a rabbit for my supper before I would have to hitch to work in the sawmill.

No rabbits bolted for the trees by the time I reached the far end of the wood and I turned to retrace my steps home, resigned to cornflakes and cheese sandwiches for supper. I held the shotgun loosely across my waist. The barrel pointed into the trees. I made no effort to walk quietly as I strode through the stubble.

As I reached the far end of the woods, where a bramble entangled path led down to my parents' bungalow, I heard a sudden cracking noise. I swung my torso towards the trees and saw a fox less than ten feet from me. It stood with a front paw frozen in mid-stride, staring at me through wide alert golden eyes. The safety was off and the gun was aimed directly at the fox. I only needed to pull both triggers and two barrels of birdshot at such close range would annihilate the fox. Twenty-five pounds from the local farmer for its tail. Proof that I had killed the fox for more than half a week's wages.

I don't know which of us was the more surprised. The fox had a disturbingly direct stare that bored hypnotically into me, as if questioning my right to be there. It held itself utterly still, a savage, almost defiant wariness about the way in which its muzzle pointed up at me, ears cocked in tawny triangles, fur and brush bristling.

Then it turned and stepped away, gone from sight in an instant. I hadn't fired. Not because I didn't need or want the money, nor from any reasons of compassion. The fox seemed to have insisted that I didn't and I had obeyed. I put on the safety, broke the shotgun and removed the cartridges.

The bandsaw shrieked as the blade bit into another freshly cut oak. The teeth of the saw, each as long as my thumb, howled in a piercing metallic scream as the rollers slowly pushed the log through the spinning twenty-seven-foot blade. I glanced across at the huge flywheels whirring the foot-wide band through the wet oak and shuddered.

I loathed the sawmill. I've always had an irrational dread of power tools. Things like hand drills and jig saws gave me the willies. When I used them I always expected the drill or blade to shear off and plunge into my eye or the jugular vein. I would adopt the most contorted position in an effort to predict which way it would fly off and so avoid blood-spattered mutilation. For me the sawmill was an inferno of howling motors and screeching blades. There were machines that could sever you at the waist in a blink of an eye.

I had been working at the mill for seven weeks, the longest I had stayed anywhere, and I was getting to the end of my tether. Apart from discovering that I had a marked distaste for any sort of work, especially dangerous and noisy work, I resented being told what to do.

The circular saw bench was a five-foot square of quarter-inch steel. The blade protruded in an evil semi-circle from the centre of the bench. I looked at the pile of chock wood I had cut the day before. There was at least as much again to do before I was finished. The chocks, used for shoring up props in the pits, were five inches square and came in two lengths, two-foot and three.

I selected a suitable piece of timber and placed it on the bench. Flicking the switch under the plate I watched the blade spin rapidly up to speed as I pulled on a pair of thick loose-fitting PVC gloves. I glanced over to see if George, the foreman, was watching. He had his back to me, one hand on the wheel that controlled the progress of the log through the bandsaw. He crouched forward, peering intently at the cutting point. The blade spun less than three feet from him, towering above him in a black belt of high-speed steel. Once, he had told me, the blade had snapped. It had probably hit some old iron stake inside the log that the tree had grown round. It snapped with a ferocious crack and the flywheels whined in protest as they span faster. There were two ways in which the blade could go, he'd said – either out into the open yard or back into the mill. It depended where the break occurred.

'Went out,' he said in his gruff Geordie accent. 'Aye, lad, right across the yard and hit that telegraph pole over there by the road.' He pointed to where a pole stood slightly askew fifty yards away.

'Went half way through that pole,' he said, examining his scarred thumb, which had been sliced neatly down the middle and out by the first knuckle. Most of the older men drinking in the local pubs had a finger or two missing.

'What would happen if it went into the mill?' I asked.

'Would have been bad, youth,' he said with a wry smile.

George couldn't see me pulling the heavy gloves on. He'd warned me not to use gloves but I was sick of having hands full of splinters. It was all very well for his calloused hands, hardened to old leather by years of abrasion. I pushed the wood through the fang-toothed blade. It passed through easily with a *zzzunk* sound when the wood separated and I swung forward slightly as the resistance stopped. I was careful to pull back, anticipating the lunge towards the saw, and kept my arms wide and straight for fear of catching the loose material of my boiler suit. The teeth were designed to pull the wood into the blade. It would pull my arm in just as swiftly.

Two hours later and the chock wood pile had doubled in size. I was getting near the end and relaxed my concentration. The repetitive boredom of the task made it impossible to be completely safe. As I fed yet another timber into the blade I felt a sharp tug on my glove. It jerked my arm fractionally towards the blade but I reacted almost instantly and wrenched my hand back. I stared mutely at the glove. The loose PVC near the thumb and the elasticated cuff was shredded.

Very slowly I leant forward and switched off the saw. It whined down to silence as I gingerly pulled the shredded glove from my hand, waiting for the gush of bright arterial blood, the grated greasy ends of shattered bone and white spaghetti tendons laid open fresh amid the meat of my hand. I felt nothing. No doubt it was the sudden shock. I had heard of soldiers feeling nothing when their limbs were blown away. It must be the same thing.

'Yer lucky bastard,' I heard George growl from behind me. He picked up the glove and looked pointedly at the one on my right hand. 'I bloody well told you lad, no gloves.'

I was staring in astonishment at my completely unmarked left hand. No ripped flesh or exposed bones, no blood. A flood of relief washed away the cold knot in my stomach.

'That's it. You're fired,' George said, and turned on his heel. He headed for the small nissan hut that was used as the office and returned a few minutes later with a brown envelope which he dropped contemptuously on the steel saw bench. It was Friday. The wages were already made up.

'I don't want Health and Safety closing me down for an idiot like you.'

I gawped at his retreating back, still not over the shock of thinking I had lost my hand. Fired. He fired me. The little shit!

Picking up the wage packet, I walked morosely across the yard and kicked the damaged telegraph pole angrily before heading into town.

'Hated the bloody job anyway,' I shouted at the mill. A high screech came back as the bandsaw engaged.

While my father was serving out his last year in the army, I was using the small bungalow in north Yorkshire he and Ma had bought for their retirement. Until I went up to university in Edinburgh I had the place to myself. It was ideally situated opposite the local pub.

As the summer came to an end and my first term at university approached I found that I was heavily overdrawn and the bank was losing patience with me. In desperation I found work in a local quarry hoping to make enough money to supplement my meagre grant cheque. The work was hard, poorly paid and, when fooling around with six hundred pounds of gelignite and a couple of thousand tons of exploding limestone, extremely dangerous.

There were three of us working at the quarry, and the atmosphere was relaxed and friendly. I spent five days drilling bore holes at the top of the one hundred and twenty-feet-high quarry walls. I worked with Ray, a 62-year-old Yorkshireman, a slow sort of man, short on words, but with a gentle kindness. A long barn-like building stood at the side of the white dusty amphitheatre of quarried limestone. It housed a huge diamond-tipped circular saw and an awesome triple-wired bandsaw for slicing the hard blue limestone blocks. Water and carborundum grit poured constantly on to the spinning three ply wire as it bit down through the stone.

My time was divided between operating the circular saw and navvying in the quarry. The saw terrified me. It seemed outrageous to be cutting solid rock. I controlled the speed at which the stone was fed into the five-foot diameter blade. There was a critical moment when the teeth first hit. If it came in too fast, the industrial diamond teeth would sheer off and the blade be destroyed. Ray and the boss seemed more concerned about the expense than the possible side-effects of shrapnel screaming round the work hut, maiming the occupants. I was extremely careful with the control wheel.

On the morning of the fifth drilling day Ray beckoned me over to a small steel chamber set off to one side.

'Got to get the jelly up to the drill site,' he said gruffly.

'Jelly?'

'Gelignite, lad. I prefer the stuff I make myself, but there you go.'

'You make gelignite?' I asked incredulously.

'Same thing,' he said, 'diesel and fertilizer, and some other stuff. It works a treat.'

He reached into the steel arsenal and lifted a heavy cardboard box from the shadows. It was marked with large red letters saying 'GELIGNITE – HIGH EXPLOSIVE – DANGEROUS'. I didn't need telling.

I had driven the dumper truck over to the armoury and stood nervously beside it as Ray carried the box towards me.

When he got near to the open rear bucket of the truck, he hefted the box into the air.

'Catch!' he yelled.

I lurched forward with a squeak of terror, arms outstretched in a desperate attempt to catch the box but, to my horror, it plunged through my arms. I closed my eyes waiting for the last blinding white flash of my life. Ray guffawed with delight.

'Yer daft bugger,' he said, 'it won't go off like that. It's safe as houses, youth. You can burn it. Here look.'

He pulled out a thick stick of gelignite as thick round as a coffee cup. It was two feet long and coated in cardboard. A greasy gunge, smelling of marzipan, protruded from the ends. Ray struck a match. I leapt backwards. He smiled at me in a teasing way as he brought the flame closer to the exposed explosive. We were standing beside crates of the stuff, six hundred pounds, and this lunatic was about to set fire to it. I couldn't believe my eyes, and at the same time couldn't make myself turn and flee. It flared at the touch of the flame and then burned steadily with a sickly, smoky yellow flame.

As the dumper rocked and bounced up the path Ray leant towards me. 'It's not the jelly you want to worry about lad,' he said. 'These are the dangerous ones.' He pulled out a handful of glass tubes – detonators.

'For Christ's sake, Ray!' I yelped. 'What have you got those for?' Even I knew the rule that explosives and detonators must never travel together. Ray had both in a bouncing juddering dumper truck.

I stood to one side as Ray prepared the charges. He punched a hole through a stick of gelignite and then tied what looked like white coated wire through the hole. It was the sort of thing into which you wired plugs, except that it was filled with cordite instead of three-ply wire. The stick was dropped down a borehole, followed by several spadefuls of gravel, then another two sticks, more gravel, more sticks until the gravel spewed out from the top of the 120-foot hole. A thin white line of flex ran out of the gravel. When each hole had been charged Ray connected the ten cordite loaded charge wires together and secured them to a long length of electrical wire. He unrolled the command lead, walking carefully backwards past the generator until he was thirty yards from the charges.

'Got to be careful here,' Ray said as he inspected the wiring.

'Why?'

'If we left the top charges too close to the surface it blows the rock up and back instead of out into the quarry.'

'What? You mean on to us?'

'Aye, could do. Best to keep your eye on the rocks when she blows.'

When he had fiddled with the two contacts and was satisfied that all was in order, he handed me the compact little plunger.

'Go on, lad, have some fun.'

I had expected some black box with a T-shaped handle but the controller was a small thing with a twist grip on it.

'Get on with it, lad. A good twist and she'll blow ... I hope.'

I hesitated, wanting to refuse the offer. After all, who would be so childish as to want to blow up two thousand tons of quarry? Me, I decided, and wrenched at the plunger.

The explosion was not as loud as I had expected since it was muffled deep down within the rock. I looked on in fascination as gouts of smoke and dust spewed out and huge boulders tumbled into the quarry. Some debris shot upwards, and I watched as it arched into the air. One piece, the size of a pool table, seemed to tumble lazily in the sky directly in front of me. A mass of smaller blocks spiralled up alongside.

'Run!' Ray yelled in an uncharacteristic display of emotion, and I turned to see him cantering across the wet ploughed field behind us. I looked back at the rocks just as they reached the top of their flight and began to fall. It was then that I realised, far from flying out over the quarry, they were spinning back towards me. I dropped the controller and started to run.

The minute I turned my back on the rocks the fear took

over. I ran blindly, too scared to turn and see where they were landing. I soon overtook Ray and pounded out across the field with huge heavy clods of soil stuck to my feet. I heard loud thumps and one metallic crashing sound behind me which galvanised my exhausted legs into a faster spurt of speed. My heart seemed to be about to burst as I tripped and fell face first into the wet earth. When I had calmed down and climbed unsteadily to my feet I heard Ray laughing in the distance. I had run a hundred yards further than he had. I stumbled wearily back and examined the diesel generator. The cowling was badly damaged.

'Where's the controller?' Ray asked.

'I don't know. I dropped it round here somewhere.'

I spotted the white control wire and followed it back until it disappeared beneath a large boulder.

'That's two hundred and fifty quid down the pan,' Ray grunted as he headed off down to the quarry to examine the results of his explosion.

A fortnight later I hitch-hiked up to Edinburgh to start the first winter term of my four-year honours degree course in English Literature.

5

APPROACHING THE SCREEN

I WAS DISAPPOINTED WITH my first taste of Scottish winter climbing. Where was all the fabled vertical ice? We were a little over halfway up Red Gully on Corrie-an-t-Sneachda after no more than high-stepping up a reasonably steep twisting snow slope. I had skied down steeper inclines in the Dolomites. The walls of the gully had begun to close in around us, adding a slightly more exciting atmosphere, but the general difficulty of the climbing remained unchanged.

I glanced up to see that Adrian had stopped and was taking in the rope. We had moved together so far, and I had discovered that he was much fitter than I was. Because we were roped together I couldn't stop for breathers but had to keep going at Adrian's pace. I was damned if I would ask him to slow down after I had disparaged Red Gully as being far too easy.

Adrian had patiently explained to me that since I had never done any winter climbing it might be a good idea to start with something easy. His suggestion that we might try Central Gully – a Grade I route – had been met with point-blank refusal on my part. I could see from the corrie floor that it was a straightforward snow plod.

'No way,' I had said contemptuously. 'I want to climb some proper ice.'

With that I made menacing waving motions with my recently purchased ice axe at an imaginary vertical wall of ice. I had seen superb photographs of people climbing stupendous cascades of ice in the Scottish mountains, and there was no fun in doing a Grade I. How would I ever climb a Grade V if I set my sights so low.

'Okay,' Adrian had conceded, 'we'll do Red Gully and see how it goes. It's a good Grade two, so it should have icy bits higher up.'

Icy bits, I thought morosely as I plodded up. *I've seen more bloody ice in a gin and tonic.*

We had set off that morning from the camp site in Glen More, near Loch Morlich. It was my first meet with the Edinburgh University Mountaineering Club (EUMC). I had been forced to ignore my natural dislike of clubs, and Hon. Secs, Treasurers and Presidents and all the petty power struggles, and join the EUMC if I wanted to take advantage of the fortnightly transport to the Highlands which the club provided. It also introduced me to other climbers, and I had a mind to find a regular climbing partner, preferably one with a car, by joining the club.

The coach had taken us up the ski road and deposited a tangled bunch of rucksacks, axes, climbers, and ropes in the Corrie Cas car park. From here a two stage chairlift took you 3,500 feet up to the foot of Cairngorm, thus giving easy access to Loch Avon in the heart of the Northern Cairngorm Mountains. As we tightened our boots and checked our rucksacks I was astonished to see a large reindeer weaving nonchalantly between the cars and coaches, until it stood patient- ly in front of us. Someone gave it a Mars bar, which it chewed thoughtfully, wrapper and all, while regarding us with an unwavering bored expression.

'What's he doing here?' I asked incredulously.

'Oh, there are loads around here now,' Adrian said as he rescued his rucksack from the reindeer's inquisitive nose. 'Come on, we're getting left behind.'

He shouldered his sack and strode off.

'Hey,' I shouted. 'The chairlift's over there.'

'I know,' he shouted back. 'We're walking. It's cheaper and the exercise will do us good.

I detest walking, always have. I've walked long distances to climb things but never just for walking's sake.

My body isn't designed for walking. It's entirely the wrong shape. The legs are far too short and the whole trunk is shaped exactly to fit into seats and be carried comfortably to its destination, preferably by something fast and exciting, such as a sports car or a helicopter. I muttered irritably to myself as I tramped after Adrian, forced to keep up with his long strides as I had no idea where we were going. I was also without a map, or a whistle, or a compass, though they would have made little difference. I've never fathomed out how to use a compass, relying instead on carefully selected partners with the ability to navigate themselves out of anywhere.

From the car park we followed the contour round the Fiacaill of Coire Cas and into the coire itself, following a path towards the head of the coire where the squat black rock buttresses of the main cliff came into view. Nestled in the back recess of the coire, the cliff rises in four distinct buttresses, seamed by shallow gullies and streaked with ice and powder snow.

After a brief discussion about which route to climb we set off up the wide snow cone at the base of Red Gully. We were the last to start climbing. I noticed that Dick Nossiter, an EUMC member, had headed off towards a gully climb called The Runnel, intending to solo it, and felt a momentary pang of jealousy. Although the Runnel was the same grade as the gully it looked more interesting, with a fork in the upper reaches of the 400-foot route that offered a choice of finish. The left fork climbed a steep narrow chimney far more exciting than anything on Red Gully, but as we were the last to arrive there were already too many climbers on it, so we were left with Red Gully.

I reached Adrian and slumped gratefully on to my axe in the soft snow. Adrian Clifford was a tall bearded young medic, approachable and friendly, and the owner of a car. His long night shifts as a junior doctor in the Edinburgh Royal Infirmary made driving north at weekends an exceedingly dangerous undertaking. Normally he wouldn't have had any sleep for about thirty-six hours and I always expected to hear that he had killed himself on the Loch Lomond road after falling asleep at the wheel.

'It's in very easy condition,' he said.

'I noticed,' I said, face down in the snow.

I looked up. Adrian was staring down at the corrie floor. I heard a distant shout, a warning cry, and then saw a body shooting out from a gully that was hidden by the rock buttress on our left. It was moving at incredible speed. As it rocketed into sight it was tumbling in a frenzy of arms and legs, axes swinging wildly on their wrist loops.

'Christ Almighty!'

'Quick!' Adrian said. 'We'd better get down.'

I couldn't take my eyes off the small figure as it sped down the long run out slopes beneath the cliffs. It slid, head down, arms stretched out to the sides in a V-shape. There was no attempt at an ice axe brake. At the end of the slope the corrie floor extended in a jumble of rocks and boulders – the shattered remains of an ancient glacier. A large black rock protruded from the snow slope and, like a bee to a honeypot the frail figure headed straight for it. I stared open-mouthed, half afraid to watch, half fascinated. The body stopped with a sickening abruptness. There was no sound, but I flinched as I saw it jerk to a violent halt as it smacked head first into the rock.

'Come on!' Adrian yelled. He had unroped and was heeling down the gully as fast as he could. I looked at the tangle of ropes at my feet and distractedly began to coil them round my neck. As I did so I glanced down at the body, fully expecting to see the snow blossoming into a red stain. There was no movement. *Dead. He's got to be dead,* I thought. *No way could he survive that.* Suddenly a leg moved.

'Adrian! He's still alive.'

Even as I said it the figure curled up into a ball and shuffled on to its knees. For a moment he was bowed forward, clutching his helmeted head and then he rose shakily to his feet. He turned and faced the silent cliff with climbing parties in every gully gawping down on him.

'I'm OKAY!' he yelled.

As the words echoed round the cliffs I saw him standing with his arms outstretched triumphantly above his head, an axe in one hand. Before the sound of his cry had faded he toppled slowly forward, flat on his face in the snow, out cold.

A large group of people who had been practising rescue techniques hurried across to him. After a protracted shouting match, Adrian discovered that they didn't need a doctor; they were members of an RAF mountain rescue team, and Dick Nossiter, the victim, had timed his fall to perfection.

We finished the climb quietly – an easy, boring Grade II snow gully, just like the Runnel on which Dick had so expertly executed his own brand of death plunge. Those endless seconds after he had stopped, when I was convinced that I had just witnessed someone fall to their death, stayed with me on the long walk back to the car park.

Dick sat in the coach on the way back to Edinburgh with a swollen face and glazed concussed eyes. There was an unusually tense edge to the humorous comments on Dick's climbing, as if the seriousness of how close he had come wouldn't go away however much we laughed.

Not long after my first foray into the Scottish mountains I took the EUMC night coach up to Glencoe, where I found the Coe warm and wrapped in cloud. It rained as we struggled to erect the tent before the bar in the nearby Clachaig Inn closed. In the stark atmosphere of the public bar we discussed which route we would do in the morning.

I was brimming with the confidence born of being a two-axe man, the proud possessor of a new ice hammer, a tool that looked suspiciously like a geology hammer and about as effective for ice climbing. I had wondered why the shop assistant had been in such a hurry to ring up the price on the till the moment I had picked it up.

Still, it had a nice curve to the pick, with teeth that I had filed to razor sharp points, and a blue rubber handle, and it felt good as I made experimental swipes with it in the tent. Nick Rose, my partner for the weekend, had prised it from me before I could shred the nylon wall of the tent. *Whatever we do,* I'd said as we hurried through the rain to the pub, *it won't be some piddling little grade two*. Nick had made no comment.

'Steep ice,' I said as time was called at the bar, 'that's what we need.'

'It's your round.' Nick replied.

As I waited in the sweaty steaming throng I noticed some colour prints on the back of the bar. One in particular caught my eye. It was a picture of a blue white cascade of ice with a climber fixed, fly-like, to the centre of the ice fall. When I looked more closely I noticed that the climber was stark naked but for boots and mitts. It seemed a bit of an extreme way of going about such a spectacular climb.

'Did you see that photo of the guy climbing the icicle naked?' I asked Nick.

'Yeah. Elliot's downfall. That's the climb he's doing.'

'Really. It looks amazing. Where is it?'

'In the Coe,' Nick said warily. 'It's on the West Face of Aonach Dubh.'

'In the Coe, eh? Well, why don't we try it?'

'For God's sake, Joe, you've only done one grade two. Leaping to grade five is a bit too much.'

'Oh. I didn't realise it was that hard.' I said. 'But you could lead it if you wanted to.'

'I don't want to,' Nick said firmly.

'Is there anything else like it but a bit easier?'

'Well, we could do the Screen, I suppose. It's grade four and pretty steep, but there's only one main pitch.'

'Right. Let's do it.'

'I don't know. It might be a bit much . . .'

'No, we'll do it. I'll lead it. No worries.'

We stumbled back to the tents in the dark of a warm moonless night.

'It might not be in condition,' Nick said as he climbed into his sleeping bag. 'After all, it's not very cold, you know.'

'Well, we'll see in the morning,' I said, cheerfully while executing a few ferocious swipes at the night sky with my new ice hammer. To say I was over confident was an understatement. I had absolutely no idea what grade IV ice climbing entailed. Up to that winter I had been better than most of the people with whom I had climbed, and arrogantly I now assumed that this ice climbing lark would be just as simple. Bursting with conceited notions of my own brilliance, I clambered into the tent and laid the hammer possessively beneath my rucksack, which was doubling as a wet pillow. I briefly toyed with the idea of telling Nick that I had decided to name my hammer 'Thor' but managed to stop myself just in time. *No need to make a complete prat of yourself.*

Next morning, after a lung-bursting race up the steep heather-covered slopes of the flanks of Aonach Dubh, we made our way gingerly across wet snow and bulges of gleaming water ice to the foot of the Screen. To my utter dismay, I saw a leader high on the first pitch. Lumps of ice clattered on to our shoulders as we dug a type of snow stake called a Dead Man into the base of the climb. Nick clipped himself to the wire coming from the small sheet of galvanised steel buried in the snow and declared himself happy that nothing would pull him off. Glancing nervously at the steep snow and ice-choked gully below, I cramponed unsteadily over to Nick and clipped into the Dead Man as well. The crampons felt very strange, as if I were teetering around on multiple stiletto heels. *Soon get used to them,* I reassured myself.

Dick Nossiter, his face recovered from the battering he had given it, smiled at me from his belay stance. His leader had climbed the first 75-foot cascade of ice and had clipped his rope through an old piton at the back of a small cave.

'Looks as if it's not going to last,' Dick said.

Water streamed down the surface of the ice. I could see from the way the leader was using his axe that the top three inches was water-logged mush. I had an experimental hack at the ice in front of me and succeeded in twisting my wrist. The point of the pick bounced clear of the thin ice with sparks flying from the underlying rock. I nearly dropped it.

'Haven't you got a wrist loop for that thing?' Dick asked.

'No,' I said sharply, annoyed that he should call my pride and joy a *thing*. 'Didn't have time,' I lied. *Why do I need a wrist loop anyway?* 'It'll be all right for this,' I said confidently, 'It's not too long.'

There was a quizzical look on Dick's face as he set off to follow his partner's lead. 'Be careful, mate,' he said as he stepped up and away.

'No worries,' I replied with a more successful hack at the ice. 'It's a good tool, this.' I muttered to Nick as I wrenched away at the hammer, trying to free it from the glutinous ice bulge into which I had embedded it.

'Should have called it Excalibur,' Nick commented drily. 'You can be King Arthur, if you get it out.'

Three-quarters of an hour later Dick had yet to reach the piton in the cave. We were soaked and shivering. Two climbers had joined us at the stance and sat to one side examining Dick's progress with grim disapproving expressions. They were older than us and their confident superiority made me feel uncomfortable.

Patience has never been one of my strong points. Perhaps it came from growing up as the youngest of five children and always having to fight to assert myself. It may be that I was born a stroppy pig- headed little bugger and never changed. I tend towards the family assertiveness theory myself.

'Oh, sod it! I can't wait any longer.' I stood up.

'What are you doing?' Nick asked. 'You can't go until he's finished.'

'Don't worry,' I replied, 'I just want to get going before it all disappears. Watch me.'

I swung my axe above me and stepped off the ice bulge. After a few bunny-hopped steps up the cascade I began to wonder why Dick was having such a struggle. It seemed remarkably simple to me. Easier than rock climbing. You choose your own hand and foot holds simply by swinging an axe here or kicking a spiked boot there.

The meltwater pouring down the cascade flowed over my axe handles and wrists and trickled in icy rivulets down my armpits. I shivered. As the angle increased I found that I had to grip the axes harder and began to worry about how well they were holding. The angle pushed me out, and my arms tired quickly. I tended to forget about my feet until the front points of my right crampon suddenly sheared out of the soft ice and I jerked down on to the picks of my axes. I kicked wildly at the ice and tried to calm the thumping fright in my chest.

Dick seemed to have made no progress at all. He pawed at the ice with an axe, unsure whether to commit himself to the few teetering sideways moves to the cave. Lumps of mushy ice thumped into my shoulders and worked their way down the back of my neck. He was spread-eagled on the cascade about twenty-five feet above me. I glanced down at Nick to see him staring intently at us. The two older climbers seemed to be laughing at me. I hammered a warthog into the cascade and clipped the rope into its eye. I didn't think the warthog − a drive-in ice piton − would be of much use in the soft surface ice but it made me feel better.

Suddenly one of Dick's feet skittered out from the ice and I flinched away. Ice and mush clattered on to my head, but no spike-footed climber, as I had expected. *Well, it's go down, or go up and pass him,* I thought, *and I'm damned if I'll go down and face those guys laughing at me.* As I came up level with Dick's feet I saw him looking down between his legs.

'Don't worry,' I said as I drove my ice hammer into the ice just below his crotch. He suddenly looked very worried. 'If you stay still I'll climb above you and then be out of your way.'

I thumped my axe in just to the left of his hip and stepped up. Dick flinched. I had some difficulty removing the hammer from between his legs but eventually it came loose and I swung it into the ice beside the axe. I noticed that Dick was less tense now that I had stopped hacking away between his legs.

Absorbed in the problem of climbing past Dick without falling off or hitting him, I didn't at first register the tightness in my right hand. At last I was past him and standing on my front points just above his shoulders. I looked at the dark cave to my right. A brightly-coloured tape had been clipped to the piton and then to Dick's rope. A few moves and I would be able to reach across and grab it.

The pick of my axe seemed well embedded so I reached across to the right and tried to get my hammer to stick. The ice sloughed away from the blows. I had reached the point where Dick had struggled for so long and was beginning to realise why. The ice was awash. I needed one solid placement with each tool to get across to the cave.

A needle-like pain started to make itself felt in the ball of my right thumb. I was developing cramp in my hand from having to grip hard on the wet rubber hammer handle. It was then that I realised why I needed a wrist loop. A loop would allow me to hang on to the hammer without gripping so tightly. The first tremor of fear shivered through me. It wasn't going as planned. It wasn't as easy as I had thought.

It happened very slowly. The pick of the ice axe suddenly ripped free and the jerk swung me out from the ice, hinging out on the desperate grip of my right hand on the wet rubber handle of the hammer. For a moment I seemed to have the situation under control, then the hammer shifted, my hand slipped slightly, and almost as the pick pulled free my cramped hand opened and I was falling. I remembered just in time to hop back slightly so as not to impale Dick with my crampons. Unfortunately I hopped too enthusiastically. I not only cleared Dick but everything else as well and found myself swooping down in a stomach clenching lurch.

It was a peculiar sensation. It seemed to happen in slow motion and I saw Dick's legs, my slack rope, white pocked-marked ice, the warthog, all flash past in what seemed like a series of snapshot photographs – images of the fall photographed through the staring shutters of my eyes and the numb feeling that I was about to be hurt. There was a slow, suspended fall and then a brutally sudden acceleration that made me feel as if I had lurched over a hump-backed bridge and left my stomach somewhere level with Dick's feet. Nick flashed past me with the deadman trailing from his waist by its wire – and then I hit.

I felt something crunch in my chest and the wind rushed out of me. My helmeted head snapped painfully sideways and something smacked into my right leg. Then silence, and no breath. I lay on my side staring fixedly at the two older climbers who scrutinized me with a mixture of concern and contempt. I seemed to stare at them for ages as I retched fitfully, quite unable to draw breath.

At last I sucked in a lungful of cool air just as one of the climbers licked the glue on his cigarette paper and rolled it down.

'Here,' he said, handing me the lit roll-up, 'you should have shouted *Geronimo!*' He grinned.

There was a rushing sound from above and Nick jumped to my side as Dick came slithering down the cascade. Unnerved by my fall he had himself fallen and his partner had been unable to hold his rope with wet icy gloves.

'See you at the tents,' Nick said as he started up the cascade. He had tied in to Dick's rope after Dick had said he would help me down. I didn't speak to the two climbers for fear of further humiliation. I grunted at Nick and set off tentatively down the hillside. I knew that I had hurt myself but the adrenalin seemed to ward off the worst effects. My right leg felt sore but strong on a straightforward step downhill. If I put sideways pressure on the leg it virtually collapsed. My chest and neck throbbed painfully.

When we reached the river Coe I realised, to my dismay, that we were too far downstream.

'We'll have to go back up about half a mile to reach the bridge,' Dick said gloomily.

I looked downstream. 'It isn't deep down there. Do you think we could get across on those rocks?'

'Might do, I suppose.'

I watched Dick leap from rock to rock until he reached the gravel shallows on the far side.

'Come on,' he yelled. 'It's not too bad.'

Like most righthanded people I tend to lead with my right leg. That is, I kick balls with it, step off pavements with the right foot, and leap across stepping stones right foot first. I forgot that my leg hurt. The minute I hit the first stone there was a rush of pain up the outside of my leg and I pitched headfirst into the icy waters of the Coe with an enraged yelp.

It might have been shallow but the water wasn't taking prisoners in its rush for the sea. I tumbled and rolled downstream, grasping at rocks and trying to dig my feet into the river bed. It deposited me very wet, icy cold, and in a filthy temper on the far bank some hundred yards downstream from a giggling Nossiter. We squelched morosely back to the pub.

Two days later I hobbled into the Accident and Emergency clinic of the Edinburgh Royal Infirmary. At first the doctors wouldn't believe I had fallen 70 feet until they found three broken ribs and three more cracked on my right side, a hairline split in the fibula of my right leg, badly torn trapezius neck muscles that forced my head on to my left shoulder and a bladder that seemed to have gone walkabout.

'Did you scream?' the young house doctor asked cheerfully as he extracted what seemed to be a pint of blood from my arm.

'Er. No, actually . . .'

'Good thing too. Here, pee in that for me, will you?' He handed me a tiny specimen jar. 'If you had screamed your lungs would have been empty on impact and your ribs would have caved in like match sticks.' He grinned at me. I handed him back a full and wet jar and wiped my hands on the bed sheet.

'Hurts when you pee, you say?'

'Sort of.'

'Ah well, it's just been wobbled to one side. Your bladder, that is — it'll find its way back. The ribs will take between three and five weeks. Try not to laugh or sneeze. Oh, and get in touch if you have any more trouble with the old waterworks. You're a lucky man, Mr Simpson. Goodbye.'

As I hobbled back to my flat, bent almost double in a geriatric stoop, with my head fixed to my left shoulder like the hunchback of Notre Dame, I wondered at some people's idea of lucky. Far from lucky, I felt as if I'd just been gang raped by the entire Welsh rugby team. Not for the first time, I had made a bloody fool of myself!

6

THE LEARNING CURVE

'WHY DON'T WE try the Dolomites first, get some rock climbing done, and then go on to Chamonix?' Nick Rose asked.

'Sounds good,' I said. 'Where abouts in the Dolomites?'

'Cortina,' he replied confidently. 'I've got a guidebook. We can go and do that.' He dropped the book on the table.

'Dolomites East, eh,' I said, picking it up and glancing at the page Nick had indicated. 'North face (Via Comici) Cima Grande, 500 meters, grade VI, A1. What's grade VI, then.'

'I dunno, but it must be hard. There doesn't seem to be a higher grade in the book.'

'Have you ever done any aid climbing?' I asked.

'Well, no, not exactly. I mean I've hung on a few things in the past, you know nuts and pegs and things, but only because I was knackered. Anyway it's no big deal. We'll soon pick it up.'

It was early July and very hot. No breath of wind stirred as I toiled in a stupefied daze up the pine-forested hillside, following the road to what I had hoped would be Misurina. I had been at it for several hours and was beginning to wonder if I had taken a wrong turning out of Cortina.

I shrugged the heavy rucksack off my shoulder and watched in dismay as it tumbled into a deep bramble-filled ditch at the side of the road. By the time I had thrashed around in the undergrowth, swearing and yelping as the thorns attacked my arms, the obstinate rucksack had jammed itself firmly in the ditch and I was done in. At last I dragged it from its lair and collapsed in a dusty, sweaty heap on the grass verge. I lay there panting in the dry pine-scented air, sprawled across the rucksack with my legs in the ditch. A car came up the hill in low gear and cruised remorselessly past me just as I managed to lift an exhausted thumb into the air. It didn't stop.

I noticed a large thorn protruding from the end of my thumb and a bloody scratch on the back of my hand. I licked the scratch and felt another thorn prick painfully into my tongue. I consulted my map and the guidebook yet again. 'Follow the road from Cortina to Lake Misurina from where a good metalled road leads all the way up to the Auronzo and Lavaredo Huts.' The map showed it to be about sixteen miles from Cortina to Misurina. *So, two hours at about three miles an hour makes it another ten miles to go, and then the two-hour slog up the hill from the lake to the huts. Oh my God . . .*

I awoke from a dehydrated coma to the drone of another car engine labouring up through the woods below. As I was closing the guide book I noticed the last line of the paragraph I had been reading.

' . . . chances of getting a lift alone and not too heavily laden are good: would-be hitchers are advised to look extremely fatigued.'

Since I was on the point of total physical and mental collapse I reasoned that all I had to do was to hide the huge sack and hold up my thumb. I succeeded in thrusting the recalcitrant baggage back into the ditch with a hefty kick. The car ground to a blessed halt and a swarthy mustachioed driver peered out curiously as I swayed weakly on my knees. I noticed that both my hands were outstretched in an open-palm imploring gesture. Forget the thumb, it was time for desperate measures; nothing was too undignified.

'Bon journo,' I stammered, 'Misurina, Lavaredo . . .'

'Si, Si.' He nodded vigorously and indicated that it was no longer necessary to kneel in supplication.

Suddenly full of energy, I turned and tried to retrieve my rucksack but the little bugger wasn't going to give up without a struggle. I heard the driver say something impatiently.

'It's okay,' I gasped with my head and shoulders thrust into the gap in the thorns. 'Uno minuto, grazie, okay.' I dreaded the sound of him engaging first gear and leaving without me. The rucksack chose this moment to lurch violently out of the ditch and I tumbled backwards, wrestling it into submission.

The gears crunched and the car began moving away even as I subdued the beast.

'No, wait!' I yelled, staggering after the car. The driver waved dismissively, said something that I didn't understand and left me standing there in despair. I was consumed by an indignant and petulant fury and ran after the retreating Fiat, yelling and swearing and giving him the finger, cursing his nationality and his mother. I stomped back to kick the dormant rucksack and heard something break inside. As I laid into the sack in an infuriated tantrum a bus chugged slowly round the bend and shuddered to a halt beside me. I looked up in surprise at a row of passengers who examined this filthy, wild-eyed man kicking seven shades of hell out of his rucksack. The doors slid open with a hiss of compressed air and the driver said, 'Misurina?' I almost hurled myself into the bus to embrace him.

Sitting contentedly by the beautiful little circular lake at Misurina, I ate my fourth ice cream between puffs on a roll-up. I checked my watch. It would be dark in a few hours. I stood up and wandered over to the metalled road where my rucksack squatted in the dust. I gave it a desultory kick and turned to see a car coming towards me.

Half an hour later I was deposited by the driver outside the Lavaredo hut. His friend, the guardian of the hut, got out and strode into the small tin-roofed stone-walled building. The car swung round with a flurry of dust, a beep on the horn, and a cheery 'Ciao', and headed down for Misurina.

I turned to gaze up at the huge towers of yellow limestone looming over the hut. A steep scree slope ran down from the broad base of rock. The Cima Piccolissima, Cima Piccola,

Punta Frida and Anticima. I recognised them at once from the photos I had studied in Edinburgh. They seemed pleasantly foreshortened from where I stood, but I knew from an awesome photograph taken looking down from high on the south ridge of the Anticima that the summits were a vertical thousand feet and more above me.

I turned and followed the guardian into the hut and ordered a very expensive beer. I had got to the Alps. Now what?

A few days later an equally filthy Nick staggered into the Lavaredo hut and we ordered two astronomically expensive beers. We unpacked his half of the tent and attached it to the makeshift half in which I had been living. After sorting out the tent into two halves – personal gear and a mass of climbing gear – petrol stove and petrol in front, boots and axes under the fly-sheet at the back, we cracked open a bottle of cheap red wine and got drunk.

So started our first Alpine season, that near suicidal baptism of fire undertaken by poor souls with enough skill and talent to get into serious trouble but no experience to help them get out of it. I had read enough of books to convince me that the Alps were big, beautiful and potentially lethal. Gazing up at the stupendous one-thousand-foot limestone column of the Yellow Edge, the Spigolo Giallo, on the Anticima, I had no doubts about how big they were, but I couldn't see the dangers. The rockfalls, the lightning storms, the harrowing abseil descents on bad anchors, and the freezing unplanned bivouacs – I had read about them and secretly, I suppose, looked forward to experiencing them in a naive sort of way. All the words I had devoured about the exploits of the great Alpine and Himalayan climbers had fired my imagination to such a fever pitch of anticipation that it never occurred to me I might become a victim of these mountains, a shattered bloody relic of overweening ambition.

Toni Kurz dying alone on the North Face of the Eiger, Gervasutti falling to his death in an abseiling accident, Herman Buhl plunging through the cornice on Chogolisa – but think of what they had done before these tragic accidents.

I saw their deaths as a loss of greatness rather than a waste of lives.

Comici's directtissima routes that followed, in his words, 'the drop of water from the summit to ground'. All the attempts on the great north faces in the Alps and the players in that glorious arena – Whymper, Mummery, Merkl on Nanga Parbat, Welzenbach, and Hillary and Tenzing on Everest, Cassin on the Walker Spur, Bonatti on the Drus, the formidable Frenchmen Lachenal, Rabuffat, Terray and Herzog in despair on Annapurna. Desmaison on the Shroud, Mazeaud surviving the Frêney Pillar epic, Bonington and Clough, Brown and Whillans and Patey – I had read them all, and it seemed as if they were showing me more love of life and adventure and challenge than I could ever have dreamt was possible. They were heroes to me and role models – people who scared me with what they had achieved, what they had dared to try.

That long hot summer was fraught with perils foolishly embraced and crowned with delight and wonder and exhilarating excite- ment. Looking back now, I wonder how on earth we got away with what we did. I will never forget that consuming sense of discovering something brilliant, something precious and life-enhancing. From that time on, I had to learn fast because I knew there was no going back.

I often asked myself why I wanted to climb mountains but soon realised there was no need. Such questions are unanswerable, and are posed only by those who have never done it themselves.

Nick was perhaps a little more pragmatic about it all. We were both small, dark-haired and slim built. Yet, whereas I responded with a fiery impatience, Nick was a calm and reserved young man. Easy going and quietly spoken, he was a perfect foil to my impetuous pig-headedness. He had read as much as I on the great climbs and climbers of the Alps but I refrained from expressing how I felt to him. I chose instead to hide behind a mask of studied assurance. If I suggested that we try such and such a route, I would always put forward a sensible reason and not the truth.

The truth seemed uncomfortably egotistical. I wanted to do only hard climbs, great north faces, impressive and daunting rock routes. I wanted a 'tick list' of hard routes under my belt. I wanted to be a great climber, craved the false glory that I thought went with being a 'hardman'. I did not realise then that I could never be something that existed only in my boastful mind. At the same time, it seemed wrong to want such things, shallow and superficial. I suppose it was only ambition, vaunting ambition perhaps, a goal which gave me incentive, but which to my guilt-ridden lapsed Catholic mind was wrong. Pride was a sin.

So I persuaded myself I climbed because the routes were good, so aesthetically beautiful, and so fine, which was partly true as well as being an easy way out. It cosily covered the real reasons.

Why else had I gone for The Screen and nearly killed myself? And that too was an uncomfortable thought. I knew it was a dangerous business, and it scared me sometimes to know what could happen, and if this were so, then surely the reasons for doing these things must be noble and right, not a matter of petty self-aggrandizement? I concealed my real feelings, or the half of them that sat so uncomfortably in my mind, and began to live the lie. Before long I could not distinguish between the two and lost all sense of why I had started, except to remember that it was good; in the beginning very good.

We started cautiously. 'For anyone venturing on Dolomite rock for the first time the NE Ridge of the Cima Grande will give a good introduction to Dolomitic rock and exposure.' It had been climbed in 1909, so we thought it must be easy – a dangerous assumption to make, I later discovered. It was 1,800 feet long – six times longer than any rock route we had tackled before – and graded III, unless we included the most difficult pitches which would make it IV. Grade IV was described as very difficult to severe. These were British grades we regarded as simple, almost climbable without a rope.

We left our tent before dawn with a water bottle each and sweets to nibble during the day. The guidebook time for the route was four hours, so we expected to be back down at the tents long before dark.

Eighteen hours later we finally resigned ourselves to a long cold night out on a crumbly ledge somewhere on the North East Face of Cima Grande. We had taken a pitiful fifteen hours to complete the 'easy' four-hour ridge. The rock had varied between good and horrific. The harder the climbing, the safer and more solid the rock. Several parties had galloped past us during the day as painstakingly we belayed and put in protective nuts and wires on every pitch. It was how we climbed in Britain. We had not realised that the only way to do the route in four hours was to move together on many easy scrambling sections. Near the top of the ridge the route traversed out across the stupendous overhanging abyss of the North Face. I had never experienced anything like it and easy grade III climbing suddenly became the most extreme thing I had ever undertaken. I couldn't haul my eyes away from the empty space below my feet. Fifteen hundred feet of teetering emptiness that dragged at my shuffling feet as I edged across the traverse. When Nick joined me beneath a crack that climbed vertically above us for seventy feet my legs were shaking. Nick had a peculiarly fixed expression on his face and very wide eyes as he glanced down.

'Oh my sainted Aunt . . .'

'Let's get out of here.'

I was glad it was his turn to lead. The feeling of exposure was paralysing. I felt capable of nothing except concentrating on my various sphincters and making sure they didn't open.

At the summit we blundered around in search of a line of descent. All around us were ominous lurking drops into the evening shadows. Though the guidebook said it was a scramble, we were relieved to discover pitons with abseil tape on them. Someone had been down this way before, but was it safe? Did he know any more than we did?

A cold rain began to lash around us in the dusk. We couldn't go on. We hadn't thought to take head-torches on such a short route and now could hardly see where the pitons were. In any case, most of the pitons were rusty and very unsteadily placed. I watched, horrified, as Nick descended into the gloom off a small soft metal leaf piton which flexed alarmingly. When I examined it carefully, I saw that less than an inch of steel was embedded in the crack. Hastily I unclipped myself. If it went, I would be left standing on a very narrow ledge without ropes or gear. Nick had all the hardware with him.

A faint cry echoed up from the shadows. *Well, if it held for him it will hold for me.* Repeating this spurious logic to myself, I gingerly abseiled into the gathering darkness, trying not to jerk on the rope. By the time I reached Nick it was too dark to continue. I wanted to curl into a foetal position and promise myself, eyes closed, that this wasn't happening. Unfortunately the ledge was too small and we were forced to sit with our legs dangling over the drop shivering miserably.

By five in the morning, when the Gods sadistically screw down the temperature control, knowing that puny mortals are at their weakest, I regretted my secret longings for adventurous bivouacs and stimulating climbs.

As we staggered down the last loose screes to the tent I felt too stimulated to speak and could think of nothing but hot sweet tea and oblivious sleep. A huge spaghetti, wolfed down with butter and fingers covered with tomato sauce, left me with warm feelings in my chest and a building pleasure at the memory of what we had done. Perhaps it was just indigestion.

'Well, we learnt a few things, didn't we?' I said, reaching for the wine.

'Yes. We're useless.'

'True. And slow.'

'And we belay too much.'

'Yup. No good at heights either.'

'Or descending . . .'

'Or bivis.'

'I wonder what those guys thought of us?' Nick asked.

We looked at each other and burst out laughing at the memory of how idiotic we must have seemed to the other parties.

'It was fun though, wasn't it?'

'It is now,' I agreed, and slurped at the wine.

Two weeks of grinding up screes and grappling with various routes soon sorted us out. We climbed the superb Yellow Edge, graded V+, and were delighted to find it easy. We abseiled off without mishap and were back at the tents by early afternoon. We avoided easy climbs and loose rock after being showered with missiles while descending the Dulfer couloir. On the climb up the Preuss Crack we found a sad reminder of mortality. By one of the belay stances, a small airy ledge perched 600 feet above the screes, I noticed a small brass plaque. There was a name inscribed on it and the climber's age, nineteen. Beneath this it read in German:

Mord in Steinschlag.
Kleine Zinnen So Grat.

'What does it say?' Nick asked when he pulled up on to the small ledge.

'Killed in rockfall. Little peak so great.'

'Oh,' he said, looking suspiciously at the rock walls above us. 'What's little peak got to do with it?'

'Well, the Italians call these three peaks the 'Tre Cime', the Germans call them the 'Drei Zinnen.' This is the Cima Piccolissima, the littlest peak, or the Kleine peak. So it's saying, Little peak but so great, so serious, it killed this lad here. See what I mean?'

'Yeah,' Nick said. 'Let's get out of here.'

The next day we cruised up the Grade VI+ south-east face direct of the Punta Frida, finishing in an hour less than the guidebook time. We returned to the tents to find that the wide horned cows which kept us awake at night with their jangling bells had up-rooted the flysheet and trampled over the doorway. We repaired a minor tear and re-erected the tent. The sky had darkened with heavy grey clouds and we had

1 Grandad Scotland in India, 1931

2 Da as a boy with Grandma Scotland and a tiger cub, 1928

3 The Simpson family at home in Gibraltar, Joe and Sarah on the right.

4 *(left)* Doug Pratt Johnson and Joe Simpson after their ascent of the North Face of the Matterhorn (Photo: Joe Simpson)

6 The North Face of the Courtes, showing the line of climb and Joe's 2,000-foot fall (Photo: Roland Gay Couttet)

5 *(below)* Snells Field campsite, Chamonix, 1982 – left to right: Sean Smith, Richard Cox and Andy Hislop. (Photo: Nick Kekus)

7 Alpine binmen Simon Richardson (back), Mark Miller, Murray Laxton and Jon Tinker. (Photo: Simpson)

8 Murray Laxton on steep ice on the Droites. (Photo: Simpson)

9 Approaching the ice field on the north face of the Droites. (Photo: Simpson) 10. Rob Uttley lies injured after a rockfall on the Grand Jorasses. (Photo: Kekus)

11 Murray Laxton in contemplative mood. (Photo: Simpson)

12 *(below)* Les Drus, Chamonix. (Photo: Simpson)

13 *(right)* Phil Thornhill climbing steep mixed ground on the Drus Couloir. (Photo: Simpson)

14, 15 *(above)* Rob Uttley in Kathmandu and Don Barr before he was killed in the Verdon Gorge. (Photos: Kekus)

16 *(below)* Ian Whittaker before attempting the Bonatti Pillar.

hardly finished with the tent before the outriders of the storm settled in a thickening white carpet.

It snowed heavily for the rest of the afternoon and through a long windy night. I was surprised to find nearly a foot of snow blanketing the area when I knocked the sides of the tent clear and peered out blearily in the morning. I fumbled with cold fingers and soggy matches until at last I managed to light the wad of petrol-soaked tissue in the priming pan of the petrol stove. We had laid a plastic sheet in the porch area of the tent to keep dust and grit out and I reached over it to fill a pan with snow. The storm had allowed me to make the tea without tramping off to the stream to collect water.

When the flames subsided I pumped up the stove and watched the burner burst into a satisfying blue roar. Nick was still asleep in his sleeping bag with his head at the far end of the tent. As I shuffled an elbow on the plastic sheet it rumpled up and toppled the metal petrol bottle on to its side. I made no attempt to catch it. As it fell I was horrified to see a spurt of petrol splash from the open top. I had forgotten to screw the top on after soaking the priming tissue.

For a moment I thought it wouldn't ignite and then there was a *whoosh* as nearly a litre of fuel flooding across the plastic ignited on contact with the hot stove. Three weeks of beard growth, my nostril hairs, eyebrows, and some of my hair vaporised in an instant. My first instinct was to get out of the tent and save myself. I lurched off my knees in a clumsy dive over the flames and fell face first into the snow outside.

From behind me I heard a muffled yelp and turned to see the red cocoon of Nick's sleeping bag thrashing around behind the wall of flames. The drawcord had been pulled tight and cinched so that only his nose had been exposed to the cold stormy night. As the *whoomph* of igniting petrol woke him he felt the heat rush back into the tent. With his arms by his sides it was a frantic effort to control his panic, find the drawcord and release it.

For a moment I gawped at the blazing tent in astonishment. It had happened so fast I couldn't really grasp what was going on. Fortunately there was snow on the ground. I scooped a double-handed pile and threw it on to the burning plastic. A second load soaked up the fuel and quenched the flames. I scrambled into the tent to grab Nick only to find him gone.

'Nick?'

'What the fuck are you doing,' was the angry response from outside.

'How did you get out there?'

I popped my head out of the door to see Nick still in his sleeping bag and clutching a penknife and a lump of salami.

'How do you think?' he snapped.

'What . . . you cut the tent? It's going to snow again and you cut the tent?'

'I thought it better than burning to death.'

'But I put the flames out, for Christ's sake.'

'Look, there was a big explosion and it was bloody hot. I didn't know what you were doing. I thought you were in the tent with me.'

He stood up out of his sleeping bag and came over to examine the smouldering remains of the doorway.

'I knocked the fuel bottle over,' I said lamely. 'I forgot to put the top on.'

It took several freezing hours to sew and patch the inner tent together with gaffer tape before we retreated to the hut with the flysheet to warm up and sew it in warmth and comfort.

Fit and strong, and no longer freaked out by the scale of the mountains, we decided it was time to attempt the Comici route on the North Face of the Cima Grande and wandered round to the foot of the wall to examine the line of the route. The lower wall overhung for some 900 feet and, although we knew people had free climbed the route, we were too intimidated to do anything other than use the many pitons on the wall for direct aid.

As we toiled up the final few yards of scree towards some dirty winter snow banked against the wall there was a high-pitched whistling sound and a cracking report behind us.

'What was that?'

'Not sure . . .' Nick was staring up at the sky and I saw his mouth drop open. I glanced up and saw that the sky above had an odd mottled appearance.

'Rockfall!' Nick yelled, and held the open guidebook on top of his unhelmeted head. There were deep thrumming sounds, whistles, and the nerve-tingling reverberating *vroom-vroom-vroom* of stones spinning over and over through hundreds of feet of space. A staccato machine gun rattle of cracks on the scree behind me galvanised my frozen legs into three lunging strides up the banked snow. Without a second thought I dived into the small crevasse formed between the rock wall and the snow, my forearms clasped over my head. Dropping five feet into the gap, I huddled into as small a ball as possible. When the bombardment subsided, I looked out from under my arms.

'Nick! Are you okay?'

'Yes. It's all right. The wall's so overhanging they were hitting about forty feet away from us.'

As I lifted myself on to an elbow I noticed a revolting stench coming from where I lay. Glancing down, I saw a piece of pink tissue and a squashed turd protruding from beneath my elbow.

'Oh, jeez . . .' I lifted my arm, keeping it fastidiously away to one side, and rose to my knees. I was kneeling in several more turds. As I stumbled to my feet the freshly released stench wafted out of the gap, making me retch.

'Oh, no. I don't believe it!'

Nick was laughing at the sight of my spattered clothes, stuck here and there with bits of soiled tissue. In a blue funk I had dived into the one place at the foot of the route where climbers had their last nervous crap before starting the climb. Now I learnt that the rockfall could never have touched me.

He kept a good distance between us as we walked back to the camp.

Three days later we basked in the hot July sun, drinking cheap red wine and feeling wonderfully degenerate and languorous after two hard days work on the face. We had been forced to bivouac on loose rubble ledges above the overhanging wall, and although we hadn't done it in the greatest of style, we had reason to be pleased. It was one of the six classic north faces in the Alps. It may be the easiest and probably the safest, but we didn't care.

Two young Oxford University climbers had turned up while we were on the wall and pitched their tents near ours. On our return they quizzed us about the route. It was their main objective before they went on to Chamonix. We told them that it was a good idea to bivouac on a small ledge near the foot of the route so as to get a head start on the other parties attempting the wall.

A few weeks later I met up again with one of the Oxford climbers who said they had climbed the Comici but not without a near fatal accident.

His partner had completed the final pitch of the main overhanging headwall and had pulled out on to the gently angled rubble slope separating the wall from the steep chimneys and cracks above. Searching around, he noticed a large boulder protruding from the boulder field and decided it would make a strong enough anchor point. He placed an eight-foot loop of tape around the boulder, clipped in, and shouted for his partner to follow.

As the second climber came up he steadily unclipped the rope from the pitons until there were no more between himself and the leader. At that point a shower of stones and pebbles sprayed out over the top edge of the wall twenty feet above him. The rope went slack and coils of it tumbled down past him.

On the scree slope above, the boulder had started to move. The belay sling came tight and inexorably dragged the terrified belayer towards the top of the wall. Since the wall was undercut all he could see was the enormous 900-foot plunge to the screes below.

There were no pitons between the two climbers to prevent them hurtling out into space. On the exposed wall below, his partner saw a huge black boulder tumble over the edge and arch out into the drop. For a dreadful moment he thought it was the body of his friend and tensed, waiting for the impact to rip him from the wall.

When eventually he pulled over on to the rubble field he saw a very shaken belayer clinging to a rock buttress. At the last moment the tape had slid under the boulder and set him free. We were delighted to hear of their misfortune not just because it was amusing but also because it made us feel better about our own efforts on the wall.

After my efforts at hitching to the Dolomites we decided to take the train from Cortina to Chamonix. It was a long and tedious journey, most of it spent squatting on our rucksacks in packed corridors and making confusing changes at Bolzano, Trento, Verona and Turin. On at least one occasion we got off the train, thinking we had to change, only to become lost and be directed back to the original train which trundled off towards Bologna and the main line across country to Turin.

As the train approached Bologna station it slowed to a crawl, then shuddered to a halt. It stayed motionless for an hour in steaming, frustrating heat. Just as we were about to make inquiries, it shunted forward and crept slowly through the station without stopping. I was astounded to see that the main platform and half the station buildings, waiting rooms, ticket offices and shops had been demolished. Groups of policemen were sifting through the rubble and there were dark stains on platform. The Red Brigade had exploded a massive bomb twelve hours before, devastating the station and slaughtering eighty people. The train clanked past with the passengers staring in mute horror at the scene outside.

Chamonix was everything I had imagined. Mont Blanc and the Chamonix Aiguilles, beautiful red granite rock spires sheathed in ice and hanging glaciers, towered above the small bustling town. The mountains here were so much bigger than the Italian precipices from which we had come, and with such a concentration of climbers from all over the world attempting so many routes each day that there was a frenetic thrusting atmosphere to the place. Helicopters clattered busily across the valley, carrying supplies for high mountain huts, building materials for the new ski lifts under construction, and going seemingly non-stop to the rescue of accident victims. This concentration of climbers distorts reality. In other areas of the Alps there are far fewer accidents simply because there are fewer climbers. In the Chamonix valley, often called the Capital of World Climbing, the average summer toll rises to one life a day and God knows how many seriously injured.

We tramped for twenty minutes out of town to camp in Snells Field, a notorious illegal free camping ground inhabited by the impoverished climbers – British, Spanish, Australian, German and American. I never once saw a French climber staying there. From time to time the French strolled imperiously through the mayhem and squalor, curiously inspecting the wretches in their plastic palaces. Usually they were the Gendarmes armed with truncheons and tear gas for their occasional pitched battle as they tried to clear away the site.

We pitched our tent next to a boisterous group of Bristol climbers. A lithe blonde-haired man emerged from the tent next to ours and walked over to a large erratic boulder in the trees. I watched him smoothly complete a difficult bouldering route up the overhanging side of the rock. He climbed with a precise, fluid action, moving from hold to hold as if in one continuous movement. It looked like ballet.

'He's good,' I said to Nick, who had stopped sorting out the gear and was enjoying the performance.

'It's Arnie Strapcans.'

'Really?'

I watched while he started another sequence of moves and felt a twinge of jealousy. I had read about his climbing in the magazines. He had been instrumental in pioneering the development of rock climbing, especially on sea cliffs in the south west of England. A week after we arrived I watched him stride confidently out of the campsite with a bulging rucksack. He was off to solo a route on the Brenva side of Mt Blanc. He was never seen again.

When his friends became alarmed at how long he had been

away, they went to the mountain rescue office and asked if a search could be undertaken. After a brief helicopter sweep the search was called off. When asked to keep looking the guides refused. They said that since no one knew exactly where he had been heading and what route he intended to climb then there was no point continuing the search. Although Arnie's friends clubbed together to hire a helicopter, no trace of him was ever found.

After the Bristol climbers left a young couple arrived and pitched their tent on the flattened grass where Arnie's tent had stood. A week later we returned from climbing the Cordier Pillar on the Grandes Charmoz to find the man being comforted by friends. It turned out that he had climbed a short rock route on the Aiguille de L'M with his girlfriend and had descended the wrong couloir on the way down. On his advice they had left their boots at the bottom and were using smooth-soled rock shoes. When they were trying to solo the icy chimney-cum-gully, the girl suddenly slipped and fell past him. She was dead when he reached her.

He had a lost and distraught expression on his face and kept blaming himself for the accident. We felt unnerved by his grief, and by the fact that he was camped where Arnie had been. For three nights he had nightmares and cried out in the early hours until our patience ran out and we told him to shut up. To our relief, he left for England the next day. It was uncomfortable to be faced with facts from which we preferred to hide.

This was not the only unsettling warning. Although I knew that climbing mountains was all I wanted to do, now I had an inkling that I had been lured into something wonderful but ominous, and that I was unlikely to escape. I would finish my degree but only out of duty to my parents. Then I would climb.

The rescue helicopters flew directly over the camp site to land in a clearing by the river Arve a few hundred yards away. On the first day in Chamonix I had come by chance upon the landing site, with a small tin-roofed building by a metalled road. As I wandered over to the building I heard a helicopter approach from further up the valley. I watched as it banked round in a steep turn and curved in to a perfect fast landing. Only then did I notice the red ambulance parked at the side of the building. A man ran out to the helicopter, crouching under the spinning rotors. At the open side door I saw him lean in and gesticulate to the pilot. A man in climbing clothes stepped out. His arm was bandaged tight against his chest and his eyes were glazed and unfocused. The ambulance man began backing away holding the handles of a stretcher. The winchman stepped from the belly of the helicopter holding the other end. As they hurried to the waiting ambulance I saw the patient's head lolling slackly from side to side. His eyes were open and lifeless. I walked slowly back to the campsite full of apprehension.

7

NORTH FACES

THE STRETCHER HUNG down the red granite wall amid a tangle of ropes. It was a forlorn reminder of some recent tragedy. I climbed carefully past it, grabbed one of the ropes and pulled myself on to a narrow ledge. The rope was tied off to three pitons to which I clipped myself before shouting down to Dave. He appeared from behind a small bulge and moved steadily towards me.

I glanced at the empty stretcher rocking in the slight wind that was coming up from the distant glacier. There was a smear of blood on one aluminium handle. By my feet lay a chaotic mess of ropes, ice axes, two rucksacks, and a red metal water bottle. I couldn't see why the stretcher would have been left. Had something gone terribly wrong? Dave seemed unconcerned.

'Must have been Japs,' he said as he rummaged through the rucksacks. 'Wow! Look at this.'

He pulled out an expensive bivouac tent. In the other sack I found a yellow headtorch with a cracked reflector, some climbing hardware and an ice axe. 'We'll never manage with all this,' I said as I stuffed the torch into my own rucksack and compared the axe with mine. I rejected the Japanese tool as being inferior.

'We could always abseil off with it,' Dave suggested.

'What, and abandon the route. We can't do that. It's in perfect nick and the forecast couldn't be better.'

'Yeah, I know,' Dave agreed doubtfully. 'Typical. We find all this free booty and we can't keep it.'

He looked at the cloudless sky. There was no choice. We couldn't abandon the climb. Any other route maybe, but not the Walker Spur – the classic hard North Face of the Grand Jorasses. It was a route people dreamed of doing; I knew that I would have to climb it. Now on our first day, with the weather set fair, I couldn't possibly turn back just for material gain. Reluctantly we climbed away from the lonely rocking stretcher. Dave had kept an axe and a water bottle. I had the torch. It had never occurred to us that there was anything immoral in taking the equipment. It belonged to anyone who found it. They were clearly not coming back for it. Only the splash of blood on the stretcher made me pause at the thought that we might be taking dead men's gear. Dave noticed my expression.

'Dead men don't climb,' he said with a grin. 'As the saying goes, no points for being dead.' He turned and tip-tapped his way across the small ice field that stretched between us and the famous 75-metre diedre.

I had met Dave Page in Edinburgh the previous winter. He was twelve years older than me and very experienced. I doubt if I would have dared to attempt the Walker without a partner of Dave's strength. It was a huge spur of rock and ice lunging 4,000 feet up from the head of the Leschaux glacier. When we approached the face in the silent darkness of early morning I felt intimidated by the looming presence of the great mountain, visible as a black shadow in the starlit sky. Rocks clattered down the central couloir as we cramponed quickly up the lower slopes.

Dave moved fast and with confident efficiency while I wobbled along behind. He was unaware that I had no snow and ice experience in the Alps, and I didn't tell him in case he chose not to do the route with me. But my fear evaporated with the fleeing dawn shadows. It was replaced with a mixture of wonder and delight at being on such a stupendous mountain. As we climbed higher I knew, deep inside, that we were going to succeed. There was no reason why I should believe this but I did. I had never before had such an exultant feeling. I had stood at the foot of a huge north wall and knew unquestionably that I could climb it, that I was strong enough and good enough, and knew as certainly as I had ever known anything that this was exactly where I should be and what I should do. It seemed wonderfully irrational and ludicrously egotistical. It needed no justification, no rationale. It had to be done, and done well, and nothing more.

I climbed in a daze of excitement, revelling in the steadily deepening abyss below me and the walls of granite and ice thrusting up to the summit cornices far far above. On the second day I tired quickly, but the sheer joy of being there buoyed me up. The weather remained settled; no storm clouds formed ominously in the familiar cap over the summit of Mt Blanc. We wound an intricate path up the great pillar, climbing the 75-metre diedre and the Grey Towers leading to the icy corniced summit. Darkness fell and we bivouacked in the icy chimneys on the upper headwall, shivering through a long cold night. When the eastern sky slowly changed from black to dark inky blue and a streamer of gold spread across the horizon, I knew that this would be the greatest day of my life. Despite the cold, the joy tingled through my veins as I glanced down at the pinpricks of light on the glacier nearly four thousand feet below. Lights bobbed tentatively across the darkened glacier signalling that other climbers were approaching the magnificent route that we were preparing to finish.

I had celebrated my twenty-first birthday halfway up, and the summit would be a perfect present.

We sat quietly on the snow, gazing out across the Mt Blanc range – south, down into forested Italy, and north, at the Chamonix Aiguilles and far away the slender outline of the Matterhorn and the bulk of the Monta Rosa. The buoyant excitement gradually subsided as I surveyed our new world laid out before us. Suddenly I felt very tired, drained.

There was a long descent into Italy ahead of us. It would be a day of concentration if we were to stay safe until we were free of the mountain's grip. As we began to traverse the steep avalanche-prone snow slopes between the summits of the Walker Spur and the Whymper Spur I realised with shock that the dream of climbing the Walker was over. The dream had become reality and the magic had gone. I had destroyed it by succeeding. *What next,* I wondered, *what will give me that feeling again?* It was strange to be filled so soon with a sense of anti-climax, now that it was finished. Wearily we climbed down the rocky Rocher de Whymper and crossed the short Grandes Jorasses glacier towards the comfort of the Boccalatte hut.

All the glory with which I had invested the route had vanished the moment I had climbed it. The reality was disturbingly ordinary and unremarkable. It was as if I had robbed myself of something perfect; an ideal had been violated. A route ticked, a summit gained, something to look back on with vain pride, but the joy had gone. To experience that joy once more I would have to find another objective, another climb, another ideal to destroy. It was a vicious circle. Where would it lead me?

By the time we trudged into the Snells field after hitch-hiking through the Mt Blanc tunnel from Italy I was nearly out on my feet. That afternoon it began to rain and peals of thunder came from the dense grey clouds as lightening struck the rocky summits of the Aiguilles far above. The bad weather lasted for four days, giving us time to recover before we became impatient with the weather. My heart jumped when Dave suggested trying the North Face of the Eiger next. I thought of Toni Kurz and Adi Mayr and forgot the Walker Spur in an instant. The Eiger. Could I climb it when it scared me so much? Was I strong enough for such an enormous route?

If I had invested the Walker with attributes that in reality it didn't possess, then the Eiger was a nightmare. *But, think of it, Joe. The Eiger and the Walker in one season. Maybe the Schmidt route on the North Face of Matterhorn as well. The big three in one summer.* Now that was worth dreaming about.

Oh, and I could dream. I dreamed so vividly I convinced myself that it was possible. Within a day my fear of the Eiger had been replaced by scary anticipation. I could do it, I knew I could.

'How would we get to Leysin?' I asked Dave in the tent.

'Oh, I don't know, hitch probably.' He seemed strangely distant, as if he were hiding something. He glanced over at Pete and Pat, two brothers who had parked their red frog-eyed Sprite next to our tent. There was something conspiratorial about the way he looked at them.

'Can't we get a train?' I said.

Dave looked embarrassed and said nothing.

'What's wrong?' I asked.

'Look,' he said patiently, 'I don't think you're experienced enough for the Eiger.'

'What? I . . .'

'You weren't very confident on the Walker when you had to climb ice.'

'But . . .'

'No, listen,' he interrupted. 'Be honest. You didn't feel confident, did you?' I didn't answer. 'There is a lot of ice on the Eiger, hard mixed climbing, and I don't think you're ready for it.'

'Well, let's do some mixed routes here until I'm better.'

'No. It's not something you learn overnight. I'm going to the Eiger with Scott.'

'What? Who's Scott?' I retorted angrily.

'He's an American climber I met in the bar.'

'You just met him in the bar and you want to do the Eiger with him? How can you know whether he's any good? At least we've climbed the Walker together.'

'He is good. I know what he's done.'

My world was suddenly falling apart. I didn't know anyone else with whom I could tackle the Eiger. We had spent the winter talking about it and now he had betrayed me and chosen to do it with a complete stranger. There was a confusing mix of anger and impotent frustration in my efforts to persuade Dave to take me. The next day he left with the American.

I took the train to Zermatt with a Canadian lumberjack called Doug Pratt Johnson, my own bar aquaintance. We climbed the North Face of the Matterhorn by the Schmidt route, one of the classic six north faces, but my pleasure was soured by the knowledge that the real prize had been stolen from me. On returning to Chamonix I was crushed to hear that Dave had succeeded on the Eiger in two and a half days.

Later I knew that he had been right. I wasn't good enough, but the truth always hurts and it took me a long time to learn the lesson. I was too reliant on single partners who would climb with me throughout the summer season. Climbing with Doug, a total stranger whom I had met only once in the bar, was an eye opener. I found that, if you were prepared to trust strangers and believe they had climbed what they claimed, then you could choose any partner who happened to be free. There is a great deal of trust involved when two people team up for a difficult climb That trust is fundamental to the whole business. You have to trust that they will watch your back, get you out of trouble, even save your life. And they must trust you.

For sure, there are always those climbers who, for a variety of reasons, claim more than they are due, perhaps out of ambition or egotism. Lying in this way is a dangerous form of deception, a betrayal of trust, an act that could lead to tragedy. Doug was everything he claimed and more – a tall bearded placid man, who was a strong, calm climber with a cheerful disposition. He wielded an ice axe as if he were felling two-hundred-foot pine trees.

On the summit a huge black iron cross threw a shadow down the south face. It was intricately wrought and the words 'Führer der Bergsteiger' (Father of the Climbers) were punctured by tiny pinprick holes caused by lightning strikes. We spent a long cold September night bivouacked on a slab of crumbling grey shale just below the summit of the Matterhorn and paid the price of going light, without sleeping bags, and trying to climb the face in one day. We hung from two dubious pitons to wake in the first light and find that one of them had fallen out.

We descended the Hörnli Ridge without ropes. The upper towers had three-inch thick hawsers draped down them to aid incompetent clients being dragged up by their terse Swiss guides. Doug was several hundred feet below me when I reached the first rope. It was white and shiny, recently replaced. I wore mitts, thick heavily-woven woollen mitts, and it never occurred to me to take them off. I grasped the rope and swung confidently out over the immense drop of the east face ready to go hand over hand down the rope. Before I knew it I was hurtling down. I tightened my grip to no avail. There was no purchase between the wool and the shiny new rope and I realised with a sense of disbelief that I couldn't stop. At the speed I was travelling I would hit the end of the rope, where it was tied to a huge ringbolt, and be catapulted off down the east face. I stared fixedly at my mitts and tried to exert more pressure on the rope. My forearms burnt with a sharp acid pain.

I stopped so abruptly that I slammed my face against the rock wall. My foot touched a ledge and I pushed down hard to regain balance. For a moment I had no idea what had happened. Then I saw the four-foot black rubber sleeve encasing the rope. Halfway down to the ringbolt a splice in the rope protected by a rubber sleeve had saved me. It had given just enough grip to stop me from accelerating to full speed. After some hesitation I hesitantly continued down slowly.

As I stepped off the last wall on to the path leading to the Hörnli Hut I heard a cry of alarm from above. Instinctively I turned to look up. The air was full of rocks. The first stones whirred past my unprotected face, cracking into the rocky path and ricocheting down to the glacier far below. I was paralysed by the sight of the rocks spinning towards me and the client staring at me with an imploring look on his face. I didn't move. I wanted to dive under my rucksack but my brain wasn't getting the message through. The rocks sang, whistled and thrummed past me, some exploded over my head, but nothing hit me.

When it was over I shook convulsively, screaming hysterically at the white-faced client a rope's length above me. He turned and climbed quickly away. Instead of shouting a warning as soon as he had dislodged the rocks he had waited to see whether they were going to hit me or not. I turned on shaky legs and walked gingerly down to the hut where I found Doug with a huge grin on his face.

'Jeez. I've just come within an ace of being killed,' I said as I joined him with a beer.

'How?'

I told him about the rope and the mitts and the rockfall.

'You know what they say about the Matterhorn.'

'What?'

'Well, there are so many people on the mountain that your best chance of being killed is by slipping on some orange peel or having a bottle of suntan lotion hit you.'

I looked up at the tiny dots of countless climbers on the Hörnli Ridge.

'I can believe that,' I said. 'I've heard that during good weather in the summer something like three hundred people reach the summit in a day.'

'Yeah, and the rest.'

On one wooden wall of the hut six plastic helmets hung from rusty nails. They were all either split from rim to rim or had fist-size holes punched through them.

Dave's account of the storm through which he and his companion had made their Eiger ascent frightened me enough to stop me complaining. Having joined forces with two Geordie climbers at the Traverse of the Gods, they had fought their way up the exit cracks in appalling conditions only to lose one of the Geordies while descending the easy west face. Tired and off guard, he had tripped and fallen to his death on ground that, on any other day, he would have walked down with his hands in his pockets. His death was a salutary lesson that I have never forgotten. *At the top you've only reached halfway*.

During the Christmas holidays I hitched out to Chamonix to join Dave on my first winter Alpine season. I met him in the Bar Nash. We had barely finished our first beers when Maurice, the landlord, approached us with two brandies. He looked grave as he placed them in front of us.

'You know a British climber called Pete, yes? The man with the red sports car, you know him I think?'

We both nodded.

'I am sorry.' He shrugged and spread his hands in a typically French gesture. 'Peter is dead. He fell on the Cherie couloir yesterday.'

Pete was dead? I was dumbstruck. Maurice said that his brother Pat had been told, but he was in a state of shock, and the authorities needed someone to identify the body.

'I see,' Dave said. I drank my brandy and averted my eyes. I had seen Pete's red frog-eyed Sprite sports car when I had walked to the bar and had looked forward to seeing him again. Dave looked at me questioningly. I reached for my beer.

'I'll go,' he said quietly. 'Thank you, Maurice.' He downed his brandy and left for the morgue. He was quiet and subdued when he returned, saying only that it was Pete.

Pete had soloed the Cherie couloir, a steep grade IV ice climb on the flank of Mt Blanc du Tacul. As he tried to traverse off from the top hard pitch he was seen to have problems with a crampon. He struggled to cross the steep thinly iced rock walls, trying to reach the easy descent route, and then fell. He wasn't wearing a helmet and might have survived the fall but for the serious head injuries.

I didn't climb that winter. The weather stayed mercifully bad. I didn't know it then but the attrition had begun. The payback for the fun. I was saddened by Pete's death and shocked by how quickly I accepted it. Once I knew how he had died it seemed I could accept it and shelve the memory away as a lesson learned. *Always wear a helmet.* Was that all there was to it? It didn't seem much for a life.

I didn't want to look any closer, just as I hadn't wanted to go to the morgue. I knew instinctively that these things, these unanswerable questions, are best avoided.

8

AVALANCHE

THE VIEW FROM the summit of the Courtes was awesome
– the sun hanging, a high violent heat in the azure sky, and
the mountains rearing up all around us. The vast Argentière
north walls lay beneath our feet, the Chardonnet, ice capped,
directly before us, and the dark north wall of the Grandes
Jorasses behind.

We sat in the sun for far too long. We were tired, but that
was no excuse. The long cold night climbing the 'Austrian
route' on the north face was a good memory as the sun
warmed away its chill dark shadows. It was only the sun,
lazing in the hot sun, that made us wait too long. By the time
we got up, packed away the ropes, shouldered our sacks and
headed for the top of the north-east face we had already
missed our last chance of safety.

The route down which we would descend swept 2,500 feet
to the glacier below, snow-covered, undisturbed and
unclimbed since the storms twenty-four hours ago. The sun
shone full on to the face. The storm snow, now heavy and
wet, rested uneasily on the hard old snow beneath it. Water
seeped between the two layers.

We knew it was too late in the day. We should have waited
until the evening cold froze the snow and made it safe. We
knew we had dallied too long in the sun, but we were tired,
and hot now, and with it thirsty and all too anxious to get
down.

I was nervous descending the first fifty feet. Warning
doubts kept urging me to stop and go back. I stood, unsure,

looking at my half-buried legs, and between them to the glacier far below. The snow slides of my last steps hustled on down the slope. I gazed up at Hugh above me and away to my left. He too was looking uncertain. I wanted him to voice my doubts, but he said nothing. Perhaps he was not scared, like me. Perhaps he thought it would be all right. I descended another fifty feet.

Doubts grew into consuming fear. There was definitely something bad about this place. Something was going to happen. I felt for a moment to be poised on the edge of the world. Just as I imagined those sailors of old had feared falling off the earth, I also felt a dark unknown threat.

Hugh hadn't moved. He was looking at me, leaving me to test it out. I didn't like that.

Penguins crowd the edge of ice floes, watching the water for sea leopards, but just to be sure they push one of their unfortunate companions into the cold green sea and then examine the outcome intently to see if it is safe to follow. I didn't like being the experimental penguin; I wished that I was doing the pushing.

I descended again, a few steps, then stopped. *No! I don't like this. I'll go back. Do it now before it's too late ... quickly.*

I didn't hear the words, only the cry of alarm that froze my heart.

I hunched down immediately, facing into the slope and forcing all my weight on to my axe, trying to push it down, down into the very rock of the mountain. I glanced up. Hugh stood motionless, staring in silence.

The crescent-shaped wave of snow was almost upon me. *Oh God! You stupid bastard! Why did you wait so long?*

I had thought that maybe it was not so big; hoped it would brush over me. The wave punched me full in the chest, threw me over backwards, ripping the axe away effortlessly as I went down.

I fell ahead of the wave, sliding fast, screaming at Hugh.

'Look at me, look at me! Follow my fall. Look ... '

I shouted it in fear, hoping he would keep his eyes on me to see where I was eventually buried. For one brief moment I saw him clearly, standing rigidly in the same spot, staring at me. He was gone the instant I saw him as the wave flipped me over, tumbled me, played games with me as its strength grew with every gathering of snow that built up in the fall.

Far below, across the glacier, a group of climbers drinking tea on the verandah of the Argentière Hut paused to look up as they heard the building roar of the avalanche. No doubt they thought the pluming rush of snow was impressive. In their time scale it lasted no more than thirty or forty seconds.

My time scale disintegrated. I heard myself screaming and felt embarrassed even though no one could hear me. But there were other things for me to worry about – how to stop this uncontrolled tumbling, how to get an ice axe brake to work, how to stop falling. Then I hit the rocks.

I screamed. I wasn't hurt, but I screamed like a wounded rabbit, screaming mad, just screaming because I wasn't going to stop. I was going to die.

Hugh watched me getting smaller, falling faster, tumbling and disappearing, then reappearing, all the time trying to follow my fall. Left above the noise and violence, he stood protected by some whim of chance to witness what might have been.

The snow, hundreds of tons of wet snow, swept to the left into a steep rock-strewn ice gully, It curled and weaved its path from side to side, spewing snow up over boulders, rolling itself over and over. I went with its fall, disorientated, lashing arms and legs, trying to control the force of it all. Smashing feet first into a large boulder in the gully bed, I was thrown up above the surging snow. Hugh saw the dark figure pirouette, then it disappeared again.

I landed back in the gully, head down the slope, as the snow poured out over the boulders, forcing me down against the ice. Wet snow jetted up my nostrils, packed my mouth, pushed me down harder. The rushing hissing of the avalanche faded, pressure pain built in my chest, sounds receded, a dull roaring in my head was like surf on a distant shingle beach, and all dimmed into grey shadows.

A numbing crack on my forehead shook me free, another rock threw me clear. The impact jerked the packed snow from my mouth and I gulped at the cold air before the weight of the onrush threw me back under.

I had seen a glimpse of the glacier below, close now, very close, and the thought that I might survive sprang to mind until I remembered the bergschrund – the huge crevasse marking the separation between glacier and mountain. I knew it was enormous, at least thirty feet across. There was no way I could clear it. I would plunge down the gaping maw and tons of wet snow would pour in after me, sealing me in, crushing, drowning and asphyxiating me. I was forced under again even as I remembered the bergschrund, but this time I fought in a blind screaming panic, full of horror at the impending burial. *I will not die, I will not die.* The words seemed to reverberate through my head like some hysterical mantra, as if just by thinking them something would happen, something, anything, would stop this awful hammering.

Swim. That's what everyone says. If you are caught in an avalanche, swim. No one told me that it would be like swimming through wet concrete, that surges of heavy wet snow would wrench and twist my body into agonizing contorted positions. *Swim?* The instruction manual writers must be bloody comedians.

I had been down too long. As sounds and feelings faded to a dull numbing ache, I had a brief moment of anger, a flooding sense of resignation, and then the odd idea that maybe Ma could help me, maybe she could stop it for me, as she had so often when I was a child. *Oh please Ma, stop it for me. I'll not do it again. I promise.* Nothing changed, and the total calm of acceptance, a placid submissiveness, allowed me to sink quietly into airless sleep.

Then, as if tired of the game, the avalanche released me. I was abruptly spat out from the gully and felt myself flying free through the air, easily clearing the gaping bergschrund, and left free to slide the last few feet on the glacier.

Hugh found me there, when at last he reached me an hour later. I hadn't moved in the time it took him to descend the face. I was sitting up in the snow, buried from the waist down, staring across the glacier and seeing nothing. At first we laughed hysterically, and then cried with relief as the tension ebbed away.

There was a circular hole in my forehead as if I had been shot, and holes in my cheek where my broken crampons had made two neat punctures. I tasted metallic salty blood in my mouth. My legs were encased in about eighteen inches of compacted wet snow which had set like concrete the minute the avalanche had hissed to a halt. Hugh had to dig them out with his axe.

A piece of green tape hung from my wrist. The axe was gone. I felt my face with a shaky exploratory hand, searching for damage, waiting for the sudden stabs of pain from broken bones. Hugh helped me to my feet and I stood on wobbly legs amid the blocks of avalanche debris.

'Hey man, yeah!' Hugh said, slapping his thigh. 'Wow! Far out. Man, that's the craziest ride I've ever seen. You should have seen yourself go. That was wild, I mean *wild*. Hot shit, yeah, did you go . . . ' He grinned at me in delight.

Hugh came from Glencoe, Illinois. I'd known him for two days. He was a likeable, easy-going person with a penchant for talking continuously in catch-phrases. 'Go for it, race the sun,' he'd hollered at me as wearily I had led up the final part of the face, and I had groaned inwardly. What on earth was he on about?

Now the shock of the avalanche and the excitement of finding me alive had triggered off an unstoppable stream of disjointed phrases as he helped me across the snow of the Argentière glacier towards the safety of the hut. I let the words wash round me, smiling at his enthusiasm, but quite unsure what was going on. By the time we reached the hut an hour and a half later my mind had begun to wander. I think Hugh noticed the dull glazed look in my eyes and the slow laboured speech of someone suffering from concussion. He set me down carefully on a wooden bench outside the hut and I smiled foolishly at him, unaware of the concern in his eyes.

'Hey, man, take care. I've got you now, Joe, I'll go get some help. Stay right here,' he said, and I grinned amiably at him. I sat in the full heat of the afternoon sun, gazing at the north face of the Courtes, which we had just climbed, and the north-east face down which I had fallen, and giggled inanely. A soft female voice spoke to me in fractured English with a strong Italian accent.

She was beautiful, with huge melting brown eyes and a gorgeous white-toothed smile. She handed me a bowl of hot chocolate and stroked my cheek. I gave her my best, most charming smile, unaware that my eyes were unfocused, that blood had coagulated on my cheek and forehead and dark bruises were swelling beneath each eye. I was in love.

For some reason the glass bowl wouldn't stay still when I tried to drink from it. I felt shivery and unaccountably cold in the hot sun. The bowl started juddering so much that hot chocolate slopped out from the sides, scalding my legs, and the firmer I gripped it the more I shook, until my whole body seemed to have gone into convulsions and her strong arms reached round my shoulders and pulled me to her. I smelt her perfume, a musky exciting smell, and stared at her full breasts beneath her thin T-shirt as she pressed my face to her bosom and hugged me. There was a moment of irritation as I realised I had lost control of my body just at the moment when I wanted to be charming and sexy – and that is all I remember. I awoke in the hut dormitory next morning with a thumping head- ache. Hugh handed me some coffee and told me that the girl had left.

'Where?' I mumbled.

'She's cruising, man, chasing the sun.'

'What?'

'She's gone climbing, man.'

'Oh.' The disappointment hurt. I never saw her again, never thanked her, never even knew her name.

Hugh left me at Les Praz, a small village ten minutes walk from the campsite. 'You okay, Joe?' he asked.

'Yes, never better,' I lied, holding out my hand. He grasped it and shook it vigorously.

'Okay, okay. Take care, friend.' And he turned to go,

shaking his head and muttering something about 'crazy rides, far out.'

It was a couple of days before my slurred speech returned to normal and I began to feel interested in life again. How close I had come to being killed didn't seem to matter. It was chance, luck, that was all, but I had learned never again to take chances with bad snow.

I had spent half my savings on a new pair of crampons to replace those lost in the avalanche and wondered how I was going to survive for the rest of the summer. There was a boisterous anarchy about the group of climbers from Sheffield and Manchester – Sean Smith, Murray Laxton, Mark Millar and Paddy Gaunt – who were camped nearby. They had few pretensions about themselves or their approach to Alpine climbing. Someone had heard that the French did not prosecute the poor for stealing food. Indeed some Paris supermarkets left foodstuffs that had passed their sell-by date out on a table for the poor to take, free of charge. This seemed a very noble, socially aware, egalitarian attitude, and we took full advantage of it.

I am a totally incompetent and fearful thief. The thought only has to enter my mind and I am blushing furiously, convinced that there is a large neon sign above my head flashing 'Thief, Thief' for all the world to see. So when the white-coated butcher handed me the ham neatly wrapped in white waxed paper, with the name of the supermarket printed on it in large blue letters, I smiled self-consciously, and treacherously.

'Merci, bien,' I said as I turned towards the deserted aisle behind me and shuffled guiltily away. With conspicuous glances from side to side, I quickly shoved the rectangular package down the front of my white shorts, feeling my ears start to glow red with shame. I picked up an item from a shelf and pretended to examine it with interest. When I realised that I was taking an unhealthy interest in a box of sanitary towels, I hurriedly dropped it and moved towards the cash tills. I had enough money in my pocket for a stick of bread, which I selected fastidiously while glancing at the cashiers to see who would be the least trouble. Eventually I sidled up to a cheerful pretty girl who was filing her nails as she waited for a customer.

After placing the baguette on the moving rubber conveyor, I reached into the front pocket of my shorts for money. The pocket was so tight that I was forced to squirm and wrestle my fingers around the small change. As she watched my struggles I saw her eyes widen in surprise. I handed her three francs. I couldn't understand why she was shaking her head and giggling, and smiled uncertainly.

'Voila, merci,' I said with a flourish, and she laughed in my face. What she found so amusing was beyond me. I thought it best to humour her, and laughed courteously, which only increased her mirth. Covering her mouth with a hand, she looked into my face and then directly at my crotch. I glanced down, following her gaze, and was mortified to see an obvious rectangular shape outlined across the crotch of my shorts and the blue words clearly visible through the tightly stretched white material. As peels of laughter broke behind me I fled from the shop and raced for the safety of the Bar Nationale.

I found Murray Laxton reading the *Telegraph* in the back corner of the bar when I walked awkwardly and with some discomfort through the open glass door, with a kilo of smoked York ham crammed into my crotch.

'How's tricks?' Murray asked as I struggled to extract the ham from my shorts.

'I've been better,' I grunted, and slapped the ham on to the table.

Murray was an unfailingly kind and courteous man, almost to the point of driving his friends to distraction when he apologised for everything that happened, even those things that had nothing to do with him. He was a quiet unflustered person, a patient and tolerant friend, with an impish smile and a flare for pyromania when the mood took him.

'Did you hear about Paddy and Mark?' he asked, helping himself to some sweaty ham and bread.

'No. Was there an accident?'

'Sort of, but they're okay now.'

Mark Millar and Paddy Gaunt had left the campsite several days before to attempt the first free ascent of the Hidden Pillar on the Frêney face of Mt Blanc. They had joined up with a team of friends attempting the classic Central Pillar just to its left. These two magnificent high altitude rock climbs on superb golden granite are among the finest and hardest routes in the range. Sean had gone with Richard Cox to attempt the Central Pillar, and behind them came four Australian friends led by the inimitable Johnny Muir. They had decided to call themselves the International Turkey Patrol, for some strange Antipodean reason.

Mark and Paddy had decided to go lightweight and fast, so light-weight in fact that, before they left the hut to approach the remote and serious upper plateau of the Frêney glacier where their route started, Paddy had borrowed a pair of rubber washing up gloves – a poor substitute for warm mitts, but offering some protection from the bitter early morning cold.

By late evening, as the sun settled on the horizon, they pulled over the last difficult rock pitch and on to the top of the pillar, having completed a very fast and the first British free ascent. They could hear Sean, Richard and the Australians still climbing on the Central Pillar and shouted a cheery farewell before setting off up the snow slopes towards the summit of Mt Blanc. They climbed unroped, moving quickly up the smooth frozen névé. Paddy followed Mark cautiously. Mark is a big strong man, much heavier than Paddy, so it made sense to keep exactly in his footsteps. If Mark didn't break through into a hidden crevasse, the much lighter Paddy would not do so either – or so he thought. Close to the rounded snow summit, with Mark gradually pulling away from him, Paddy carefully placed his foot into one of Mark's prints and, with an abrupt rustle of snow and scraping of clothing, disappeared into a suddenly gaping circular hole.

Fortunately for Paddy, the crevasse was narrow and zig-zagged from side to side, so that, as he plunged 120 feet into the bowels of the mountain, his velocity was slowed by the constant battering from one icy wall to the other. He crashed into the floor of the crevasse, winded, bruised and lacerated, but otherwise unhurt.

After a while Mark became aware that Paddy was no longer following him and retraced his steps in the gathering gloom of nightfall to find the hole made by Paddy's fall. Shouting into the crevasse he was relieved to hear the distant echo of Paddy assuring him that he was all right. Digging the rope out of his rucksack, Mark tried without success to lower it to his friend, but however much he flicked the rope, it kept coiling on a small ice ledge 75 feet above where Paddy stood shivering at the bottom of the crevasse. Realising it was hopeless, Mark set off to get help, climbing rapidly over the summit of Mt Blanc in the dark. For several hours he awaited the rising moon so that he could find his way down past lurking crevasses to the Gouter Hut to alert the mountain rescue teams.

As the long night hours passed Paddy tried to keep warm by jumping up and down, slapping his arms around himself, and keeping his washing-up-gloved hands in the warmth of his armpits. Ten hours later a faint glimmer of dawn light entered the crevasse and in the eerie gloom he made out a possible escape route along the floor of the slightly shelving icy vault. It rose steadily towards the surface until he reached a point where an ice ledge ran across one wall of the crevasse. Shuffling gingerly along the narrow ledge, he arrived at a spot directly beneath his entrance hole. He was standing on the ledge that had stopped the rope reaching him. His hands, encased in yellow rubber gloves, were numb with the first effects of frost-bite as he began bridging up the narrow ice walls – feet on one side, shoulders pressed against the other. He heard the sound of rotor blades growing louder above him. Eventually he popped his head out into the sunlight of early morning and saw the helicopter swinging down towards him.

When Mark and Paddy trudged into the campsite to tell of their extraordinarily lucky escape they were met with howls of merriment. Paddy's fingers were frost-nipped but they soon recovered, as did the bruises and lacerations. After he had returned to Sheffield Mark sold the story to a British washing-up glove manufacturer for £250, even though it was Paddy who had been wearing them. I had suffered the same humorous gibes after my escapade in the avalanche and was relieved to find the focus of attention switched to Paddy. As a figure of fun he was far better qualified than I. Paddy had stepped closer to that fine line between extinction and life than most. He had barely recovered from blast injuries suffered in Spain when a terrorist bomb had exploded beside him in a railway station two years earlier. On that occasion he had been blown off his feet and knocked senseless. As the smoke cleared his two friends had rushed into the room to find a scene of devastation. Five people were sprawled in a bloody lifeless mass to one side, others groaned and screamed as the shock of the explosion wore off and the pain surged through them. Paddy lay among the dead, breathing raggedly, with severe blast injuries and shrapnel embedded in his back. He was lucky to survive. The shrapnel injuries were not as bad as they looked, but both his lungs collapsed from the shockwave of the initial blast, which also caused terrible bruising all over his body. It was the bruising that nearly killed him. Once he was fully recovered and on the way to strength and fitness, he had resumed Alpine climbing only to fall down a crevasse on the summit of Europe's highest mountain.

Coming down to the valley after spending two or three days on a hard and dangerous route always gave a strangely separate view of life, as if your perspectives had been subtly altered, momentarily frozen into those black and white decisions given to you on the mountain. Things that before had seemed important, had made you worried and anxious, now seemed quite insignificant. Money, bills, future prospects, security – all those things that seemed to be the root of modern life – were irrelevant. Reality for a short time was just being alive, luxuriating in unexpectedly easy pleasures like plenty to eat and drink. The tourists that traipsed past the shops and bars of Chamonix seemed aimless and lost, achieving nothing. There was far more to life than what we had been taught to expect. Maybe for the first time I learnt in the avalanche exactly what it was to be alive, how precious, and how fragile. There was so much to be lost from a moment's careless mistake but so much more to be gained by knowing the value of life.

In the West we live in a safe society, a world of vaccines and high tech medicine offering longevity for its own sake. We are encouraged to be careful, to avoid risk, to build secure safe lives, comfortingly backed up by pensions and life assurance and anything that would shield us from the reality. We are taught to look ahead to the future and work towards a perceived idea of what we want from life. We are rarely told to live for the present, to take what we want and give nothing back. Societies cannot operate on such selfish principles. Occasionally illness, bereavement, redundancy and accidents impose on people and bring them up short with a shock of recognition that, however hard they try, nothing can be permanently safe.

When I walked away from the avalanche I was somehow committed irrevocably to a chosen path. I knew what I wanted, and that was to climb. I wanted to be good enough to go to the greater ranges, the Andes, the Karakoram and the Himalaya, and to climb on those mountains. I wanted to travel, and to see other people's lives and cultures, to climb their mountains and keep putting myself back into that transient perspective I had found in the Alps. I didn't want a career, or marriage and a family, or anything that would tie me down and hold me back. I simply wanted to be free, and being in the mountains was the most liberating experience I knew. It was quite the opposite of everything I had been brought up to think and do. The fact that non-climbers could never understand made it all the more special, like a secret held within the minds of a select few.

There is a perverse delight in putting oneself in a potentially dangerous situation, knowing that your experience and skill makes you quite safe. To stand with a friend in eerie moonlight at the foot of a vast mountain wall and be certain that you can safely reach the top – that is a wonderful feeling of self-confidence. It might seem an absurdly pointless thing to do, but to have the nerve to go and try it, just to see if you can, is an affirmation of everything noble in humanity. The task has been rationalised, and carefully weighed, and now you must act and do it right; it is a suspended moment. As you step up on to the first hold or drive the first axe blow you step into a new perspective, a world that is absolutely and cruelly real. The power of it is indescribable, as vital on the first step as it is on the last, at the base or on the summit, and the intensity only gradually fades on your return to the valley.

Jean-Paul Sartre once wrote: 'Man is nothing else but what he purposes, he exists only in so far as he realises himself, he is there- fore nothing else but the sum of his actions, nothing else but what his life is ... In life, a man commits himself, draws his own portrait and there is nothing but that portrait.'

If memory could recall exactly the sense of a past experience nothing would be done. We would sit out our days and fantasise about the past. Why challenge the present if the past can be so good? Fortunately our memory is kind. It blurs the bad times and softens the good. And as life in the valley, in the real world, if that is what it is, erodes the transient lingering memory of your last climb you understand that you must go back and stand under the shadowed wall again and commit everything.

At the same time there is a taint of insanity about it. How can I possibly justify losing my life, or that of a friend, in the pursuit of something so ephemeral as a passing state of mind, an achievement of the truly irrational? Why ascend a mountain by its hardest, most dangerous face when you can walk, hands in pockets, up the other side? Or, in some cases, sitting in a train or a cablecar. If it were simply adrenalin you were after, you could take a ride on a roller coaster, snort a line of cocaine, indulge in a fraught extramarital affair, any number of things that have thrills without kills. Why be a conquistador of the useless, a compulsive addict of the absurd?

The eighteenth century theologian and philosopher, Jeremy Bentham, developed a theory he called 'Deep Play', whereby what the player stands to lose is completely disproportionate to what he can possibly gain. In climbing there is the death of yourself, or your friends, or the loss of toes and fingers, to set against the transitory pleasure of a summit, the thrill of the adventure, the fleeting satiation of an irrational desire. The fact that the desire can never be fully gratified is the addiction. Perhaps the desire is deeply rooted in the very absurdity of the undertaking. It is so wonderfully pointless and meaningless that it has to be done.

9

ALPINE BINMEN

AT THE END of the summer I returned to university in Edinburgh to resume academic studies. I found the work boring and uninspiring. I didn't want to read endless tracts about what other people thought, what intended meanings could be detected in this play or that book, to learn to quote them by rote so as to pass exams and convince my teachers that I knew or cared anything for literature. I was tempted to abandon my degree but Catholic guilt and a sense of duty to my parents made me stick at it. I had no intention of using the degree to start a career of any sort.

It was while glancing through a climbing magazine on a windy day of lashing rain and rotting autumn leaves that I saw Richard Cox had been killed in the Garwhal Himalaya in India while attempting a first ascent of the north face of Shivling. He had fallen a full rope length on to the upper ice field while on the first pitch of the frighteningly steep headwall and had sustained serious injuries. Nick Kekus had managed to hold his fall but during a desperate attempt to retreat down the face Richard had become detached from the rope and plunged to his death during the night. Nick was left to complete a lonely descent the next day. It was Richard's first expedition to the greater ranges – a bold attempt on an extremely difficult and still unclimbed route that had ended in tragedy. I put the magazine down and thought about Mark and Paddy, waving to the teams on the Central Pillar of Frêney, the International Turkey Patrol, and Sean and Richard Cox enjoying life on sun-heated golden red granite.

Shortly after reading of Richard's death on Shivling I became deeply depressed. It surprised me since I had never been depressed before and could find no good reason for it. The more I tried to work out what was happening to me, the worse I became, until I seemed to be spinning in a spiral of vicious circles.

On another wet and windy evening in early December I found myself standing on Dean Bridge, looking down the eighty-foot drop to the sandstone slabs far below. Traffic passed noisily behind me. I couldn't recall how I had got there. The bridge was close to home but I could remember nothing of leaving the flat. I wondered whether the jump would kill me. I had fallen almost as far on the Screen.

Jump? What on earth was I doing? I must be going mad!

I turned away from the parapet and hurried back to the flat, hunching my shoulders into the wind. After closing the door to my room, I slumped on the bed and began to cry. It had been going on for weeks now and was getting worse. I wiped my face and reached for the whisky bottle. With the first fiery slug I knew what I was going to do. Get out, and get out fast.

I sensed it was the city, the university and the awful weather that was doing it. If I was slowly going mad, I was determined to do it in better surroundings.

The following day I went to see my course tutor, Professor Savage.

'I'm leaving,' I said flatly.

'What? Why?'

'I think I'm going mad.'

'But, the course. You've nearly finished. Another six months and it will be over. You've finished your dissertation, your marks are good, so why leave it now . . .?'

'Professor Savage,' I cut in, 'I nearly topped myself last night.'

'You did what? Topped yourself?'

'Yes, topped myself. You know. I nearly threw myself off Dean Bridge, for Christ's sake!'

'Why?'

'Oh God, I wish I knew,' I said wearily. 'I really wish I knew.'

'You could get help,' he suggested kindly.

'No, I don't need help. I need to get away from here, away from this country.'

'Where will you go?'

'To the Alps. I've got friends staying out there for the winter. It'll do me good.'

'So that's it then, is it? Three years work down the drain. A good honours degree almost in your grasp and you're going to throw in the towel. Doesn't sound like you Joe, eh?'

'I know. I'm sorry. I just can't go on.'

'Come on, Joe. It's such a waste. The dissertation is good. Look at all the merit certificates you've earned, look . . .'

'Listen, Professor,' I said curtly. 'I'll be dead if I stay.'

Perhaps there was something in the way I looked at him, for he put up no more arguments. He promised to keep open a place for me if I wanted to return but warned me that I wouldn't be able to complete the senior honours year. The syllabus would change. I could get a masters degree in literature and some other subject if I did another year studying another subject.

'Like what? Psychiatry?' I asked sarcastically,

'Could do,' he laughed, 'or Philosophy. Much more apt, don't you think?'

Two days later I stood at a roundabout on the A1 with a cardboard sign saying 'Dover', an enormous rucksack and a light heart. The further south I travelled that day the better I felt. As the white cliffs of Dover receded into the wake of the ferry I knew that I had made the right decision. Sean and Murray had wangled a seasonal job as binmen in a large apartment complex in Chamonix. A one man studio flat came with the job. I was sure there would be space for one more.

I had phoned my parents in a disturbed state and sensed their deep disappointment. They had spent their lives trying to put all the children through the best education they could afford. It seemed a pretty shabby way to treat them and I put down the phone burdened with guilt and failure. On my father's advice, I called his younger brother, my uncle, who was a doctor in the army. When I finished the conversation a great weight seemed to have lifted from me. In his opinion I was suffering the side-effects of concussion received in the avalanche on the Courtes the previous summer. Delayed effects, particularly depression, were quite common with head injuries – something to do with chemical imbalances in the brain, he said. I was relieved to know that I wasn't losing my mind. It was deeply frightening to find myself in an inescapably dark and desolate state of mind such as I had never suffered before, nor have I since.

Twenty cold hitching hours after the ferry docked in Calais I walked slowly down the Rue de Pacard towards Chamonix-sud. The town had a bleak deserted atmosphere. The winter season hadn't begun. There were no tourists, most of the bars were closed and shuttered, and a damp misty rain fell on empty streets. Two days later the first heavy snowfalls laid a three-foot carpet of snow on the town, the lights went on and the beer prices shot up. Winter had come. With the snowfall my depression disappeared.

Murray Laxton and Sean Smith were the original binmen. They had secured the job, and the one-man apartment that went with it, the previous summer. Mark Miller, Rob Spencer and I joined them for the winter, sharing their dustbin duties in exchange for a free floor on which to sleep. The weekly turnover of winter skiers meant that the whole complex of two-, four- and six-person apartments had to be cleaned every Saturday, and this was our chief source of earnings as well as our scavanged food and drink. So much food, and in such a wide variety, was left behind in cupboards, fridges, and dustbins by departing tenants that we needed to buy little more than fresh bread for our entire stay.

Every evening the rubbish bags were gathered on two-wheeled trolleys and brought up into a dark winter night and dumped by the main road for collection. It was a full-time job for one man but, when divided among five, it often turned into a frenetic race to see how quickly it could be finished. Visiting friends who stayed at the apartment made the job even faster, and consequently dangerous. A wipe-out on one of the trolleys in the underground car park broke Mark's ribs and crashed Murray into the ceiling. After that the process calmed down. At one time there were as many as twenty-one, all with their climbing and skiing equipment, crammed into the tiny flat. A room fifteen feet square became a chaos of gear, skis and clothing, the floor lined wall to wall with multi-coloured sleeping bags, under tables and chairs, even two in the bathroom. The bath became a much sought after sleeping spot. As there were no spare cupboards, the five binmen kept their personal clothing in plastic bin bags, which seemed sensible until it came to recognising which of the identical bags was yours. Often the contents would be emptied, strewn around, repacked, sometimes into the wrong bag, while someone tried to find a lost shoe – a search that could take as long as an hour.

No one could afford skiing tuition, so novices taught themselves in a typically aggressive style that consisted largely of aiming directly downhill and falling over, or colliding with another unfortunate skier when they wanted to turn or stop. Early in the winter season Mark Miller and Sean Smith made a fine ascent of the North Face of the Pelerins while the rest of us confined ourselves to the choatic warmth of the apartment.

Our idea of Après Ski was almost as dangerous as winter climbing. On the night of New Year's Day someone had the idea of going tobogganing on the nearby ski jump. It was one of those brilliant ideas that tend to occur soon after you've eaten the worm at the bottom of the tequila bottle. It was snowing lightly and the air temperature had dropped dramatically but, in our twisted state, this was the least of our worries. Staying upright and climbing the vertiginous slope required all the concentration we could muster.

In a more sober condition it would have been obvious that cramming yourself on to a small child's plastic sledge and hurtling off the end of a ski jump was a quick way of dying young. In fact, years later, a friend told me how six of his companions had jammed themselves into a wicker laundry basket and gone off a 90-metre ski jump in the Alps and were killed instantly. Fortunately the ski run we chose was a beginner's practice jump. Murray and I managed to stay airborne for about thirty-five feet on our individual jumps before crashing painfully on to the steep run-out slope and tumbling, at a terrifying speed, two hundred feet into the valley below.

For a brief instant as I flew off the edge of the jump, I had thought that I would be all right. Unfortunately it soon became clear that the sledge wasn't designed to fly. In the air it exhibited the same lack of control as it had on the ground, as well as taking on the aerodynamic qualities of a large house brick.

I bit back a squeal of alarm as it began to topple forward, executing a neat half-front somersault through the snow-flaked winter night. I had a momentary glimpse of the spangled lights of the town, a view of the lurching drop of the run-out slope, and then I was upside down, with my feet jammed, my knees on either side of my throat, and the improvised seat-belt tape cutting tightly across my waist, preventing me from falling out. I waggled my wrists optimistically, but I couldn't release my arms.

The flight seemed to take a long time – long enough to start congratulating myself that I would clear the thirty foot flat space – but not enough to finish. My head smacked with stunning force into the snow, and lights danced before my eyes. My neck was forced forward and my nose flattened with a nasty bone-crunching sensation. The sledge toppled over and almost came to a rest on the edge of the run-out. I peered hopefully out from the side of my helmet which had been knocked askew as I began to tumble sideways down the slope. The edge of the sledge caught in the snow, flipping it over, and pounding my face and sensitive nose back into the icy slope. My forearms remained firmly trapped, and however hard I thrashed, I couldn't get free. I slid to a halt, breathing heavily and trapped in the infernal sledge.

Undaunted, Murray decided that my take-off technique was fatally flawed and headed up to make a better job of it. He crashed face first into the snow, not without some style, but with equally damaging force. His descent of the slope, face down on his knees and chest, with the sledge glued like a turtle's carapace to his back, was a faster and more direct line than mine. Bruised and wet, we tramped into town and headed for the bar, and a form of Après Ski with which we were happily more familiar.

By mid-January the weather was settled and very cold. It was late enough in the season for many of the covered crevasses to have good strong bridges over them. Murray drew my attention to the description in the guidebook of the direct route on the South-east Face of Mont Maudit, a fine mountain connected to Mt Blanc by the remote and high Col de la Brenva. It was said to be a difficult mixed climb on 2,000 feet of excellent granite that had yet to have a winter ascent. This last fact was the clincher, and we set off from the Midi Téléphérique station with enormous rucksacks bulging with axes, snow shoes, food, fuel, and hardware. We immediately discovered the strenuous efforts required to ski with such unwieldy burdens on our backs and abandoned the skis at the foot of a stupendous pillar of overhanging golden granite.

The Grand Capucin towered above us as we struggled to strap plastic snow shoes to our boots. Awkwardly we waddled up into the Maudit-Tacul glacier bay beneath the granite spires of the Capucin and Point Adolphe Rey. There were several large gaping crevasses on the left as we struggled up the steepening wall of névé towards the Col de la Fourche. There our route began. We intended to stay in a small bivouac hut, called the Trident Hut, which stood on the ridge to the left of the Fourche.

We made slow progress, the snow shoes more of an encumbrance than a help, and were not roped together, which was reckless since the heavily crevassed glacier was a minefield of gaping holes covered with a deceptively smooth skin of thin snow. As evening fell a biting cold wind sprang up, blasting icy spindrift into our faces. We couldn't bear to look directly into the full force of the wind. There was no sign of the hut, only the sulphur yellow beams of our headtorches flitting through the maelstrom.

'It's got to be here somewhere,' Murray shouted into my ear.

'Are you sure we're on the right col?' I yelled back.

'Yes. Certain.' He looked intently into the vortex of blasting ice particles.

'It said go left a little bit along this ridge.'

'Yes but left from which way?' I asked. 'I mean, if you're looking from the other side it would be right from here.'

'Eh?' Murray looked perplexed.

He clambered off to the left and soon disappeared into the murk. I started to follow but the pool of light from my torch abruptly flicked out and I cursed myself for buying cheap batteries. By the time I had replaced the cell I saw the flickering glow of Murray's torch move slowly towards me.

'Can't see a thing!' he yelled.

'I'm freezing. Let's bivi. We'll never find it in this visibility.'

He nodded in reluctant agreement and we resigned ourselves to losing the cosy shelter of the little hut. A short distance to the right we found a suitably wide patch of snow and began to dig a rectangular hole big enough to fit the two of us side by side. It wasn't deep enough for a snowhole but the walls would provide some shelter from the wind. We worked silently both aware of the debilitating cold and the icy wind stripping the warmth from our bodies. Despite the warm work I shivered uncontrollably.

Murray had taken off his boots and was struggling into his two sleeping bags as I finished my sleeping area. With a last sweep of my axe I cleared away some blocky snow and then leant wearily on the axe. Suddenly it plunged down and I buried my face in the snow. My arm was embedded in some sort of hole. I peered down, trying to probe it with my torch beam. Spindrift kept blasting into the hole, making it difficult to work out what I was looking at. For a chilling moment I thought we were on the roof of a crevasse, but dismissed the idea. *Stupid prat! You don't get crevasses on top of rock ridges,* I thought. I quickly shovelled some snow into the hole and then laid my insulated sleeping mat over it.

It was a long windy night. At dawn a faint washed-out blue sky rose above the ink black of the retreating night, the wind subsided and a weak sun began to warm us into life. Murray got up first for a pee. He stood with the two sleeping bags coiled around his feet delivering a steaming yellow arc off the edge of the ridge. As he turned to get back into his bag I saw his mouth drop open in surprise.

'You'll not believe this,' he said.

'What?'

'Stand up and look.' He was laughing now.

I stood up and looked to the north. Fifty feet away I saw the black wooden railings of the hut. Fifty feet! I kicked away my sleeping bag and crossed to some nearby rocks to relieve myself.

'Murray,' I said quietly as I turned back to the bivi site, 'I'd get away from there if I were you, and do it softly.' He looked at me quizzically.

'Why?'

'Because we dug our bivi on the top of a bloody great cornice, that's why.'

I could see the curled ice cream lick of snow hanging out over the three hundred foot slope above the Brenva glacier plateau. My abandoned sleeping bag was only a few feet back from the edge. It suddenly dawned on me. *So that was what that hole was last night.* In the turmoil of gusting snow we had mistaken the whale-backed cornice for a flat safe col. Why it hadn't collapsed under our weight was beyond me. I sat in the feeble morning sun while Murray gingerly retrieved our equipment from the bivi hole that now we hardly dared to approach.

As we climbed down the steep snowfield leading to the glacier I glanced up at the underbelly of the cornice that hung out over the ridge. There was a scuffed mark in the smooth curl of snow at the point where my axe had broken through.

'Pretty dumb, eh?' I said, and Murray burst out laughing.

A few hours later we had reached the bergschrund beneath the south face of Mt Maudit. This long thick-lipped crevasse ran the full width of the face in an undulating, gaping gash of hard blue ice walls, topped by a creamy whip of snow. We approached the narrowest section and Murray struggled to bridge across it. Large chunks of snow broke away beneath his scrabbling feet and rustled into dark echoing chambers below him. With an exhausted grunt he hauled himself on to the slope above and stood up.

'I'll just go up a bit and make an axe belay,' he said, and had barely stopped speaking before a sharp report broke the silence. We both glanced in the direction of the sound. Fifty feet to the right an immense block of ice and snow, the upper lip of the bergschrund, crashed into the open maw of the crevasse. A crack line snaked rapidly towards us cutting a fracture line swiftly through the crisp snow level where Murray was standing.

'Sheiiit!' Murray howled, and began running away from the advancing fissure. Luckily I didn't have the rope in a belay device so I could let him run free and fast, arms pumping, head down, with his huge rucksack threatening to up-end him into the gaping jaws of the bergschrund. He disappeared over a rise in the slope and was followed attentively by the crack line. Eventually the rope stopped. For a second there was absolute silence, and then a deafening roar as about one hundred feet of the upper edge of the bergschrund thundered into the depths, spraying a cloud of ice particles over me.

The collapse conveniently filled the gap between me and the upper lip of the bergschrund. I stepped easily across the debris and followed the slack rope over the rise. I found Murray lying flat on his back. His face was puce and his chest heaving, as if he were trying to vomit up his lungs. I crumpled to my knees in a mixture of amusement and hysteria. I was all too well aware that the collapse could have killed Murray, and it began to dawn on me how fortunate I was that it all went down the slot and not over me. We should have been smeared messily across the upper Brenva glacier plateau.

The start of the direct route was an intimidating ice-filled ramp line cutting diagonally from left to right across a vertical granite wall. Murray made a half-hearted attempt to climb the ramp before surrendering to my suggestion that it might be easier on the left. We had to ascend a steep rock wall that separated us from a large pear- shaped hanging glacier. The line then followed the edge of this glacier and up into the intimidating headwall. I had spotted a small chimney a little way to our left. It was choked with hard water ice in its bottom reaches but then opened up into what appeared to be easy dry rock climbing. I thought there was a way back to the top of the first line so long as one could climb the chimney.

I used a Friend, an expanding camming device, in the narrow gap at the back of the chimney. Testing it by tugging on the rope, I noticed that the teeth bit deeply into water ice on the wall of the chimney.

'It might melt out under pressure,' I said to Murray. 'Still, I'll only be on it for a moment.'

With that, I clipped a sling to the Friend and stepped slowly up. Ice crunched as the teeth of the cams expanded into the crack. I reached as high as I could and tried to get a placement with my axe. It was hopeless. Sparks chipped off the pick as I thrashed at the ice. It was hard brittle stuff and shattered as soon as the axe struck it. What I had taken as vertical turned out to be overhanging and I was being pushed relentlessly out from the rock. I felt the sling shift fractionally down and glanced at the Friend. One side of the cams had melted deeply into the ice under the pressure created by my weight. I had just begun to wonder if they would grip into the rock when I saw the aluminium device burst out of the crack in a spray of ice fragments. I flew backwards, flailing my axe hopelessly at a cruel and empty sky.

Murray hauled me up towards him as I tried to brush the snow out of my collar. I had fallen twelve feet on to my back. Surprised but unhurt, I felt the snow melt and trickle in icy rivulets down my back.

An hour later we jumped over the bergschrund and trudged dispiritedly back towards the Col de la Trident. I had managed to climb twelve feet up the face and Murray had reached an impressive high point of forty feet before conceding defeat. It had taken us one and a half days of slogging to fail after forty feet, and then the same again to get back to Chamonix. Not an impressive performance.

10

CHEAP THRILLS

IT WAS DARK when we reached the summit of the Droites
after climbing wearily out from the cold inhospitable gullies
at the top of the north face. Murray moved off to the right
without saying anything. I followed the sodium yellow glow
of his head torch as it bobbed from side to side, occasionally
blotted out by a blast of spindrift-laden wind. Three tugs
pulled at the knot on my harness and I clambered to my feet
and followed the twin lines snaking through the snow.

'Where are we?' I yelled when I could make out the darker
shadow crouching in front of me.

'On the Brèche des Droites. It's the col between the east and
west summits.'

'Any bivi sites?'

'Can't see any,' Murray replied as I slumped down besides
him. 'But if we go straight down the south side of the col it
leads down to the Talèfre glacier. That's the usual descent
route.'

'Should we try it in the dark?' I shone my torchbeam down
the couloir. 'I can't see a thing. Didn't the guide say there
were abseil slings in place?'

'Yes, further down. On the righthand walls. I don't fancy it
in the dark, do you?'

'Not much.'

Murray sat astride the col with one leg down the north face
and the other down the descent route to the south. The night
sky was clear of clouds. A milky opacity on the horizon
heralded the rise of an almost full moon.

133

'The weather's set fair. The meteo was good for three more days. I can't see the point of continuing in the dark.'

'No. It's silly. Let's see if we can dig out some space here,' Murray said as he shrugged the rucksack from his shoulders. 'I'll go and fix up a belay.'

He tramped off towards the summit, heading for a large rock outcrop thirty feet from the col. I began to dig into the sugary crystalline snow, keeping my back to the bitter winter wind that tore viciously across the col. A few minutes later I hit hard ice.

After three quarters of an hour's hard digging we had managed only to round off a small area of the sharp-edged col, barely enough for the two of us to lie down. The rope had been attached to the rock outcrop and ran away from us along the crest of the ridge. If either of us fell off the col, we would be dragged into a gut-clenching pendulum either across the north or the south face of the mountain. It wasn't the way I wanted to wake up – dangling above a 3,500-foot drop while still trapped inside a tightly closed sleeping bag.

Murray quickly arranged his sleeping bag on top of his insulating foam mat and struggled into it. I noticed he had grabbed the inside spot, leaving me to set out my bed on the very edge of the north face. The south side was at an easier angle, although just as high. It meant that I took the full brunt of the bitter wind which came screeching over the col.

As the tiredness of two day's hard climbing up an extreme Alpine north face took hold I made an almost disastrous mistake. Sitting cross-legged on my bag, I was fighting to get the plastic shell of my double boots off my right foot. It had become jammed on some part of the felt inner boot. Just as I was about to abandon pulling and undo the inner boot the plastic shell shot off my foot and soared into the air. Both of us dived at the spinning boot, missed it, collided, and I knew I'd lost it. Losing my boot at 13,000 feet in the middle of winter was worse than falling off the damned ledge. How was I going to descend? I would get frost-bite for sure!

I sat back, swearing in frustration at my carelessness. Murray had a look of polite astonishment on his face as he stared at me howling at the wind. I glanced down, averting my face from the ice-laced blast. My boot was balanced precariously on the outside edge of my sleeping bag, held in place by the slight grip of the vibram sole on the shiny nylon fabric. I dived over it, smothering the boot with my body and searching for it with my hand. I held it up triumphantly and grinned at Murray. He smiled, shrugged himself down into his bag and muttered 'stupid bastard' from inside the hood.

We got little sleep. Exhausted snatches of unconsciousness were rudely interrupted by the slide of the bags, or a sudden harsh blast of wind tugging us out of balance. Dawn came quietly as the wind faded. The sun hit us early, warming away the cramped stiffness of the bivouac. We sat basking in the warmth, sipping at sweet black coffee, smoking the first cigarette of the day and quietly watching the rising sun spill its light into the darkened valleys and glaciers below us. There was a tremendous view of the Argentière basin with the huge north walls spread out to our right. I saw the face on the Courtes down which I had hurtled in the avalanche and beyond the long snow crest of a ridge running away towards the distant north face of the Aiguille de Triolet. Beautiful white-capped gendarmes, golden granite sentinels, spiked up intermittently from the ridge.

Immediately in front of us the symmetrical summit of the Chardonnet was iced with a delicate winter white fringe on the broken rocky ridges of its south face. The pyramid of the Argentière rose to 13,000 feet from a col joining it to the Chardonnet. It too was frosted and etched with a lacework of ice. At the far end of Argentière glacier Mt Dolent rose in an almost perfect cone shape above the A Neuve glacier. It had an ethereal quality about it in the soft early morning light, almost as if an artist had water-coloured it into place. Close to its summit there was a junction of ridges that marked where the frontiers of France, Switzerland and Italy met. It had been worth the long cold night to awake to such an overwhelmingly beautiful scene, with white-shouldered peaks marching away from us in a seemingly limitless horizon of jagged mountains.

'There's the Matterhorn.' Murray pointed towards Switzerland.

'Where?'

'There, that pointy one with the big one, the Monte Rosa, on the left.'

'You can't see that far from here, can you?'

'Course you can.' He flicked away the dregs from his mug and turned to light the gas stove again.

I caught a glimpse of the North Face of the Triolet with its huge double bands of ice cliffs threatening all who approached.

'I've always fancied doing the Triolet,' I said as Murray prepared another brew.

'Not me,' he said over his shoulder. 'Those seracs are too dangerous, and it's just an enormous ice slope. Boring and risky.'

'Those cliffs are pretty solid. Big, I grant you, but they look pretty safe to me,' I said, feeling disappointed with his dismissal of the route.

'Those things are never safe,' he said emphatically. Several years later our friend Roger Baxter Jones was swept to his death with his client when the seracs collapsed.

I sipped the hot coffee he had given me and stared reflectively at the distant profile of the Triolet, wondering whether Murray was right. Maybe I only wanted to do it because it was a big north face; for the cachet it might bestow on me. I just wanted another tick on my list of big routes. Murray had swiftly exposed that conceited and boastful side of my climbing aspirations. I couldn't imagine him doing a climb for such shallow reasons and felt a pang of embarrassment.

It was useless to try to analyse it. If we did it only for fun or for aesthetics, why on earth choose the hardest routes in the most difficult season? Why not just climb those routes that are well with- in your ability rather than struggle up horror stories that leave you unsure of the likely outcome from the very first step? Because, as Murray had so succinctly pointed out, it would be boring. There was no point doing what you knew you could do. Much better to test the limits; it was the only way to improve and learn.

And, to be honest, I needed the thrill and the fear. Uncertainty was addictive. So much of mountaineering was harshly uncomfortable, miserable and exhausting that, without the exciting flush of fear, it would become almost unendurable. For sure, the glorious morning on the summit with the panoramic view as we perched on the edge of the abyss of the north face was enjoyable, but getting there had been hard. Twenty hours of tip-toeing up ice fields, cascades and steep mixed ground, two uncomfortable bivouacs, and always the anxious glances at the sky, searching for signs of bad weather, all too aware of how committed we were. On the summit my memory edited out the anxiety and tension and fed me happy recollections of the superb climbing, the spectacular positions we had been in, feeling confident and safe, knowing we were going to succeed. I didn't care why I had chosen to do the route. Whether it was boastful egotism or the genuine desire to climb a splendid line up an extreme face didn't matter now. It had been done, and done well, and that was enough.

Murray interrupted my thoughts. 'Come on, better get down before the sun makes the south slopes dangerous.' I glanced up to see him stuffing his rucksack with the tail-end of his sleeping bag.

Three hours later we had descended the snowy couloir to its junction with the Talèfre glacier. A bergschrund lay between us and the glacier, with a fragile-looking snow bridge stretching across the gap of about fifteen feet. This crevasse between the glacier and the mountain didn't appear to be very deep but I knew better than to be deceived so easily. Many a climber had slipped into such slots, to be killed in the crashing fall, ricochetting between the hard rock of the mountain and the slick ice of the glacier, finally becoming inextricably jammed, sometimes hundreds of feet below the surface.

'Do you think we should rope up?' I asked Murray anxiously. We had soloed down the last half of the easy descent gully with our ropes neatly coiled and packed away in our rucksacks.

'Naw,' he said, stepping forward, 'looks okay to me.'

I was about thirty feet back from the edge of the bergschrund and stopped to watch his progress. He made an awkward step down on to the bridge and then gingerly took a stride forward.

There was a startled yelp, a rushing sound and he had disappeared with shocking abruptness. It was so fast that it seemed as if he had simply evaporated into the sun-heated air in front of me.

'Murray?' I spoke tentatively, barely able to grasp what had happened. There was no answer. The day seemed to have become uncannily silent. 'Murray!' I took a few steps forward and saw where the bridge had collapsed.

'Oh Christ, no! MURRAY . . . are you okay . . . ?'

There was no reply. A slow cold dread began to seep through me. *He's gone. Just like that . . . gone.* I approached the bergschrund warily. I was suddenly afraid of it, as if somehow it would come alive and grab me too. I checked the snow, anxious now that everything I stood on was frail and brittle. It is an awful sensation to lose all confidence in the solidity of what you're standing on.

Very gradually, and without a sound, the head of a red shafted ice axe rose like Excalibur from the maw of the bergschrund and swung forward embedding itself in the far wall of the glacier.

'Murray! Are you okay?' It seemed an absurdly inane thing to say.

'I will be in a moment.'

The voice seemed strangely disembodied and unemotional. There was a scraping sound and Murray's helmet appeared beside the axe, as if he had been lifted vertically by some invisible hydraulic lift. He scrabbled in the crusty snow on the lip of the hole and hauled himself up and out of the bergschrund.

'I wouldn't use the bridge.'

He had a funny lopsided expression on his face and his eyes

seemed to be glazed with a distant stare. I stepped forward and looked down into the depths. Pretty honeycomb ice structures bridged across the walls in a flimsy barrier. Beneath their lacy web I sensed rather than saw the lurking shadows of the chasm.

'What stopped you?'

'I don't know. I didn't look down to see.'

There was nothing down there that looked remotely strong enough to hold a falling man.

'I'd jump if I were you.' Murray said, getting to his feet.

'Yeah? Well, you're not me, and you don't have to try it,' I said, measuring the gap with suspicious eyes.

'Not there, you fool. It's an easy jump to your right.'

I landed with a satisfyingly solid impact face down in the wet snow of the glacier and felt my axe head jab painfully into my ribs. As I stood up and brushed the melting snow out from my neck I saw Murray standing at the edge of the bergschrund, doubled over and holding his right leg with both hands.

'What's wrong? Are you hurt?' I asked.

'No,' he said in a quivery voice. 'My leg won't stop shaking.' He let go his grip and I saw his leg vibrating with rapid shivers. Murray laughed. 'I can hardly stand up. Must be a reaction of some sort.'

'I know. I feel a bit wobbly and I only witnessed it. God, I really thought you were gone there, you know.'

'Mmmm . . . me too.'

Several cigarettes later we had calmed enough to begin the long trudge down the Talèfre glacier where it joined with the large mainstream of the Mer de Glace, and on down to Chamonix.

At last we had made our first winter ascent and felt justifiably proud of ourselves. It hadn't been so long ago that winter attempts on the North Face of the Droites had taken several weeks and been achieved with Himalayan-style fixed rope siege tactics. As we entered the Bar Nash for a welcome beer, dropping our bulging rucksacks outside the door, we looked forward to a pleasant bullshitting session and quietly glowing with the satisfaction of our achievement. We had barely taken our first sips of cold lager before someone said,

'Hey, did you hear that Andy Parkin soloed the Droites in five hours last week?'

Even as I was choking on my beer someone else replied that Stevie Haston had soloed it in four hours soon after Andy. We finished our beers and slunk out into the winter sunshine. As we tramped wearily back to the madhouse of our apartment I couldn't help laughing at myself. What an idiot! Good thing neither of us had opened our mouths. It is so easy to spot bullshitters in the climbing world and we had so very nearly fallen into that trap.

Soon afterwards the weather broke with a heavy ten-day snowfall. The Christmas rush of visiting friends was over and five people in the one-man studio now seemed like palatial luxury. When the weather improved Sean Smith and Mark Miller set off to climb the North-east Ridge of the Droites. The day after they left, I decided the time had come to change my underpants. It was a momentous decision, made all the more significant when I knew that I was the only one of us who had had the foresight to bring two pairs for the six-month stay in Chamonix. The pair I had worn for two and a half months had finally succumbed to the ravages of wear and tear. The rubber waistband was attached by a few threads of sweat-rotted cloth. I searched the apartment three times, sorting through a mass of filthy clothing, but found nothing. I was about to start again when Rob Spencer came in.

'Hey Rob! Have you seen my shreddies anywhere?'

'What?'

'My grollies, my underpants, you know.'

'Oh, the black pair?'

'That's right.'

'Clean ones. Looked new to me.'

'Yes, yes, that's right,' I said testily, 'where are they?'

'Mark nicked them.'

'What!'

'Yeah. He was searching for his and couldn't find them, so he took yours.'

'But he didn't have a spare pair.'

'I know, he was quite pleased with them.'

'Bastard. The selfish grabbing little . . .'

'It's all right, he'll give them back when he gets down.'

For the next four days I grumbled moodily about private property and individual rights while the others laughed and enjoyed themselves winding me up. Mark and Sean were overdue and there had been a bad weather forecast on the morning of the fourth day. Murray, Rob and I were unsure what to do. If we called out the rescue and it wasn't required, Mark and Sean would have to pay for the helicopter flight. If we didn't, and they were in trouble, and the storm was bad . . .

In the early afternoon the door crashed open, and Mark stomped heavily into the apartment. He looked tired.

'Sean's in hospital. Is there a brew on?' he said, matter-of-factly.

'Here.' Rob handed him a mug of tea. 'What happened?'

Mark grinned and told us about the descent. Sean was desperately anxious about his frost-bitten fingers which he needed for his burgeoning photographic career. They had reached the glacier when they heard the faint buzz of a small sight-seeing plane. It swung left, up the glacier, and circled once above the tiny figures of Sean and Mark. Not one to miss out on such an opportunity, Mark had held his arms above his head, spread in the international distress signal. He hoped the pilot would see his signal and radio for a helicopter, but to his amazement the plane circled once more and then came in, landing on its skids on the glacier.

When he had recovered his wits, Mark walked over and asked for a lift. The pilot refused, saying they would be too heavy to take off. The tourists clicked away happily with a battery of telephoto lenses, delighted to see a real climber in the wild instead of a tiny speck of colour spread-eagled on a vast rock and ice wall. Shortly after the plane flew off a helicopter clattered into the cirque and hovered in to pick up Mark and Sean.

As Mark came out of the bathroom, I remembered my underpants.

'Hey Mark, have you got my shreddies?'

'Yeah,' he said, drying his head. 'They're in the bathroom.'

'Thanks,' I said, getting up.

'Unfortunately we ate chocolate and dried fruit for four days and it plays havoc with your guts. Sorry, couldn't help myself, you'll have to give them a wash.'

'Great. How considerate of you.'

I went into the bathroom, picked up the noisome soiled cotton between thumb and fingertip and dropped them in the bin. I wondered if I could patch my present pair.

The Easter rush of visiting British friends was made all the more hectic by coinciding with the appearance of a coach-load of twenty impoverished Czechoslovakian climbers. Their food appeared to consist solely of barrels of sauerkraut that they brought with them. The fact that East and West did not understand each other's language presented no great difficulty. Animated sign language and an obsession with alcohol solved most problems.

After being ejected from the Bar Nash, our inebriated crowd tottered off in the direction of a bar called the Choucas. Murray staggered past me with a bed sheet draped over his head, tied with a piece of green climbing tape, as Lawrence of Arabia for the evening. A car carrying a middle-aged couple cruised carefully past our unstable group. The passenger window was open, and an attractive, elegantly dressed woman looked out at us with an expression of feigned amusement and Gallic disdain.

'Salut! Ca va?' Murray hollered as he galloped up to the car with the bed sheet flapping wildly. The woman smiled uncertainly. Murray grabbed the roof-rack, hopped up on one foot, thrust a sodden, odorous shoe through the window and settled himself comfortably on the window sill. Hunza, a short powerfully-built Czech, and I lunged for the roof-rack.

We clung on tenaciously to the ice-coated metal struts, boots dragging in the snow, as the car increased speed. I heard an abusive French voice from the driver's seat and saw Murray topple from his perch in a billowing cloud of bed sheets. At the same time the stressed metal of the roof-rack gave way, bent flat across my fingers, and then flew off the roof. The car sped away without stopping, an angry fist waving from the driver's window as Hunza and I tried to disentangle ourselves from the roof-rack.

Having been deposited somewhat roughly outside the Choucas well ahead of the others, we staggered inside to order the beer.

I awoke the next morning convinced that I was about to die. It felt as if someone were standing on my head. Squinting through painfully bloodshot eyes, I realised that Mark was in fact standing on my head in an attempt to reach the toilet. When he had finished I sat up gingerly and peered at the chaos of twenty-one hung-over bodies sprawled in the cramped space of the flat.

During the Easter holidays Rob Uttley turned up at the apartment with the usual monstrous rucksack. He was a brilliantly talented climber from Sheffield, where he was studying at the university. He had been training hard in preparation for his first Himalayan expedition to Annapurna III the following autumn and had come to Chamonix on a flying visit, hoping to make a winter ascent of the Walker Spur. But, with the face out of condition, he resigned himself to an expensive fortnight of debauchery.

Rob had a ready smile and a quick dry sense of humour. I was in awe of his climbing ability and slightly tongue-tied when I first met him, but his easy-going nature quickly put me at ease. He was small, compact, wiry-muscled, and seemed to exude an electric vibrancy, as if there wasn't enough time or space in his life to contain his dynamic spirit. There was a bright boyish gleam to his eyes, suggesting irrepressible exuberance and a zest for life. In a group, he quickly became a focal point of attention. When he left to resume his studies in Sheffield we missed his charismatic energy.

Shortly after Rob left I teamed up with a Dutch climber who appeared one day sporting a punk hairstyle that looked like a badger's bum badly shorn by a lawnmower. I immediately felt an affinity for him. During a long spell of bad weather, boredom finally got the better of me and I dyed my own hair. I had thought that pure hydrogen peroxide would do the job and after soaking my head I emerged from the bathroom in some pain.

'What does this say?' I said as I passed the small bottle to Murray. He read the French instructions slowly with an impish grin on his face.

'Well. If I've read it correctly, it says it is concentrated enough to clean sixty toilets. It's burnt your skin off,' he said, pointing to my chest.

There were thin white lines running across the suntan and down my forehead. The peroxide had bleached my skin. I whipped the towel off and stared distractedly into the mirror. My hair was exactly the same colour. I grabbed a handful and gave a sharp tug. Nothing happened, which was a relief since I had expected the whole lot to come away in a desiccated thatch of dead hair.

'You need a reactive agent, I think,' Sean said.

'What's that?'

'Oh, it's something that, when combined with the peroxide, reacts to bleach the hair.'

'Well, why didn't you tell me before?' I snapped in exasperation.

'You didn't ask,' he said with a grin, 'but you'll get a kit at any hairdressers.'

An hour later I returned clutching a small box purchased from a very expensive hair salon. I had some difficulty persuading the svelte and foppish hairdresser that I wanted to do it myself. He insisted on stroking his fingers through my hair, patting my bum and fluttering his eyelashes at me.

'Non, non, non ... ' he tutted and made a few more adjustments to my hair. He showed me the colour he preferred.

'No thanks, mate, I want the blond one, you know. Le blanc.'

I jerked away as his hand caressed my buttocks. His mood changed abruptly at my rejection and he became haughty and dismissive, thrusting the blond box at me and demanding an extortionate price in a sharp angry voice.

I kept my eyes tightly closed as I energetically towelled my hair.

'This time it had better work,' I muttered, as I opened my eyes and stared in disbelief at the mirror. My hair was incandescent with the brightest most outrageous orange colour I had ever seen. It produced a weird shimmering aura around my head.

'Good God!' I yelped. 'The little bastard sold me orange.'

After the jokes subsided, I slowly came to accept the new look. It was immediately obvious that my Belisha beacon head aroused considerable emotion in the good citizens of Chamonix. At tobacconist's, supermarkets and bars that I had previously visited without complaint, I immediately sensed an aggressive response. At least it made the punk Dutch primary schoolteacher, who drove a 2CV with CHAOS scrawled all over it in dayglow lettering, and me an unusual looking team. The Dutchman suggested we might try to make a first ascent of the direct start and direct finish to the Shroud on the North Face of the Grandes Jorasses. It was a bold choice. This line had repulsed many climbers far better than us. Emboldened by our hairstyles, we decided that we wouldn't know if we could do it unless we tried.

Having agreed on our objective, the Dutchman dragged me off to the supermarket for some hill-food.

I followed him round the shop while an astonishing amount of produce disappeared into the pockets of his jacket. Unable to stand the tension any longer, I tried to sidle away from him. I was well aware that we were the most conspicuous people in the shop, in the whole town in fact. This tall Dutchman with the white-striped mohican haircut, three ear-rings, in his rag-tag mixture of clothing styles, and me with a bright orange head, a huge red feather ear-ring, a punkish black and white angora jumper and red snakeskin-patterned jeans. He waved conspiratorially at me, cutting off my escape plans. I shuffled uneasily back to where he stood by a counter full of tins of pâté

'What do you want?'

'Stand in front of me while I readjust these things.'

Judging by the fact that he towered above me, and was writhing, Houdini-like, in an attempt to organise his acquisitions, I doubted that I would be of much use as a screen. I stood there, thinking of the bubble-gum-heist with Sarah, and wishing I were somewhere else. There was a loud clattering sound from behind me, followed by some Dutch curses. A tin of pâté rolled past my feet. I gave it a surreptitious kick, hoping it would disappear under the opposite counter but, to my dismay, it richocheted off and span crazily down the centre of the aisle. I raised my eyes despairingly to the ceiling only to find myself staring at the blinking red light on a security camera that was aimed accusingly at me.

'Oh shit, it's spotted us,' I said.

'What has?' the Dutchman asked, pulling his jacket round him.

'That.' I nodded towards the camera.

'Oh, it's nothing. They never monitor them.' He strode confidently towards the cashiers clutching a small baguette.

I followed ten minutes later, convinced that I would find the gendarmes indulging in baton practice on the pavement outside. I found the Dutchman calmly making himself a ham sandwich in the Bar Nash.

'Ah, there you are,' he said through a mouthful of bread, 'I thought maybe you had voluntarily surrendered. You're not very good at it, are you?'

'It's not my idea of fun,' I admitted.

We emerged from the ice tunnel at the top of the Midi into blinding sunlight. The Grandes Jorasses loomed ahead of us with the steep profile of the Walker Spur dominating the surrounding mountains. A couple of skiers barged roughly past us and heeled down a steep ice ridge leading to a small col. They seemed unconcerned about the 3,000-foot drop on the left. We descended slowly and carefully. Our enormous rucksacks, and the skis across our shoulders, made us feel alarmingly unstable.

At the col we prepared for the ski descent of the Vallée Blanche. This superb off-piste route takes skiers through fabulous mountain scenery in the heart of the range. In winter it also allows mountaineers fast, easy access to some remote routes.

As we were about to set off a guide dressed in a smart red ski-suit covered in badges asked where we were going. Two clients stood quietly behind him.

'Jorasses,' I replied curtly.

'Jorasses?' He snorted contemptuously. I glanced at him in annoyance.

'Oui,' I said, 'Jorasses. Linceul [The Shroud].'

He laughed, and said something to his clients, who laughed with him. With an exaggerated swing of the hips he curved off down the slopes leading to the start of the Vallée Blanche.

'What did he say?' I asked my Dutch partner who was glaring after him.

'Something about punks and idiots, I think.'

As darkness approached, we sat in the snow beneath the ice-streaked walls of the Walker Spur. We had dug an open pit, building the walls up to form a wind break. Our bivouac site was directly under a route called Rolling Stone (a desperate Czech route up the left flank of the Walker).

'Do you think we'll be safe here?' I asked as I climbed into my sleeping bag.

'Why not?' the Dutchman said from the downy depths of his.

'Well, the name Rolling Stone does suggest rockfall to me.'

'No, not in winter, and not at night,' he replied with reassuring confidence.

I awoke with a start at midnight. Opening my eyes, I stared at the star-studded sky, and strained my ears. *What was that? What woke me?* The answer came immediately. There was a whirring, high-pitched whistling sound, and then a rapid series of thuds. *Rockfall!* I squirmed inside my bag trying to find the drawcord.

'Quick!' I shouted. 'Move, we're going to get hit!'

There was a muffled reply, and more thuds that seemed to come from dangerously nearby. Then silence. So sudden it seemed that it made me wonder whether I had imagined the thudding sounds. I found my headtorch, pulled the drawcord open, and peered out cautiously. I couldn't see above the snow walls we had built. *Maybe it hadn't happened, and if it had it was probably miles away from us.* I settled back apprehensively in my pit.

'What was all the shouting about?' the Dutchman wanted to know.

'I think we nearly got hit by rockfall.'

'Rubbish. Not in winter. Go back to sleep.'

We managed to climb about 450 feet of the route before being repulsed by an impossible powder snow overhang. Twenty feet from the overhang I knew that I couldn't go on. In fact, I doubted if I could get back without falling. On top of the rock overhang there was a ten-foot bulge of powder snow, like whipped cream, though not as solid.

'Watch me,' I shouted.

Glancing down, I saw my partner smiling confidently and paying close attention to me. I looked past him at the 400-foot drop to the open shadows of the bergschrund. However strong the peg was, I didn't want to take a sixty-foot fall down that slope. Breathing heavily, from fear and effort, I eventually made the safety of Edmund's stance.

'Let's get the hell out of here.' I said.

We reached our bivouac pit after several hair-raising abseils. I noticed a handful of rocks embedded in the snow near the snow walls. I hadn't seen them when we had left in the darkness of early morning.

'There, look at those,' I said triumphantly, 'I knew there had been a rockfall last night.'

The Dutchman examined the stones curiously. They lay within a few feet of where I had been lying. I knew that such impacts didn't simply break bones; they splintered them into fragments.

'Ah well, at least they were all on your side,' he announced with some satisfaction.

After an alarming ski descent through a narrow, twisting tree-lined track littered with tree roots and stones we emerged on to a small ski slope by the edge of the town. The Dutchman skied smoothly out on to the slope ahead of me while I careered, virtually out of control, from a small copse of dwarf pine trees. Trailing branches and pine-needles over the snow, I was horrified to see a ski school of toddlers lined up directly in front of me. The ski instructress had just got the helmeted six-year-olds into some sort of order when I burst from the nearby forest. I knew that if I attempted to turn I would fall and slide into the kids. The exposed spikes of my axes and crampons could cause terrible injuries.

One little lad was facing me with an expression of innocent curiosity on his face when I spread my arms and legs and scooped him up against my chest. I flashed through the line and, once clear, slowed down and let the boy gently down. He grinned cheekily and looked behind me. I turned to see the whole class slowly topple like falling dominoes away from either side of the place where I had bisected the line. I knew I hadn't touched any of them or caused any injury. The instructress was advancing on me with a murderous expression on her face. I shoved the boy away and hastily made my escape.

Retreating to the safety of the apartment I found an alarmingly battered looking man drinking tea with Murray. His face was swollen and bruised, with puffy bloodshot eyes and lumpy purple swellings bulging from his cheekbones. There were lacerations on his forehead and the sides of his face. He looked up when I came in and gave me a painful lopsided grin.

His name was Pete Barrass, and he had just survived a double avalanche while descending the steep slopes of the Pas de Chèvre with his partner, Andy Nisbet. The snow had suddenly broken away dragging him down in a long tumbling fall. The first avalanche spat him out leaving him relatively unscathed. He stood up and waved at his now distant partner shouting, 'I'm okay!' As his words echoed off the gully walls another, much larger, avalanche had thundered down, sweeping Pete another four hundred feet in a lacerating, bruising descent. Luckily he wasn't buried, and after Andy Nisbet reached him, was quickly evacuated by helicopter.

Pete left for home a few days later. Seven years later, a man approached me in a local pub in Sheffield and asked how I was getting on. I stared at him in confusion. I couldn't for the life of me recognise Pete without the scars, bruises and swellings.

As the heavy wet avalanches of spring cut scars down the forested valley walls I began to think of returning home. I wasn't sure what I was going to do. Since impulsively throwing in my degree course and escaping suicidal depression by hitching to Chamonix, I had given no thought to the future. Should I go back and finish the course? I felt a stab of remorse for letting my parents down, as well as a deep and insistent sense of failure.

My parents could not appreciate what climbing meant to me. I had tried to explain it, and had been careful to emphasise the seriousness of it all. If something were to happen to me, I wanted them to understand that I had accepted this possibility. I couldn't bear the thought of leaving them hurt and confused, unable to comprehend the death of their youngest son. Above all I disliked the idea that they might think it a waste of a life and never understand the truth – that for me it was the most life enhancing thing I had ever experienced, that the very nature of the pursuit made me and all my climbing friends the characters we were. The mountains were inextricably woven into the fabric of our lives.

In much the same way I had decided in my mid-teens that I didn't want to do those things that society expected of me. I didn't want to compromise anything and rejected the idea of marriage and parenthood for fear that these would rob me of the selfish desire to do what I wanted with my life; a life lived once, with no reincarnation, no afterlife, heaven or hell, finished at death. Grab the chances that come your way and run with them. That had become my credo, and there was no going back.

It never occurred to me that these early certainties would themselves become eroded by time; that self doubts and too many questions would make a mockery of what I once was and had set out to be; that time would change me, would betray everything I once believed in. If I succeeded in avoiding regret, I failed to realise that I would look back and sneer at what I once had been.

It wasn't that I expected to die. Far from it. If I had thought that, I would have quit immediately. I didn't want to deceive my parents in any way. It seemed acceptable to delude myself, to build up however shaky a rationale for myself that enabled me to participate in something which had claimed the lives of so many friends, but this was because I was in the midst of it. Tunnel vision helped. I thought that, if I were absolutely honest, it would help them understand how important it was to me. In truth, I never managed to explain it to them and succeeded only in loading myself with yet another burden of guilt. It was a selfish pursuit that left the agonizing worry on loved ones while I enjoyed myself.

I was aware of this, yet there was nothing I could do about it short of quitting. I couldn't very well stay tied to my mother's skirts, I reasoned. There had to come a time when you launched out to do what you wanted, whatever the cost. I knew that Ma had already begun praying earnestly while I was away climbing. She talked to me of Guardian Angels that looked after me through her intercession. My faith in a God of any sort had long since been destroyed, yet I had tremendous respect for Ma's belief, and as far as I was concerned every little bit of help was welcome.

There is an element of masochism in the Catholic upbringing, particularly one closely associated with convent and monastery. Perhaps it is the constant exposure to pain and suffering. I could find little sense of joy, of simple delight in living, in the crucifixes, the stations of the cross, the myriad icons of pain attached to a religion that seems so harshly punitive and castigating; only a catalogue of rights and wrongs, sins and guilt. It seemed as if you had to reject everything that was good about life in an effort to achieve an afterlife whose existence couldn't be demonstrated.

I resented priests preaching to me about real life when they could have no concept of it from their own blinkered cloistered lives. Most of all I despised them for giving me something to believe in, something that was precious to me as a child, yet were unable to prove it to be true when I was a questioning adolescent. They could only fall back on faith. And blind faith, like burying your head in sand, gets you nowhere. I resented the sense of betrayal, of failure, that has infected me since I realised that I had no faith; that the fairy tale had evaporated. It was the ultimate deceit, and I couldn't stomach deceit.

'You could always try to become qualified as a guide,' Murray suggested when I was musing over what to do when I returned to England.

'I haven't any paper qualifications, mountain leadership certificates, that sort of thing.'

'Well get them.'

'But I loathe all that bureaucratic rubbish. Half those certificate holders are just a bunch of willy wavers, like those guys who join mountain rescue teams just for the kudos of being some self-important swinging dick . . .'

'That's a bit extreme. They're not all . . .'

'Yeah, okay, maybe not. If the truth be told I resent them because I dislike tests like that and think I would fail them.'

'Why? You're a good climber, better than most of those who have certificates.'

'Well . . . I don't know. I can't navigate to save my life, never could figure out compasses and I know nothing about rope work. Not formal rope work, by the book, that sort of thing. The trouble is we may be able to climb but we're all self taught. Our methods wouldn't go down very well.'

'It can't be that hard to learn and navigation is a doddle. At least give it a try,' Murray said, as he put the finishing touches to the small bomb he had been making on the kitchen table. He was fiddling with a dodgy-looking fuse at the time, trying to insert it into the top of the bomb and check that it would work properly. One of Murray's more endearing qualities was his childlike delight in anything to do with fire and explosions.

'Do you think that thing will work?' Rob Spencer asked dubiously.

'Only one way to find out,' Murray said with an impish grin. He picked up his bomb and hefted it in his hand. We all moved away.

'Why have you made it?' I asked from behind a bin-bag full of clothes.

'Why not?' No-one could think of an answer.

The bomb was about the size of two sugar bags and appeared to consist of large quantities of sugar, petrol, flour and other unidentifiable ingredients. The weather had been overcast for ten days, and boredom had set in quickly. So why not make a bomb?

Murray opened the window of our third floor flat and tried to light the fuse. It refused to ignite at first, and we laughed with nervous relief as we watched from various hiding places in the room. Then with a sizzle and a flash of flame it caught, surprising even Murray, who lobbed it hastily out of the window. There was an expectant silence in the room. Murray peered cautiously over the windowsill. There was no explosion, no flash of flame.

We hurried over and looked out. The bomb, looking like an innocent bag of sugar, sat in the snow with an unimpressive curl of smoke twisting up from the fuse.

We trooped outside and stood to one side of the smoking bomb, considering our options. No one was eager to pick it up. Poking it with a ski stick was suggested but rejected because no one could be bothered to go and get one.

'Go on then, Murray.'

'What?'

'Well, it's your bomb, you have to do something with it.'

This passing the buck went down well with us but Murray

seemed oddly unsure of himself. Then, with a typically abrupt change of mood, he ran up to the bomb and gave it a mighty kick. It soared into the air, partially ruptured by the kick, and landed with a thump and a whoosh of flames on the bonnet of a brand new car parked by the flat. The ingredients spilled out and burst into flames, melting the sugar, and igniting the paper containers.

Luckily we managed to douse the fire with armfuls of wet snow, and sweep the bonnet clear. There didn't seem to be any damage done to the bodywork of the car, so we tramped back inside, and Murray sat down to design a more effective bomb. I went down to the Tourist Information Centre and booked a seat on the coach back to London at the end of the week.

II

LIVING DANGEROUSLY

THE SUMMIT OF Snowdon was shrouded in a bleak damp mist. There was nothing to see but a tatty-looking cafe and dimly through rents in the cloud a white concrete triangulation point.

'Is this it?' A shaven-headed thug asked in a voice loaded with contempt.

'Yes Wayne, this is it,' I said wearily.

'What a load of toss . . .'

'Quite!' I snapped, cutting off the inevitable stream of obscenities. I had had enough of Wayne's aggressive posturing for one day. I was tempted to punch his face. Unfortunately, Wayne, the little darling, was one of twenty similar horrors given in to my charge. I was their instructor, their guide. Punching clients was generally frowned upon. *Anyway,* I thought, watching Wayne strut away from me, *the little bastard would probably beat the tripes out of me.*

Guide! That was a joke. Unpaid slave might be a better descrip- tion. Dragging twenty unwilling teenagers from the rough sides of Manchester and Liverpool up Snowdon every week wasn't my idea of guiding. I was working as a volunteer instructor based at a centre in Llanberis in North Wales. The outfit had a contract to take on children from a series of youth training courses. The idea, as far as I could make out, was to introduce the kids to the great outdoors; make them do exciting things, such as abseiling, raft building, river running and rock climbing. The reality was less idyllic.

Trying to teach a thug like Wayne how to rock-climb and

to persuade him that it was exciting was absurd. He thought ropes were an unnecessary proof of cowardice and real excitement could be found in climbing over twenty-foot-high glass encrusted walls with several video recorders under one arm. Better still would be to drink ten pints of snakebite (lager and cider) and then go on the rampage – as one group was to do in the centre, smashing up the new pool table and games room while we, the less than heroic instructors, cowered nervously in the attic kitchen.

If Wayne was bad, the girls were worse. Attempting to tell them that high heels and tight skirts were no use while climbing Snowdon resulted in howls of screeching outrage. They would compromise and wear wellingtons and mini skirts and stomp morosely up the miner's track, fending off lewd comments and assaults from the likes of Wayne with obscene one liners. All the time they kept up their endless litany of complaints.

'Can we stop, sir . . . how much further . . . I can't go on, sir . . .'

Then at the summit, be it fine weather or foul, came the inevitable 'Is this it?' I must admit to sympathising with them. I have always detested walking and the summit of Snowdon isn't something I have found to be soul stirring. But yes, that was it. That was guiding, apparently.

I had taken Murray's advice but things didn't turn out quite as I had expected. Without any paper qualifications I needed some experience, and working at a centre for a couple of months and then guiding with the organisation in the Alps seemed an ideal way of gaining it. It would look good when I applied to take the stringent series of tests set by the Association of British Mountain Guides for those who wanted to qualify as a guide. Unfortunately Murray hadn't told me about the Waynes, nor had he elaborated on what it was like to live on ten pounds a week as a volunteer. I calculated my average earnings to be ten and a half pence an hour.

It was a good way to start, I was told by Jim Lyons. Everyone should come up the hard way, get some experience, start at the bottom. If I wanted to be a guide, this was the way to do it. So I had thought, until gradually I sensed that maybe I was being used. Now I was growing tired of being patronised.

After a long spring in Wales in the company of Wayne and his chums I set off for the Alps, paying my own way out there, and joined a ten day Alpine Course as an apprentice guide. The fact that I had a fine Alpine record behind me made five pounds a day for guiding three or four clients seem pretty mean.

I was well aware that I was unqualified but then none of our guides at the time held the ABMG guide carnet. John Yates, the director of the courses, was himself in the process of successfully qualifying, but his superb Alpine and Himalayan experience almost made that unnecessary. John was cheerful and easy going and seemed to accept my Alpine credentials as sufficient to guide clients on my own. I was flattered, although I also knew that he had no choice. There was only he and I in Chamonix at the time to run a course for nine clients. I guided four clients along the spectacular Midi-Plan traverse with the frightening exposure of a 3,500-foot fall down the icy North Face of the Midi. Two days before, a father and son had plunged to their deaths down the north side, so I was pleased when I led my clutch through in good order and time. I was later to take clients up the Couloir du Tour, and an American photographer up the Milieu Glacier on the Argentière, which nearly cost me my life. He had been contracted to photograph the area for an American winter holidays company. I tried to teach him the basics of moving together and how to use coils of rope while doing so, but he seemed more interested in his motor wind. At one point, high above the daunting bergschrund at the foot of the face, I was alerted by the buzz of his motor wind and glanced down. He had dropped the coils around his feet and was snapping away at the surrounding mountains as he absently climbed up the icy steps carved in the névé. I screamed abuse at him, more out of fright than annoyance. A fall would certainly have killed us both. How could people be so unimaginative?

After the Midi-Plan traverse Jim Lyons returned from taking a party across the Haute route high level tour between Chamonix and Zermatt. John gave him the low-down on progress and we were both astonished by Jim's sudden outburst on hearing that I was guiding alone. John had suggested that I take the two most competent clients up the 4,000-foot Frendo Spur on the North Face of the Midi, a superb classic Grande course that I had climbed the previous summer. For some reason, Jim objected strongly to this plan, and I found his abrasive manner highly insulting. He kept insisting that I was unqualified, despite John pointing out that we all were. I think it also offended John since it rode roughshod over his authority as director of the course. I thought he was about to walk out on the whole schedule of summer courses, but patiently he stayed on. I had had enough and left. I could tolerate low pay in exchange for experience but I couldn't accept an offensive attitude from someone for whom I had little respect. I don't think we liked one another. As a young and ambitious climber, I resented what I regarded as old men lording it over me and was too quick-tempered to bite my lip and ignore the condescension. As usual, I responded with a knee-jerk reaction and stormed off, convinced I would get nowhere if I stayed on the course.

I had also discovered that I detested guiding. I can now see how useless and intolerant I was with people, just as I have always been unable to relate to children. If I am more patient and less dogmatic now, after some hard lessons learnt, at twenty-three I was quite un- able to understand why some people were so utterly pathetic when climbing.

Guiding seemed to consist of being tied to clients of wildly varying ability on terrain that was easy but unforgiving in the event of an accident. Some of the routes were horrifically dangerous. Roped to three clients on easy névé slopes, I frequently looked at my harness and wondered how to tie a guide's knot – the knot that looks safe but miraculously falls apart when an impact comes on to it. Many were the situations in which I knew with a chilling certainty that if any of the clients tripped over their gaiters and fell it would pull us all straight off the mountain. Hurtling down névé slopes and into deep crevasses tends to be a brief and terminal experience.

It wasn't that I resented the clients. I found the job to be unacceptably dangerous and was unable to comprehend their fear and their lack of ability, and consequently failed to improve their skills. I think that I was too selfish to be a teacher. At times I would stare at a client in difficulty and find myself lost for words, wondering why, if I found it easy, they couldn't do it. I was as baffled by it all as I was by the French shopkeeper who didn't understand a word of my carefully enunciated questions in English.

I teamed up with a Lancashire climber called Ian Whitaker, also known as Bolton because of his almost unintelligible accent. He was a short cheerful young man, with a mop of dark curly hair and a ready smile. After a while, I found I could generally understand him if we were talking face to face, but once we were more than fifty feet apart I couldn't make out a word he was saying.

We had decided to attempt the Bonatti Pillar on the Petit Dru. Walter Bonatti had made the first ascent of this stunning route alone over five days in 1955. I had read Bonatti's account of it in his autobiography, *On the Heights*, in which he speaks of his fear and exhilaration while fighting his way up the 2,000-foot golden granite pillar. It was a legendary mountaineering story, perhaps one of the greatest exploits in the history of Alpinism to rank alongside the first ascents of the north faces of the Eiger and the Grandes Jorasses.

Ian and I decided to climb the south face of the Dru to reach a gap on the Flammes de Pierre, the rock of flames, a jagged, crenellated rock ridge abutting the summit spire. It derived its name from the way in which it blazed with fiery explosions as lightning blasted up its shattered crest. Our plan was to abseil from the gap down 800 feet to the foot of the pillar. At the bottom of the abseil we had to rush across a shadowed and icy couloir. Bonatti first pioneered this approach in a successful attempt to avoid having to climb up the couloir which had a reputation for ferocious avalanches and almost constant rockfalls.

Only after completing two irreversible abseils did we realise that we had taken the wrong line. We should have been descending a series of loose walls and broken chimneys. Instead we found ourselves swinging in space due to the rock walls leaning out from vertical and overhanging. I was alarmed to find myself dangling twelve feet away from the rock. As I neared the ends of the ropes I cursed myself for being so stupid as to forget to tie a knot in them. One rope was longer than the other and I could see that it almost reached a small ledge. There was no alternative but to try to swing into the wall and look for some sort of anchor point.

Burdened by a heavy rucksack, I found the attempt to get up some momentum exhausting. I threw my axe back and forth on its lanyard and, curling my feet around the slack rope, eventually managed to swing close enough to the rock to grab at hollow flake. With no other anchor points, I reluctantly threaded a tape sling behind the flake and gingerly lowered my weight on to it. There was a creaking sound and a hollow thumping echo, but it held. Ian quickly joined me and then abseiled down into the bed of the couloir. It was a frightening place. The huge sunlit pillar of the south-west face towered above us, beckoning us away from the high-walled cold shadows of the couloir.

As Ian crossed the hard black water ice that was crusted with granular snow I heard the first stomach-clenching sounds of rockfall. I screamed a warning to Ian, who was over halfway across the ice, and saw him hunch his shoulders. He began a frantic sideways scuttle towards the shelter of a rock buttress. There was no cover on my side. I decided to keep looking up. If I could see the rocks coming I might be able to avoid them. The air around me exploded with black spinning shrapnel. There was a peculiar knock-knock-knocking sound as well as the familiar thrum and whistle. The stones were all flying far above me, perhaps as much as forty feet up, as they ricocheted from side to side off the walls of the couloir and the pillar. The hollow flake where we had hung half an hour earlier was strafed by a handful of rocks. It was over almost as soon as it had started. Silence crept back, broken only by the muted echoes of the stones cracking their way down the thousands of feet of couloir below me. The air had a charged electric feel to it and there was a smell like cordite and sulphur from the explosive impact of the rocks.

'Are you okay?' Ian shouted.

'What?' I yelled back, not understanding him.

He waved me across and I teetered out across the black marble shine of the ice, tip-tapping my axes and crampons as fast as I could without falling off and feeling the tingle and spinal shudder of hairs rising on the nape of my neck. I shivered with the anticipation of being caught in the open by more enfiladed stone bombardments.

As Ian led up the first pitch on the pillar I spotted a butterfly lying motionless on a patch of snow by my feet. I leant down and touched it gently with my finger. It was dead. This was a harsh and hostile place for a creature of such delicate and exquisite beauty to meet its end. It must have been caught in an upwelling turmoil of heated valley air and spun helplessly up into these high cold regions to die at the first touch of night's black chill. Bonatti wrote of finding a dying butterfly at the start of his solo ascent of the pillar with a poignancy and philosophy typical of his approach to the mountains.

I saw a poor butterfly, lured there by the day's warmth, which fell helplessly to the snow a few feet away from me with a last beat of its wings. Poor living thing, what bad luck you had to find yourself about to die in this cruel world, whose existence you never suspected! In that last beat of its wings I saw before me an almost human drama. Who knows, I thought to myself, with what terror your little eyes watched the last rays of the setting sun, the unexpected metamorphoses of their colours? Who knows with what horror your senses warned you of the fateful bite of the frost, the atrocious certainty of death and, like me, the same infinite regrets? Wretched insect, my brother in misfortune in this place of death, how much I feel for you and with you. Your tragedy is mine too; what I am searching for in the conquest of the Dru is similar to the intoxication which brought you here. The Dru which I was about to challenge was naught else for me than that last ray of sunlight which only a few minutes ago you saw set for ever. If tomorrow I do not succeed in mastering myself, I will share your end.

I could see how climbing was never a death wish for him, more an intoxication with life. I felt ashamed that my butterfly had not moved me at all. Later, high on the intimidatingly Red Walls, I was showered with tiny silver insects – silver fish they were called – which came tumbling down the golden red granite and across my bare arms, making me pull back in fear. Where had they come from? Two Alpine choughs cawed and span acrobatically in the thermals below us, feeding swiftly on the sudden falling bounty. Those that they missed fell softly into the icy couloir below to die of cold.

We climbed fast in glorious sunshine on the slabs, corners and cracks of the rough granite. The Dru is a truly extraordinary pinnacle of rock. It sports an icy north face, one of the six classic Alpine north faces, a phenomenal 3,000-foot west face of slabs, smooth vertical walls and overhangs, the spectacular south-west pillar, and a superb modern mixed route up the north-east couloir between the Petit Dru and the Grand. Few mountains offer such a variety of magnificent lines on them or appear so hypnotically arresting. Crusted with a winter lacework of ice and gilded in the golden pink of Alpen glow, it is one of the most beautiful sights in the Alps.

The Bonatti Pillar rises in a series of steep columns, presenting fissures, overhangs and, here and there, flat-topped pedestal ledges. Slightly off vertical at first, it gradually rears up towards the massive capping overhangs just below the summit. We quickly dispensed with the lower slabs and climbed the diedre known as the Lizard. Bonatti had given it the name because, from the valley, it appears as if a huge green lizard is trying to slither up the Dru. There was little shade from the hot sun on the exposed pillar. By late afternoon we had reached 300 feet on intimidatingly blank granite wall, split by a thin hairline crack that bristled with old pitons. We were tempted to bivouac on a series of terraces and ledges at the top of the walls, but confidence got the better of us and we decided to climb past the huge roofs looming above us and then settle down, knowing that the main difficulties were all below. We knew, if we got that far and the weather be- gan to break up, we could escape from the pillar via an airy traverse to the right towards the spot where the Flammes de Pierre abutted the summit ridge of the mountain.

As darkness began to close around us we found ourselves in forbidding territory, with no sign of any ledges. The dark shadow of the roofs blackened the early night sky above and tendrils of mist began swirling up from the depths, thousands of feet below. I stood uncomfortably on a small stance, dancing from foot to foot, trying to revive the circulation and peering anxiously into the dark shadows of the corner above me. I heard the distant jangle of hardware and shouted up to Ian, asking if he had found a ledge. The reply was as unintelligible as they had been all day. The rope moved up uncertainly and then dribbled slackly down again, a sure sign that the climbing was hard. After what seemed an age I felt the rope tighten and there was a muffled call from above.

The rope tugged three times and I began to follow stiffly, clutching in the darkness at unseen holds and shouting anxiously for Ian to keep a tight hold. After about forty feet the vertical corner seemed to pinch out into a smooth wall. Groping my fingers to the left, they slipped into a reassuringly sharp-edged crack, and with help from Ian I struggled up twenty feet until I saw the dark shadows of his legs hanging in space above me. He was sitting on a narrow ledge about four feet wide and six foot long.

'Well, this looks all right,' I said.

'Yeah. We can just about lie foot to head with a squeeze.'

'It's an odd looking ledge, don't you think?' I asked when I had got my torch out and glanced around me. 'It looks detached to me?'

'It is,' Ian said. 'It's a sort of pedestal on top of that last corner. We used the crack on its left side.'

I shone my torch down between my legs which dangled over the edge. Our ropes hung down in two huge coils that swung gently in the slight breeze. I could just make out the top of the corner appearing through grey spectral streamers of mist. The ropes vanished into the dark chasm below. I clipped myself to a handrail rope that Ian had fixed above the ledge. It had been knotted into an old ring peg and stretched across to the far end of the ledge where he had tied it to a small flake of protruding granite.

'Do you think it's safe?'

'Sure, solid as rock,' Ian said confidently. 'I gave it a good few kicks and it didn't move.'

'Suppose you're right.' I could see nothing suspicious about the pedestal. We had climbed past dozens of them all day.

An hour later, as Ian was preparing to do something smelly off his end of the ledge and I was zipped into my bivouac bag, there was a sickening lurch accompanied by the grinding sound of splintered granite plunging into the abyss. I had my arms outside the bivi bag as I fell and flailed blindly, trying to grab something. The drop must have taken only a fraction of a second but it seemed to last for ever.

I heard a cry of alarm and pain above the roar as tons of granite went thundering down the pillar, echoed and then died to silence. The rope brushed my arms and I clamped them down by my sides as the falling stopped and I bounced on the springy stretch of the rope. The handrail had held and for a confused moment I desperately tried to remember whether I had clipped myself on to it. I was momentarily disorientated. Where was Ian? I remembered that sudden yelp during the fall. Had he gone with it?

'By 'eck!' I heard close by in gruff Lancastrian. I struggled to get out of the tightly squeezed bag. Close beside me Ian's head lolled down on to his shoulder and his torch reflected a sodium yellow light off the surrounding rock walls. There was blood on his neck.

'Are you okay?' I asked

'Banged me 'ead.' He groaned and then lifted his head.

'It's okay,' I said, inspecting his matted hair. 'It's only a small hole.'

It took a while to realise that the whole pedestal had detached itself and dropped straight off the mountain face. There was a good deal of swearing before we became aware of the seriousness of our position. We hung side by side on the tightly stretched V of the handrail rope. Shining our torches down, we were horrified to see the remains of our two ropes, cut to pieces by the falling rocks. All our equipment, including our boots, had gone with the ledge.

We looked at each other and giggled nervously. *No ropes. Two thousand feet up and no ropes!*

The handrail shifted suddenly, causing us both to squeak with fright, hearts hammering at the thought of falling again. I turned and shone my torch on it. There was something wrong. I twisted round, grabbed the rope and hauled myself up towards the ring peg. The rope shifted again and the ring peg moved. I lowered myself gingerly back on to the rope.

'Oh my God,' I whispered.

'What?'

'The peg's knackered. It's coming out.'

'Christ! Where's the gear, let's put something in.'

'It's gone. The hardware, boots everything. We can't do anything.'

Ian was silent. I looked at the flake above him to which the handrail had been tied off. Tiny pebbles trickled from the sheared off base of the flake where it had been attached to the pedestal. We were suspended against a smooth vertical rockwall. There were no handholds or small foot ledges and both attachment points could break at any moment. If either one went we would be hurled into the abyss.

'I think we had better stay very very still.'

'Aye,' Ian muttered, taking a last swig from his water bottle and then flicking it into space. The tinny clangs of the metal bottle rang up from below in decreasing volume. There was nothing we could do.

To attempt to climb up or down would be suicidal. Fifty

feet above us loomed the huge roofs and 200 feet below lay some ledges. We couldn't hope to climb down in our socks and there was too little rope to make an abseil. There was no chance of making the fragile safety line that was keeping us alive more secure.

We hung there for twelve interminable hours. It was an endless night. Fear rose and fell between bouts of hysterical giggling and a hollow dread. It was not long before we were suffering agonising cramps from where our sit harnesses cut deeply into our thighs and waists. Inevitably one of us would shift position to try and relieve the painful pressure, the handrail would shudder, and for a heart-stopping second we would be convinced that we were about to fall into the abyss. We hardly spoke. The tension would not allow it. We silently endured the waiting, unable even to comfort one another. There was no escape from it. If you were standing at the very edge of a high cliff and a friend gave a slight push, then immediately pulled you back, you would gasp with shock and your heart would beat furiously and it would not be very funny. Each time our handrail rope moved we felt this exquisite shock of fear. The wire tightrope transmitted the faintest of movements and our fevered imagination did the rest – Was the peg pulling out? Did I hear the flake move? Like condemned men shackled and strapped, awaiting the drop of the trap, we waited for someone, anyone, to help us.

The helicopter hovered directly in front of us, its rotors edging nearer, we flinching back in fear. The pilot gave us a thumbs-up signal, and then the machine rose effortlessly above our lonely stance. We watched in awe as the tiny figure of a man was lowered on a silk thin wire from the belly of the helicopter. Four more figures followed. They had deposited the rescue team on to the summit two hundred feet above the roofs.

Yves, the last to descend, span crazily on the silver thread of wire. Looking down, he saw his four colleagues crouched over the Troyes winch. The black wrought iron Madonna on the summit of the Petit Dru flashed past his eyes as the wire lowered him towards the four guides. Glancing up at the red belly of the helicopter he noted how thin the wire now looked. Swaged wire cable six millimetres in diameter appears as thin as a silver silk thread when a man hangs from the end of sixty feet of it. Yves pushed from his mind any thought of it snapping. He knew the breaking strain of the wire, he knew it wouldn't snap, but even so it was best not to look at it. The prospect of a 3,500-foot freefall was hard to ignore.

Earlier Yves had relayed instructions from the helicopter as it had hovered mid-way between the guides and the climbers. The two men had looked pathetically small, hanging on the vast walls of the pillar. The pilot had inched the helicopter in towards them until Yves could plainly see the expressions on their taut, hopeful faces. Their arms were outstretched, and one climber was pointing to his feet. Both had socks but no boots, and two short lengths of rope hung below them. He could see where the white core had been exposed by the shearing force of the rockfall. A fresh rock scar began above the climbers and extended to just below where they hung on what appeared to be a fragile handrail.

'I've tried to get them off directly,' the pilot had said through Yves' headphones. 'It's not possible. Those roofs are too close.' He pointed to the huge stepped overhangs fifty feet above where the climbers were hanging, and 250 feet below the summit. 'The winch is the only way.' He turned and grinned at Yves, who glanced back at the roofs.

The fall line of the pillar drew Yves' eyes inexorably downwards. The shadowed couloir lay far below, a thin dirty ribbon of ice snaking between dark rock walls. He spotted the chimneys on the far side where they had worked all morning.

During the night the climbers stranded under the roofs had alerted the rescue team by flashing their torches at the Charpoura Hut, but when the first helicopter had gone to investigate they discovered two more severely injured climbers three-quarters of the way down the abseil descent from the Flammes de Pierre. After a long complicated rescue the two victims, a guide and his client, had been hauled to safety. One was paralysed from the neck down, the other from the waist. They had inadvertently pulled rocks down on to themselves while retrieving their abseil ropes. It had been lucky for them that the two hanging climbers had needed help. In the dark depths of the couloir, with no line of sight to any huts or places of possible help, the two paralysed climbers would never have been able to attract the attention of the rescue teams.

'At least these two are not badly hurt,' Yves said as he dragged his eyes away from the hypnotic sweeping fall of the pillar.

'Still wouldn't like to go down over those overhangs.' The pilot smiled at some private joke as he eased the aircraft into a climbing turn towards the summit and Yves prepared to be lowered down to his colleagues who had already been ferried to the summit.

'Bon chance,' the winchman said, clapping him on the shoulder.

I hope it doesn't come to that, Yves thought as he was lowered beneath the helicopter. Once safely on the summit he moved quickly over to his four colleagues by the Troyes winch. They had sited the winch with care so that the wire would run directly over the overhangs down towards the two stranded climbers. The leader of the team issued a few curt orders, nothing that Yves hadn't already gone over endlessly in his mind. The winch was hand operated. Two guides on each side of it controlled the speed of descent and kept in touch with him by radio. When the time came they would winch him back by turning two handles on each side of the machine.

'Okay. I'm ready. Let's do it,' Yves said standing up and leaning back on the thin wire.

His team mates smiled encouragingly and began to release the brake on the cable. Yves stepped back and over the edge of the first wall below the summit. The cable ground noisily on the edge of the rock, setting Yves' nerves on edge.

Ignore it. It is nothing. It will not snap. I have done this many times. It will not snap. He repeated it like a mantra, vocalising it in his head, pushing the fearful thoughts away, convincing himself. While he descended short broken walls, the true verticality of the pillar did not affect him. He kept glancing up the wire cable and then down below him in an attempt to visualise his position on the face as he had seen it from the helicopter.

'Slow down, slow down.' He spoke calmly into his radio. The reply crackled back in his headset. 'Okay. Approaching the roofs now, wall is steepening, keep it steady.' He found that relaying the instructions back with a non-stop commentary on the geography helped him to forget his fear.

The last smooth vertical slab of granite led him to the lip of the roofs.

'Stop.' He said it too sharply. The abrupt view of the abyss between his legs had made his heart lurch into a sickeningly fast rhythm.

'What's the problem?'

'Uh . . . wait . . . one minute, please?' He tried to gather his thoughts and his courage. The thin streak of the couloir was visible nearly 2,000 feet below. Nothing obstructed his view. *Oh my Lord! And to think I had ambitions to climb this route!* He squeezed his eyes shut and took several deep controlled breaths. Gradually he calmed.

'Okay,' he said quietly, 'let's go again.'

The wire crunched horrifically as he stepped down into space and hung suspended. It grated over the sharp granite edge of the roof. The sound, like that of finger-nails scratching a blackboard, shivered down his spine. He glanced down. Two pale faces stared up at him. 'I see them,' he said into his mike with a note of triumph. 'Bang on line. Keep going slowly.'

He watched the two men carefully. There was blood on the neck of the one without a helmet. The other appeared to be uninjured and was watching him with catlike intensity. Yves saw the ring peg with the handrail attached to it but could not make out the other anchor. He was being lowered in line with the peg. He had already decided to clip it when there was an abrupt shout of alarm.

The uninjured man was shouting something in French but he couldn't understand the words because his companion was yelling in English. Something had alarmed the men but he did not understand what it could be. He continued to descend towards the peg. As his left boot came towards it the uninjured man hit out at his foot.

'Touche pas, touche pas, il est très mal. *MAL!*' he screamed.

Yves glanced at him and realised that only utter terror could produce an expression of such intense ferocity.

'Stop,' he ordered into his radio. The man visibly relaxed, his shoulders slumping.

'It is about to break. There is no strength,' the hanging climber said in poor French, pointing to the ring peg. Yves glanced at the far end of the rope. The shattered flake with the rope looped over it appeared to be on the point of detaching.

'Merde!' he swore in a whisper. So that was why they were so scared. He felt a momentary pang of guilt at the thought of how long they had left these two men hanging on such a fragile thread. The rescue of the paralysed climbers below had taken nearly seven hours. It was at midnight, twelve hours ago, that the alert had come through. He shook his head.

'Qui est blessé?' he asked, despite knowing which was the injured man.

The climber nearest him answered in appalling French. 'Er . . . he is, but it's nothing really. Not bad, just a little hole.' He reverted to English. 'It's nothing to worry about. I'd take me first since I'm nearest, and heaviest.'

The talkative man grinned hopefully at Yves who couldn't help but laugh, admiring the humour under such stress.

'No, I must take your injured friend first. It is a rule.'

He shrugged eloquently.

'Ah . . . A rule, you say, eh? Can't break it then? Just this once . . .'

'No.' Yves laughed as he swung across the wall towards the injured man. 'I would lose my job if the injury turns out to be serious.' He bent forward to examine the man's head. It was a superficial scalp wound.

'You see. It's nothing. Come on, let's toss a coin for it.'

Yves ignored the noisy one as he prepared to clip the injured man to his harness. He spoke quickly into his radio.

'Okay, okay. Listen.' The uninjured man was no longer joking and Yves turned towards him. 'This rope is no good, right? So when you suddenly lift his weight off it I will drop down. I don't know if it will hold the sudden jerk. Do you understand?'

'Yes. I understand. I will move him slowly, softly. Do not worry.'

'That's easy for you to say.' The man muttered and looked pointedly down at the couloir far below. Two choughs wheeled across the thermals, spinning extravagant acrobatics through the air.

'Up. Slow and smooth.' Yves spoke into his radio and at once he heard the harsh crunch of the cable on the overhang, his harness tightened and he began to rise. He braced his feet against the granite and swung the climber awkwardly round so that he hung below his back.

'Return soon,' he called, glancing at the remaining climber. 'Do not worry, my friend. I will come back soon.' Judging by the man's expression, he clearly wasn't convinced. His eyes were wide in a white face, staring fixedly at the ring peg. Alone now, he looked vulnerable and scared, like a child.

Once over the roofs Yves swung across the granite wall above to a small ledge perched above the awesome fall of the west face. He lowered the injured climber on to the ledge and clipped him to two pitons.

'What is your name?' he asked, looking into the man's eyes and checking to see that he was stable. Suddenly he appeared very tired, drained by the abrupt release from his hanging.

'Ian.' He said it quietly.

'Okay, Ian ... ' Yves faltered, trying to remember his English. 'I leave you here. I go for your friend. You are safe, yes?'

'Yes,' Ian said, shaking his head as if trying to clear it of confusing shadows.

'You are safe, okay? Stay here and do not move, understand?'

171

'Yes, okay. I'm not going anywhere.' He smiled at Yves.

'Good, good.' Yves spoke once more into his radio and the cable tightened and swung across the wall. 'Au revoir, Ian.' He called as he went back down over the roofs.

When he returned to the ledge with the second climber they began an animated laughing conversation while Yves called the helicopter. It curved round from the direction of the Grandes Montets with a clattering of rotor blades. The silver cable extended slowly towards him. At first it swung tantalisingly out of reach, forcing Yves to lurch out from the ledge in an attempt to grab it. He caught the shackle on his third attempt. The shackle was a simple and very small snaplink attached to the cable. A metal ring fixed two feet above it allowed a handgrip to prevent toppling over backwards. Turning to Ian, he unclipped him from the pitons, keeping his body between Ian and the drop. Once he had secured the shackle to Ian's harness, he lifted his arm and made a turning motion with his hand. As soon as he felt the cable tighten and begin to lift he twisted round and, with a violent swinging movement, hurled Ian out into space. There was a yelp of fear as the man launched away, riding up, and fast, as the helicopter climbed swiftly clear of the mountain to escape the danger of rocks falling into the rotors.

'Was that necessary?' the remaining climber asked anxiously, staring at Ian spinning crazily above the void, with his woollen mitts still covering his stockinged feet. The climber raised his camera and took a photograph.

'I suppose you were worried that he might panic, which of course I completely understand. And with a head injury you never know of course.' Yves knew what was coming. 'I assure you that I am very calm. Rock solid, I promise you, and there won't be any need for throwing me off the ledge. Just let them lift me off, nice and steady. You know?'

'Yes. Do not worry. I will not push you.'

'I wish you would stop telling me not to worry ... Aaaahh!'

'Salut!' Yves yelled, as he hurled the protesting climber off the ledge and grinned as a stream of obscenities came back to him. He watched, shading his eyes from the sun, as the helicopter rose up far above the summit. *That must be some view*, he chuckled to himself.

After two attempts I abandoned trying to climb up on to the metal ring in the wire. The Nant Blanc glacier spun giddily below my feet. There was a fall of some four thousand feet beneath me. I stared up the wire. *Oh Jeez, it's gonna snap, I know it'll snap*. I shut my eyes and didn't open them until I was sprawled on the floor of the helicopter and staring at an utterly deranged-looking man huddled on a small metal bench. It took a while to realise it was Ian. I scrambled over to the seat, reaching it as the aircraft curved round in a sickening, dropping turn. The centrifugal force seemed to be dragging me towards the open door. I felt Ian's body slide against mine, pushing me closer to the exit. We both grabbed at the seatbelts but in our panic got the wrong ends. In desperation I tied a granny knot in the two buckled tapes and braced myself against a ridge on the floor.

We met Yves two days later. He shook our hands and laughed when we presented two crates of beer to him and the rest of the guides. He said that no one had ever brought them a present after a rescue and seemed genuinely enchanted with the gift. We decided not to tell him that since we were penniless we had employed cunning logic and borrowed it from the local supermarket – disguised as Spaniards, just in case we were caught. It's the thought that counts.

A few days later Ian left for home. He was deeply disturbed by how close we had come to a painful end. I too felt unnerved by the accident.

A fortnight after our ledge had collapsed I witnessed a massive rockfall on the Dru. I had taken a temporary job washing dishes at the Montenvers Hotel, which was perched 6,000 feet above the Mer de Glace had a spectacular view of the West Face of the Dru. I heard a commotion on the balcony and, poking my head out of the window, saw everyone pointing up at huge blocks that were tumbling down from the summit. They were bigger than helicopters, plunging straight into the white snow-filled Niche on the north face and then catapulting out into space again. I shuddered to think of anyone on the mountain, knowing that I would be witnessing their deaths. A dust cloud gradually formed, rising a thousand feet up the face and extending for half a mile on each side. Fortunately only two climbers were caught in the rockfall and miraculously they escaped with only minor injuries. The summit of the Dru had changed shape for ever.

It was one of those massive rock collapses caused more by crystal changes in the granite than by the freeze and thaw action of the elements. It had been a hot dry summer with the freezing level staying at an unusually high altitude. As a result many routes were bombarded with rockfalls.

Not long after the collapse on the Dru a friend of mine, who was guiding a party of clients on their first visit to the Alps, came across the bodies of two climbers who had fallen from high on the rocky spire of La Pouce in the Aiguilles Rouges. It was an unfortunate introduction to the Alps but there was nothing he could do about it. He led the party back to the téléphérique station and alerted the rescue teams. At the station he met two English climbers who were there to photograph mountain rescues. They set off at once for the scene of the accident to record the grisly recovery of the bodies.

That night in the bar one of the photographers, Don Barr, brought us news of the accident. There was a general chorus of protest along with good humoured warnings about insulting the dead and receiving just retribution.

'No worries,' Don said cheerfully, 'I'm off to the Verdon tomorrow. It's too dangerous here. Too much rockfall.' He was right of course. The memory of Simon Horrox's death in a rock avalanche on the Fou the previous summer was all too fresh.

'I'm off to do some nice safe rock climbing on sun-bleached limestone,' Don announced with smug satisfaction.

Not long after this came the terrible news that he had been

struck by lightning and killed while climbing on the huge Verdon cliffs. It was sobering news and it was hard to forget our morbid warnings about dire retribution. Perhaps we shouldn't have joked about it.

Although Ian had gone home vowing never to return, he was back the following summer, cheerful and eager to climb. We teamed up again for another route on the Drus, which wasn't a very sensible choice. Despite climbing fast and free, reaching a point just below the Jammed Block on the American direct line up the west face, Ian was suddenly overwhelmed with a sense of exposure and memories of our accident on the Bonatti Pillar. His self-control abruptly disappeared. Once we had begun a hurried abseil retreat he pulled himself together and coped well. He left for home and his formidable collection of pets, wanting to start breeding deer hounds. I never saw him in the Alps again.

In September, I returned reluctantly and with apprehension to Edinburgh to complete a Masters degree in English Literature. Half-way through the Christmas term I picked up a copy of *High* magazine and read that Rob Uttley was gone, dying alone on his first Himalayan expedition, abandoned because no one could help him in the lonely snow cave, coughing a brilliant life into unconsciousness and a slow cold death from altitude-induced pulmonary oedema. I could scarcely believe it.

They had set out to climb Annapurna III by its 9,000-foot south-east pillar, which was a challenging and seriously remote objective typical of Rob and Jon Tinker, Nick Kekus and Trevor Pilling. But it had gone tragically wrong. Another accident, another life. Trevor had been forced to fight his way down from the snow cave, leaving Rob semi-conscious but incapable of movement. The storm was slowly killing him too and he only just made it to base camp where Jon Tinker and Nick Kekus were preparing a rescue attempt. The weather deteriorated, forcing them back. Early vicious winter weather had hit the mountains and soon the route up to the cave was cut off. In the end they were forced to accept that Rob must have died. For Nick Kekus it was a terrible blow, coming as it did after his tragic experience on Shivling when Richard Cox had died the previous year. Trevor Pilling had done the only thing possible, and had been lucky to survive, yet he was burdened with a sense of guilt for abandoning Rob, despite there being no other choice.

In truth, it was unjustifiable. Sensing this, I preferred to dupe myself. I built up a clever rationale, a pyschological buffer against the possibility of it ever happening to me. If someone had an accident, there was always a reason, and it was inevitably human error. If a climber was killed because he made a mistake, however unwittingly, then I could learn from his error. It wouldn't happen to me like that. The self-deception held up when the victims were strangers. Then it was easy to be callous, and to distance myself from the reality of the death. It was a different story with friends and acquaintances. What mistake had Rob made? I didn't know. He was talented, strong and ambitious. He was so much more accomplished than I. It unnerved me to realise he had gone so swiftly, leaving me with the empty feeling that, if him, why not me?

Something had gone awry in his body. A vestige of a bronchial infection not fully cured, a chemical receptor not firing off the right signals to the brain, trapped fluid slowly waterlogging the lungs. No amount of training could have forestalled being trapped by a storm and gradually succumbing after five days to the insidious fatal grip of pulmonary oedema.

The invisible cumulative effects of high altitude mountain sickness had always spooked me. I could grasp the idea of avalanches, falls, lightning, cold, rockfalls, and so on. They were tangibly obvious. The cause and effect of their occurrence was visible and most often predictable. There was a logic to them. Altitude sickness seemed unpredictable, almost random in the way it struck some and not others.

Early in the following summer season Duncan Elgin fell to his death, and Andy Parkin sustained terrible multiple injuries while guiding clients for Mountain Adventures. There are few people who could have survived such appalling injuries.

Eventually Andy pulled through after emergency operations on his heart, spleen, liver, hip and elbow. Roger Baxter Jones stood in for Andy, guiding his two clients through the rest of their course and donating his fee to a fund set up to help Andy's girlfriend stay close to the hospital in Bern.

I managed to shelve the experience of our collapsing bivouac ledge, pushing it carefully to the back of my mind where it could not ambush me with sudden doubts. Soon after hearing of Andy's accident I climbed Mt Blanc for the first time. I went by the way of the superb Central Pillar of Frêney, a huge candle of perfect granite soaring up the Italian side of the mountain. I also climbed the American direct on the West Face of the Dru, and the hard mixed route of the Dru couloir with Phil Thornhill in a record slow time. I soloed the North Face of the Aiguille Blanche de Peuterey with Simon Yates and then we continued up the magnificent Peuterey ridge. It became an epic crawl since I was suffering from heat-stroke. In a greedy frenzy I tackled three more classic routes before I was ready to move on. I wanted to get away from the hustle and bustle of the Alps where the helicopters buzzed and climbers queued and jostled their way up classic routes. Coming down from the summit of Mt Blanc, following a knee-deep trench punctuated every so often by vomit and faeces and rubbish, made me yearn for something more remote, a place that was higher and more challenging, where there were no rescue teams or helicopters and only your own judgement and ability to save you. After Richard and Rob's deaths in the Himalayas, Simon and I decided that the Peruvian Andes would be our best bet – larger than Alpine- size faces, ease of access to 6,000-metre peaks, lack of bureaucracy and low cost.

Back in Sheffield, where I had decided I would set up home, we consulted Al Rouse about a possible objective in Peru. The unclimbed West Face of Siula Grande seemed to offer the challenge and excitement we were looking for. We set about planning and funding the expedition.

12

THE BRUNSWICK STREET
COCKTAIL RIOT

I WAS LOST AGAIN. The windowscreen wipers swept almost soundlessly across the glass. I looked out through a thin slit of rain smeared window between two huge loud speakers at the back of the Mini. I couldn't see anything. For a moment it was silent as the track on the car stereo ended. I wound down the side window and peered out into the rain. I had stopped in a street of gloomy red-brick, terraced houses. There was a silver wash of light from my headlights on the wet black road. I heard the heavy bass thump of reggae music pulsing out from one of the nearby blues clubs. The lights of a car flashed past the junction ahead of me. I tried to see whether it was John. I had been following him until he had disappeared at the last set of traffic lights.

'He's probably at the party by now,' I muttered as I wiped the rain from my face.

The girl was standing in the doorway of the pub. Light sprayed out from the open door through a curtain of rain. It formed a white iridescent halo around her. I eased the car up against the kerb and leaned out of the window.

'Do you know where Brunswick Street is, love?' I asked, but she didn't seem to hear me. I ducked back into the car to turn the music down and when I looked out again she was standing by the door, leaning down to the open window.

I saw a pale rain-streaked face with a crude bright slash of lipstick. There were goose pimples on her exposed stomach in the gap between her mini skirt and cropped Lycra top. Her thighs were fat, white and streaked with veins. The hem of her skirt had hitched up and I saw a flash of yellow knickers at the junction of her thighs.

'It's ten quid and I don't do oral,' she said.

'What? I . . . er, I just want to know where Brunswick . . .'

'You a talker then?' she sneered.

'No, I . . .'

'Waste of fucking time, you!' She straightened and turned away.

'Up yours, darling,' I yelled, slipping the car into first gear. The music exploded from the speakers as I accelerated away grinning as I saw her giving me the finger.

Eventually I found Brunswick Street in the heart of the Broomhall area of Sheffield. I parked behind John's car and watched the rain spattering across the window. I turned the music off and listened for sounds of a party. The deep reggae beat was louder as I climbed out of the car and locked it.

At the end of the street two girls were illuminated by a street lamp. They wore skimpy tops and short skirts and held their arms tight across their chests, shivering in the wet chill of an early spring evening. I watched them, thinking of the Yorkshire Ripper who had been arrested in these streets. A car eased up to the kerb and there were swift exchanges between girl and driver. She kept her head cocked to one side, alert for the police, as she gave the prices fast and hard. I couldn't see the driver. He was a fleeting dark shadow inside the car. I saw his hand wave briefly in the street light as he haggled over the price. The girl hesitated, looking to her companion for help. She shrugged dismissively. It wasn't her trick.

The girl reached for the door, pulled it open, and slid into the passenger seat. The car pulled away in a wash of headlights. Her friend stepped back into the lamplight, and cupped her hands round a cigarette, protecting it from the rain, and inhaled deeply. She seemed to notice my stare and turned towards me, lifting her chin in a defiant, challenging manner. I walked hurriedly up the dark street, examining the houses for signs of a party. Half the street lights were broken. I kept glancing back nervously. A friend had been mugged twice here in the last ten days and I had just cashed my dole cheque. The street was empty. I passed the underground blues club, selling ganja and Red Stripe lager and pulsing with a deep bass beat.

I recognised the house from the chipped holds on the brickwork of the ginnel. It was the climbing wall. I heard a shriek of laughter and an odd clattering noise mixed with the high-pitched whine of an electric motor. I knew Murray had made a cocktail mixer out of coat hangers and a vacuum cleaner's electric motor. A blast of sound rushed over me as I pushed open the front door. The girl on the corner was talking to the driver of a black taxicab as I stepped inside and shook the rain from my hair.

Both the sitting-room and the kitchen of the house were lined with wall to wall shelves that were bending under the weight of books. Large speakers were propped in the corners and wired to an impressive stereo system stacked amid piles of tapes and records in a doorless shelved side-closet. People were packed densely into the small space. I saw Murray bent over his mixer, vibrating furiously. Large jugs of cocktail mixes were being passed round. Smoke hung in a thick blue smog at chest height, swirling in eddies as people moved about the room.

The party had been in full swing for several hours and the front room throbbed with a heavy bass interrupted by peals of laughter and the occasional thrashing cacophony of the mixer. The cocktails had become more outlandish as the evening progressed, several jugs doing the rounds at any one time. Someone had decided that a fish cocktail, consisting of tinned pilchards and sild beaten into a creamy chocolate-coloured consistency, would be a good idea and that did the rounds as well. The front door was open and anyone was welcome to join the party.

The mixer consisted of an electric motor mounted on three aluminium strips that were bolted to the kitchen worktop. It was connected by dangerous looking wiring to the mains. An ingeniously twisted wire coat hanger had been attached to the working end of the motor to provide the shaking and stirring effect. The idea was to fill a large jug with whatever ingredients of fruit and spirits seemed attractive, place the coat hanger into the jug, flick on the power and then hang on. It worked with violent and alarming efficiency so long as you could hold on to the jug for long enough with one hand to be able to turn the switch off again with the other.

Having just been sandbagged by the fish cocktail, I hurried to the sink to wash out my mouth. Finding an empty glass jug, I began preparing another cocktail from the impressive array of bottles and fruit cartons by the sink. I sliced the last of the oranges with a wickedly sharp vegetable knife and added them to the jug along with a carton of cream. Murray had just finished with the mixer and had turned to offer his latest recipe around the room. I fiddled the jug under the motor and gingerly flicked the switch. The coathanger clattered against the jug, threatening to shatter it into a mess of fruit, alcohol and glass. It seemed to be less a matter of deciding when the cocktail was sufficiently blended and more a case of having to turn off the infernal machine when one's nerve failed.

I was chuckling to myself as the wire threshed to a standstill. The hum of conversation and the piercing wail of a Frank Zappa album rushed into the sudden silence left by the mixer. I turned to face the centre of the room. Simon Yates was sitting on a sofa between my girlfriend, Jacky Burley, and Sean Smith. The three of them were laughing. Around the room there were animated, arm waving, gesticulating groups. Large jugs passed swiftly from hand to hand. Through a blue layer of pungent smoke I saw Murray go out to the hallway with an impish grin on his face. I turned back to the mixer and released the jug from the coat hanger. As I was about to wipe the spilt cocktail from beneath the mixer an angry voice hissed close by me.

'Hey guy, you messed my jacket, huh? You got that shit on my jacket.'

I turned to see a short moon-faced West Indian wearing a loud checked, broad shouldered jacket. He stood square on to me, legs apart and chest thrust forward aggressively. At a guess, he was about five feet high and I had to look down at him, which was an odd sensation for someone who was used to being the small guy.

'What?' I said, confused by the noise and babble around me. I was trapped in the corner of the room, pressed against the bottle-covered work top. I hadn't seen the man before.

'My jacket, man.' He grabbed my arm with his left hand and held the jacket open with his right. 'You sprayed that crap on my jacket.' He pointed to the jug in my hand.

I looked stupidly at the jug and then at his jacket, trying to sober up. The man seemed very agitated. There was something frightening about his posture. He held himself tight, as if anticipating a sudden move. There was a menacing vibrating tension in his body that I recognised immediately despite my drunken state. He was trouble.

'Look, I'm sorry mate. I didn't see you there. It was an accident, okay? I mean, look at that machine. It's been spraying all night . . .'

'Shut it, eh! Just shut it. What you going to do about my jacket, hey? You tell me, heh? I ain't paying for no dry-cleaning. You are, man.'

I would have laughed if it were not for the look in his eyes. They scared me silent. His face was remarkably childlike and soft and his teeth were perfect, brilliant, white and even. His stare was ferocious, totally at odds with the rest of his face. I seemed to be looking into madness. I glanced away, breaking eye contact. Behind him I could see the party going on. Smoke drifted and swirled as people moved round the room. The music blared. No one had seen the altercation. A tall emaciated black man and an evil-looking weasel-faced white man were standing near the door. Both held personal stereos and were staring at my antagonist's back. I began to sober up. We were being rolled. The small man in front of me pulled my left arm to- wards him, tugging my body round and in close to him.

'I want money for my jacket and now, okay?' He said it in a menacingly quiet but oddly high-pitched voice.

'Look, I'm sorry. It was an accident. I haven't got any money. I'm . . .'

I didn't finish the lie denying the cash in my back pocket. The knife was suddenly there. It sprung into his right hand from nowhere. He didn't reach into his pocket or move his hand but suddenly it was there, pointing at my stomach, and I was instantly sober, instantly cold at the thought of the blade.

It was a thin blade, concave-sided, without a point. It mesmerised me. He moved it with slight nervous jerks. Light flickered off the shiny metal, and as he turned his wrist I realised with a sickening dread that it was a razor, the old style cut-throat razor. He was talking to me but I couldn't hear him. I stared at the razor.

'Hey,' he hissed and pulled me towards him. I resisted and sucked my torso back away from the blade. Suddenly I was talking, babbling at him, talking fast trying to give him the blarney, desperate to get away from the knife even if only by talking it out of my mind. I stared into his eyes as I talked, hoping he would recognise my sincerity. *No money, I'm sorry, no money, there's no need for this, sorry, try someone else . . . please . . .*

He pushed me back with his free hand, swopped the razor to it and reached across the worktop. He moved with astonishing speed. I had transferred my attention to his left hand only to find his right hand swinging into view with the vegetable knife in a stabbing grip aimed at my solar plexus. The razor came up towards my face, weaving slightly. I pulled my face away and sucked in my stomach. I could see the party going on behind his back. I was being mugged, maybe stabbed and razored, and no one would notice until it was too late. I stared back at him and he held my eyes in his glittery, liquid, obsidian stare. I wanted to plead, wanted to cry even, just so long as he would go. The brilliant gleam of the razor and the dull used blade of the vegetable knife enthralled me. I could feel them sliding in. It made my stomach cold and empty. I waited for the movement of either arm, anticipating the stab or a scything slash across the face. I knew what the razor would do to my face or my throat. Did he know he could kill me by mistake? Had he thought of that?

I remembered a black and white film I had once seen in

which a razor cut across an eyeball and the gel burst out, looking like a full moon sliced across by a streamer of cloud. It was a Man Ray film, I thought, and then wondered why I was thinking such things. The blades waved in the party light as the man stared me down with manic, angry eyes and here I was thinking of surrealism and Man Ray.

His left arm, the razor arm, jerked forward and I threw my head and neck backwards with terrified force. The cut never came. In the same motion he had spun round and taken two strides towards Nick, who was talking to a couple of friends, oblivious to what had been happening. I saw the man threaten Nick, saw the two by the door push violently at someone and rush out into the hall. People suddenly sensed there was something wrong. I could see their confusion as they looked to the knifeman, then to the doorway.

The knifeman had his back to me. He was within reach of a swinging arm and I stood beside a work surface littered with full, empty and half-empty bottles. I reached towards a full bottle of vodka. My hand hesitated, moved towards an empty tequila bottle and then stopped, resting open-palmed and powerless on the wet surface. I couldn't do it. I didn't know whether a full bottle might kill him, and if an empty bottle didn't knock him out it would infuriate him and he would turn, slicing and cutting and hurting me. It was no use. I had never been good at fighting. What little I had done had always been in self-defence. I lacked that hardness, the vicious killer instinct, that made a fighter win. Don't imagine the consequences, don't care or even think about them, only be hard and fast and ferocious. I couldn't be like that. Instead I stood helplessly and watched the little man terrorise Nick. I felt relieved, almost glad, that it was Nick who would get stabbed and not me. *Thank God he's left me . . .*

I watched him turn swiftly away. There was no blood on Nick as the man bolted for the door, stuffing Nick's dole money into his loud and tasteless jacket. I sagged back into my corner. Someone came up to me and asked what had happened. Nick was talking loudly, his face unnaturally pale. I wondered what I looked like. The music continued to blare and the smoke eddied around a room full of startled and dazed people. I reached for a cigarette and lit it, feeling weak and giddy as the smoke sucked into my chest. I held it down, exhaled slowly, shook my head like a drying dog, and began to giggle.

There was a loud crash outside the house. The music stopped. Someone shouted in panic, the sound muted and distant. I made for the door, crossing the room to the right of the window which overlooked the street. There was a sharp crash and a white spray of glass fragments burst into the room, back-lit by the sodium yellow flare of the street lights. A brick flew past my shoulder and crashed into the wall. In a small room crowded with people neither the glass nor the brick had touched anyone. For a moment everyone froze and then, as if galvanised by a collective signal, they lunged for the safety of the side walls.

All except Nick who, to a chorus of anxious and distressed cries of alarm, stood on a chair and carefully inserted his head through the jagged splintered hole in the window pane. The hairs on my neck shivered as I watched the vicious slivers of glass touching his throat and the nape of his neck. He started yelling obscenities at our attackers in the street who, to no one's great surprise, began hurling more bricks at the window. I could hear them thumping into the brickwork by the window frame. Nick continued to scream despite our pleas for him to take cover. We couldn't drag him away without risk of lacerating his face on the broken glass.

Abruptly he ducked his head back into the room and stepped down.

'They've just stabbed Keith and Murray's unconscious.' He said it in a blunt disbelieving voice.

'Get the police! Where's the phone?' Someone moved towards the phone.

'My Walkman's gone,' a voice complained.

'My purse . . .'

'What about Murray?' Neil Milne said forcefully.

'My purse has gone . . .'

'Come on, we've got to help them,' Neil insisted. 'We've got to get them inside.'

185

He pulled at my arm and I followed him into the hall and down the stairs. Someone had bolted the door shut. The glass fanlight was shattered across the stairs. A stone lay on the mat. There was the sharp crack of something hitting the door. I looked fearfully at Neil. He had an uncharacteristically determined and angry expression.

'Are you ready?' he said, opening the door without waiting for my answer which was going to be an emphatic 'no'. He ran into the lighted street. I followed instinctively.

Murray sat slumped on his haunches. He was looking at us as we came through the door, his eyes dull and unfocused. There was blood on the side of his head. He seemed to be talking to himself. We moved quickly towards him. There was a shout and, glancing up, I saw the moon-faced knifeman standing in front of Neil. I was on the point of shouting a warning about the knives when the man's arm shot out with startling speed. His fist cracked the side of Neil's jaw in three rapid punches that he never saw coming. His head sprang back on his neck in three jerks.

Neil went down. Ahead of him I saw Keith, Sean Smith's brother, slumped in the low hedge fronting the road. The weasel-faced man ran across the street and swung a vicious kick into his chest, pushing him deeper into the hedge. I felt a stunning blow on the side of my head and a half brick dropped on to the ground. Dazed, I sank to one knee as someone ran at me, kicking. I tried to put up my arms to protect myself but succeeded only in tripping my adversary, who knocked me on to my back. He was on me at once, punching and kicking, forcing me to squirm on the ground as I tried to avoid the blows. I knew I had to get to my feet but couldn't. I curled into a protective foetal position and waited for it to stop. Suddenly the memory of the knife sprang into my mind and it seemed to catapult me into action. I threw an arm out, hitting something, and twisted up on to my knees. Neil staggered past me towards the door. I lurched after him, feeling a rock crack painfully into my temple.

For an endless moment we beat against the door, screaming to be let in, and nothing happened. I was about to start

17, 18 *(above)* Fear shows in their eyes after Ian and Joe had hung for twelve hours over the abyss. (Photos: themselves)

19 Yves Sandoma rescuing Ian from the rope. (Photo: Simpson)

20 Ian and Yves being winched over the Bonatti roofs. (Photo: Simpson)

21, 22 Ian suspended above Mt Blanc by a silver thread, with 3,500 feet of open space beneath him. (Photos: Simpson)

23 *(left)* Photograph of the Bonatti Pillar taken by Stephen Reid from the summit of La Petite Aiguille Verte on 23rd July 1983 and given to Joe Simpson nine years later. The timing indicates that the dot suspended beneath the helicopter is undoubtedly Joe, the second to be rescued.

24 *(above)* Making the ascent of Sinla Grande in Peru, 1985. (Photo: Simon Yates)

25 The agonising mule ride in Peru. (Photo: Yates)

26 *(left)* The truck ride to Lima. (Photo: Yates)

27 *(below)* Filming a reconstruction of the rope cutting for American television. (Photo: John Stevenson)

28 Simon Yates, who cut the rope. (Photo: John Muir)

29 *(below)* Joe and Simon re-enact the rope cutting for television. (Photo: Stevenson)

30 The Silk Road team – Steve Ralph, John Stevenson, Joe Simpson and Tom Richardson. (Photo: Simpson)

31 *(left)* Glorious Leader, Richard Haszko. (Photo: Simpson)

32 The Topopdam team, Arabian style.

giggling again. *What the hell is going on? This is madness. The two smallest men in the house and we decide to come out here and now we can't get back!* The nervous giggles were catching in my throat when the door opened a fraction and reaching arms dragged us roughly inside. Rocks clattered against the woodwork. The hallway was a scrum of people.

'What's going on?'

'Don't know. I was too busy being hit.' I replied.

'Sean's out there.'

'What?'

'Sean went out when we dragged you in. He saw what was happening to Keith.'

'Oh Christ! Has anyone called the cops?'

'Yeah. Ages ago.'

'Where the fuck are they, then?' Neil shouted as we all ducked away from a brick coming through the shattered fanlight.

'Look, we've got to get them inside,' Neil said. He hadn't lost his look of stubborn determination. I edged away from him, uncertain whether he planned to drag me outside for another futile beating.

'Murray looks really bad,' he went on, staring at me for con- firmation. I nodded mutely. 'And they were kicking the shit out of Keith. He could be killed.'

'We need more people, bigger people,' I added, hopeful for some volunteers. There was another rocky thump on the door as Mark Millar pushed his way down the stairs.

'Come on. Let's do it.'

He pulled open the door and ran in a crouch towards Murray. For some utterly inexplicable reason, Neil and I followed him. I heard the door shut behind us. Mark had grabbed the discarded lid of the dustbin and held it above Murray's head like a clansman's shield as he dragged the semi-unconscious man towards the door. I hesitated for a moment, feeling scared and vulnerable, as Mark passed by.

'Back to square one,' I muttered as I followed Neil towards Sean who was leaning out over the hedge with his arms protecting Keith's chest and his head bowed over shielding his brother's face. The moon-faced man directed a karate-style kick which thudded into Sean's shoulder. Keith appeared to be unconscious. The weasel-faced man began another run at the helpless pair and then stopped. Moon-face shouted something and waved his hand urgently. The three of them turned and ran off in the direction of the dual carriageway and the city centre. There was a distant wail of sirens.

As quickly as it had started it was over. The street was shockingly silent. I looked at Neil, who started laughing. I swore. Sean got slowly and unsteadily to his feet with a dazed expression on his face, as if surprised to find himself released from the maelstrom. Keith looked up from his perch in the hedge and smiled wanly. He held out his hand. It was daubed with dark congealing blood from the stab wound in the ball of his thumb. He had protected his stomach from the knife with his right hand.

Murray swayed unsteadily at the foot of the stairs. He kept muttering unintelligibly. There was a streak of blood near his ear. I couldn't tell whether he had or had not been wounded. Rachel talked to him softly but he didn't understand. His skull had been fractured. As Murray had stepped out of the door one of the raiders had struck him across the temple with a tree branch as thick as a baseball bat. Keith said he was being friendly in a typically Murray manner. He hadn't seen the knives or the thefts in the room, only the angry threesome charging down the stairs as he came out of the lavatory. Murray had run after them to assure them they were welcome, it was an open party, and any problems could be sorted out. They had struck him down and stabbed Keith as he came to Murray's aid.

Murray mumbled as the ambulance man loaded him on to the stretcher. Keith followed him into the back of the vehicle, clutching his hand protectively to his chest. As they left, lights flashing, we turned to look at the devastation while the remaining party-goers walked hurriedly away. They didn't want to be around when the police arrived.

We sat in the back of the police van and cruised the area. The two officers slowed whenever we approached a black man on the streets and we stared at them. There was no sign of our attackers. From our description, the police said they thought the moon-faced man was responsible for at least two razor attacks outside local blues clubs. The victims had been left severely injured with disfiguring facial scars.

That night shattered my illusions. When we talked about it afterwards, people said we probably shouldn't blame the attackers. They would be socially disadvantaged, unemployed, black, from broken homes, needing help and sympathy. Neil and I stared at them dumbly, until Neil cracked and shouted,

'Don't be so fucking stupid! They don't need help. It's Murray and Keith who need help. Where do you get these dumb ideas? Those guys are bastards. I don't give a toss about how bad a time they've had, it can't excuse them. Black, white, unemployed, whatever, it doesn't take away the fact that they're mindless, violent, thieving, vicious bastards.'

'And the rest,' I added, glancing at Neil whose grossly swollen jaw made his outburst sound strangely distorted. He was right of course. They were bastards, and I hated them bitterly for making me so scared, so helpless and weak, unable to hurt them in return because I had some concept of pain and injury and couldn't bring myself to inflict it on others. In a house full of climbers, with an arsenal of ice axes and hammers hanging in the hall, none of us had thought to arm ourselves. Partly because we didn't know how to fight but mostly because we were too frightened of the possible consequences. We didn't have the blighted zero mentality of the thugs who had attacked us. If they ever killed someone, and I wouldn't be surprised to learn that they did, it would be an accident; the mindless kick to the temple which caused unconsciousness and brain haemorrhage, or a burst and bleeding spleen. They would never stop to imagine the effect of their blows.

After the riot I never felt comfortable in the Broomhall area. It was silly really. Nothing had changed. We had tangled with a group of evil men. It could have happened anywhere. Nothing had changed externally, internally everything was in turmoil. I felt threatened by black men as I had never felt before. I distrusted them for no reason other than the fear that small moon-faced man had induced, and I hated him for it, for making me feel racist when I knew that I wasn't, for poisoning me.

Two years later he appeared in the dole office while I was queueing to sign on. I recognised him at once and glanced away when his eyes met mine. My heart began hammering in my chest and the fear returned. *Had he recognised me?* I risked another look. He had turned away from me. There was no doubt that it was him, and as I examined his broad shoulders the fear changed to anger. I remembered Murray's dull pain-filled eyes as he recovered from the head injury in the curtained darkness of his room. *This bastard needed punishing.* Although hateful and bitter, I hesitated. I wanted to leave the queue and get to the nearest phone, to call the police and wait for them to appear. I wanted to point him out and get him charged. I wanted him banged up, beaten, scared, all the things he had done to us, but I couldn't do it. What if the charges didn't stick, if nothing could be proved, what then? He would know my name then, and my face, and he would come for me. So I signed on and walked away, impotent and feeble, and even angrier than before.

The party had been a farewell bash for Simon and me. A week later we left for Heathrow and the long flight to Peru, heading for the sun-drenched southern hemisphere and a world of fairy-tale mountains sculpted in flutings and pillars of gossamer powder snow. We left a bleak cloud-wrapped Sheffield filled with buoyant excitement, flying south across the north Atlantic past Cuba and the West Indies to swing in over a moonlit oily-calm sea and land, smooth and gentle, at Caracas. By then all memory of the riot had gone. All connections with home were severed, as if we had stepped into a time capsule.

Flying on south, down the spine of Latin America, with the Pacific Ocean suddenly gleaming blue to starboard as the mountains came into view and cut off the vast Amazon rain forest from the thin strip of desert running down the coast,

Simon was convinced that he could see Siula Grande, the mountain we had come to climb, and pointed it out to me. I wasn't sure whether it was the the Cordillera Huayhuash or the Blanca, but Simon was adamant. It wasn't important to me. We were there. We had arrived at a stepping stone to the greater ranges. The Karakoram and the Himalayas would be next. Nepal, India, Pakistan, the Canadian Rockies, Alaska, Africa — they all beckoned now that we had made the first step. No longer would I read of other people's expeditions and hope wistfully that someone would invite me along. I knew that the only way to go was to do it yourself.

'Why not the Huayhuash?' Al Rouse had suggested the previous winter. 'Try the west face of Siula Grande. It's unclimbed, and hard. You'll like it.' He had said with it with a conspiratorial grin, so we went, travelling on a shoestring, full of confidence and naive excitement, convinced we could succeed where at least four other expeditions had failed. We had served our apprenticeship in the Alps. We were good climbers. It was time we expanded our horizons.

Four weeks after saying goodbye to Murray in his darkened room I found myself in the gloomy depths of a crevasse with no apparent means of escape, staring at a cut rope and realising that Simon was either dead or had given me up for dead.

Two days earlier we had succeeded in climbing the west face of Siula Grande but as we descended the desperately unstable north ridge I had fallen off a small ice cliff and badly fractured my right knee. In the freezing chaos of a storm Simon had lowered me thousands of feet down the mountain until he was forced into the terrible decision to cut the rope that joined us in an effort to save himself from being pulled to his death from his collapsing snow seat. I had plunged one hundred feet into a crevasse at the foot of an overhanging ice cliff. Gradually, I came to accept that either Simon was dead, or that he had left believing the fall had killed me.

I was utterly alone, abandoned to a fate I couldn't accept,

crying in the cold darkness of an implacable, icy tomb. With a shattered leg, there was no way out by climbing up. I had tried and failed. There seemed to be no escape either by lowering myself deeper into the crevasse on the remaining 150 foot of rope. When the hysterical tears and screams for help had finally been exhausted I sat still and strangely calm on the narrow ice ledge on to which I had fallen after the rope had been cut. I was exhausted, hungry and very thirsty. Yet in the shelter of the crevasse I knew that it would take many days to die. Four, maybe five days of lingering agony, being driven insane, before dying alone.

To this day I cannot understand why I was so convinced that Simon had died or left me for dead. If there had been the slightest doubt, I would never have had the strength to abseil off that ice ledge. I would still be there, frozen in an icy tomb, preserved as long as the glacier existed. Instead I left my last remaining prussik loop on the ledge and deliberately did not tie a knot in the end of the rope. I knew that, with my frozen hands, there was no possibility of regaining the security of the ledge if there was nothing but emptiness at the end of the rope. I didn't have the courage to stay on the ledge and wait to die, alone, maddened by pain and fear and loneliness, and I was too scared to throw myself off, unroped, to a mercifully quick death.

I try not to think of that time now. The decision was taken in a state of madness. I had lost touch with life, with any sense of it, for a few terrible hours in that crevasse. Now there is just a void in my mind, a place where some memories have been locked away so that I can never recall them fully. I remember parts of it with startling clarity but I can never quite remember exactly how I felt, how empty and desiccated I became, with a mind split between extremes of deranged insanity and cold rationality, my body shrinking visibly.

After it was over, after Simon had dragged me sobbing from a snowswept darkness into a candlelit tent, I tried to pretend it hadn't really happened. It worked for a short time. The agony of the mule ride to the road head and the truck drive to hospital in Lima diverted my mind from unbearable memories.

In the hospital it came back in flashes. During the warm bright sunny days I dozed between morphine injections and looked around my small ward with wonder at the sudden luxury. I watched a man slowly die beside me and joked with another patient about his chances. I never saw him. They kept his bed concealed behind curtains but we could see the two glass bottles filling with the poison that was killing him.

I spent time writing down the details of my survival on the mountain, writing a dispassionate chronicle of events with shaky frost- numbed fingers. When I was tired, or the drugs made me smile helplessly on my pillow, I would stare at the curtained bed and watch the drips of pus filling the bottle. A woman sat by the bed for three days and nights. She rarely moved. Once I saw her reach forward past the curtain. I realised she was holding his hand and looked away.

At night it was different. At night the nightmares came and the morphine made me sweaty and feverish. I dreamed of the hours alone in the crevasse and woke crying like a child. Each time I jerked awake I would see the curtained bed lit by the soft yellow glow of a night light and the woman sitting there motionless. She knew he was dying. You could tell that she was waiting for it. She had already accepted her loss. I watched quietly like a voyeur. I wish I could have seen the man, watched him die. I knew where he was.

Slipping back into sleep, I saw the stars wheeling above me as I lay in a rocky cleft. The sense that I would lie there for ever came over me again and I struggled to wake from the dream. The star-spread blackness seemed to press down on me, pushing me relentlessly into the ground, and I felt as if I had died. I fancied myself lying on the moraines for centuries staring blindly at the star-spread vista above my corpse. I knew I was dying but it was not such a bad thing. There was nothing to be done about it. A voice told me I was too late and part of me agreed. It hadn't been so bad . . .

I felt a hand on my forearm shaking me and came slowly awake to see the nurse smiling as she injected antibiotics into the drip in my arm. I looked past her at the curtained man and wondered whether he was dreaming of a star-spread blackness and feeling the heaviness of his life seeping down into the earth.

The dreams stopped on my return to England, or maybe I simply stopped remembering them. They had been in colour and were experienced with such intensity and vividness that I couldn't separate them from reality. Perhaps it was the morphine.

PART TWO

13

DOWN AND OUT

HE WASN'T MUCH of a drug dealer – short, like all
Peruvians I had met, and stocky, with slick oiled black hair
and bright glistening eyes. His teeth were very white and he
smiled a lot. His smile was his strength. It made him seem
honest and trustworthy. I wanted to talk to him as soon as he
approached our table. Simon looked up and smiled at him
and showed him the empty chair near the stool which
propped up my plastered leg. My toes were a livid dark
purple colour and protruded from the white plaster in five
swollen tubers. I couldn't make out any creases at the joints.
They looked like purple gherkins. When I wiggled the toes
they moved together, as one. I stopped wiggling and
examined the drug dealer. We didn't know then that he was a
drug dealer, but because we were bored we would have talked
to him anyway.

I had been released from the Clinico Americano hospital
six days before. The pain had gone by then and the doctors
had grown tired of Simon fetching me in the afternoons and
wheeling me out into the bright sun and feeding me beers in a
nearby bar.

In the hospital I could still get morphine when I wanted it. I
would press the buzzer and one of the student nurses would
come and inject my thigh. It made me feel sticky and feverish
but it helped me to sleep. I could have used the pills we had
but they made me dream. Temazepam produces glorious
vivid dreams in colour but my dreams were of crevasses and
crying out in the night. The nurses would wake me and the

197

other patients complained loudly in Spanish. So, after beers in the afternoon, Simon would take me back to the private ward where the other men lay waiting for the nurses to bring round the evening meals. The three middle-aged men had problems with their stomachs and intestines and ate thin soups and light snacks while casting envious glances at my double rations of steak or roast chicken.

There had been a fourth man, but he never ate. He came in unconscious with blood septicemia and his bed was always shrouded with drawn curtains. I assumed the woman who sat with him day and night to be his wife, or his lover – we didn't talk to her. We saw only the big glass bottles, like cider flagons, under his bed. Each morning we checked the contents; one held thick oily saffron pus and the other an ominously dark and mottled-looking blood. The fat man opposite – all yellowed teeth and sweaty scalp – would smile sadly and shout over to me in the morning.

'Hoy! Gringo! Como eres tu? Mecor, dolores . . .'

'Yeah, a little pain; better . . . a poco mas,' I would reply, and we would both glance at the bottles and the curtained bed.

'Si, si,' he would say quietly, nodding his head politely to the woman who smiled a wan, ashen face at him. She had been there all night, motionless on her chair, legs crossed demurely at the ankles, hands clasped limply on her lap, sitting quiet and sad-eyed like a shadowy ghost on the edge of my morphine consciousness. Every morning this cheerful, fat hernia patient would extend his hands, palms up, and weigh them up and down, as if indicating the change in levels of blood and pus, and he'd take on a serious face and slowly shake his head. He always did it when she wasn't looking, this silent mime with his hands, telling me the life expectancy of someone behind a curtained bed whom I had never seen. After three days I awoke to find the bed empty, the curtains gone and the mattress bare. The fat man nodded his head and drew his finger across his throat in an obvious gesture. He had died in the night when the morphine had me, and I hadn't noticed them taking him away. I wondered whether his wife had cried. I doubted it; she didn't look the type to make a fuss in public.

They took the drip from my arm two days after the operation and for a week injected me with antibiotics – and morphine if I wanted it. I remember waking from the operation with my memory gone. My head lay heavily on the pillow as if there were a large rock pressing it down. On my back, my face to the ceiling, I saw the fan swinging lazily and the big glass drip bottle hanging on its stand. Then the pain flooded up my leg and I gasped and began to pant quickly, sucking in abrupt frightened lungfuls of air as the agony built and built and I waited for it to level out and stop. But it didn't stop. It kept growing worse and worse. Far sharper and hotter than on any of those endless days I had spent crawling and falling on the glacier. I must have groaned because I heard one of the men ask me something that I didn't understand. He spoke Spanish, and my tongue was thick and dry from the anaesthetic. My breath smelt of the sweet gas and I couldn't form words in English, let alone in Spanish.

I recall searching for the buzzer but they hadn't replaced it on the bed and I couldn't lift my head from the pillow because something was pressing it down. I lifted my left arm and my hand swung into view, trailing plastic pipes with a hard transparent tube threaded into a vein on the back of my hand. There were various extra plugs – for injecting other substances – protruding from the pipework so that the whole contraption looked like a see-through cap on an oil well when I held it close to my face and squinted at it. Reaching above and behind me, I tried to find the electric cable with the buzzer on it. The pain was getting worse. It seemed that there was acid or molten metal spilling across the inner thigh of my right leg. It felt solid and immovable. I could see where the white sheet rose up in a tunnel over my leg. They must have put some basket over it to protect me from the weight of the bedclothes. I couldn't see my foot, or feel it. I wondered for a moment whether they had amputated the leg. I knew only a few words of Spanish and I hadn't been certain of what it was the doctor wanted to do when he had shown me the X-rays and explained the operation. He could have made a mistake. I remembered trying to resist the anaesthetic and being pushed back by the nurse with the green face mask. The pain kept flooding up into my groin. *What had they done? What the hell could they have done?*

I cried out, more a scream than the word 'nurse', and the man opposite said something. The buzzer was nowhere to be seen. I shouted again, and tried to raise myself on to my elbows, but this pulled my leg up the bed and dragged at the bandages, making the pain flare. There was a busy clatter of heels and the door swung open.

'Que es tas?'

A young nurse looked quickly round the small ward, seeking the source of the shouting. The man opposite said something and she walked over to me.

'What is the matter?' she said, smiling and touching my forearm gently. I asked in English for a pain killer. She didn't understand me. Her brow crinkled and her smiling eyes clouded in confusion.

'Pain. I am in bad pain.' I said it slowly, as if talking to a child. I heard the words come out, slurred by the anaesthetic, and closed my eyes, feeling heavy and sleepy. Her cool hand pressed my arm again and I heard her heels on the floor.

'No,' I said as I opened my eyes to see her by the door. 'No, I need something now. Please . . . por favore.'

The door swung shut and I groaned.

I think I might have slept a little, but I'm not sure. Suddenly I found myself surrounded by three nurses. They smiled expectantly at me while the pain stabbed at me. I must have called out again. I asked for a pain killer, for morphine, and they looked at each other blankly and then giggled. Angrily I pointed to my arm to indicate an injection and said 'dolores, dolores', which I thought was 'pain, pain' in Spanish. The pipes hung down from the oil well cap in my left hand, and there was a sudden bright understanding in the faces of the three girls and laughter as they held my hand and removed the pipes. I lay back relieved that they were going to get rid of the pain that was beginning to make me cry. I turned my face away while they fiddled with my hand.

The sharp stabbing pain in my hand made me look round. One nurse had replaced the thick needle at the end of the pipe work into another vein. She taped it down with white zinc tape and smiled beautifully at me. They hadn't given me anything. They thought the pipes had been painful so they had replaced them.

'No, no,' I said loudly, trying to sit up. One of them pushed me back into the pillows. 'No, it's the pain in my leg ... mucho dolores.'

They replaced the drip twice more into my left arm and I swam in and out of lucidity, fighting the anaesthetic and the pain. When they tried to put the drip back into my right hand I lost my temper and screamed as loudly as I could.

'PAIN!'

Swinging my left arm out hard, I knocked the drip stand over. It was a heavy metal stand with a litre glass bottle hanging from its hook, and it toppled over to the side. I saw my neighbouring patient throw his arm out to protect himself as it fell towards his fat, round, recently-stitched stomach. A nurse caught the bottle and the stand before they hit him and struggled to put it back upright as the other two shouted at me. But I was gone then, I didn't care, and I shouted back, angry and violent and full of pain and frustration, until they hurried away.

I kept shouting and swearing, loud and obscene, despite the fat old man opposite who kept saying 'Calme, calme ...' in a soft musical voice and wafting his hands, palms down, in a gentle conciliatory manner. I was still yelling when the door burst open and one of the nurses hurried towards me, looking determined and scared. I think I was telling the old man to fuck off when the needle went into my buttock and a sluggish warm feeling crawled up my back. The pain was still there for a while but its fire was dying, and with the injection and the anaesthetic my eyes closed and I slept with an obscenity on my lips.

After four sweaty humid nights, full of strange dreams and sudden wakenings, convinced I was still in the crevasse, the pain eased to a mild throb. I kept asking for the injections now that the nurses understood what I meant, but I became the model patient. The morphine helped me to pass the time and made me forget.

One day a woman came to visit me. She was the Vice Consul from the British Embassy, and she spoke with a delightfully posh voice, all cucumber sandwiches and colonial tea parties, assuring me that there was no longer a problem with my insurance. She asked me what had happened. When I finished telling her about the rope being cut, and the crawling, and the reunion, she clapped her hands with joy at the wonder of it all. She said how amazing it all was, and how pleased she was to have met me, because of all the nine mountaineering accidents with which she had been involved, mine was the only one with survivors.

'Most of them just disappeared. Sometimes I had to deal with a body or two, but really you are the first live climber I've met. Isn't that jolly?' She said it with girlish excitement and swept out of the room, all floral skirts and loud commanding voice bidding farewell.

Yes, how jolly, I thought as the nurse slid another needle of smile juice into my buttock and Simon came in with a grin and a bunch of bananas. I had a permanent grin on my face for the week until, on the twelfth day, they said I should leave. Simon came and helped me to wobble down the stairs on crutches and out into the blinding sunlight and the hot interior of a dilapidated Volkswagen beetle taxi.

The airline had said it would try to get us on an early flight home, but that meant a wait of at least two weeks. I moved into the cheap run down hotel off San Martin Plaza that Simon had searched out. We had a double room on the ground floor, close to the noisy toilets where I moved in a state of constant terror on the slippery wet stone floor, with the rubbers of my crutches skating sideways. At least I didn't have to climb stairs, and it was easy getting to restaurants and bars in the nearby streets. The streets were dry. Only rubbish and rotting vegetables threatened my slow crutching steps. I felt weak, as if my muscles had dissolved. I had to stop and rest frequently, breathing heavily as if at altitude, which seemed strange. I should have been fit.

I should have been, but I wasn't. Selectively I forgot what I didn't want to remember. I had lost more than three stone in weight, 40 per cent of my total body weight. My muscles had dissolved, had been absorbed, eaten by my desperate body. The memory of crawling among the boulders and the shale had been neatly erased. Little more than a fortnight had passed since I had crawled deliriously back into Simon's life after days of despair and yet everything about me now was so astonishingly normal and unchanged that it felt as if nothing at all had happened. Even the hospital dreams seemed to have nothing to do with waking reality. Simon behaved as if all was just as usual, which, in a way, I suppose it was. I had broken my leg in the mountains and we were waiting to catch a flight home. I might have appeared a little hollow cheeked. My eyes perhaps had a manic glint that was not usually there, a morphine glaze, or the thousand yard stare of someone who has drifted too far over the edge, for too long, and is struggling to get back. Otherwise, everything seemed fine.

We would check with the airlines each day, stump round the local market buying fruit, Simon administering motherly attention, and then head for a bar. The hardest part of the day was getting up. If I sat up suddenly after a night on my back, the blood would rush to my feet. My swollen and plastered right knee caused a great restriction to the blood flow and my toes would rapidly darken until they were almost purple and a terrible bursting sensation would build in my foot. The only way to avoid the black toes was to rise very gradually, propping the pillows higher and higher, until I sat almost upright, slowly lowering the heavy stiff leg by degrees to the floor. It could take as long as an hour. I would smoke steadily through the process and listen to others making hollow noises in the toilets that echoed in the empty central atrium of the hotel.

After an hour the toes were simply swollen but not purple and the pain killers had begun to take effect. I would crutch cautiously into the now empty but flooded toilet and wash myself while standing on one foot, brush my teeth, swallow the antibiotics with the rinsing water and examine the neat hairline crack in my front tooth where the icicle had hit me on the second day. I examined it every day and watched it gradually shade into the dull grey-blue colour of a dead tooth with the nerve canal cut off. The dentist hacked it down and capped it soon enough.

Every day we called the airline and every day they said there were no available seats for another month. Only when they suddenly realised that I wasn't a stretcher case, and would occupy only one seat and not four, did they reveal abruptly that there was a flight via Bogota and Caracas leaving at the end of the week. We grabbed the chance. We told the Vice Consul and she gaily offered to escort us to the airport in the Embassy limo – as a precaution, she said, to stop the customs people searching inside my plaster with wire probes. It was a common method of smuggling drugs, it seemed, and I winced at the thought of the probes thrusting across the stitches around my knee.

Many were the horror stories that circulated about European travellers buying drugs for personal use in Peru. Often the dealer would receive a reward by reporting the buyer to the police the moment he had made his sale. Some embassies warned of the terrible conditions in the central prison in Lima. They estimated a life expectancy of about four years for the average westerner. The sentence for being caught in possession of one marijuana joint could be as severe as seven years. It proved that the Peruvian authorities were doing something about the drug trade by incarcerating the occasional innocent hippy traveller while the main culprits, the cocaine barons, dealt on, secure behind a complex intrigue of bribery and corruption. All the same, when the smiling young man had asked whether we wanted to buy some coke, we had grinned and showed interest. We were bored with waiting, bored with drinking beer, so why not have a fling? I doubted that things could get any worse than they had been a few weeks before, and as the young man talked, my heart began to pound with the thrill of the deal. The idea that we might get ourselves into deep trouble was as much an incentive as the possible delights of abusing ourselves with narcotic excess.

He had come from Bolivia, he said. He was a student and needed money, so he had brought some cocaine with him, to sell in Lima. It seemed plausible to us, and he had a winning smile. We haggled about the price and whether to pay in dollars or solis. He kept saying it was of the finest quality, the purest we would ever taste, and we grinned expectantly at him and quickly drank our beers.

'We'll have to test it first, though,' Simon said, and the man smiled and nodded in reply.

'We can't do it here,' I protested. The sight of the white powder on the brown paper held under the table had been brief. I knew only that it was the right colour. The man was understandably nervous about showing us his wares. I felt my pulse throbbing in my swollen toes.

'I'll nip back to the hotel,' Simon suggested. 'It's only round the corner, and you can wait here and keep an eye on him.' He stood up and folded the paper packet into his pocket. I reached for my crutches and moved slowly out on to the pavement. The sun glared a fierce white on the street opposite our cool shadowed alleyway. The drug dealer asked for money and Simon handed him a few dollars.

'I'll give you the rest if it's good stuff,' he said, and the man nodded and smiled reassuringly at me.

'Best quality, sir,' he said, 'the very purest quality.'

'Okay, Joe, keep an eye on him, I'll be back shortly.'

Simon headed for the sunlit street where motes of dust thrown up by the traffic glinted in the sun. The moment he turned the corner and was gone from sight, the drug dealer was off. I saw his grin as he turned and ran down the alley, ignoring my shout and the futile waving crutch. He was gone at once. I stood leaning my armpits on my crutches and stared stupidly down the alley. *Why on earth had Simon decided that the cripple should guard the dealer?* I began to laugh, and felt the tension of the deal wash away. It had become so natural for Simon to look after me, to fetch and carry, that it had never occurred to him not to be the one to go.

I reached the hotel room just as Simon was snorting furiously, with his eye streaming from the effect of testing some concoction of washing powder and rock salt. He looked up as I stumped up to the door, caught my eye and burst out laughing.

Two days later we boarded the aircraft for the long flight home. While the Andes floated ethereally past us, we smoked cheap rough cigarettes and drank beer with gin chasers. We talked idly about whether that really was Yerupaja we could see down there on the right, just as we had done on the way in, and I wondered if it had all really happened. I mixed sleeping pills and a pain killer with the beer and the gin and began to go a bit hazy. My mind was numb. For the moment it was refusing to acknowledge how close I had come to that void. Simon was peeling the blackened skin off his frost-bitten fingertips with my Swiss army knife, the knife that had cut the rope and saved us both from death. The skin came off like wax-dipped finger prints. There was no pain as the bare fresh pink flesh beneath was exposed. My fingers had been black and numb since the fight down Siula Grande. I watched him pausing to drag on his cigarette before carefully cutting again. The passenger beside him looked on with fascination and disgust. I wondered whether we could ever explain to anyone exactly how it had been. I doubted it.

I spent a week at home with my parents in a state of shock. There were nightmares and tears, sudden attacks of the shakes whenever memories rushed back of days filled with dread and the long dark nights of waiting for the sun to rise. I felt ashamed and struggled to convince my parents that Simon had saved my life even if it appeared to them that he had tried to kill me.

In the local hospital a condescending orthopaedic surgeon removed the plaster from my knee. He examined the incisions for signs of it going septic and then fitted me with a plaster braced at the knee so that I could bend the joint. He dismissed the Peruvian X-rays as irrelevant. There was something infuriating about this man, a conceited arrogance that all too many doctors seem to have. The questions I asked about the seriousness of the injury were waved aside. His whole attitude spoke of the general public being too stupid to understand anything of medical matters. Patients were to be seen and not heard. I wanted to storm out, screaming abuse, but this is hard to achieve effectively on crutches. Instead I kept my silence and seethed. In a way he probably did me a favour. I became incensed by his manner and determined in future to ignore all doctors' advice. They could put me back together again, perform their surgery, but after that I was damned if I would listen to one pompous word they uttered. When he swept regally from the cubicle I reached for the crutches, shoved my X-rays under my arm, and headed for the door. I didn't make the requested appointment at the desk. There was something about the man that convinced me he had made a wrong diagnosis. It just didn't tally with what I had been told by the Peruvians. I went to Sheffield the next day for a second opinion.

Mr Kay looked at the Peruvian X-rays with a frown on his face. He was a tall smartly dressed man with curly greying hair and gold half-frame spectacles. He chewed thoughtfully on the one thin gold arm.

'Is this what they did to you?'

'Yes.'

'Hmmm . . . not good, not good at all.'

'The doctor in York hardly glanced at them.'

'Really,' Kay said with some disdain. 'First thing, I think, is to get that brace off.'

He looked up brightly and said something inaudible to a junior registrar. They huddled forward, pointing to the X-ray with pen and spectacles. I leaned forward, trying to catch what they were saying. Mr Kay kept shaking his head, then he straightened, slid his spectacles into his pocket and turned to me.

'Well, it's a bad break. A tibial plateau fracture, quite rare I'm afraid, and it has left this piece sticking into the articular surface of the mortice.' He pointed to a spot on the X-ray.

What the hell was he on about, I wondered, as I

examined the fuzzy black and white image on the wall with the hard white line of the bolt outlined starkly.

'And this is very crude' he added, pointing to the bolt. 'They did their best I suppose, but they're years behind us. You should really have come home for the operation, you know.'

'Yeah, well, it wasn't as easy as that, what with difficulties over the insurance and my weak state. Anyway, I just thought it was a normal break. They didn't speak very good English. It was difficult . . .'

'There is no such thing as a 'normal' break, especially not where joints are concerned.'

'I didn't go to medical school, did I?' I said sharply.

'No, quite so.' Kay pulled his spectacles from his pocket and swung them by an arm. 'I favour fusing the knee myself. You see, it's been over three weeks since the Peruvian operation and this piece of bone has revolved on the bolt and is now protruding up into the joint here.' I peered hopefully at the X-ray.

'Er . . . what exactly do you mean by fusing?' I asked tentatively.

'Ah yes. Well, we literally fuse the joint together so that it can't move. We use bone grafted from the pelvic area to help and so . . .'

'You mean I would have a stiff leg, no bend at all?'

'Yes. We would set it at a slight angle, but yes, it would be stiff.'

'A solid bone from hip to foot?'

'Yes. I said it wasn't good.'

'No.' I said firmly. 'No way. If you do that I'll never climb again. I won't even be able to walk normally.'

'I don't think we have much choice, Mr Simpson. You see, this displacement has already begun to fuse.'

'Well, break it back. Cut it open and snap it back in place . . .'

They asked me to leave while they considered their options and return in a couple of hours. I sat morosely in a nearby pub. Although after the accident I had vowed never to climb again, it didn't feel right to have the choice taken away so harshly.

Mr Kay seemed cheerful and confident on my return.

'Right, Joe. It is Joe, isn't it?'

'Yes.'

'Good, right! Well, we have decided to try to break the displaced bone back into place.'

'Great, wonderful. Will you be cutting the knee open again?'

'Oh no, that's the last thing we want to do. In fact they should never have done that in the first place. We'll try to snap it back by manipulation.'

'And what exactly is that?'

'Well, we get your leg like this,' he said as he demonstrated on my good leg, 'and we bend the joint up like this.' He pulled my foot up towards me while holding the upper thigh firmly on the bed. My leg began to bend back at the knee and the hamstrings tightened.

'Ow!'

'As the leg hyper-extends, like so . . .'

'Yeow.'

'. . . we think the displacement on the tibial plateau will be crushed back into place by the femur, like so!' He rolled the knuckles of his fist together to demonstrate the breaking point, allowing my aching leg to flop back on to the bed.

'Looks painful,' I suggested massaging the back of my knee, 'and what happens to all the tendons and ligaments in my knee? I suppose they all snap, do they?'

'No. I hope we can avoid that situation, especially if the fracture breaks early enough.'

'Good.'

'The one problem, of course, is that after a three week gap it might not be possible to break the displacement. The bone will have hardened too much. If that is the case, we will have no choice but to fuse it.'

'And if it works, will my leg be back to normal?'

'No.' He said it confidently. 'In fact the outlook is pretty bad even if it does work.'

209

'Oh well, it's nice to have a choice, I suppose. By the way, what would happen to the knee joint if we left it in this braced plaster?'

'It would never work. You can see that from the X-ray. Judging by these dates, it had moved one day after they operated.'

'So the consultant who put this thing on would have crippled me?'

'Er, no, it's not so simple. Each doctor has a different approach to treatment.'

'And his was to cripple me . . .'

I was talking to a departing white-coated back. It always fascinated me to witness fence-sitting of such peerless quality.

Four months later, after two attempts to re-break the knee and umpteen changes of plaster cast, I sat once more in front of Mr Kay as he peered at me over the top of his lenses and told me the prognosis.

'Well Joe, it's still a very bad knee but I'm hopeful that you will get some movement now. Five degrees bend at the most I would say. Climbing is out of the question, of course. It's doubtful whether you will ever walk without a limp. Osteo-arthritis is inevitable where the cartilage is damaged by the fracture point and this reduced displacement grinding into the femur. It's better than fusing however, and you could consider yourself fortunate not to be able to climb again. A longer life span maybe, although not for the old knee I suspect.'

'Perhaps,' I agreed dubiously. 'But you never know, people have suffered far worse and got over it.'

'True, but I wouldn't raise your hopes too much. Right, I'm discharging you now, so off you go – and keep away from mountains.'

In that long summer of operations and painful recuperation Simon had gone to the Alps and climbed the North Face of the Eiger. It had caused me a momentary pang of envy, which surprised me. I had decided unequivocably never to climb mountains again, but somehow I had expected my resolve to be eroded as the months passed and feel the familiar yearning for high places once more. The opposite occurred. With each new bit of depressing news concerning my leg and the medical evidence that it would never work again the more resolved I became against climbing.

I had come to terms with the accident and the terrible struggle to survive. It continued to amaze others, but to me it was simply something that had happened half a year ago. If asked about it, I found that I could tell the story in about a minute and a half, describing details of the ordeal without a flicker of emotion. It meant nothing to me. I had shelved it far back in my mind, leaving only a thin skeletal story devoid of any feeling. I decided that dwelling on the events, wondering what might have happened, was a negative cul de sac up which I didn't want to go.

Simon went on from the Alps to Pakistan and the Karakoram range. I didn't care. Whatever aspirations I'd once had were gone, seemingly for ever. When I heard the news that Roger Baxter Jones had been killed while guiding on the Triolet, I found myself shocked as much by my inability to accept it as by the fact that he was gone. In the past it had seemed easier to accept the attrition; now that I wanted nothing to do with climbing it was impossible. I had no need to convince myself that such risks were justified. I had abruptly become a non-climber, and suddenly it seemed incomprehensible to me.

With trips to Shishapangma, Makalu, Broad Peak and K2, he had established himself as one of the finest of British alpine-style Himalayan climbers. He had said he was taking a break from the big expeditions to be with his wife, Christine, and his young daughter, earning a living by guiding in Chamonix. He seemed to have grown tired of the strain of long expeditions with their huge expense of time, money and energy. A break from it would do him good, replenish the batteries, and placate the bank manager, he had said. I had never been over-awed by him because of his natural humour and friendliness. When I remember him, it is of someone always smiling, always cheerful, ready to help selflessly, as he did when Duncan had been killed, and later when Andy Parkin was critically injured in Switzerland. Now it seemed a whole generation of British climbers had been wiped out.

Pete Boardman and Joe Tasker had disappeared on the North-north-east Ridge of Everest in May, 1982. In the autumn of that year Alex MacIntyre, a bold and talented climber, had been killed by a single falling stone on the vast South Face of Annapurna at the end of a year in which Doug Scott, Roger and he had made a superb alpine-style ascent of the South West Face of Shishapangma. Three years later Roger was to die on the Triolet, and the following summer Al Rouse, who had encouraged Simon and me to go to Peru, died with twelve other climbers during a tragic summer on K2. There is a telling picture of Boardman, Tasker, Rouse and Bonington after their ascent of Kongur in 1981, standing on the summit in one-piece red down suits. Within five years all but Bonington were gone.

Suddenly climbing seemed to be a very silly thing to do. If climbers that good could be snuffed out so swiftly, then what on earth had I been hoping to achieve in Peru? The combination of the deaths of friends and associates and the terrifying experience of being left for dead on Siula Grande had stripped me of all my previous perspectives. It was a shock to find myself so abruptly alienated from a way of life that before had seemed so positive and enhancing. Seeing it with different eyes was uncomfortable. I didn't like to feel that I had been fooled, that we all had been fooled, and that the lives lost had been no more than a pointless waste. Yet I couldn't escape from the insidious idea that really it was a mug's game, that we had simply been blindly chasing our tails.

I knew that this feeling was true only for me. Simon was as keen to climb as ever, and so were all my other friends. Feeling as if I had silently ostracized myself, I watched them going away on expeditions and waited for the inevitable news that yet another accident had happened. I did not yearn to go with them.

Meanwhile the accounts of our adventure in Peru were doing the rounds by word of mouth, and consequently the story become grossly distorted. I overheard some astonishing versions that bore no relation to what had happened. There was a peculiar fascination in cutting the rope. It seemed to mesmerise people. Perhaps it touched on a sensitive part of the climber's pysche; the cutting of the umbilical lifeline between partners was taboo. How could it possibly be the right thing to do? To some climbers, it was anathema to hear that such an act was not only possible but justified and absolutely necessary. This was threatening stuff. As a result it appeared to me that Simon, who had risked so much to save my life, was being vilified for something he didn't do, for something that had become twisted by idle chatter.

Later I was to discover that a member of the Mount Everest Foundation Selection Committee had moved that Simon be barred from ever again receiving a grant on the grounds that his actions in Peru were unacceptable. In that closed meeting an article written by me for *High* magazine, explaining what had happened, was presented as proof of Simon's wrongdoing. Fortunately our friend Andy Fanshawe, the National Officer for the British Mountaineering Council, was present at the meeting and successfully argued that Simon's accuser was woefully out of touch with modern mountaineering. Without Andy, Simon would never have known the reason for his ostracism. Something had to be done to correct this injustice.

'Write a book. That's the best way to get things straight,' John Stevenson announced as he bent over to address the balls on the pool table.

'Oh, sure,' I replied sarcastically.

He missed the black ball, cursed under his breath, and then straightened up.

'Why on earth not? You've written a few things.'

'I've written a couple of thousand-word articles for *High* magazine. That's not exactly a qualification for a book, is it now?'

'Well, every writer has to start somewhere. You'll never know if you don't have a go.'

'How long's your average book?'

'Somewhere between eighty and ninety thousand words, I guess.'

'Ninety thousand! I can't write that much. Hell, my dissertation was only ten thousand and I thought it was never coming to an end.'

'No, no,' John said dismissively, 'you don't think of it like that. You take it one day at a time. You decide on a target of say two thousand words a day, right? So that means you've finished it in forty to forty five days, and that's only five and a half to six weeks – or eight if you don't work weekends. See, that's not so bad, eh?'

I stared at him. 'Not so bad? How many books have you written then? None.' I addressed the cue ball and won the game by potting the black into the middle pocket. 'Oh, and that's a pound please,' I said, holding my hand out for my winnings on the game.

'How do you think books ever get written, for goodness sake?' he said, handing me the money. 'People just sit down and do it. No one said it's easy.'

'Okay, say I complete this eight-week masterpiece, what then? I hawk it round the publishers and wait for the rejection slips, right?'

'Wrong. You go to the publishers first, persuade them you have a story worth telling, sign a contract that commits them to publish, ask for an advance of, oh, several thousand pounds, and then start writing.'

'You're joking!'

'No, that's what people do.'

'They actually give you money in advance?' He nodded. 'Well, what's to stop me buggering off with the cash and not writing a word.'

'Oh, you would have to pay it back, if they could find you. But why not write it and see. A thousand a month is pretty good pay, and you never know, it might be a good read.'

I couldn't believe he was being serious – though if the contracts John had talked about really did exist, then perhaps I should give it a go. No – it was ridiculous! Even if I did (as

John pointed out) have nothing better to do, was unemployed, crippled, without previous work experience, was surviving on dole cheques, housing benefit and a bit of ducking and diving. The local hospital had refused to buy my body for medical science even at the bargain price of forty quid, and I had bottled out of selling my sperm halfway down the corridor to the artificial insemination donor room. Why not write a book? At least it would pay my way in The Broadfield for a couple of months.

I started to cast around for advice on publishers and editors. Jim Perrin, an author and a columnist for *High* magazine, encouraged me to contact Tony Colwell at the publishers Cape. They weren't close acquaintances but Jim had liked a couple of books Tony had brought out and Jonathan Cape was rather a smart literary publisher.

At first the response was encouraging. Tony was easy to talk to and he gave me confidence, but after several telephone conversations I was still without any commitment. He seemed to want me to write the book but something was holding him back. I began to think it was all a daydream. I said I needed the stimulus of a contract to get me started, otherwise I would never have the nerve to make the effort.

Eventually a modest advance was agreed and, in March 1987, a contract was signed. I then had to face the first hurdle – the blank sheet of paper. By the time my first cheque arrived I had written almost twenty thousand words, decided they were rubbish after showing a sample to Tony, and threw them away. He seemed undismayed. I wanted to start again with as honest and direct an account as possible of what had happened. I would simply let the story do the talking and get it finished quickly.

By the time I reached the moment when I had to describe the breaking of my leg on the tricky descent from the summit of Siula Grande I was in despair, moaning on the phone to Tony that I couldn't go on with it. He sounded somewhat shaken by my anguished state and, after urging me not to stop now, left me alone with my frustration. I had hoped the writing would have a cathartic effect on me, sweeping away the ghouls from my mind and releasing me from painful memories. It was more in anger with myself than fear that I finally went back to it.

Several weeks later the last words were written and I posted off the script. The writing had not been cathartic at all – quite the opposite. The suffering and loneliness had come flooding back and I was shocked by what had gone down on paper, almost as if someone else were setting down the worst things about me. It put a distressing burden on my girlfriend as well as me. I felt as if I had forced myself to dig up the midden and was retching as the noisome odours wafted up. Once the script had gone I was filled with trepidation and anxiety. What had I produced? What would people think? Had I been too honest, said too much about the fear and the pain? Would I be slaughtered by the reviewers? The questions and self-doubts overwhelmed me. I wasn't accustomed to being so unsure and out of control and I found it an unpleasant and disturbing experience.

Gradually I realised I had never been in control. I chose a direction and dealt with whatever was thrown at me as a result. Control lay only in the choice to go. Then it seemed to become a lottery. In the end I was responsible for whatever happened to me because I had made choices that directly created those events. Yet I never really knew what would happen, and could therefore never be in control.

14

THE MOMENT OF TRUTH

IT WAS TWO years before I shook myself free – twenty-four
months of insisting that I never wanted to climb again, a
suddenly empty life; a life without plans and ambitions. Yet
there was a lot to be done. Trying to walk and writing the
book took up most of my time; and both were equally
painful.

The gloomy prognosis of my doctors hadn't helped me to
recover quickly. Indeed their cautious approach meant that
for a long time I was faced with a psychological battle more
than a physical one. Being told that I would never walk again
without a limp and never get more than about five degrees of
bend was a hard obstacle to cross. And the only way I could
see to achieve that was to disbelieve the men in white coats,
disregard their authority and experience and presume that
they were wrong.

White coats always represent certainty and power. They
cannot be questioned, let alone disregarded. The men wearing
them – and for me it was always a man – assume this air of
superiority and unassailable conceit and on the whole the
public is happy to believe in it. People must trust the white
coats with their lives, invest their pain and fear in these god-
like figures, and hope that they will manage to keep their lives
going. I used to believe in them implicitly. Until my return
from Peru I thought of doctors as almost infallible; secretly I
still do, for like everyone else I need to be able to have faith in
their skill. Since Peru I have learnt to distinguish between
repairing the pure mechanics of an injury and the physical

217

and psychological side of making the traumatised injury site work again. Surgeons can cut and saw and graft and sew, and put back together as best they can a shattered body, but once the repair is done then it is the physiotherapists and the patient who make the body work again.

My sessions with the physio were painful and for a long time seemed fruitless. After so many months in plaster my leg had shrunk to skin and bone. When the last cast was taken off, I remember staring at the white stick of my thigh, no thicker than my forearm, covered in long black hairs. The thigh muscle seemed to have disappeared altogether. For a long silent moment I believed them when they said it would never work again. I almost cried for its loss, then I became angry.

One day, while the physio tried to crank one more degree of bend from my knee and I tried not to hit her, a middle-aged man crutched slowly into the room. There was a chorus of laughter and surprised greetings. The man grinned sheepishly, put his crutches against the wall, and sat on a nearby bench. He was thin, with a gaunt pinched face. He wore a singlet and a pair of shorts from which fragile legs poked towards the floor. His right knee was swollen and inflamed. The machine-gun punctures of stitches criss-crossed his knee. He leaned forward, placed a small sandbag across his foot and began to perform a series of straight leg raises with his injured limb.

Later I found myself beside him in a group exercise session and, during a lull in the training, I asked him why there had been such a raucous greeting for him. His reply did much to make me realise that there were others far worse off than me and that I had to stop being so negative about my knee. He had been in a car accident eight months previously, he said, and it had been a long and painful road back to recovery. Two days after being discharged from physiotherapy and pronounced fit, he went to a local firing range with a friend who had suggested that target shooting was an enjoyable pastime. Within an hour of arriving on the range his friend had somehow contrived accidently to shoot the poor man straight through the recently healed knee joint. It had been his first visit to the physiotherapy class since getting out of plaster after the knee-capping. He seemed genuinely amused by the incident and quite unperturbed about having to go through it all over again. Within a week of meeting this man my knee joint began to move, having been blocked for more than a month. A fortnight later I had gained nearly fifty degrees of flexion, ten times the amount suggested by my doctors, and at last I began to think positively and believe that it would work properly again.

A month later I was staggering out of a blues club in the Broomhall area with Neil Milne, severely the worse for wear after celebrating the completion of his final degree exams. I lurched forward unsteadily, tried to correct myself, and tumbled backwards, sitting heavily on my haunches and bending my stiff knee forcefully through its block. There was an audible gristly ripping sound and a flood of agony boiled up my thigh.

I cannot recall getting home. In the morning I awoke to find a knee the size of a cabbage attached to my right leg. Three days later the swelling had reduced sufficiently for the doctors to assure me that no damage had been done. In fact I had managed to perform a manipulation on myself, forcing the knee to bend beyond its range. This operation is usually carried out under anaesthetic rather than the effects of an indeterminate number of Red Stripe lagers. When the inflammation dissipated I discovered that I had accidently increased flexion by another fifteen degrees.

Tentatively I began to rock climb in the Derbyshire Peak District. With Richard Haszko's insistence and encouragement, I managed to struggle up a few very easy climbs. I knew that I was capable of much harder routes, but mentally I couldn't cope. Although I had acquired the ideal rock climber's body – skinny legs and strong arms and several stones lighter, my upper body strength greatly improved from seven months on crutches – I was simply terrified. It was not just a fear of hurting myself again. I felt extremely vulnerable, as if I had never climbed before. I was a novice, with no faith in the ropes or the hardware, let alone myself. My confidence had evaporated, and with it my ability. Fear made me weak, impotent. It was not the fear we had always dealt with, the fear in which a climber learns to operate, that you control as you climb, checking always how far you are willing to go, how close to the edge, the fear that keeps you alive. This new dread was corrosive, destructive and so strong at first that I simply couldn't face it down. I was as anxious about what, potentially, I was letting myself in for as I was of the thought of falling again and hurting myself. I was afraid that I might enjoy climbing again and wake the demon that would begin to prod me back towards the mountains. I wanted no more mountains. I had had my fill of accidents and death. I was fearful of temptation.

I kept repeating to myself that I didn't want to climb mountains ever again.

Rock climbing was just for fun. With modern equipment and common sense, there is no good reason for being badly hurt or killed while rock climbing. I had never taken it very seriously except as useful training for the mountains. It gave me greater confidence as well as fitness, but there was no comparison with mountaineering. There were no comparable dangers. Rockfall was minimal, and in Britain there was no danger from storms, avalanches, lightning, and all the other hazards of the high mountains.

I would rock climb for fun and nothing else. I had to do something, and it had to give me that rush of adrenalin which made the body work and the mind think quickly. Safe fear was what I needed, safe sanitised fear. Nothing serious.

I became frustrated with my inability to cope. It didn't make sense to know that I was now physically strong enough to be climbing extreme grade routes and yet barely able to get off the ground on the simplest of rock climbs, with or without the use of a rope. The moment of truth came in the spring when, on the spur of the moment, I joined some friends on a climbing weekend in North Wales.

As I hadn't been climbing with Dave Walters, he was unaware of my difficulty. I decided not to tell him. I had come to the conclusion that the only way to get past the block was to outflank it by ignoring it. Dave was set on a classic extreme grade rock climb on the popular Bwlch-y-Moch buttress of the Tremadog cliffs. I had a moment of doubt as we headed up through the trees towards the impressive cliff face, with the distinctive hanging ochre-coloured slab of Vector in the centre of the buttress. This awkward and very polished slab was the crux section of the 250-foot route and a far cry from the easy fifty- foot climbs I had been doing on the gritstone crags of Stanage and Froggat.

I had told Dave in a moment of what now seemed to be insane bravado that I would lead the crux pitch. To admit at this stage that it was about eight grades harder than anything I had climbed since my injury seemed a bit foolish. I was about to confess my fears but held my tongue. Resigning myself to an honourable defeat on the pitch after a token effort at climbing the slab, I plodded slowly behind Dave, feeling my knee ache in the cold April morning air.

To my astonishment, I found the climb remarkably easy. I had built such anxiety about it in my head that the reality, a pleasant day on the rocks, came as a complete surprise. As the climbing became harder my concentration tightened, and I found myself enjoying the intricacies of the moves, making adjustments for the way in which my knee couldn't bend, solving the puzzle of the ochre slab and the stiff overhanging groove and the flake crack at the top of the buttress. The sun was beaming a pleasant warmth on to the cliffs as we wandered down through the trees to the base of the rocks with the tingling sensation that comes from unexpected success.

There was also a sense of release, an escape from fear through facing it head on and pushing it confidently away, laughing at the bogeyman, winning the mind game at last when for so long I had been crushed by it. It wasn't a big climb, or a serious one, but in its way it was as challenging as any I had ever attempted. Even on a sunny day it had become one of those looming dark shadowed walls under which I had chosen to stand, sure in the knowledge that I could climb it, fear or no fear.

Over the next two days Dave and I romped up Vector, The Weaver, Nimbus, The Snake and Pincushion – nearly a thousand feet of hard climbing. In a weekend I had brushed aside a mindful of imaginary horrors and fearful memories. Even if I did not know it at the time, my vow never to return to the mountains had begun to crumble.

At last I had managed to shelve the experience of Peru in a dark corner of my memory and could now be selective about recollecting it. All the terrible dreams I had conjured in my mind during the first months after the accident had left the conscious world. I would wake each morning cheerfully refreshed from undisturbed sleep. Gone was the moaning sleep-talking and the screaming that John Stevenson and Neil had heard coming from the attic bedroom of John's house where I had slept while I struggled to write down the memories of Peru during the day.

Later that summer Andy Parkin arrived in Sheffield from his home in Chamonix to visit his mother. He was eager to go rock climbing despite the pronounced swinging limp he suffered as a result of an appalling accident in Switzerland. The fall had shattered his right hip and elbow joints, ruptured his spleen and punctured his liver. It had so displaced his heart that he was fortunate to have survived the helicopter flight to the hospital in Bern. It looked as if the accident had finished Andy's career as one of the world's up and coming alpine-style Himalayan climbers. He had climbed Broad Peak with Roger Baxter-Jones and Al Rouse and gone on to reach a high point of 7,500 metres while attempting the first ascent of the South Rib on K2 with Doug Scott, Roger and Jean Afanassieff. Andy took his misfortune philosophically and while recovering from his injuries turned his attention and energies into painting. He now makes a living as a talented and successful professional artist.

I was well aware of Andy's reputation as a rock climber and felt nervous about making a fool of myself in front of him. Once we reached the quarry, I found that his presence gave me a tremendous boost in confidence. Here we were, both limping around and making jokes about our infirm and crippled state, while I prepared to lead on a rock route at a standard I had never before climbed. If Andy could climb at such extreme standards after injuries far more serious and incapacitating than my own then there was no reason why I shouldn't be able to climb as well, if not better than before. I set off in fine controlled style, unlike my usual frantic thrashing efforts, completing the climbs with no falls or practice moves.

It proved how much of one's capabilities rest within the mind. Andy showed me that I had been blinkered and narrow-minded about my injuries. The experience of surviving in Peru had been so drawn out and full of dread that I had applied the same extreme to my shattered knee. The doctor's conservative approach had served only to reinforce my attitude. It was as if I were the only person ever to have suffered such an injury, and it took on a significance far greater than it deserved, until I had become obsessed by it. It was through Andy I saw that most of the injury was to the mind. If I could deal with that, the rest would follow.

For a few hours on the walls of that limestone quarry I climbed harder and better than I have ever done simply because I allowed myself to believe that I could. With a pang of guilt I saw that it was pathetic to let self pity rob me of the chance of realising my full potential when many others would never have such a chance.

A month after Andy had returned to France came the awful news that Al Rouse had died after reaching the summit of K2. He had died alone at camp IV after he and six other climbers had been trapped by a ferocious storm. Julie Tullis, the first British woman to climb the mountain, lay dead in an adjoining tent. When, after six days pinned down at 8,000 metres by one hundred mile an hour winds and heavy snowfall, the five surviving climbers struggled out into sunshine on August 10th, they were forced to leave a delirious Al, who was incapable of moving, to die alone. Of the five only two, Willi Bauer and Kurt Diemburger, managed to reach base camp.

Five hours' walk down the Godwin Austin Glacier and

along the Upper Baltoro Glacier, another group of climbers were taking shelter from the storm. At the base camp of the British Chogolisa Traverse Expedition Andy Fanshawe, Ulric Jessop, Liam Elliot, Hamish Irvine and Simon Lamb were patiently waiting out the prolonged spell of bad weather, unaware of the desperate tragedy unfolding high on K2. They had visited the K2 base camp only a fortnight earlier and had talked to members of the British K2 team. Al had been insistent that he was going to have one last attempt on the summit via the Abruzzi ridge. The K2 climbers had given Andy a tip before he returned to his own camp under Chogolisa.

'Go for it when the wind blows from China. Look for the plume on K2.'

August 10th – when Al was left at camp IV on the shoulder of the Abruzzi ridge, the day on which it is presumed that he died, the day on which Alfred Imitzer and Hannes Wieser also collapsed and died in the deep storm-laid snow a hundred yards from where Al's tent lay half buried in the drifts, and the day Dobroslawa 'Mrufka' Wolf, (Al's Polish climbing partner) disappeared somewhere on the fixed ropes above camp III as Bauer and Diemberger fought their way down to safety – had dawned clear and fine. For Andy it was a day of bright optimism as he rose to examine the clear blue skies, with the beautiful pyramid of K2 etched perfectly at the head of the Godwin Austin glacier, and saw a plume of cloud blowing from its summit. A China wind! So the young British climbers set off on what was to be the first successful traverse of Chogolisa, a mountain of breathtaking beauty, aided by the advice of a friend who on that very day lay dying on the pyramid in the sky. They set off up Chogolisa, a mountain first attempted by the great Hermann Buhl and Kurt Diemberger in 1957, just as Diemberger himself was desperately fighting for his life on K2 ten miles away. In a bizarre reverse symmetry of events, the British team went on to make an illegal attempt on Broad Peak after their success on Chogolisa and tragically Liam Elliot fell to his death when a cornice collapsed on the summit ridge. In 1957 Buhl and

Diemberger had already made the first ascent of Broad Peak when Buhl died falling through a cornice while later attempting to climb Chogolisa.

There was a tragic irony about those weeks in the summer of 1986 in the Karakoram. I was visiting my parents when the dispassionate voice of the BBC Radio 4 news reader reported the accident. It happened so quickly I wasn't certain that I had heard it correctly. I phoned John Stevenson and knew at once that Al Rouse was gone.

Al had wanted to climb K2 with such intensity and passion that it seemed nothing would stop him. I stared out of the kitchen window at the flower beds and the lush lawn in the last of the August evening sunshine and wondered if it was his passion that had killed him. I thought how dangerous it can be to want something too much, especially to want something without knowing why you wanted it. That was the trap into which I had fallen so easily.

Had it been a mountaineer who had coined the childhood taunt 'I want never gets'? It would make sense, for so often quirky truism surfaces in the mountains. The moment your hopes are raised by a possible improvement in the weather, or the sight of an easy way ahead to the summit, something happens to dash hope to pieces. The easy way turns into a lethal avalanche slope. The clear sunny sky reveals a powerful mind-numbing wind once you pop your head above the ridge line. Think for a moment that you are safe and it may well be your last thought. Sometimes it is possible to feign indifference, to pretend not to want it, and by a sneaking sideways motion outwit the mountain before it has the opportunity to strike, before it recognises your soft footfalls on its heavy flanks.

But this is nonsense! Al was killed by a storm. It trapped him high for too long, and the elements did the rest. It must have been bad luck; wrong place, wrong time – that sort of thing. Al was too brilliant to be caught out in any other way, I assured myself without much confidence.

As the summer faded damply into a leaden autumn Richard

Haszko began a protracted assault on me. He had been working as Chris Bonington's assistant and had come across a photograph of a mountain called Tupopdam. It was a peak that Chris had passed on his way to attempt an ascent of Karon Koh with Al Rouse in the seventies. Richard was eager to get together a team of friends for an attempt the following year. He approached me in the pub one night.

'What do you think of that?' he said, showing me the colour print of Tupopdam.

'What is it?'

'It's a mountain, a large pointy thing that juts into the . . .'

I cut into his irrepressibly childish sense of humour. 'Yes, thank you Richard. What's it called?'

'Tupopdam. It's just off the Hunza valley, six thousand metres, so far unclimbed, and we're going to climb it.'

'Oh really. Well, good for you.'

'Eh?' He looked puzzled. 'Don't you want to come?'

'No. Why should I? I told you, I've given up mountains.'

'Yes, I know you said that, but you didn't mean it, surely?'

'I did, and stop calling me Shirley.' I turned to the bar and ordered a pint of bitter.

'You'll enjoy it. John's coming, and Tom, and Andy. It'll be a scream.'

'I know, that's what's worrying me, I've done enough screaming, thanks.'

We left it at that, and the conversation changed to weightier matters, such as the price of a pint and whose round it was. Unfortunately the seed had been sown and it germinated in the fertile warmth of a mind starved of the high and beautiful places and forgetful of the past. Within a week I had called him to ask if there was still room on the team.

During the winter we applied for a Mount Everest Foundation grant and sent off hundreds of begging letters asking for sponsorship and donations. Neil Milne and I were still renting rooms in John Stevenson's huge unheated and barely habitable house in the Netheredge area of Sheffield. We took this opportunity for Himalayan cold climate training in a stoical manner. Neil complained – on the grounds that he wasn't going to Pakistan so why should he suffer with the rest of us – but I assured him that it would stand him in good stead. In any case, he had no choice.

John himself deftly avoided such a fine chance to adjust to high altitude conditions by spending the winter months at his girlfriend's centrally-heated home. Occasionally he was seen warily approaching his own house while keeping a sharp lookout for a man in a silver jump suit who had been tracking him for months on his moped. I was told the man was a private debt collector, working for John's bank.

When he was at home, John made a point of never answering the door, in case it was the moped man, and we became adept at lying to strangers with dead pan faces while John skulked behind various articles of furniture. This was not an easy manoeuvre since most of the furniture had been burnt accidently in a bonfire during the memorial party held in Al Rouse's honour.

One late November evening he returned hungry and weary from work, ordered a large ham and mushroom pizza over the phone, and slumped in front of the television. A while later the doorbell rang, and responding to Pavlov's law and a grumbling stomach, he leapt to his feet and rushed to collect his pizza, forgetting all about the creditors lurking in the shadows.

To our undisguised delight, we eavesdropped on two policemen at the door as they arrested our starving landlord and led him off to the station for a night in the cells to await judgement for non-payment of fines. He had enough money in his pocket at the time to pay the fines three times over but the police were not interested. He had to be detained. It was the law. As we watched happily through the sitting-room window, the pizza man turned up. John grabbed his dinner, paid for it, and carried on arguing with the police, waving handfuls of money at them to demonstrate his ability to pay as they shoved him unceremoniously into the back of the black Maria. It was fine satisfaction for years of having the telephone, gas or electricity cut off for weeks at a time while our friend and landlord mysteriously disappeared to enjoy his comforts elsewhere.

Helped by strenuous training in the gym, my knee steadily improved. Owing to the damage in the joint and loss of meniscus cartilage, I was unable to run. This meant that I was forced to undergo long and tedious sessions working my leg muscles on various weight machines, most of which seemed to have been designed by the Marquis de Sade. The advice from my physiotherapist was to build as much muscle as possible around the damaged joint. This was essential to protect an already distorted and injured area.

By late winter I felt strong enough to cope with ice climbing and led Neil up Point V gully on Ben Nevis in the Scottish Highlands. It was an exhilarating climb up near vertical pitches of blue water ice on a rare day of winter sunshine. On the summit we waited in the lee of the ruined Observatory, sheltering from a bitter wind laden with spindrift that scythed across the summit plateau. The visibility had rapidly deteriorated and we studied the map carefully. It was late in the day and darkness was no more than a couple of hours away.

'Have you got a compass?' I shouted into Neil's ear.

'No,' he yelled, 'Have you?'

'No. I don't now how to use them.'

'Great.' He shook his head in despair. 'And you're the glorious mountain leader, eh?'

'Well, it's just commonsense,' I defended myself. 'We'll take it slowly, move roped together to try to find the abseil posts at the top of number four gully.'

'What if we can't?'

'We'll head down west from the col between the Ben and Carn Dearg and get on to the pony track via the Red Burn gully. We can get down into Glen Nevis from there.' I stood up and turned my face away from the icy wind. Neil tugged at my jacket.

'How will we know which way is west without a compass?'

'Er . . . it's on our left as we go down.'

'Yeah, but how will we know that if we can't see anything?'

'Ah . . . well, that's not important right now. The important thing is to get off here and down into Glen Nevis before we freeze to death.'

'But we need to get down into the other side. We've left the car at the dams. Remember?'

'Don't worry,' I shouted through cupped hands, 'we can cross over into the Allt a' Mhuilinn where the track crosses the saddle. What- ever happens we must keep close in on this side. We don't want to drift towards Five Finger Gully.'

I saw Neil's expression change and a sadness seemed to cross his face like a fleeting shadow. He nodded silently and turned, head down with his back to the wind, and began the descent.

A month before, on New Year's Eve, Andy Fanshawe and John Taylor had been trying to descend from the summit in similar conditions. They had the use of a map and a compass and had elected to get off the mountain via the Red Burn and down into Glen Nevis. They walked on a bearing first a short way south and then west, hoping that it would bring them out at the top of the Red Burn. Unfortunately they were walking on the wrong bearing. After a thousand yards of progress through the wind-blasted ice and snow they found themselves on the edge of steepening terrain that led down to the left. This was the top of Five Finger Gully, a wide-fanned easy-angled gully at the top which rapidly became a steep twisting couloir with short rocky buttresses breaking the sweep of ice. They recognised their mistake and began to contour the top of the gully tied together on a shortened rope. Suddenly, either due to an inadvertent slip or a small wind slab avalanche, they were both falling towards the narrow mouth of the gully. Unable to brake their accelerating fall they plunged into the darkness beneath them. Andy awoke to calm windless darkness in a haze of shock and pain. Crawling along the line of the coiling rope, he traced his way back to John who lay dead at the foot of the gully. John had taken off his helmet before starting the descent and had suffered fatal head injuries in the fall. Andy, with punctured lungs filling slowly with blood, both wrists badly sprained and a leg broken, was lucky to survive long enough for Andy Black and Mal Duff to find him.

John Taylor had been a lifelong friend of Neil Milne and

Simon Yates. They had grown up together in Leicester and had all started climbing at an early age. I had known John through chance meetings in the Alps, at parties in Sheffield, and on cragging sessions in Derbyshire. He was an easy going, friendly man and a calmly proficient climber. He had an impressive list of hard Alpine ascents to his credit, both in winter and summer. Behind his laughter and twinkling humorous eyes always lay his impressive calmness. It seemed to transmit an utterly dependable quality, something that would be good to have on a mountain when things went wrong.

Neil told me how safe John had always been; how he would climb hard but had no time for stupid risks or madcap schemes. He climbed as much for the aesthetic quality of the lines up the mountain faces as for gaining the summits. Reckless risk-taking seemed to sully this approach of his. I was saddened to hear of John's death, but Neil was distraught. Perhaps I accepted the loss as one of those inevitable things that come with the territory. It felt callous to be so detached but it is the only way to deal with it if you want to carry on climbing. Learn the lesson of his mistake, shelve the memory of his life, and swiftly reassure yourself that all is well.

There is a tendency among climbers to think that fatal accidents happen only to people we know while they are abroad in the greater ranges. It seems strangely unfair, almost wrong, that anyone should die at home. It's too close, too accessible, and leaves us vulnerable and exposed. Neil had lost one of his oldest friends. There was no possibility of detachment and I watched helplessly the trauma and pain of his grief, and felt ashamed that I could not also grieve for John.

Neil was caught off guard by the fact that it was John who had died. He had always reckoned that of the three of them – John, Simon, and himself – it would not be John or he who would die. Neil said he was too scared and cautious in the mountains to get into serious trouble. I always admired Neil's straightforward approach to climbing. He never pretended to like tackling things which intimidated him, just to show he could do them. He was unashamed of fear, which is probably one of the hardest and most honest attitudes to take. It also made him extremely safe in the hills. John was prepared to push much harder than Neil, but always he too stayed safe. He was not easily put off but that did not mean he would rush madly into anything. Simon was as strong and safe a mountaineer as I have ever known but, for some reason, Neil was convinced that Simon would be the one to die.

The astonishing thing was that he had chosen to assume that one of them would actually be killed. For years he had braced himself for the moment when he would be told that his childhood friend, Simon, was dead. Now it turned out to be John, and as I witnessed his confusion and grief I felt a shudder of revulsion run up my spine, despite sometimes thinking in this way myself when friends go off on expeditions. I don't necessarily think that any one particular person will be killed, but one does get a certain intuition when the risk is high. You can look at a handful of friends and work out which are most likely to go. Sometimes there are those who have all the potential for being killed, but somehow it just doesn't feel as if it is their time. They have a sort of aura protecting them and you think, quite irrationally, no, it won't happen to them. So far, no one of whom I've thought in this way has died, but that means little enough in the light of Neil's misjudgement.

This way of thinking about death prepares you for the worst, allowing you to come to terms quickly with the loss. It is a psychological defence mechanism that enables people to do something as irrational as climbing. The acceptance of the risks and the gradual attrition of friends over the years are inextricably entwined; one can't exist without the other. It is essential to convince yourself, however illogical it might sound, that you will play no part in those figures. It is as if the potential for disaster lies only with others, never with yourself.

Perhaps this sense of fatalism is a way of coming to terms with what you are really doing when you go up into the mountains. The reality of death is paradoxically very life affirming. It is not something that you are seeking, that you wish for, but it is necessary. Faced with death, the mountaineer will try his hardest to survive and, if successful, will return to mountain after mountain, year after year, to dance the same weird jig along the very boundaries of life. You create the potential for death by going to the mountains and taking the risks, and yet you do not want to die. It seems to make no sense. It makes no sense until you have stepped too close to the edge. Then you understand why you went there and perceive that you have enhanced your life, affirmed what it is to be alive by realising what it could be like to die. It has been argued that climbing mountains, tip-toeing along the knife-edge between life and death, is a way of looking into the ultimate unknown.

In his book, *The Great Blue Dream*, Robert Reid wrote:

> In the curious playgrounds of their sport, mountaineers learn what primitive people know instinctively – that mountains are the abode of the dead, and that to travel in the high country is not simply to risk death but to risk understanding it.

He goes on to suggest that the reason for death being so essential to the mountaineer is that it enables him to see life for what it truly is. Climbing prepares one for death, leads one towards the edge of another world into which one can look without fear. In the urban world our greatest and deepest anxiety is the fear of death, but in the natural world of the mountains it is possible, he argues, to overcome this fear. Far from being separate from life, Reid believes that death is really a smooth continuation from life, and for this reason the mountaineer can move easily to the edges of each world. In so doing he can discover the true beauty of life through having experienced the essential nature of death.

Without death a great many mountaineers would pack up their axes and boots and head for home. Without climbers the mountains would still be remote and ethereally beautiful, the soaring knife-edge ridges laced with winter icing and the pristine sweep of vast ice fields fluted by delicate blue-grey shadows no less perfect. Yet, without the lurking threat and the hollow fear of death, that is all they would ever be — pretty pictures, chocolate box covers. The promise of new perspectives beyond the vision of natural sight would cease to exist and to a very great extent the most powerful unconscious motivation for climbing would evaporate like hoar frost touched by the morning sun.

Unfortunately this introspective discourse on the nature of our sport hadn't occurred to me when I watched Neil vent his anguish and rage at being duped on any breakable object he could find in the back yard. As he dispatched a broken television set with a lump hammer I quietly hoped that what he had suspected would be Simon's fate would not now come true. These clever theories about death have a strong taste of truth about them when contemplated at a comfortable distance. When compared with the reality of enraged grief taking place before you, they became no more than silly notions, word play, and climbing is once again reduced to the status of a mug's game.

15

THE SILK ROAD

'DID YOU GET the rabies vaccination?' John Stevenson asked as he deposited the pints of bitter on the table.

'No,' I said before taking a deep draw at the foaming liquid.

'I must say I reckoned that sixty pounds was too much,' John said, making me splutter into the foam.

'SIXTY!' I wiped the remaining froth from my mouth while the others fastidiously brushed the spray from their arms and chests.

'Yeah, that's what I thought, and anyway that typhoid jab nearly finished me off. I didn't fancy another one like that.'

'I know, and not in the stomach either.'

'I don't think they do them in the stomach any more . . .'

'Did you know,' Jungle interrupted, 'that there were over forty thousand deaths from rabies in Asia alone last year?'

'Oh, shut up, Jungle!'

'Or was it the world?' He looked at us with a puzzled frown and began scratching at his beard. 'Perhaps it was snake bites and not rabies . . .' He examined something alien he had dug from the straggly ginger and grey hair.

'So, you had one of these jabs then, did you?' Tom Richardson asked.

'Not really, no,' he answered, flicking the offending alien away.

'And why not, if you're so clued up on the death statistics?' John asked as he fished in his beer for the drowning alien.

'Well, if you look at it logically and divide the total

33 John Stevenson retreating in a high wind from a 600 ft power station chimney. (Photo: Simpson)

34 Hanging a Greenpeace banner on Harrods. (Photo: Tom Stoddart)

DIEU ET MON DROIT

BY APPOINTMENT TO HER MAJESTY THE QUEEN
SUPPLIERS OF PROVISIONS AND HOUSEHOLD GOODS
HARRODS LTD. LONDON

35 *(left)* Unfurling the message on the second ascent of Nelson's Column, London. (Photo: Greenpeace)

36 *(right)* Simpson and Stevenson after a Greenpeace action. (Photo: Simpson)

37 *(below)* Instruction for flying the pago-jet. (Photo: Simpson)

38 The beautiful pyramid of Ama Dablam. (Photo: Simpson)

39 Joe above camp II on Ama Dablam in a snow storm. (Photo: Perpetual Collection)

40, 41 Mal Duff, who saved Joe's life on Pachermo, helps him after his fall.
(Photo: Mal Duff)

42 *(left)* Fitted with crude bamboo splints after the Pachermo fall, Joe rests in the sun. (Photo: Duff)

43 *(below)* Joe being carried down the slope to the Pachermo base camp. (Photo: Duff)

44, 45 *(right)* Wobbly but determined crutching takes Joe to 20,000 feet on Pumori. (Photos: Duff)

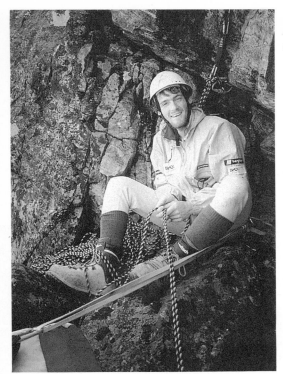

46 Andy Fanshawe, 1963–92.
(Photo: Fanshawe Collection)

47 Victor Radville and Mark
Miller on Nanga Parbat, 1992,
before they died in an air
crash near Kathmandu.
(Photo: Rob Spencer)

population by the number of deaths and the number of infected dogs . . .'

'And cats . . .'

'Yes, and cats, well, if you add them and really think about it, there is almost no chance of contracting the disease. In fact it's much more likely that you would be killed in a road accident.'

'So that's why you didn't have the jab, is it?'

'Oh no,' Jungle said brightly. 'I didn't have the money.'

Two weeks later we stood outside the Hotel Star at four in the morning. The air was heavy with humidity. A huge pile of rucksacks spilled over the cracked pavement and into the road. There were six of us standing motionless in the crushing damp heat. No one spoke. Jet lag from yesterday's flight, a ferocious whisky hangover, and the suffocating atmosphere of Rawalpindi had paralysed us. We waited for the van in silence. Ahead of us lay a sixteen-hour journey up the Karakoram Highway to Gilgit. The fabled Silk Road continued on from Gilgit through the Hunza valley past where Tupopdam, our mountain, rose above the valley, and on to the Kunjerab pass on the border with China. It promised to be a fine adventure, except that most of us were too ill to appreciate its potential.

In the distance there was the sharp toot of a scooter horn. A man sleeping on a wickerwork bed on the opposite pavement stirred, scratched himself in his sleep and rolled over.

Jungle stood up from where he had been sitting on a rucksack and wandered sleepily down an alley beside the hotel.

'When's this van arriving?' I asked.

'Four o'clock,' Richard answered, adding, 'God, I wish we could get some tea from somewhere.' He put out a yellow furry tongue.

'It's gone four now. I hope he's got the right address.'

'He'll get here.'

'Glad to hear it. I'm going for a pee. Don't leave without me.'

I followed Jungle down the dark alleyway. At the back of

the building it opened on to a small side road that was bordered by a high brick wall, partially obscured by a large hedge. There was no sign of Jungle. I walked cautiously along the road, picking my way past broken glass and rotting vegetables. There was a strong smell of urine and decaying rubbish. I came to a junction at the far corner of the hotel where a wide street ran across my path. Closed shops, with their fronts shuttered by metal doors, lined each side of the street. I looked to the right where owners of the shops slept upon wicker woven beds on the pavement. As I turned to retrace my steps down the alley a large black shape detached itself from the dark shadows of the overgrown wall and moved silently towards me. I pulled up with a start when I saw the dog approaching from the alley. It had an ugly deformed gait and reminded me of something diseased and evil.

Rabies!

It crept cautiously forward, its head hung low between its bony shoulders, dark eyes fixed on mine. I felt naked in my flip flops and shorts and lowered my hands, palms against my thighs, ready to ward off the snapping jaws. I stepped backwards slowly, suddenly afraid of the dog's menacing hyena-like posture. When I moved, it stopped and lifted its snout to sniff the air, swinging the heavy head slowly from side to side. A deep rumbling growl reverberated from the back of the creature's throat, and then it coughed harshly. I saw its flanks heave convulsively, the ribs sliding beneath the skin. A thin stream of spittle dribbled from the side of its jaws. The dog retched again and looked up at me. The fur around the jowls was matted and slimy with bubbles of spit and mucus. I noticed a large open sore on its side. It locked eyes with me for a moment and I felt a tremor of fright tingle up my back. I wondered how best to defend myself without getting bitten.

This is one sick dog! Oh God, why didn't I get that rabies injection? Sixty quid, what's sixty quid?

I looked at the wall beside me, hoping to see some way of climbing up and out of reach. There was only crumbling flaky brickwork. Again I stepped back, feeling my spine tingle and a rush of adrenalin. I shivered as my skin contracted with a bizarre eruption of goose pimples in 80 per cent humidity, as if I had been sprayed with a fine mist of iced water. It was almost pleasant but for the fear.

Again the dog moved towards me in a low stealthy prowl and steadily I was yielding to its advance. I should have stood firm, proved that I was the more powerful threat, but I was frightened of the jaws and the saliva. I glanced quickly behind me, hoping to see Jungle in the street. It was empty.

As I turned back towards the dog a blur of dark movement rushed towards me. I hurled myself backwards stretching my arms protectively across my face. The dog flashed past me in a frightened charge for freedom and sprinted swiftly across the street behind me. I lay still for a moment, feeling where sharp stones had cut into my palms and grazed my knees, staring across the street at the point where the dog had disappeared. I stood up and brushed the dirt from my trousers, trying to ignore my thumping heart and shaking hands. I wondered whether the dog felt like this; whether it was panting heavily behind the secure shelter of a bush and shivering with fear.

Once I had calmed down I headed back along the alley for a place to pee. At a point where I was partly hidden from the main street I turned and stepped towards the foliage at the back of the side road. There was a loud rustling noise to my left and part of the hedge swayed alarmingly. I jumped back, expecting another slavering dog to appear, and was about to sprint for the safety of the street when Jungle emerged from the depths of the bush, grinning cheerfully.

'Hello there, Joe.' He beamed happily at me.

'Ah, Jungle, right, hello.' I said in confusion. 'Er, tell me, what are you doing in that hedge. I mean you've been here some time now, haven't you?'

'It's not a hedge, you fool, it's a bush.'

'Okay then, bush. What on earth were you doing ... ' I tailed off as I caught a closer view of the bush. 'Bloody hell.'

'Exactly. Bush, as in wild weed, free ganja, smoking tokin heaven. Amazing, isn't it?' Jungle laughed happily and proffered his bush hat to me in one hand. I peered in and saw that he had carefully filled it with flower heads.

'I've never seen one this big before,' I said, looking down the side road and the eight-foot-high by twenty-foot-long growth of marijuana bushes.

'I know, it's wild!' The voice came from deep within the adjacent bush. 'I noticed huge areas of them growing on the way in from the airport yesterday.' There were brief rustling noises, the foliage shook and then Jungle's arm appeared at head height.

'Here you go.' He waved a handful of leaves and flowers. I put the bush hat against his hand and he deposited his collection.

'What are you going to do with this,' I asked stupidly.

'Well, smoke it. What else?'

'Right. Yes, I thought so, but it's a bit . . . sort of fresh, damp, you know.'

'I'll dry it out in my hat on the front window ledge.'

There was a shout from the front of the hotel. The van had arrived. I left Jungle thrashing his way deeper into the pungent undergrowth and went to help with the loading.

The driver was a young man with dark teak-brown skin and a quiff of silky black hair. He had a strangely expressionless face. His deep set eyes gave him a vacant motionless air, as if he were deeply tired or sedated. We couldn't communicate with him but things became obvious when he climbed on to the roof of the transit van. By the time we had finished the van had almost doubled in height and seemed grossly top heavy. As the driver tied the rucksacks firmly into place the van rocked from side to side with alarming ease.

Once everything was secure the driver retrieved a couple of brand new tyres from inside the van and tied these also to the roof. I could not help noticing that the rear tyres on the van were worn smooth, with no trace of tread left, so that they resembled the 'slicks' of a formula one racing car. Down the centre of each tyre there was a deep-cracked groove. I pointed this out to John who laughed and caught the driver's attention.

'Is okay,' the driver said, rolling his head from side to side. 'All is okay.' And with that, he headed for the front of the van and climbed in behind the steering-wheel.

'It's okay,' Richard said with the authority of a born leader. 'He's from the Punjab.'

It was apparent at once that this driver liked speed. Admittedly the traffic was sparse at that time in the morning but any vehicles he did see he immediately endeavoured to overtake. If the quarry was approaching, the driver's instinctive reaction was to set the van on a collision course, lean his hand on the horn, and stare fixedly at the oncoming vehicle. If it was one of those huge ornate Pakistani lorries resembling motorised Spanish galleons he would swerve out of the way at the last possible moment. We were thankful that one small part of his brain recognised the notion of mass winning the day. With anything smaller he would bore on relentlessly until his adversary had swerved and hurtled past, all squealing wheels and blaring horn, and we had thrown our arms up and screamed in fright and alarm. Anyone up front in the passenger seat would be treated to a triumphant and arrogant smile and the words: 'Is okay.'

At first his driving techniques caused terror and mayhem, but this gradually abated as we observed the peculiarly dangerous manner in which the other road users drove. It is astonishing how quickly one adapts to an abruptly alien and scary environment. What a moment before had been regarded as suicidally dangerous now became accepted as normal practice and something to be endured; if everyone else thought it reasonable behaviour, then it must be.

Launching on to a dual carriageway heading north-west from the city, our driver seemed to choose whichever carriageway he fancied at the time, as did all the other drivers, so that it became two parallel single carriageway roads, with interesting views of self-destructive manoeuvres on either side. We stopped howling and yelping every time death hurtled past us when we realised that the driver was paying us no attention. After three quarters of an hour we were all either reading or sleeping, with the exception of the unfortunate passenger in the front who was forced by the mesmerising view to sit in a state of buttock-clenching terror until the chance came to swop places.

An hour after clearing the outskirts of Islamabad, while we were rocketing down a straight metalled road lined with dust-whitened trees, there came a loud noise, like the whipcrack report of a rifle. We shrieked in unison as the driver fought the sudden lurching swing from the back of the van and the load of rucksacks on the roof tried to drag us over sideways into the trees. He stepped firmly on the brakes, ignoring accepted skid theories. The abrupt change from capsize to spin threw everyone to the floor with a chorus of yelps and curses. Books, personal stereos, cassette boxes and the flaming cinders of cigarette butts filled the air. I caught a flashing glimpse of Jungle slewing down sideways with one arm fully extended, fingers splayed in a desperate attempt to catch the bush hat full of flower heads.

We skidded to a halt in a cloud of dust besides a small shack selling tea and cold drinks. There was no need to wake the proprietor since the sight of the van bearing down on his wicker bed had made him scuttle for the rickety shelter of his tea shack. Throwing open the side door, we bolted after him, half expecting the van to explode. Jungle followed, clutching his hat to his chest like a man attending a burial, but with a look of ecstatic relief on his haggard face.

The van was jacked up and a wheel removed. After some complicated manoeuvres the driver managed to prop the unstable vehicle on a precarious pile of exfoliating bricks. They splintered and made crunching noises as in shocked silence we watched the driver wriggle beneath the chassis and begin hammering with great enthusiasm at something hidden from view. He seemed quite unconcerned by the way the van was rocking above him. If the bricks collapsed the full weight of the engine unit would crush his chest in an instant. I could hardly bear to watch, yet I was transfixed by the sight. Either he was astonishingly stupid or had such a deep faith in the will of Allah that such risks did not bother him. The latter turned out to be the case.

We witnessed similar roadside repairs later in the journey, with the same disregard for danger. Once we stopped to watch two men trying to mend the huge axle of one of the gaily decorated lorries on a section of the Karakoram Highway that had been badly damaged by a landslide. The vehicle was jacked up at such an angle that it overhung the road and a crowd of some thirty men squatted on their haunches besides the two who were toiling. There was a narrow, unstable and rutted area on the ravine side for other vehicles to inch their way past. Looming over them was an immense load of timber protruding from the sides of the lorry which visibly wobbled as the men beat at the axle with a small sledge hammer. Eventually our van teetered past on the outside edge of the crumbling road and we kept our fingers crossed that our passing wouldn't unsettle the flimsy props and send the lorry and its load crashing on to us.

Having detected the cause of our own breakdown, our driver waved a greasy lump of metal at us and called out 'Is okay' to indicate that he would walk back to Islamabad to fetch the necessary spare part.

'Is okay,' we chorused sarcastically as he trudged off down the road trailing a thin cloud of dust. So much for our crack of dawn start.

We returned to the shack and ordered more tea and a round of omelettes and chapattis, resigned to a long hot wait. Jungle took the opportunity to lay out his crop on the parcel shelf of the van which already was burning hot from the fiery blaze of sunlight through the front window. Then he wandered purposefully towards the tree line.

After an hour he returned from his foray into the local undergrowth with the news that he had found a lost temple. He had been alerted by a plethora of signposts pointing to the nearby Buddhist temple. Throwing caution to the wind, we agreed to follow him in search of this enigmatic discovery.

The sun had risen and the full blistering heat had begun to bake the countryside. We walked through a small grove of scrubby trees, emerging into a dusty clearing with another rickety tea shack propped in the shade of a plane tree. The proprietor poured sweet milk tea into chipped glass cups as he indicated the way to the temple.

It was a disappointing structure of exfoliating brickwork and the remains of several broken stairways. The temple had been built on a small lozenge-shaped mound and its upper walls gave an unprepossessing view of grey trees, sand and the exhaust clouds rising above the nearby road.

At various points, either set into niches in the walls or upon plinths in the centre of open quadrangles, were small neat signs announcing a type of statue, its origin and date. We opened the creaking wooden shutters to find only empty dusty spaces and another sign saying 'Removed to Lahore Museum.' The tea shack proprietor seemed inordinately proud of displaying the emptiness with grand expansive gestures.

As we wandered apathetically back towards the road we found our way barred by an immense water buffalo. It was no ordinary beast. Its huge bossed horns were held defiantly forward and the beast sniffed the air through wide distended nostrils. There was something distinctly menacing in the way it stood blocking the road, swinging its armed head ponderously back and forth and fixing us with a baleful glare. The brute's eyes were cornflower blue, with an odd translucent appearance giving the animal an unnerving alien appearance. Mucus dribbled from the huge nose ring as it snorted and pawed at the dust.

'I thought these were friendly?' Rickets said, taking a quick step backwards. Rickets was our star climber, an emaciated ex-miner who had retired at twenty-one, and knew nothing about water buffalo. There were no buffalo in Barnsley.

'Of course they are,' Richard assured him confidently. 'You see kids playing with them in ponds and paddy fields all the time. There's nothing to worry about . . .'

He jumped swiftly and with great panache into the undergrowth to his left as the buffalo swung towards him and began enthusiastically thrashing a track through the scrubby foliage. We had no choice but to follow our brave and glorious leader until we emerged streaked with sweat and caked in dust on the roadside. A loud metallic clanking noise and the van rocking unsteadily on its pile of bricks indicated that our driver had returned with the replacement part. It took several hours before the repair was complete and so by the time we set off once more on the Karakoram Highway to Gilgit it was early afternoon.

As we headed deeper into the mountains the landscape became spectacular, the scale immense. The highway itself, twisting along the steep unstable valley gouged out by the river Indus, was an engineering marvel. It had been said that a man had died for every kilometre of road built, and as we snaked our way further into the heart of the mountainous northern areas I felt painfully aware of how many hundreds had died. Our driver seemed to reinforce the point by attacking the frightening hairpin bends with ferocious speed. He kept his hand almost permanently on the horn to warn others of his approach – invariably in the absolute centre of the road.

On the few occasions he let go of the horn it was to flick over the cassette tape of high-pitched nasal whining and wailing sitars that constituted Pakistani pop music. The sole recording that our driver owned shrieked at full volume for the entire journey, with a raucous accompaniment on the horn. In desperation we began stuffing our ears to deaden the sound or turned our personal stereos to their maximum volume and wrapped scarves around our heads. That high-pitched woman's voice ululating in a mind-twisting lament drove us all to distraction until we began to take on the glassy eye, thousand yard stares of people who had been pushed too far and heard too much.

As the van approached a corner at high speed the driver would crouch over the wheel, waiting for the last possible moment to brake. At the very apex of the corner he would stand on the brakes and the top heavy van would lurch round, skidding on treadless rear tyres towards the edge of the road. Just when it seemed we were about to launch into space and plunge seven or eight hundred feet into the roaring Indus, our man would slam the lever down a gear, stamp on the accelerator, and we would catapult round the corner and hurtle unerringly for the next hairpin. On one particularly dangerous bend he sped round with one hand on the wheel, braked, changed gear and accelerated as he grinned conspiratorially over his shoulder and shouted, 'Twenty men dead,' and pointed over the edge. 'Is okay,' he yelled maniacally and threw the van into a neat slalom swerve to avoid an oncoming lorry. If we had the time and the nerve on such occasions we would glance down at where he had pointed and spot the crushed and charred remains of buses, lorries and jeeps that had taken the five second free plunge to the bottom of the ravine. Anyone who survived the crash would have had little chance of rescue in such remote spots.

Sometimes the pathetic wail from the front seat would indicate not another crash site but one of the team pleading to be allowed to swop places with someone in the back. Expressions of polite but help- less concern would be returned as we buried ourselves in books or magazines, averting our eyes from the hapless victims. Only when there was a brief halt for fuel or tea did the team leave the van. On re-embarkation there would be a short and vicious struggle for places in the rear.

When the sun sank behind the high valley walls and darkness flooded the Indus gorge, we were still far from Gilgit. We had been on the road for sixteen hours and yet were barely halfway to our destination. Major Asadu Alah Khan, an acquaintance of Richard's and our normally silent interpreter, informed us that the journey was taking twice as long as usual. This was due partly to a plague of mechanical breakdowns and partly to the fact that the driver had been without sleep for nearly forty-eight hours. This information was passed on to me when I was trapped in the front seat, pinned there by the hypnotic effect of the van headlights cutting swathes out in the black abysses beyond the edge of the road. I glanced nervously at the driver. He was wiping at his tired eyes and shaking his head in a manner characteristic of someone falling asleep at the wheel.

Fortunately we came upon another landslide where a long

stretch of road had been swept down into the river. Forced to progress at a walking pace, the van crept along the very edge of the crudely bulldozed track. It lurched from side to side as the wheels dipped into the pot holes gouged in the muddy surface where streams cut across the road. The sight of the drop on the driver's side made me push the door open, ready to leap out the moment we began to topple over. This luxury wasn't afforded to the team in the back since their sideways sliding door opened on the side of the ravine.

At the head of the valley a sprinkling of lights betrayed a small village. As we inched past the final section of damaged road the driver yawned deeply and accelerated up the steepening incline towards the village. There was a surprisingly crowded atmosphere on the streets as we rolled into the small settlement of houses that lined both sides of the highway. Dark bearded Pathans stood in the light of hurricane lamps hanging in their shop fronts and offered every imaginable type of goods for sale. There seemed to be no shortage of shops selling guns of every description. Other stalls displayed brightly coloured bolts of silk and brocade, or shelves of soap and cigarettes, or spices and vegetables. We stopped outside the most sinister looking restaurant in the village and the driver turned to us with a cheerful grin and said 'Is okay.' He pointed inside.

As I left the van I saw the driver take a large lump of hashish from his shirt pocket and pop it into the corner of his mouth. After a few seconds' chewing he noticed me staring and said, 'Is okay.' He put his hands by his cheek imitating sleep and then waggled his finger, grinning at me. I wasn't sure how long a quarter ounce of opiated hashish was going to keep him awake but I felt pretty certain that it wouldn't improve his driving skills.

Jungle pronounced the meal we were served as excellent, and the rest of us pushed our dishes hurriedly towards him. Flies rose from the greasy cold slurry in the bowls and hovered around Jungle's head. We contented ourselves with chewing on some cold chapattis.

At the entrance to the restaurant a man stood behind a

wooden counter asking a few questions of every customer who entered the room. Usually he was rewarded with a weapon of some sort, the guns and knives handed over for safe keeping. 'No weapons allowed while eating' seemed to be the accepted etiquette. The doorman's arsenal of pistols, AK47s, shotguns, ancient muzzle-loading rifles and what looked like a rocket-propelled grenade launcher was enough to set anyone's nerves on edge. We wandered out on to the street with a wary eye on the heavily armed inhabitants. It was curious to see that so few appeared to be armed until challenged by the doorman, only then producing a vicious array of weapons from the folds of their clothing.

The van had broken down again, and with it our driver. We found him sprawled across the front seat with his hands buried in the transmission area of the engine. There was a glazed, befuddled look in his eyes. I told the others about the hashish and they all groaned in unison. We gathered round as the prone figure, oblivious of our presence, tried to tie a knot in the fan belt. When this failed, he attempted to meld the two ends with his cigarette lighter. This was just as unsuccessful, and we watched in fascination as he became mesmerised by the dancing flame of his lighter. He kept looking at it in a narcotic haze until he burnt his thumb and dropped the lighter into the transmission.

Richard, our glorious leader, slumped to his knees and began hitting his forehead against the van in despair. Tom asked Major Khan if it were possible to find another van – and with luck another driver. Jungle asked me what sort of hash the driver had eaten and whether it was any good. He seemed disappointed when I snapped angrily at him in response. By that time the driver had fished his lighter from the transmission and stumbled off in search of a new fan belt. John climbed into the van and lit a cigarette with a weary expression on his face. Andy Cave, our emaciated ex-miner known as Rickets, was slumped in a sort of catatonic trance on the floor of the van. The Karakoram Highway was getting to us.

Suddenly the night sky was rent with the thunder of rifle

fire and the explosive crashes of heavy artillery echoed from the black hills.

'Jeez ... ' John yelled, leaping to his feet and stunning himself on the low roof.

There was a hubbub of shouts and people moved hurriedly down the road. The restaurant at the end of the universe quickly emptied, with the doorman working frantically to re-arm his departing customers. Bearded warrior types hurried out wiping dahl from their mouths with cold chappatis and slinging their armaments more comfortably across their shoulders. They shouldered past the small group of bewildered English climbers and headed up the road.

'What's going on?' Tom yelled above the gunfire.

'Dunno. I just don't know. Really, why ask me, why ... ' Glorious leader moaned and began rocking to and fro.

'It is no problem,' the Major answered calmly, 'just one of those small domestic disputes. These things happen, you know. Everyone has family disputes, no?'

We stared at him incredulously as what appeared to be the siege of Beirut erupted into the night sky. Richard, like a born leader, uttered a despairing groan at the Major's feet.

'Family argument? Is that what you call it?' I asked.

'Oh yes, sir. No doubt it will be quickly made better. Someone has given offence, maybe to another man's daughter, or mother. Whatever it is, no problem. Soon it will be happy again. No problem at all, sir. Do not worry yourself.'

I flinched as a sudden crescendo of shots crashed around the darkened hillsides. A police jeep with two blue lights flashing on the roof drove very slowly up the road towards the source of the gunfire. The two extremely anxious and unhappy policemen sitting in the jeep clearly thought it was a problem and wanted nothing to do with it.

In the midst of the uproar our driver reappeared clutching a brand new fan belt and smoking a large and noxious-looking joint. The fan belt was fitted and tightened by the time the firing had ceased and the police jeep returned with two delighted and relieved constables. This was a mixed blessing since it meant that once again we had to launch out on to the treacherous darkened Karakoram Highway with a driver who was virtually speechless from narcosis and the lack of sleep.

Somehow I lost the battle for a seat in the back and found myself wedged once more alongside the driver who leered as he failed to enunciate 'Is okay.' For a short while, as he conned the van through the crowded streets, I hoped that the combined effect of tiredness and drugs would calm him down, mellow his addiction for speed. If I could just keep him awake then all would be, as he said, okay. Unfortunately, temporarily blocked by a tractor on the outskirts of the village, he reacted with his usual dazzling acceleration, throwing about the passengers in the back with the g-force of his manic swerve round the obstacle.

We quickly built up to maximum speed on the short straight leading out of the village and exploded into the first hairpin bend with the engine screaming at maximum revs and a banshee squeal of burning rubber. It was a virtuoso display of suicidal cornering that by most accepted laws of physics simply shouldn't have succeeded. We powered out of the bend and into another short straight with the slingshot whiplash technique at which our man was so adept.

For several hours this progress continued as he smoked the short joints he kept in the top pocket of his shirt and flicked the cassette tape over. The rest of the team slumped into an exhausted torpor in the comforting blackness of the back of the van. Glancing back, I could see their shadowy forms occasionally illuminated by the glowing end of a nervously inhaled cigarette. Sometimes there were yelps and the sounds of people slapping at themselves as a dried flowerhead in one of Jungle's joints exploded in a burst of glowing cinders.

I watched the driver's eyes gradually close, despite his efforts to keep them open by rubbing them and shaking his head. At the last moment I would reach across and shake his arm. He would jerk up in his seat, look furtively at me, and say 'Is okay' in a slurred voice. It was far from okay! The gaps between his waking moments steadily shortened until it became a full time job to keep him conscious.

'Listen, up there,' I shouted into the darkness. 'Come on, wake up. I think we're in trouble here.'

There were a few grumpy sounds from the darkness. I turned to look at the road as it snaked ahead, illuminated by the headlights. There was less than forty feet before it ended abruptly and the beams of light shone out as two shafts cutting into blackness. I screamed with genuine terror and hit the driver across the chest as I dived for the steering-wheel. I missed but felt the van lurch sideways as the driver reacted. I fully expected to feel the abrupt stomach-emptying fall as the van plunged off the road. Instead there was a chorus of screams and various thumping noises from the brutally awakened team as the driver elbowed my nose and fought the steering-wheel round the bend.

'Fucking hell!' I screamed at the driver as I pushed myself upright. 'Stop, you crazy bastard! STOP!'

'Okay. Is okay.'

'It's not fucking okay at all,' I shouted. 'You bloody nearly killed all of us there.'

'No, is okay,' he replied, reaching for another joint.

'Oh God Almighty!' I turned to the others. 'Look, he's got to stop. He can barely stay awake and he's stoned out of his brains. I mean . . .'

Rickets suddenly threw himself up from his seat and forward at the driver's back. Jungle had crammed his foliage-filled bush hat firmly on his head and was squatting on the floor between two seats. The rear wheels squealed as the van leaned horrifyingly into another left-hander and I fell back against the door. There was a loud thump as Ricket's forehead connected with a metal bulkhead joint in the roof and he flew backwards, unaware of what he had hit. The road ran straight for about half a mile during which time we harangued the driver to stop, but he clung grimly to his steering-wheel, muttering 'Is okay' with increasing anger and vehemence.

'Why don't we rip the keys out of the ignition? That'll stop the bugger.'

'Could we grab the wheel and steer it into the opposite bank.'

'Don't fancy that . . .'

'Let's go for the keys,' Rickets said forcefully.

'Can you reach them?'

'I think so . . . Oh Christ! Here we go aga . . . ' He was staring past me at the road ahead. A series of hairpins were picked out by the crawling red tail lights of several lorries ahead in the darkness. The van shuddered and swung right as Rickets threw himself at the driver once more.

'Stop!' Crack. 'Unnhh.' He slumped across the backs of the seats, felled by the ceiling bulkhead joint, his right arm reaching out for the driver's hair.

The van made a sequence of horrifying swings on the downward sloping road and suddenly we came upon the looming bulk of one of the slow moving lorries, crawling towards us laboriously up the steep incline.

'No . . . Aaahh . . . stop him!' Pandemonium exploded in the darkness of the van as the driver, unable to effect an inside manoeuvre between rock wall and lorry, and loathe to brake, threw the van at a minuscule gap on the edge of the abyss. There was an abrupt shriek of terror, and then the crunching sound of the wheels skidding on the gravel edge of the road. At once there was an expectant silence, a sudden moment of utter calm.

I was vaguely aware of the shadowy wall of the steel-sided lorry, the heavy straining roar of its engine and the constant blare of the van's horn but these seemed to be external things outside of my existence. I could feel the tyres scratching for grip on the slithering gravels. The van began to tilt to the right. All these physical sensations seemed to have nothing to do with me. They failed to break into the bubble of tranquillity that had washed over me. The silence and the sense of time being suspended scared me deeply, helplessly. We all knew what was happening. We were powerless to avoid the inevitable.

'Is okay!' the driver yelled.

My hearing cleared as if I had swallowed and the pressure had equalised in my ears. The bubble popped and time rushed back into furious motion. Still alive was my first thought; still in the van was my second as the roaring cacophony flooded back with a rush.

'What?' It came out as a high pitched shriek.

'Is okay. Yes?'

He was grinning at me, eyes glazed, pupils huge and black. The sweat on the dark skin of his face had created strange reflections in the bright glare of the lorry's headlights that were already fading behind us. I turned to look at the others.

'He's mad. He's totally fucking MAD. We've got to get out – now!'

They stared back with distant blank expressions. Rickets seemed to shake himself free from the torpor of shock and once again lurched for the driver and again his head crunched into the ceiling joist. He swayed in his seat with an expression of polite surprise. An ugly weal was rising across the centre of his forehead.

'What do we do? What do we . . . aaah.'

I fell back as the rear end of the van slid wildly round another corner.

'I always wanted children,' Tom said in a sad and toneless voice.

'You what?'.

'I really just always wanted them. Do you know what I mean?'

'Er . . . well, not exactly.'

'It's not important now,' he said with such conviction that I couldn't answer him. There was an odd moaning sound that rose and fell, depending on the severity of the vehicle's manoeuvres. I spotted our Leader rocking back and forth, clutching my seat with claw- like hands.

'How do we stop him?' I asked. He rocked harder and shook his head.

'Well, you're a fat lot of good.'

'Open the door,' John suggested. 'At least the lights will come on. It might slow him down.'

When I pulled on the handle the lights flooded the van in a wash of harsh electric light.

'No, is okay!' The driver shouted angrily, letting go of the wheel with one hand and leaning towards me. The van veered towards the rock wall from which the road was carved. I slammed the door shut and darkness returned.

'It worked,' John shouted. 'He slowed down. He almost stopped.'

'He almost crashed,' I said sharply.

'Do it again ... Oh not again. No.'

I turned to see the tail lights of another slow climbing lorry flash past as the van lurched for a tiny gap on the inside. At least we can't go over the edge, I thought, as the sheer metal side of the lorry threatened to smear the van across the rock wall. A shadow pitched towards the driver and I heard Rickets crumple bonelessly into the aisle with an odd gurgling sound. He started retching and curled himself into a foetal position, moaning pitifully.

'What's wrong with him?' someone asked.

'He keeps hitting his head.'

'Is he going to be sick? I don't want him puking on me as well as this.'

'Shut up, Richard, and get off your bloody knees, you're in the way,' John snapped in the darkness. 'Joe. Open the door. We need light.'

As the light flooded in I anticipated the driver's reaction and pointed back at the prostrate wretched figure writhing on the floor.

'Is sick, is very bad,' I said, doing a passable impression of a wildly messy vomit. The driver glanced at Rickets, then back at the road. The engine slowed and the van pulled gently into the shelter of a rock overhang at the side of the road.

Before the vehicle had stopped Rickets had lunged for the sliding door, grabbed the handle, pulled it and flung his body out on to the road in one neat movement. There was a whooping, screaming war cry and suddenly the team was jammed in the doorway fighting to escape. I tried to climb over the front seat since my door was too close to the rock wall to open but was blocked by a scrum of struggling bodies. Suddenly the obstacle cleared and we fell through the door in a heap of limbs.

Rickets stood in the middle of the road with his arms raised above his head. His pitifully thin body was silhouetted cruelly by the harsh lights of the lorry we had just overtaken. At the moment when I was convinced he would be run down the monster shuddered to a halt in a hiss of air brakes. A man leaned out of the high cab and shouted at Rickets, who stood defiantly in the way, determined not to have to get back into the van.

With the help of the Major we managed to persuade the lorry driver that our man was too dangerous to travel. Our man was enraged and yelled abuse at us, the Major and the lorry driver, but we were unshaken. We were effectively going on strike, boycotting our own transport. The lorry driver eventually agreed to take the team in his spacious cab and we started to climb gratefully aboard, leaving a dispirited van driver in the road.

'Hang on,' Tom said suddenly, 'all our gear is on that van. Money, clothes, the lot. We can't just abandon it.'

'Well, what do you suggest?' I asked as I struggled to climb into the cab. John was blocking the way in front of me.

'Someone had better stay with it,' our leader announced bravely from the depths of the cab. 'And since you two can't fit in here it may as well be you.'

'No way!' John said.

'Come on, out you go.' Richard was being uncommonly decisive. 'We'll instruct the driver through the Major that on no account is he to overtake this lorry.'

'And what guarantee is there of him sticking to it?' John asked as we looked up at the hurriedly closed and locked door above us.

'Do not worry,' the Major called down. 'I will impress on him strongly that he must keep to the plan.'

The lorry rumbled slowly forward with a belch of blue exhaust.

'Here.' John passed me a cigarette and glanced at our driver. 'I think you'll need it.'

The van crept slowly forward, keeping pace with the lorry on the steep hill start. I glanced at our driver. There were beads of sweat on his forehead and his eyes were fixed determinedly on the red tail lights ahead of him. The ruby glow on his face gave him a diabolic appearance. As we approached the first bend at a walking pace I sat back and relaxed, confident that he would do as he was told. I inhaled deeply and blew the smoke through my teeth with a hiss. The driver's arm pumped forward on the gear lever, there was a shriek of engine noise and the van hurtled sideways and forward. The lorry was behind us before either of us could react.

In the cab of the lorry the team saw two white faces staring in anguish from the van as it disappeared round a sharp lefthand corner. Two hours later it rumbled to a halt beside the van parked on the side of the road where the gorge opened out into a sandy desert area. The driver was slumped comatose across the wheel.

'Well done, lads,' Richard said as he jumped down from the lorry. John gave him a vicious look and flicked his glowing cigarette at him. 'May as well get some sleep until he recovers,' he said brushing the embers off his shoulder.

Thirty six hours after leaving Rawalpindi the van rolled to a blessed halt outside the Hunza Inn Hotel in Gilgit. We climbed wearily out of the side door and gathered on the street, waiting for our luggage to be unloaded. As the driver stepped from his seat a tall heavily built man reached out and grabbed his collar. He hauled the driver towards him and landed a solid punch on the side of his jaw. We looked on, bemused but appreciative. Another man, a young man, stepped forward and threw a second punch, catching the driver on the top of his head to which he held his arms up protectively. The tall man berated him in rapid fire Urdu and when the driver risked a look from under his arms he caught a full blow on the side of the temple and went down in the dust. The young man aimed a vicious kick to the kidneys. Astonished and unsure of what was happening, we remained silent. Then the Major informed us that news had travelled ahead with the lorry driver and now the man's father and brother were punishing our man for being so late. We began laughing and clapping as the poor wretch was dragged off down the street.

The van was unloaded and we dragged our rucksacks into the cool shelter of the Hunza Inn's courtyard. Four days were spent buying supplies and looking for more reliable transport into the Hunza valley. We had recovered and were looking forward to getting to grips with the mountain. Unknown to us at the time, by far the most dangerous part of the expedition had already been survived.

We spent our last day in Gilgit lazing in deckchairs on the lawn of the Hunza Inn, ordering green tea and biscuits and trying to forget the horror of the Silk Road. At midday a boy called us to lunch and we settled down to a feast. Halfway through the meal I felt someone pushing the back of my chair in a soft rhythmic movement. I looked round and was puzzled to see that there was no-one behind me. Turning back to the table, I noticed that everyone else was swaying back and forth. The wall lights made tinkling noises as they swung against the plaster wall. Richard was staring at me with a horrified expression. The others looked perplexed. He mouthed the word 'earthquake' at the same time as it dawned on me what was happening. We lurched to our feet and dived for the safety of the doorway at the exact moment that the rocking motion stopped. We collided and stumbled on to our knees. The other diners looked at us curiously and laughed. A few minutes later John came into the dining-room looking very shaken. He had been dozing on the upstairs balcony when the quake struck. It had stopped as he was about to break his legs by leaping into the courtyard below.

The following morning we gratefully left for the mountains. It was to be a wonderfully happy and successful expedition. The mountain was even more beautiful than the photographs suggested. It was not a technically difficult climb, nor one that was especially dangerous. The whole pace and atmosphere was much more relaxed than it had been in Peru, and for the first time I realised how intensely we had pushed things on Siula Grande when the two of us on our first expedition had thrown ourselves at an extreme route which had rebuffed at least four previous expeditions. Taking the absolute minimum of equipment, food and fuel, we had been lucky to survive. I was proud that we had completed the ascent in good style and managed to extricate ourselves from a desperate situation, but I was ashamed of the mistakes we had made. Now, on returning to the mountains, I recognised to some extent how narrow-minded I had been. It had seemed so overwhelmingly important then to make a first ascent, to achieve an extreme new route, more important almost than my life. It was a blindly stupid attitude, competitive, ambitious, and overconfident. What had I been so desperately trying to gain? There was more to the mountains than their hardest faces and most challenging ridges. Simply being among them was a privilege worth seeking.

In an effort to save weight on Siula Grande, we had taken such a small rack of equipment – six ice screws, two home made ineffective snow stakes, and a few pitons and wires – that once into the mixed ground above the icefield it was impossible for us to have retreated. We had allowed ourselves less than half a gas cylinder per day for making drinks, only five dried prunes, half a bar of chocolate and half a freeze dried meal each per fourteen-hour climbing day. The whole trip had been run on such a shoestring that we had been unable to feed ourselves adequately at base camp, let alone on the mountain.

The lesson came home to me forcibly when we unloaded our gear at Tupopdam base camp. There were mounds of chocolate, fifty-six pounds in weight of Thorntons' fudge, boxes of sweets, cans of tuna fish and salmon, sacks of fresh spinach, potatoes and onions, rice, porridge, packets of freeze dried meals and soups. There was also a huge seven-foot tall cook called Kooshnoor, with his awesome double burner paraffin stove, and the expedition sheep in tow. In Peru our only luxury item was one small sweet lime each per day.

On the third day of our approach to base camp we staggered up on to a high shoulder where a few mud huts perched. Dropping our massive rucksacks to the ground, we stood silent and motionless at our first sight of the mountain looming above us. It was much bigger than we had expected and so much more beautiful. I felt the old familiar tingle down my spine as the mountain beckoned me at the same time as it repelled me. I knew at once that Richard had been right to encourage me to return. I felt at home here. It was where I needed to be.

In an inexplicable way it was like a great shadow lifting from me – a far more cathartic and healing experience than writing or psychoanalysis could ever have been. It filled me with a sense of joy and relief to discover that I loved the mountains; if I had rejected them and seen only menace and terror in their ridges and faces, then all the things I had experienced on them in the past would have become meaningless. All the summits reached and fears felt, and all the friends lost would have become worthless; everything would have seemed a senseless waste. Suddenly I realised that my fear of returning was as much a fear of this sort of disillusionment as it was of what the mountains could do to me.

'Hell fire,' Richard muttered as he looked fearfully at the East Face of Tupopdam. 'I didn't realise it was going to be that big.'

This first view after the ordeal of the previous week came as a sudden icy wash of cleansing rain. It caught us by surprise. One moment we had been head down, toiling up the dry rocky valley, the next we had rounded the corner and there it was, piercing the cobalt sky. First sightings are always strange bitter sweet affairs. The objective suddenly becomes real and focused. The plans and dreams are suddenly staring you in the face and a whole mixture of contradictory emotions flood through your mind.

'Looks as if we could do a new route up that face,' I suggested after a long thoughtful silence.

'You've got to be mad,' Tom said in amazement.

'Why not do the lefthand shoulder? It's much easier.'

'The face would be quicker and more direct. It's a much better line.'

'It's lethal. Look at those ice cliffs. They threaten the whole face.'

'No, they don't. If you keep to that central rib, break up that short gully and back on to the rib, nothing can touch you. It's quite safe.'

There was a distant sound of thunder and a small puff of snow appeared high on the mountainside. In seconds it had mushroomed out and swept down the centre of the face, obliterating the rib and gully of my safe line.

'Right,' I said with false bravado. 'That settles it. We go for the lefthand shoulder route.'

Four hours later we established our base camp on a small rib of moraines directly beneath the east face. While we pitched our tents and built rock windbreaks around them, three avalanches thundered down the line I had proposed. In an attempt to escape from the mocking laughter I set off with Tom to reconnoitre the start of a gully line that led up to the lefthand shoulder. We returned two hours later confident that it was possible to reach the shoulder on the north-east ridge by a slanting traverse up into the gully. The porters and Kooshnoor had arrived with the rest of the supplies and the kitchen tent had been pitched.

The porters ran back down the moraine spit, anxious to return to the valley before dark. Their whoops and cries of farewell, echoing off the hills, gradually faded, leaving the mountain to ourselves. Our cook, Kooshnoor, sat by the kitchen holding the sheep's rope. The sheep stood by and examined the camp with a jaundiced expression as if the three-day mountain walk from the valley boded ill to it.

'What's he saying?' Tom asked as Kooshnoor rattled off a few quick fire sentences in Urdu.

'I think he wants a knife,' Rickets said.

'Why?'

Kooshnoor employed some very explicit mimes to indicate what he would do to the sheep. The sheep looked at the cook and then at us with an oddly quizzical expression on its face.

I moved towards the sheep. 'He wants to slaughter it in the muslim style. What's it called?'

'Halal,' Tom said, and Kooshnoor nodded happily.

'Halal, that's right. I can't remember agreeing to that when we bought it, can you?'

'How else would we kill it then?' Jungle asked.

'Quickly, that's how,' I said sharply. The sheep seemed to realise I was defending it and shuffled towards me, keeping its wide golden eyes fixed on whoever was speaking. It gazed at me with unnerving directness. 'Halal slaughtering is bloody cruel. The animals are bled to death.'

Kooshnoor said something emphatically and with an angry slashing gesture. The sheep looked anxious.

'I think he's saying he won't eat it if we don't halal slaughter it,' Tom suggested.

'All right, then. We'll eat it. It won't go far between the six of us anyway.' A pair of golden eyes stared piteously at me, making me feel uncomfortable.

'Look, if he doesn't kill it, who will?' John said ignoring the sheep.

'I will.' I avoided meeting the sheep's eyes. 'We have to be as humane as possible.'

'Let it go, then,' Tom suggested. 'I never wanted it in the first place.'

'You should have told us you were a veggie before we bought it, shouldn't you, eh?'

'And how are you going to be humane. Killed a lot of sheep have you?' Jungle asked.

'I'll make it quick so it doesn't know about it,' I said testily.

'If you ask me,' Richard interrupted, 'it looks as if it might just keel over anyway.' The sheep had lain down and was looking decidedly ill. It had been a miserable looking specimen down in the valley; here at base camp it looked positively woebegone.

'How will it be quick?' Jungle persisted.

'With a bloody great rock,' I snapped. 'Or an ice axe. Yes, an axe will be quick. A damn sight quicker than cutting its throat . . . and stop bloody staring at me,' I shouted at the sheep.

Kooshnoor stood up and started waving his arms and

shouting angrily. He was a tall well-built man from the Hunza valley.

'Now look what you've done,' Jungle said. 'Never upset the chef, it's a golden rule, you know.'

'What's he saying now?'

'I think he's saying that he won't cook it if we kill it,' Tom said.

'Why not?'

'How should I know? It's probably unclean, defiled, something like that.'

The argument with the cook raged for most of the afternoon until eventually, with Kooshnoor about to leave, I was forced to capitulate. The unfortunate sheep was led away with one last despairing golden-eyed look at me.

By evening we had forgotton about the poor sheep as we waited expectantly for our food. The delicious smell of roasting liver wafted over the tents. Kooshnoor handed out the small chunks of meat that he had roasted on kebabs over a wood fire. They were superb, and we anticipated hungrily the main meal, imagining what delights were in store for us. Rogan josh style curry, shami kebabs, spinnach and lamb korma, maybe even lamb tikka. We were given a plate of rice with a serving of lightly stewed intestines on top.

Somehow Kooshnoor managed to produce the same dish for four days on the trot and we were running out of rocks under which to shovel it. The sheep seemed to have infinitely long guts, and by the time a few scraggy bits of meat appeared on our plates it had a high, over-ripe smell and taste to it. The carcass, stored in a hessian sack in the hot sun, was begining to stink. For some reason the head, minus the golden eyes, was placed on one of the kitchen walls.

On the sixth day we began to make forays into the kitchen for food when Kooshnoor was away from the camp. Our morning meal of porridge was also thrown discreetly under rocks without the cook noticing because it had been contaminated with paraffin on the walk in. It was a risky business, as Rickets discovered when he was surprised by an enraged cook and shooed out of the tent empty-handed.

When, on the seventh day, we saw that the skull had been split open and the contents emptied, we went into open revolt and refused to eat any more of the sheep.

Nine weeks before I had flown out to Pakistan the doctors, with exquisitely bad timing, had chosen to clear a mess of fibrous growths and bone chippings from my damaged knee. The knee cap had been removed and the debris washed out of the joint. It was the fifth operation on the knee in two years. I went to the Karakoram without much hope of being able to climb. A month before departure I could barely walk. In fact the knee felt so weakened by the operation I doubted whether I would even reach base camp. When we discovered that we had miscalculated the cost of porterage and could afford only half the required number of porters, it meant we had to carry ninety, and in Tom's case, one hundred pound rucksacks. I was convinced that my knee would not be up to the strain.

There was nothing else to do but to see how far I could get. The three days were purgatory for us all but, to my astonishment, I not only reached base camp but grew stronger and stronger as the weeks went by, eventually joining John and Rickets in a summit attempt. Then I had to drop out. The strain on the knee finally took effect and it became dangerously unstable. It would have been madness to continue with the climb. I watched my two companions carry on up the mountainside from the vantage of a high camp with a mixture of disappointment and happiness. Above all I was delighted to find that my love affair with the mountains was stronger than ever.

When John and Andy got back, having successfully made the first ascent, I knew I had to return, if not to Tupopdam, then certainly to the mountains. If I could no longer climb, then simply being among them would suffice. This was a radical change in thinking for some- one who detested walking unless there was something to climb at the end.

I walked away from that first visit to the Himalaya with warm memories of an expedition full of laughter and pleasure. Andy Cave travelled to Nepal from Pakistan to join an expedition on Ama Dablam, one of the world's most beautiful mountains. He and Andy Perkins were forced to retreat from high on the mountain with the hardest sections climbed because of lethal snow conditions. He returned to Sheffield to learn the devastating news that Trevor Pilling and his girlfriend had been reported missing, and presumed dead, probably on a mountain called Fluted Peak in the east of Nepal. Whatever new conclusions I had come to about mountaineering, the attrition was as unrelenting as ever.

Two years later Tom and I returned for a second crack at Tupopdam but failed once again, driven back by a combination of stormy weather and dangerous avalanche conditions. We spent a long night at a high bivouac watching a lightning storm flashing silently above the mountains in China. Fortunately it kept away from us and we tramped down from our high point thwarted again but determined to return and climb the mountain at some time in the future.

16

AVOIDING THE TOUCH

WHEN YOU CLIMB a chimney, you don't at first notice the peculiar sense of perspective you get as you look down. Once you are suffiently high, however, you suddenly become aware that the curving walls of the chimney below seem to be converging to a distant point on the ground and above they are running together into the sky, in the way that railway lines do horizontally across a flat desert plain. When you reach the top of the chimney and look down, you experience a mildly sickening sensation. If it is a very tall chimney, and also a windy day, it will be swaying with a slow sweeping rhythm that is deeply frightening.

A similar thing occurs when you abseil off very high bridges. At first there is the comforting view of the side of the solid span of rivetted steel girders on either side and the reassuring massiveness of design. Then suddenly you drop beneath the span and all you can see is space, empty space that swings around you as you spin on a thin spider's thread of rope dropping far away beneath you. Looking down, you see the silk-thin end of the rope snaking in empty air above the surging stream of the river, or the tidal flow of an estuary. The undulating swirl of the water distracts your eye, and you cannot properly adjust yourself to the sense of exposure. When you turn, as you would on a sea cliff, to look at the comforting solid wall of rock you see only empty space in all directions, and there is always a wind under a bridge to push you out at an angle while the bridge shivers and rumbles with passing traffic. The whole situation, bridge, space, wind and

263

water seem to conspire to unnerve you. The thin rope vibrates like a plucked guitar string as lorries roll overhead and it is hard not to be frightened.

Trying to deal with fear is instructive. Your mind seems to split into two opposing arguments; one warns you of every possible or impossible peril while the other encourages you with firm orders not to listen to such nonsense. There is no logical reason to be alarmed. The bridge is not about to collapse, the rope will not snap, and the wind cannot harm you. But something small and mischievous within your imagination begins to conjure up any number of disastrous consequences.

What if someone fiddles with the anchor point on the bridge?

Don't be silly, the police will guard it.

Is my harness slipping, or is the knot coming undone?

No, get on with it.

Will someone cut the rope for a laugh? What if a ship comes and the rope gets entangled in its mast and it drags me down?

Of course they won't, and you'll see the ship miles away and pull the rope up. Okay?

Would I survive a fall that far into water?

No, so forget it.

Fear seems to exist only in our imagination. Without imagination, without the ability to see our place in the future, to work out the consequence of a particular event in all its gruesome detail, we would be quite fearless. I suppose that is why serious violent accidents, such as car crashes, avalanches, and long bouncing falls are frequently described as not frightening while actually taking place. It's as if so much is happening to you, so much information is rushing into your mind that you have no time to imagine what the outcome might be. Things seem to happen in slow motion, as if the speed at which your mind is operating is affecting your perception of time.

The future is simply a matter of fact, an emotionless reality – you will be dead – and that is that. Only the present, what is happening to you at this very instant, concerns you. Because of this, you are unable to extrapolate what the future will be like as a result of what is happening to you now. All you can do is to experience the present, nothing more. Deprived of the ability to imagine the future, you are fearless; suddenly there is nothing to be scared about. You have no time to ponder on death's significance or fear what it may feel like. In the cataclysmic violence of the accident you lose not only the future but the past as well. You lose all possible reasons for fear, unable as you are to understand the loss of what you once were or what you could become. Time is frozen for you into the present events and sensations, the knocks, and bumps from which you can draw no emotional conclusions. *I'm crashing. I'm falling fast. I'm about to die. This is it.* In truth you have far too much on your mind for such frivolous luxuries as fear.

I once drove too fast in patchy fog on a dangerous stretch of road in North Wales. It didn't seem fast at the time, or not until I hit the slate wall at fifty miles an hour. I was heading for Llanberis, anxious to get there before the pubs closed. John and Eileen were asleep in the back of the car. Beside me in the front Tim Carruthers was leaning forward, changing the tape in the music system that I had fitted in the glove compartment. I had told him to fasten his seatbelt but he had ignored me. We were near the Silver Fountain when the visibility deteriorated suddenly.

I accelerated into a clear space of night air and my headlights lit the start of a curling lefthand curve in the road. I swung round the bend into a cloud of thick fog. There were no road markings so I kept my eyes on the side of the road and began to slow down, unaware that I was driving into an unmarked lay-by. I spotted the squat solid slate wall at the end of it a split second before the car hit it. I felt calm and devoid of emotion. There was no time in which to shout. We hit hard and the world began to shatter around me.

I remember hearing the crashing sound of music and thought what good timing Tim had to get the tape turned on before we crashed. I saw him surge forward off his seat. The windscreen exploded silently in a spray of icy fragments, backlit by the white glare of the headlights. It seemed odd that the headlamps hadn't smashed. Tim's forehead crunched into the dashboard and his head flopped up and back with a heavy slow wobble. It was like seeing a slow-motion replay of a boxer being punched unconscious, with the hair and sweat spraying back and the head flopping disjointedly on nerveless neck muscles. With Tim, it wasn't sweat but blood; a great gouty spray of blood from a jagged laceration across his forehead.

I watched in fascination while I brought my arm slowly across my chest and the seat belt cut in tighter and harder as slowly I crumpled up against the steering-wheel, feeling my sternum go with a crack and the dense meaty impact of John's body pressing into the back of my seat, bending the metal of the framework so that, in spite of the belt, I hit the wheel hard.

A shower of cassette boxes came streaming backwards from the open glove compartment. They seemed to float past, as if weightless, turning slowly in the air. The can of beer in Tim's hand toppled back and joined the stream of plastic boxes as his brain was punched asleep. The headlights glared dementedly off the white fog banks. Eileen's head whipped forward between the seats to hit the gear stick and lash back again, keeping a crazy rhythm with Tim's blood as it surged forwards and backwards.

Then it was over. Between seeing the slate wall and stopping had been a fraction of a second yet it had gone on for a lifetime. All was momentarily silent. The red tail lights of a car flickered past and two fleeting crimson eyes faded into the fog. It was very still, and I felt as if I were holding my breath. My chest hurt with a needle-sharp stabbing pain. There was a bubbling noise. I thought I could hear bleeding in the silence.

Real time rushed back in at me with a woozy sensation and the sound of Tim's gurgling breath broke the unnatural quiet. My past and the future returned with a vengeance. I looked at Tim. He lay unconscious, slumped forward on the dashboard, and bled with vigour, and I thought, *I told you. You should have worn your belt, you stupid prick!* I might even have said it aloud. I wondered whether he was dying and then, feeling the pain in my chest and my arm trapped behind the wheel, a flicker of panic ran a tingle of fear up my spine.

I thought coldly, factually, without emotion. Then fear overwhelmed me as I imagined what could have happened. I realised that we were alive though we should have died. Was Tim going to die, and why hadn't the others said anything; were they dead too? All at once I had the time in which to imagine what had almost been and I started shaking. I squirmed and tried to move but the pressure of the seat trapped me tight.

Suddenly Eileen was at the window, looking in at me. Her left eye was closed and both lids were swollen into two blue-black plums. I remembered her head whiplashing forward on to my arm and the gearstick and I had a flashing memory of the plastic boxes floating past weightlessly, as though in a space craft, and the white glare of the headlights.

'Are you okay?' she shouted. A car went past in the fog with a sodium yellow glow of lights. I watched the smudges of red tail lights fade.

'I'm trapped,' I said. 'Tim's bleeding. He's unconscious.'

'I know. We need help.'

'Where's John?'

'Asleep.' She smiled. 'He hasn't woken up.'

'What?'

'He's so pissed he hasn't woken up yet.'

'Can you get me out of here?' I asked, struggling to reach the door handle. 'I need a pull to get me out sideways.'

I slid out easily. Eileen helped me move Tim into the back of the car where he gurgled and bled profusely on my jacket. I resented him for that. It seemed petty but I wasn't myself. John had woken up on the floor behind my seat and, after shaking himself down, had wandered unsteadily round to the front of the car. We found him passing his hand slowly back and forth where the windscreen had been with a puzzled look on his face.

'Yes, John,' Eileen said. 'We've had an accident.'

'Right,' he said, brightening up, 'I thought as much. Amazing what those treble gins can do. Didn't feel a thing, not a scratch.' He said it with satisfaction and went off to examine the front of the car, or rather the lack of the front of the car.

The man who hauled us off said the road had an inverse camber. According to the police, there had been seven accidents on the bend in the past two months. After treatment at the hospital in Llandudno we were taken to the police station. They suspected that I had been drinking but the breathalysing machine came up negative, as I knew it would. They said I must have been driving too fast. I complained about the lack of road marking. Then they lost interest and told us to go away. I was numb with fright over what nearly happened. I had bought the car for £550 three weeks before. The scrap merchant gave me £17 for the remains and charged me £40 for towing away the wreck.

Fear, like balance, is not innate but painfully learnt. The fight and flee instincts of all animals are not intuitive responses but carefully controlled actions. In the same way as they are learned, they can be unlearned. Fear can be controlled, rationalised away, understood for what it is and ignored. Some people are better at doing this than others, but everyone does it. Crossing the road is a fine exercise in self control, battening down the impulsive imagination and refusing to let it pull a fast one on you and convince you that, yes, that truck will hit you after all.

At the same time, fear is usually a positive, helpful mechanism. It posts warnings to you all the time – watch out here, don't do that, slow down, mind the step – without which you would soon be dead. In a world full of loud conflicting information, increasingly filling up our addled minds, it is a good thing to have fear as a lookout in the mind, checking for the accident that is waiting to happen, alert for the slightest danger signals.

The trick really is to sample fear. That's where the self control lies. Select the fear you want or need to react with and dispense with the rest. Examine each fear as it builds up, understand what it's warning you about and act accordingly. For the climber, this often means operating continuously in a state of controlled fear. Only when the level of fear becomes intolerable does the climber know he is moving close to or beyond his limits and had better do something about it. Retreat, lunge for the handhold, remain motionless, whatever seems the best way to avoid the cause of the fear.

Ladders, like chimneys, are extremely frightening things to climb. Ladders on chimneys are the living end. John and I had climbed a lot of ladders for Greenpeace, and our fair share of chimneys. I once climbed a very long ladder up a tall thin steel chimney and slept on the top for three days, alone with my thoughts, the biting north-east wind scything in from the sea across the grim tangle of the chemical works below. It was the first time I had climbed as a protest action on behalf of Greenpeace, and it was the least enjoyable of them. The spiteful winter wind brought black rain squalls in over the mouth of the Humber, smudging out the view of Spurn Head and Sunk Island. At night, with navigation lights twinkling from the dark estuary and the bleak industrial landscape of Cleethorpes and Grimsby momentarily hidden, I almost liked the wind but for the way it made me frightened. Workers in the chemical plant banged the steel chimney with scaffolding poles to keep me awake and nervous. Hollow booming echoes shivered up the chimney while the wind made it sway six long inches from side to side. My imagination kept telling me it was falling over, or that the ropes holding the portaledge had shifted, or that the acid cloud was coming, and I kept telling myself that it wasn't true, despite the self assurance being hard to believe.

On the first day a man was murdered in the nearby town. No one could remember when last there had been a murder in Cleethorpes and it made big news in the local papers. There was no mention of me on my chimney, trying to save the Humber estuary from death and destruction and massive pollution by acids and heavy metals. I stayed up there hopefully. After a long night, with the truckers calling me on their radios, calling me Santa Claus, 'breaker one-nine for a copy', and the workers banging the chimney, keeping me awake, I watched the sun rise through a cloud of sulphuric acid steam from an adjacent chimney. I peered through the misted goggle eyes of my gas mask and kept one thumb jammed in the hole where one of the two filters had fallen out during the night and became scared of being asphyxiated.

If someone had been with me, I wouldn't have been so scared, I theorised as the acid clouds drifted by, because I could have been reassured, through seeing a partner, that everything was okay.

Later, when the wind shifted and the acid drifted away, I checked the ropes for damage and tried not to imagine them melting. I reminded myself that they were polypropolene ropes and wouldn't be affected by the acid, but something answered me back, questioning whether I was sure this was a fact or maybe just hearsay, and I began to worry again. During the day a nearby chemical plant had to deal with a leak and an explosion that made big news. The plant manufactured the same chemical as had been produced by Union Carbide at Bhopal in India when that went up and thousands died in their sleep. No one could remember such a near disaster in England and the papers were full of the story. It was depressing not to be in the news.

As no one seemed to care about the dead estuary I told the Greenpeace team that I would stay another night and day to see if we made the news. Late the following afternoon I climbed down the rusty swaying chimney and surrendered to the police. I was cold, my skin felt clammy from the wet acid air, and I was exhausted by the continuous effort of trying not to be fearful for three days on end. Workers from the plant stood in white overalls in a circle at the foot of the ladder, some holding scaffolding poles. I felt intimidated. Then they started cheering and clapping, and some moved closer and slapped me on the back. As I walked towards the police car I heard shouts of 'Well done, lad' and 'Good on you, kid'. Everyone except the managers seemed to be smiling. They stood to one side in their three-piece grey suits, looking silly with white plastic construction helmets on their heads, and tried to appear stern. I gave them the finger before I ducked into the police car and the workers laughed and cheered louder. As we drove out of the compound I heard one of them banging the chimney with a scaffolding pole, as if to say we meant you no harm, we were only following orders. Glancing round, I saw through the back window a besuited manager gesticulating angrily at the man.

The police took my camera and exposed the film with the pictures I had taken of the illegal fly dumping of chemicals and told me with taunting grins that, as the miners had just abandoned their year-long strike, I wouldn't get into the news at all. They let me go without charge and I didn't make the news. But I remembered their stupid laughter, and the single remaining fisherman who said that nothing lived in the River Humber any more, and I was converted to the cause.

Years later, I found myself perched on the very last rung at the top of a forty-foot ladder with John pressed against the back of my thighs. The ladder was leaning at a precarious angle and below us were the sharp granite edges of steps. A fine rain was blowing coldly from the north-east and the stone plinth against which the ladder rested was wet and slipppery. I stepped warily off the top rung and on to the sloping stone. At once my feet began to slip and I tried to get back on to the ladder which had shifted further to the side and John stared at me fearfully as I stretched my foot back towards the top rung. It was obvious that, if I made the step, I would push the ladder away and he would fall. Since I was roped to him I would fall too.

'I've got to get back,' I pleaded, 'it's wet and covered with pigeon shit.'

'You can't. You'll push me off.' There was a loud shout from below and John's arm jerked. 'Shit!'

'What?'

'One of the coppers has got hold of the ropes.'

'Tell him we need them.'

John shouted down and his arm was jerked again.

'God! If he's not careful he'll pull us off.'

'What did he say? Has he still got the ropes?'

'He's not buying it at all. I think he's angry, very angry.'

'Look, I'll try to reach that ledge,' I said, 'I'll be safe there and they won't be able to see me. Then I'll start screaming.'

'Con them into thinking you're about to fall, you mean?'

'Yeah, and you ask them for the rope. Be desperate. You know.'

'I *am* bloody desperate!' John snapped. 'If he pulls me like that again I'll be off.'

When I reached the ledge and made myself safe, I started screaming and hollering at John. I put everything into it until my voice was cracking with terror and the people on the ground stopped struggling and fell quiet. They knew someone was in mortal danger and the knowledge paralysed them. Even the policemen froze – all except the barmy Inspector who had hold of the rope. I screamed so loud and so well that I scared myself. The sound of my panic convinced me that I really was in trouble and I became sure I was slipping. I wasn't, of course, but my head told me I was. I gripped the slimy granite harder, screamed the harder and became even more scared.

I heard John shouting at the policeman. He sounded genuinely frightened and angry, while for me it was all make believe – or it was supposed to be. The policemen began remonstrating with their officer, trying to persuade him to let go of the rope and, as he turned to face them, he lost concentration. One rope flicked from his hand. John had it up and away in seconds, hauling in hard and yelling exultantly. Once the rope was safely clear he untied the remaining rope, which the police inspector still held, from his harness and threw it down with a contemptuous laugh.

He quickly joined me on the ledge and tentatively we edged round the wide base of the column. An ornate carving of a rope offered some muck-filled slimy handholds and clouds of pigeons swung round the square in agitated circles, occasionally sweeping towards us and strafing us with their wingbeats. It didn't bother us. We were free to continue the climb up the lightning conductor on Nelson's Column in

London's Trafalgar Square in what was to be one of Greenpeace's most successful land-based direct actions. We were arrested by an apoplectic officer when eventually we abseiled down seven hours later, but there was little he could do. We had been careful not to cause a breach of the peace, or any criminal damage, and could be fined only £10 for breaking a local bye-law pertinent to Trafalgar Square.

Together John and I have climbed chimneys, buildings, bridges, skyscrapers and monuments and hung a wide variety of flags and banners from them in protest against the injustices of the world. The Houses of Parliament, Harrods, Australia House and Tower Bridge have been bannered to save pilot whales, kangaroos, fur-bearing animals and the ozone layer. We have romped up a huge three-hundred-foot fair wheel in Vienna and, unaware that machine-gun-toting members of the elitist Cobra force were after us, had hung a banner protesting against atom bomb testing. In Canada we were caught three hundred feet up the sky-scraping walls of the Toronto nuclear power industry headquarters. We were charged with piracy and convicted of stowing away after boarding the acid-dumping ships in the North Sea. Using poorly fitting ice screws, we have climbed nervously up the six hundred feet of chimney at the Ferrybridge power station in a sixty mile an hour gale and abseiled in a blue funk off the Clifton Suspension Bridge with a massive banner demanding that Britain's rivers be saved. We even learned to fly parachutes with 450 cc propeller-driven engines on our backs in the mad hope of boarding an aircraft carrier carrying nuclear weapons at sea.

In short, we prostituted ourselves at first not to the enviromental movement but to the adrenalin surge of fear and exhilaration that comes with these actions. Our approach was soon tempered by the terrible facts revealed to us by Greenpeace campaigners of a world on the brink of self-destruction, a planet on which one species of animal had managed in a fraction of the time of its existence to bring the whole system to the point of collapse. While the Cold War still firmly gripped the world, an enviromentalist described the condition of the earth with a chilling analogy.

Planet Earth is 4,600 million years old. If we condense this inconceivable time-span into an understandable concept, we can liken earth to a person of 46 years of age. Nothing is known about the first 7 years of this person's life . . . only at the age of 42 did the earth begin to flower. Dinosaurs and the great reptiles did not appear until one year ago when the planet was 45. Mammals arrived 8 months ago and in the middle of last week man-like apes evolved into ape-like men and at the weekend, the last ice age enveloped the Earth.

Modern man has been around for four hours. During the last hour man took to agriculture. The Industrial Revolution began a minute ago. During those sixty seconds of biological time, Modern Man has made a rubbish tip of paradise. He has multiplied his numbers to plague proportions, caused the extinction of thousands of species, ransacked the planet for fuels and now stands like a brutish infant, gloating over his meteoric ascendancy, on the brink of a war to end all wars and without regard for this oasis of life in the solar system.

If today the threat of nuclear war has diminished slightly, the destruction of the planet goes on apace. To think that we have managed to damage not only the climate but also the structure of our atmosphere and the vast oxygen producing rain forests is appalling. Somehow man has managed to unbalance the fragile system that makes the earth a place of life. It is a far more frightening reality than any mountain I have been on.

I make no apology, and nor does John Stevenson, for saying that our Greenpeace actions are the most worthwhile things we have ever done. For once in our lives, we set aside our selfish ambitions, took the moral high ground and protested to the world with right on our side. We were rewarded with criminal records and didn't give a damn. We are usually apathetically apolitical in outlook, and the fact that we became so committed is more a tribute to what we were taught by Greenpeace than any moral or ethical zeal on our part. Having taken part in 18 direct actions, some of which were life-threatening, having been arrested almost as many times, fined and on occasions assaulted, we still look forward to the next call for us to perform some crazy stunt to bring attention to some new environmental disaster.

I have one reservation. I will not fly motorized parachutes again. After experiencing partial engine failure while high over Derbyshire and suddenly taking on the aerodynamics of a breeze block, I suffered a disrupted disc in my back as a consequence of the impact into fortuitously thick and springy heather. The experience firmly convinced me that fear of flying would never be a fear I could control.

I suppose it is only the belief of being in control that keeps us all on an even keel. The moment we suspect that we are losing control is the moment when fear edges into the fragile balance of our sanity. Death by drowning, burning or falling are archetypal fears that we all recognise, though few alive know of them from experience. We shudder at the imagination of pain before ending in the unknown and wrongly think of them as our worst fears. The violent and numbing reality of crashing a car or plunging down a mountainside is in fact so brutal that there is no time for fear. More often than not it is an experience of deep calm resignation, an utter helplessness so profound that knowing we can do nothing leaves us emotionally empty.

Uncontrolled fear is a corrosive emotion, something that gnaws away at the fabric of your mind, screws you up to a frightful aching state of anxiety, and leaves you with nothing good. *Will I win or lose? Where will I get the money for the mortgage repayments? Are my children safe? Do people like me? Am I a failure? Will I appear foolish or boring? Am I good enough, strong enough, brave enough? Am I making a serious mistake?* There is nothing but sickness in this sort of fear; sickness of the mind which produces no answers to your questions and leaves you in an agonising limbo. At least there is the fight and flee surge of adrenalin in the archetypal fears and the sense of achievement and confidence that comes with confronting the beast.

If you choose to stand under a vast icy mountain wall and make that committing step up, then you have the comfort of choosing your fear. It is something you go to willingly. Embracing the near future and all that it will throw at you with open arms and a clear mind, confident that you will succeed, you will control it. There is no control over parental anxiety, or the stressed businessman's self-doubts, or the world of the lonely and the heartsick. Once indulged, imagined fears of this kind hold us prisoner. They are the penalty of thinking, the penance of life.

In a curious way, maybe the climber stops living when he begins to climb. He steps out of the living world of anxiety into a world where there is no room, no time, for such distractions. All that concerns him is surviving the present. Any thoughts of gas bills and mortgages, loved ones and enemies, evaporate under the absolute neccessity for concentration on the task in hand. He leads a separate life of uncomplicated black and white decisions - *stay warm, feed yourself, be careful, take proper rest, look after yourself and your partner, be aware.* Be aware of everything until there is nothing but the present and there are no corrosive fears to eat away at confidence.

Living for the moment, for nothing but the present, brings with it an unexpected bonus. It seems to me that if you can escape from the need to know the future and free yourself from the constraints of the past, and in so doing act in and only for the present, then you achieve an absolute freedom. If you manage simply to exist you are more free than you could possibly have imagined. In believing this to be true I come as close as I ever will to understanding the existentialist view of the world. Jean-Paul Sartre claimed that 'reality alone is reliable' and that all hopes, ambitions, dreams and expectations are deceptive. He wrote that 'man is no other than a series of undertakings' and that 'he exists only in so far as he realises himself, he is therefore nothing else but the sum of his actions, nothing else but what his life is'.

In the absolute freedom achieved by living solely in the present, however temporarily, I sense that I experience what he meant. The climber chooses to accept a high degree of risk and in so doing the entire responsibility for his existence rests exclusively upon his own shoulders. Although this is true for every moment of his life, it is never more clearly obvious than when he has stepped into that suspended world of present reality. Whatever action he takes directly affects him, and therefore also his partner, to whom he is as committed as he is to himself. Sartre says that existentialism 'is not a philosophy of quietism since it defines man by his action; nor (is it) a pessimistic description of man, for no doctrine is more optimistic, the destiny of man is placed within himself. Nor is it an attempt to discourage man from action since it tells him that there is no hope except in his action, and that the one thing that permits him to have life is the deed. It is an ethic of action and self-commitment.'

There are moments on high cold mountains, life-enhancing moments, when this is precisely so. They are fragile transient times, when the borders between living and dying seem to overlap, when the past and the future cease to exist and you are free. It is because of this commitment to the present that it is so difficult to look back at what you have done and explain why you chose to do it. Perhaps you have to accept that at some point your future self will look back and mock at all that you once were; this is time betraying everything you once believed in. In looking back you lose the perspective of the present, and you can never truly explain yourself.

As the climber edges along the fragile line between the worlds of life and death, peering cautiously into the other side, it is as if he were immortal, neither alive nor actually dead. When he comes down off the mountain and steps unsteadily back into life he tries, with little success, to comprehend what he has just experienced. He has a tantalising memory of those days but is unable to say exactly what has happened. He cannot quite put his finger on it and yet he is in no doubt that something happened. But, with the return of time, of the concerns for past and future, this certainty fades until it appears to be no more than the nebulous recollection of a ghost half-glimpsed in a far away time-worn corridor. At one time he knew what he had seen, knew it to be real, but now he is not sure, nothing seems real and he trembles on the verge of going back for a second look to be sure that he did see it. The uncertainty tickles at his mind until he is forced to go back. When the corrosive fears and anxieties of the present crowd around him once again, he remembers that elusive state when time stood still, those days when his perspectives shifted into another dimension of living, and he hungers to go back there.

I never succeeded in losing that shadowy memory of the mountains. Even when I persuaded myself after Peru that I would never climb again, I couldn't get rid of those haunting memories and the feeling that I had once been somewhere ethereally beautiful, seen an intangible world that I wanted to see again.

17

OUT OF CONTROL

WHEN *Touching the Void* was published in the summer of 1988, a launch party was held in the Sherratt and Hughes bookshop in Sheffield. Seeing it stacked up in the shop filled me with a sense of childish delight. I had written a book and it was there for others to see. I was inordinately proud of myself – not because I thought the book was anything special but simply for managing to write it at all. When I started, my ambitions had been very modest. I wanted to tell the truth about what happened to Simon Yates and me on Siula Grande in Peru, to write honestly and with feeling. At the back of my mind there was a flicker of hope that, maybe, the book would be short-listed for the Boardman Tasker Memorial prize for mountaineering literature, but I kept pushing the idea back and telling myself not to be so foolish. It couldn't possibly happen.

My publisher organized a two-week whirlwind publicity tour which involved rushing round the country to tell the story of Peru to countless journalists and over the radio until my head span with banal questions about climbing and death wishes. I felt embarrassed by the sudden flare of media exposure and the flicker of fame that came with it, but I felt sure it would soon be over and pass. I also felt guilty. It seemed all wrong to become well-known for a serious accident: surely renown should arise from deeds, not screw-ups? My inability to separate the book from climbing caused me a great deal of anguish.

There was also a darker reason for my unease. I was all too well aware of how many close calls I had experienced in the mountains. I dared not think of the long odds I had beaten to survive them. There is no doubt in my mind that the 2,000-foot fall in the avalanche on the Courtes should have killed me. Why it didn't I cannot say. Why the handrail didn't snap on the Drus, or why I hadn't landed four feet to the right in the crevasse in Peru – these are questions without answers to them, only a welter of frightening thoughts. The book and my sudden small celebrity only made me more painfully aware of the friends and acquaintances who had not been graced with such good fortune.

So many of them had died in a short time, and almost all in their very first climbing accident. If you include the fall on the Screen, I had come through four such potentially lethal falls and, deep down, I knew with certainty that I would not survive another. There was a profound sense of guilt about simply surviving. While on the one hand I was pleased with the book's reception, I was also developing a deep sense of anxiety about what was happening to me. I felt out of control.

At first, sales of *Touching the Void* were slow. This came as no surprise to me. On top of feeling guilty, and a fraudulent climber, I began to feel I was an imposter as a writer.

One evening, in the pub, I played a game of snooker with a very serious young man who began talking about books and writing. It turned out that he had been a struggling author for years, pumping out radio plays, short stories and novels and sending them to anyone who would look at them. He had met with little success and had received a great many rejection slips. When he asked me what I did for a living I muttered into my beer something about *Touching the Void* and tried to change the subject. He kept asking with a mixture of admiration and envy how I had done it. I was overcome with remorse. I had not taken the writing seriously and everything about it had just fallen into my lap, whereas this man had tried so hard for nothing. I beat him at snooker and felt even worse. It was a bad night for the Catholics.

Soon afterwards I received a phone call from Dorothy Boardman who told me politely that the book had won the 1988 Boardman Tasker Award for Mountaineering Literature.

She offered me her congratulations. All I could say limply was 'thank you' before putting down the phone with a feeling of utter disbelief. Until then I had not even known the book had been short-listed. I held the Boardman Tasker prize in high regard. It came as a form of approbation by my peers, by the people who climbed, who actually knew what climbing was about. Buoyed up with exhilaration and pride, I went to the pub intent on breathing not a word but getting paralytically drunk. Keeping secrets and getting drunk are mutually incompatible feats, so I was mighty relieved to walk into the pub to a chorus of 'Well done', and to discover that, as so often, I was the last to know.

A short while after the award I gave a slide lecture about the Peruvian adventure to the Royal Geographical Society as part of a symposium on survival. Over lunch, which the audience took with the presenters, John Stevenson and I found ourselves without any wine.

'Well, this isn't so good, is it?' I said, enviously eyeing the three nearly full bottles spaced out along the table to our right.

'I'll just see what I can do about it,' John said with a mischievous glint in his eye.

He leaned over and spoke softly to the woman on his right. Her expression changed from one of polite interest to an appalled look of concern. I saw her lean forward and glance discreetly at me before saying something to John and pursing her lips in a disapproving manner. She turned away and spoke to her neighbour and a ripple of conversation went down the length of the table. Suddenly three bottles appeared in front of me while a whole row of concerned expectant faces peered down the table at me.

'What the hell did you say?' I hissed at John as he quickly filled my glass. I took a sip to hide my embarrassment while he filled his own.

'Oh, it was nothing really,' he said airily. 'I just told them that as a result of the desperate experiences you so graphically described in your slide show you had developed a drink problem bordering on alcoholism . . .'

'You what?' I yelped, spilling my wine.

'Sssshh!' he soothed. 'Don't make a fuss. It worked, didn't it?'

'Yes, but . . . but you can't say that . . . it's . . . they'll think I'm a total pisshead.'

'Well, you will be when we've finished these,' he said cheerfully, filling my glass once more. I gulped at the wine, uncomfortably aware of the expectant faces monitoring my slide into abject alcoholism. I managed a weak and what I hoped was a convincingly ravaged smile and tried to make my fingers shake.

'Cheers,' John said, raising his glass. I glared at him, and he grinned back.

I had spent so many penniless years ducking and diving to make the little cash I needed for climbing, existing in a happy anarchic state on the dole in between, that I gave no thought to the possibility of the book making any money. I dismissed the prize as a one-off fluke, not something that could materially change my life. The one thousand pounds prize money disappeared with astonishing speed into the tills of The Broadfield, my local pub. When Tom Richardson had tried to introduce me to the notion of tax, I pointed out that the book hadn't earned its advance yet and I wouldn't receive any royalties until it did. But he only replied that simply because the potential to earn money existed, that was enough for the DSS to withdraw my housing benefit. This was deeply upsetting.

For a few weeks I dithered uncertainly. I had never felt any sense of stigma about shamelessly accepting handouts and I didn't like the idea of losing the security of a regular welfare cheque. At the back of my mind I knew that one day I would have to get regular work and then I would be paying back these early years of indolence. Now forced into the unpalatable prospect of working, I enrolled in the government's Enterprise Allowance Scheme, despite my view that it was no more than a cynical way of removing numbers from the unemployment figures while guaranteeing little hope of success. The truth more probably lay in the fact that this was how I approached the scheme rather than what it was like. I set up a company called 'Cunning Stunts', but there was no way I would make any money out of writing and as soon as my year on the scheme was up I expected to be back on the dole.

This comforting assurance was swiftly shattered when I went to meet my editor, Tony Colwell, for lunch in the Groucho Club in London's Soho.

'I've got some good news for you,' Tony said with a broad smile almost before we had sat down.

'Oh yes,' I said as a svelte waiter sidled up and looked condescendingly at the pair of us. He had a naturally disdainful expression with the contemptuous curled lip of the professionally rude. His eyes swept me from head to foot.

'Drinks, sir,' he stated in a frosty voice, haughtily ignoring me. I bristled.

'Ah, yes,' Tony said, looking up from the menu. 'What would you like, Joe? Some wine?'

'Wine? No, thanks. Don't fancy it at lunch time.'

The waiter raised an eyebrow and looked wearily away at the other diners. I was begining to dislike the man intensely. 'I'll have a pint of bitter, please,' I said with what I hoped was a cheerfully disarming smile.

'We do not serve pints, sir,' the waiter said with more than a hint of a sneer. 'Nor do we serve bitter.' Did he see the word bitter as conjuring up the worst images of coarse uneducated northern manners?

'Right,' I said, keeping tight control on my temper, 'what do you serve?'

He reeled off a short list of Spanish and Mexican beers, none of which I knew and all of which I was certain would come in small fancy bottles and taste like watered down rat's piss. I wondered as I glared at him how long this waiter would last in Sheffield pubs.

'I'll have two of those and one glass, please.'

'Which do you want first? The good news or the very good news?' Tony asked.

'What?' I said, surprised from a vicious glare at the departing waiter. 'Oh, let's have the good news.'

'Okay, we've got a paperback offer for the book from

Pan . . .' He rattled on about the advance and the staggered royalty percentages and the publication date a year after the hardcover edition. I was pleased, of course, since I hadn't expected the book to come out in paperback, and the extra advance would come in handy. It didn't change my view about the dole queue in twelve months' time.

'Don't you want to hear the *very* good news?'

'Go on.'

'We've sold the American rights to Harper and Row in New York . . .'

'Oh good,' I said with most of my attention on the waiter.

' . . . for a very large advance.' In almost a whisper Tony enunciated the amount in dollars with great deliberation. He laughed, delighted at the expression on my face.

'*WHAT*? . . . This isn't a wind up, is it?' I said, convinced that it was some silly game.

'Not at all. All we're waiting to know is if you'll accept the offer.'

'ACCEPT?' I yelped, seeing a few heads at other tables turn to see what all the noise was about. 'What do you mean, accept? Course I'll accept. Gimme a pen.' And then a thought struck me. 'This advance thing . . . who gets the money? I mean has Cape sold it? Do the publishers take the money?'

'No. It's yours. We just keep the agent's percentage.'

'Oh my good God . . . I don't believe it . . . bloody hell. Are you sure they've read the right book?'

'Yes, they've read it.'

'Right then. That's okay, isn't it? Not bad at all, I'd say. I'll have another two of those funny beers please, mate,' I said to the passing waiter. For a moment I was lost for words.

'How much is it exactly? In pounds, I mean.'

'Oh, somewhere in the region of . . . let's see, yes . . . ' Tony was gazing at the table cloth as he concentrated on the calculations before naming a figure.

'Jesus, Mary and Joseph!' I exclaimed. 'You're kidding?'

He was not kidding. We left Groucho's and I headed off towards the Greenpeace office in Islington. I felt numb with shock. I kept trying to tell myself that in real terms it wasn't all that much money really; only a bit over two year's salary for a lot of people. But it was a hollow lie. To me, it was a fortune. I'd spent years happily living on less than four thousand a year. Ten times that was inconceivable. *And just for a book, and not a very big book at that. This is scary . . .*

A week later Larry Ashmead phoned me from Harper and Row to tell me I would have to keep January free for a publicity tour of the States. If it wasn't for the satellite delay on the phone and his accent I would still have suspected some cruel prank. I was losing control of my life. Things were happening that seemed to have nothing to do with me. The money was alarming. I wanted it, but it frightened me. *What on earth could I do with it? How do I explain to the tax people my sudden increase in income? I've never filled a tax form out in my life. What do I do?* Steadily I worked myself into a state of gnawing debilitating anxiety. On the one hand I loved what was happening while on the other it churned in my guts as I tried to ignore it. I was perfectly happy before this. I hadn't sought it and I didn't like the way it was changing my life without my consent. On the surface I gave the impression that I was taking it in my stride, but inside I was becoming increasingly confused and unhappy.

I confided in Tom. He was highly amused by my predicament, especially when I expressed so much dismay at having to relinquish the comforting normality of the weekly housing cheques.

The next few months were a blur of crazy experiences. In mid-January I left Manchester airport for New York, convinced that when I arrived at JFK airport the Americans would tell me it had all been a big mistake and that they had got the wrong author. Instead I was met by a man holding a placard saying 'Joe Simpson. Harper Row'. I edged cautiously around him without revealing myself, to check him out. He wore a chauffeur's uniform, complete with peaked cap, and when I introduced myself, he waved me towards the exit doors and took the small suitcase from my hand with a deft and practised flourish.

Parked outside was a white stretched limousine with

smoked windows and a TV aerial. I walked past the beast, expecting some rock star type to emerge, and headed off, looking for the chauffeur. There was a shout from behind and I turned to see him holding open the rear door of the limo. I could only laugh, and as I climbed in I tripped on the sill and fell headlong into the vast dark interior. The chauffeur politely leaned in and indicated the facilities, the television and radio channels, the drinks cabinet, and all the different controls for the privacy window and the air conditioning, while I giggled helplessly on the floor in the back.

Ten days went by in a jet-lagged daze. I didn't fully recover from the first flight since I was never in one city for longer than a day and I seemed to be flying the wrong way round the time zones. I went through a bewildering variety of live televison and radio shows – four or five a day in addition to countless interviews with journalists, either on the phone or in noisy newspaper offices. I was put up in the best hotels – the Westin St Francis in San Francisco and the Beverly Hills Hilton – but, despite the luxurious amenities, they were dull and lonely places in which to be. A suite can never be anything but somewhere to sleep for eight hours. I drank alone in the hotel bars, feeling at a loss.

Each night I talked on the phone through the satellite delay to my girlfriend Jacky and wished I wasn't in the States. Once, about halfway through the tour, I decided to ring my friend Jim Curran for a chat. It seemed as if a lifetime had passed since leaving home, though in fact I'd been away for only four days and he had forgotten that I'd gone. Convinced that I was calling to find out which pub everyone was going to, he answered my call with a brusque 'it's the Byron' and put the phone down.

After New York – Boston, Pittsburg, Cleveland, and still I hadn't seen America. Downtown areas were all the same – immense walls of glass and concrete seemed to merge into one. I could remember only the Manhattan skyline. Seattle tomorrow, and more stupid questions about why I climbed, and death wishes, and bravery and things I'd never thought about in accents that sometimes I couldn't understand.

Everyone was so cheerful, so wonderfully, absurdly pleased to see me, which was nice until you realised it was all part of the job. I knew that I was just one in a thousand guests to take part in these shows and the brief five-minute camaraderie was merely oil in the machine, but it started to work on me like an acid. I preferred the straight talking of the climbing world to this false love.

I had a rest day in Seattle. Determined to avoid the hotel monotony, I asked the doorman where would be a good place to spend the evening. I had to interrupt his litany of high-class, high-cost packaged culture and say I wanted to relax with a beer and a game of pool. I ended up in a seedy bar by the waterfront, playing pool until late into the night with a group of intimidating though not very good hustlers. They were far easier to relax with than the people I had so far encountered. I tottered back to the hotel richer from my pool winnings by $50 and glad that it was all nearly over.

Denver, Los Angeles, Pasadena, San Francisco, Chicago, and then home. I landed in rain-drenched Manchester in a baffled state of jet lag and overload. *Touching the Void* was dragging me ever deeper into a cauldron of self doubt. Unwittingly I seemed to have created a huge white elephant and realised with dismay that I might never be allowed to forget it. I would always be the man who fell off a mountain, crawled home and wrote a book about it. And there seemed to be nothing I could do to beat it. Translations into foreign languages came in thick and fast, and negotiations for a film deal were soon under way. My naive attempt to tell the story as it happened for the sake of ourselves and to entertain fellow climbers had gone haywire.

In March Simon Yates, John and I flew off to the Bugaboos, a range of mountains north of Banff in the Canadian Rockies, where we spent five alcoholic days zooming around in helicopters re-enacting the accident for a fifteen minute ABC television show. Simon acted out the cutting of the rope, with me taking a far too realistic stunt fall off a huge overhanging ice-cliff and pretending to crawl with a broken leg as wind machines blasted a blizzard of snow at us. It seemed so ludicrous that we laughed at ourselves and, for the first time, I realised that whatever had happened in Peru was over. Somehow the book had become more significant than reality and it was ruling my life.

Yet another surprise came in May when Tony phoned me with more good news. I was immediately suspicious.

'You've been short-listed for the NCR Award.' He announced it gleefully and I breathed a sigh of relief. I'd never heard of the award and couldn't see why Tony was getting so excited.

'Oh good,' I said cautiously. 'What exactly is the NCR Award when it's at home?'

'It's the biggest book award in the country at the moment. It's the non-fiction equivalent of the Booker or Whitbread prizes, and worth more than either of them.'

'I've never heard of it. What's this NCR bit?'

'National Cash Registers. It was launched only last year,' Tony said. 'I know it sounds a bit odd put like that, but it does come with twenty-five thousand pounds tax free.'

'WHAT?' I yelped. 'Oh, this is absurd.'

'You have to come down to London at the end of the month for the judging. By the way, you get £1,500 just for being short-listed.'

'What else is on the list?'

'Oh, let's see, there's Stephen Hawking's A Brief History of Time, then Tolstoy by A.N. Wilson, and a biography of T.E. Lawrence by Malcolm Brown and Julia Cave.'

'Well, that's that, then,' I said confidently. 'There's no way mine competes with any of those. Hawking will win. He's won everything else.'

'Possibly,' Tony conceded, 'but you never know. You could be in with a chance.'

Convinced as I was that I wouldn't win, I kept being ambushed by sudden wild daydreams. I could not get the prize money out of my head. All the others were professional writers, and Hawking, especially given the success of his book, had to be the favourite. It made no difference. There was a one in four chance of winning the twenty-five grand and it began to drive me crazy.

The night of the awards was a glittering occasion in the Savoy Hotel which seemed to consist of solid drinking from five in the afternoon until the announcement at ten thirty that night. I had invited my parents to join me and we sat with Tony and my agent Vivienne Schuster and several hundred others in our black ties and evening gowns, listening to the four judges – Barbara Amiel, Professor Colin Renfrew, Jane Asher and Brian Sibley – read out their individual assessments of each of the short-listed books. By then I was getting happily drunk, confident in the knowledge that we were only there for the free booze. When Magnus Magnusson, the chairman of the judges, stood up the room fell silent. I pushed away the fluttering nervy feelings in my stomach.

I'm told he did it extremely well, milking the moment for all its suspense. It was not until he began his very last sentence that any of my companions twigged and threw their arms around me, shouting congratulations. I had heard hardly anything and felt profoundly embarrassed. A ring – either my mother's or Vivienne's – stabbed me painfully in the eye just as the audience erupted into loud applause. I sat rigid in my seat, partially blinded and trying to put back my contact lens. There was no way I was going to stand up. If I did that and the real winner stood up, I would be left with burning ears to hide beneath the table cloth. When I saw Magnusson gesticulating, it finally dawned on me that it was true.

I leaned over and whispered in Tony's ear. 'This is ridiculous.'

After walking unsteadily up to the stage to offer my slurred thanks to everyone for their help and support, especially Tony, I threatened to report NCR to Amnesty International for cruelty to authors. There was a roar of laughter, but I wasn't merely joking. It was a strangled cry from the heart. Relief that it was all over was the most powerful emotion I felt. It was only much later that it began to sink in.

In many ways the award was a turning point. It was useless to become frightened about a turn of events over which I had no control. It is not possible to turn back time, and I didn't regret writing the book. If, against all odds, it was going to be so successful, then so be it. There was nothing I could do about it. Why not enjoy it? The publishing business seemed to be as random as a tombola, though there must have been something in what I had said that touched people, just as I had been touched by living through the painful times I had described. It made more sense to be grateful for what I had and to stop worrying about why I had it. The best thing I could do was to set about reclaiming my life, actively deciding what I wanted to do and how I could go about doing it.

With my knee already well past its sell-by date, I had decided to write another book, a novel that could not be compared with *Touching the Void*. At once I felt back in control. As soon as I was actively doing something, rather than sitting back and allowing things to happen to me, the worries disappeared. My first love, climbing, I could keep for myself. I no longer had any overweening ambitions in the mountains though I wanted to keep visiting them, to keep stepping out of an absurd unpredictable world into a place where I felt at ease, at home.

In the following spring, I stood on the summit of Ama Dablam with my friend Ray Delaney. It had been a very successful and happy expedition, with an earlier ascent of Island Peak, when we had stared in awe at the massive 11,000-foot south face of Lhotse. From 23,500 feet at the top of Ama Dablam, we could look out over the Lohste and Nupste ridges to the black summit pyramid of Mount Everest.

I had always dreamed of climbing in Nepal, long before we had set out off for Peru. After Peru, I had thought that the dream could never materialise. Now, not only had I climbed two mountains, but had stood at the top of the one which I most coveted. Like the Matterhorn and Mt. Assiniboine in the Rockies, Ama Dablam is one of the world's most beautiful mountains. It stands in sublime splendour overlooking the monastery at Thangboche – a fearsome tooth of rock and ice jutting up from spread ridges like arms embracing the valley below.

As we descended wearily, trying to wind up our

concentration so as to avoid the common fatigue-induced accidents that so easily take place on descents, I felt as if I had come full circle. From a time of chaos and a few years of pain and despair I had swung back to a point of normality. The book had helped me come to terms with Peru, finally burying the last lingering nightmares. Through climbing Ama Dablam, I regained a sense of self respect that I thought I had lost.

The old confidence was coming back. There were mountains to climb, books to write, so many things to do. If Peru had been a baptism of fire, then the years that followed were an incineration. I seemed to have pulled through, and once again I liked myself, enjoyed what I was doing and what lay ahead. There was another expedition – to the Indian Garwhal Himalayas – in the autumn and my novel *The Water People* to finish. There were plans to attempt an unclimbed peak in the Langtang region of Nepal and Everest's neighbour, Pumori. There was even talk of an Everest expedition the following year. I was savouring the pleasant prospect of flying to Delhi to join Simon for the Garwhal expedition when John introduced a note of caution.

'Don't you think you're pushing it a bit?' he asked.

'What do you mean?' I said in surprise.

'Well, you've been going a bit mad with expeditions lately, haven't you? And all those you're planning next year as well?'

'Yes, but I don't see why I'm pushing it. I'm not doing desperate routes or taking big risks.'

'Maybe not, but you are taking risks by going so often. That means you're putting yourself in potentially dangerous situations much of the time. Probability comes into it, you know. However good you are, you can still come unstuck.'

'I suppose so, but somehow I can't see it happening again. I've had my share of bad luck . . .'

'And good.'

'Yes, and good. I take your point, and thanks. Thanks for the warning and the concern, but it will be okay. I know it will.'

18

Déjà Vu

THE WIND HAD blown in hard and cold for a week. It was no hesitant gusting wind but a constant dense force from the west. Above the sound of the tents crackling under its pressure you could hear a deep booming coming from high above the base camp. We sat in the sunshine, huddled behind our crudely erected rock walls, and watched the mountain.

The 4,500-foot East Face of Pachermo is a complex broken black buttress sweeping down from left to right, a spider's web of gully lines and iced rocks covered in snow and a huge slanting area of ice cliffs wedged between the summit rocks. These seracs threatened most of the face. We watched carefully, guessing which way rocks would fall, or which areas of ice would be pulverized by avalanches.

If we wanted to climb the face we would have to accept that not all the route would be safe. The danger would be lessened if we started early in the frozen blue-black dawn and climbed the lower third of the face quickly. We had to be above the first thousand feet of rock buttress before the sun rose and loosened the mountain. The prob- lem then was to find a fast easy line through the steep complicated ground. After a week we decided that we could see 90 per cent of a possible line.

The crucial 5 per cent, of which we knew nothing, lay in the lower rock buttress. There the suspicion of a gully cut deeply through the black rocks and up into a fan-shaped couloir that pierced the centre of the face. We guessed the gully's position by reading the rocks, knowing from past

292

experience that there would be a weakness, a fault, that hid it. We would have to find that gully in the dead of night. A thin moustache of snow, crossing the lower buttress 300 feet above the glacier, seemed to lead towards the imagined spot, a faint tenuous broken line of white hinting that there was a ledge system which we could teeter across to get to it. I hoped we could find it in the dark. There was nothing else we could do. It wasn't possible to be certain, so it came down to a hunch, a gut instinct, an intuitive conviction that we would get through, and up, and down again safely without being swept away.

We were fit and acclimatised and bored with waiting and watching, listening to the howling boom of the wind from the west. The weather was settled and each day dawned cloudless. The sun was warm when you escaped from the wind which came from Tibet in an unbroken banshee scream, hurling itself across the frozen Tibetan plateau to smash into the mountains, stripping the snow in eddies and whirling white dervishes from summits and ridge lines. I wondered what it was like on Everest. Andy Parkin was attempting the north-north-east ridge, and that was the first obstacle the wind would meet.

There were no tell-tale mackerel skies or thin high cirrus marking the outriders of a new weather front. We had waited and watched the sky for the change, but nothing came. The wind was not heralding new weather. It simply blew, and from the west, which was odd. It shouldn't have been coming from that quarter. But we could deal with the wind, we decided, for sure it wouldn't be a problem. We had the clothes, and we could take a tent on the climb. On an east face we would be sheltered from the westerly gale, we reasoned.

Vast spirals of spindrift were whipping off the summit ridge and curling out like a diaphanous white tidal wave that hurled itself back in to crash against the east face at half height. We could see snow being sucked up by the vortex of air until it seemed that avalanches were streaming up towards the summit. Out of the westerlies, we should be safe on the east face, we assured ourselves as we tried to ignore the wail of the wind.

It wasn't a wind you could ignore. Everything danced to its tune. The tents bowed and flapped, and glacial dust pattered like handfuls of sand against the straining nylon. Through the loudest music on my earphones I could hear the wind symphony frantically grabbing for my attention. I thought of climbing in this maelstrom and of what it would be like tottering down the exposed north ridge, and whether we could be blown off. I had not known a wind that could lift a man, but Mal told me how, in a gust of more than a hundred miles an hour, he had been lifted and blown thirty feet on Ben Nevis

'What was it like?' I asked.

'Frightening,' he said as he gazed at the fury of the attack on our mountain.

'Do you think it's that bad up there.'

'I hope not. I really hope not.'

I wondered what it would be like when we stuck our heads over the summit ridge and stared into the teeth of the storm.

I looked at Mal. He was tugging at his beard as he looked up at the mountain. There was a quizzical expression on his face and he was very still. Then he turned and said, 'It'll be fine. Let's do it.' I agreed, and felt a little shiver of fear, then a full warm rush of excitement. *Yes, let's do it. I know we can. I know I can. The time's right. We'll do it, fight the wind and do it.*

I felt strong and hard and determined. I wanted to be the first to climb the east face. We had climbed Lobouche Peak (20,500 feet) within nine days of leaving London. Mal Duff had asked me to go with him and try a hard new route on a mountain called Taweche, but we failed to attract enough trekking clients to make the trip financially viable, so instead we had opted to climb Lobouche and then to try a new route on Pachermo.

Mal was a highly experienced climber who made his living as a guide. He climbed all the year round, taking clients to the ice of the Scottish mountains, the Alps, and in Alaska and

Nepal. He was a fiercely proud Scotsman, and I suspected he had little time for people who didn't match up to his strength in the mountains. I had got to know him on the Ama Dablam trip and immediately liked his irreverent humour and his no nonsense approach to the hills. I was also impressed with his climbing record. Although he had frequently failed, they were notable failures which, in themselves, were more striking than other people's successes. Privately I doubted that I could keep up with him, but I felt strong enough to give it my best effort. Decades of continual exploration in the mountains gave him a hard edge and a deep strong pool of stamina. We seemed to laugh a lot in one another's company, and that was reason enough for me to climb with him.

I looked across at Cholatse, a beautiful and frightening mountain draped in flutings and wild mushroom cornices and chaotic ridge lines. The sun threw delicate pale blue shadows across its north face. I linked the couloirs and ice gullies together, patching gaps with steep ice cascades, until my eyes rested just below the summit cornices. We had looked longingly at it for a fortnight, making plans, speculating – not very seriously – about climbing it.

We watched it at dawn, at midday and in the evening, studying the potential line through Mal's binoculars, waiting for the sun to shift round and throw shadows on to different features. Like painters, we waited for the light to illuminate different facets of the route, to give apparently smooth snow a depth and contour, to reveal hidden bivouac sites, and allow us to see the greenish-blue ice at the back of a crux section of ice cascades. We decided that it would be possible to get up Cholatse but were uncertain about the descent.

I found myself wondering at my change of heart. I had convinced myself that I would never again try a two-man ascent on an unclimbed route as hard as the one we had climbed in Peru. I would not have the confidence to set out. Yet here I was, looking at Cholatse with covetous eyes, assessing a route just as dangerous as Siula Grande had been. I turned away and examined the east face of Pachermo.

'Shall we go tonight?' Mal asked as I lowered the binoculars.

'Might as well,' I said. 'The weather looks set for the moment.'

'Aye, there's been no change for three days now,' Mal said as he checked the barometric pressure on his altimeter. 'Midnight start then?'

'Right. You know, if we do this it will be only my second first ascent?'

'Oh aye? What was the first?'

'Siula Grande in Peru,' I said, and we laughed.

'Well, let's hope we don't make this another epic,' Mal said as he began to sort out his gear.

I retrieved my crampons from the back of the tent. On the descent from the summit of Lobouche one toe bar had fallen apart on two occasions. Fortunately I had been on easy ground when it happened and had been able to make running repairs. Before the climb I wanted to ensure that I had solved the problem. I fixed them to my boots and adjusted the tension to make them grip harder. After tinkering for half an hour I was still unhappy with them. I switched the bars on each crampon, inverting them, and with some judicious blows from my ice hammer managed to fix them to my satisfaction. They were now extremely tight and difficult to put on but I felt confident that, once on, they wouldn't easily come off again. Unknown to me, there was a design fault in the crampons, but that was discovered only after we had left for Nepal. A hole had been drilled three millimetres too big and this meant that under certain forces the toe bar released. The company producing them had put a notice in the magazines, recalling all crampons made in the last twelve months, but I had missed it.

I saw Mal packing gas cartridges and food bags into his rucksack. His axes and crampons lay outside his tent.

'Have you had any trouble with your crampons, Mal?' I asked, seeing that his were the same as mine.

'No, none at all,' he replied. 'I've used them for the last six months, and they've been fine.'

'These were okay on Ama Dablam,' I said as he looked at my handiwork. 'I can't see what made them fall apart on Lobouche.'

'Probably all that soft snow balling up.'

'Yeah, probably.' I remembered how repeatedly we had had to knock the balls of snow from our crampons with our axes. I dismissed the problem while I prepared my gear for the climb.

When a faint ribbon of light blue appeared on the horizon of a black sky we edged across the traverse line. I could hear the tinkling sound of karabiners rattling against ice screws and the scraping of Mal's crampons on the rock. Occasionally, looking back, I saw a flare of light from his headtorch as he tried to pick out where I had gone. The ledge from which we had started grew smaller and then merged into the rock buttress. I peered round to the left. The dark rock walls seemed to curve inwards. It was the gully all right. I could see a streak of dirty snow just below and to my left where the gully ran out to- wards the glacier. The ledge stopped just before reaching the gully. I searched for a way over the blank wall but found no cracks or holds of any kind. Mal came along the ledge and peered silently past me at the impasse. There was a tik-tak noise of a rock cracking off the walls of the distant gully and I flinched away instinctively.

'What now?' I asked, feeling slightly foolish.

'A diagonal abseil, maybe,' Mal muttered as he shone his torch below us. I peered down, watching the beam as it swung across the shadows below.

'Looks as if there might be a traverse line, about fifty feet down,' I said as I spotted a flash of white snow in the darkness.

'Might as well give it a go.'

We hurriedly set up the abseil, nervously aware of how much precious time we were wasting. The sun would be up in an hour and the ice cliffs cracking into life under its melting glare. From high above there came the ominous booming of the relentless wind. It was sheltered here under the face, becalmed in darkness, only a hint of the violence above.

'Okay, Joe.' Mal's voice echoed up from the darkness. 'Come on down. I can see into the gully.'

When I reached him I saw that he had found a belay point right on the edge of the gully which swept up in a narrowing fan of dirty rock- pitted snow until the way was blocked by a thirty-foot cascade of ice. On each side huge black walls crowded over the thin fan of snow, giving the place an oppressive, menacing feel. Anything falling from above would be funnelled by the contours of the face straight into the mouth of the gully. A broken mass of ice and rock debris spread out far below us – a testament to the ferocious violence of avalanches.

We climbed with anxious haste, sometimes moving together, sometimes taking belays as we tackled short ice cascades that were blocking narrow sections of the gully. Once the sun had risen, we stopped to rest and look down on the glacier still in night time shadows while we absorbed the warmth. Across to our left we could see the first huge bands of ice cliffs. The ice on the cliff walls was honeycombed and fractured from recent collapses. We were beyond their threatening reach and established in a wide open couloir.

For the rest of that day we climbed steadily into the heart of the face. As we got higher so the sound of the wind increased. Snow began to whip around us in crazed flurries. We climbed into the vortex, following the righthand edge of a prominent broken rib of rock. By evening more than half the face lay below us. We found a precarious ledge on which to pitch our small tent and set it close against a rock wall for shelter. It was to no avail. The wind came from every direction, hammering at the tent walls so that they buckled from above and then from the sides, threatening to get under the groundsheet and whip our fragile thin blue home off the mountain. We got little sleep, snatching only a few precious moments between the heavier assaults.

In the morning we huddled over mugs of tea and talked about continuing. The wind had battered our confidence as well as our tent. Occasionally we looked out and up at the plumes of snow that blasted over the summit ridge 2,000 feet above us.

'What do you think, Mal? Do we carry on?'

'I don't know. It's bad down here. I'm wondering what it will be like in the full force of it on the ridge.'

'That's what I was thinking.'

We had planned to descend the easy north ridge marking the right side of the face. It led down to the Tesi Lapcha col that separated the Rowaling valley from the Thami valley where our base camp was sited. I remembered how we had concentrated on the difficult face in Peru and had dismissed the descent of the supposedly easy north ridge as a foregone conclusion. I wasn't keen on making the same mistake again.

'The trouble is,' Mal said, 'we might have no choice.'

'How do you mean?'

'Well, I don't fancy descending under those seracs again. Once is pushing it far enough.'

'We could try traversing off at this level and reach the col from here.'

'Yeah, I thought of that, but I'm not sure if there is a way past the rock buttress on the right, and if there is whether there are wide open snow slopes after that. With the sort of windslab conditions we met yesterday it could be a bit risky.'

In places, where the couloir had widened into an open slope, snow had been compacted by the wind and every footstep had sent cracks across it. We had hugged the shelter and security of the rock bounding the left side of the couloir, placing pitons where we could to protect us from a fall or the sudden surge of a windslab avalanche. On open slopes there would be no protection at all.

'So, it's down into serac falls, or across on to windslab, or up into the wind? Not a pleasant choice, I must say.'

'Up, I reckon,' Mal said with a grin. 'Bit of wind never hurt anyone.'

'A bit might not, but this lot could be altogether different. Okay, up it is.'

We struck camp late in the morning, fighting with the thrashing blue tent as we pummelled it into a rucksack. For most of the day we swopped leads, taking turns to break trail up exhausting knee-deep snow. The wind howled dementedly around us, preventing communication. We moved in our own worlds, meeting one another at the end of every rope length, often passing by without a word. By the late afternoon I was begining to tire. My legs became leaden and exhausted. On the last four rope lengths Mal took the lead and broke trail all the way to the summit ridge, following a faint rib of snow and then a wildly corniced ridge up to the last open slope below the cornices of the north ridge. I followed, guiltily aware of failing him, but it wasn't important. As the stronger, it was better for him to forge ahead.

The last flat white light of the evening made the cornice on the ridge appear twice its actual size. I kept looking up wearily at the rope snaking through a weakness in the bulge of snow and hoping to see that I was almost there. The more often I looked, the more I became convinced that the ridge was moving away from me as I climbed. I knew that Mal was exposed to the full fury of the gale as he waited for me to trudge wearily up the final pitch of windslab snow. Mercifully, the cornice was hard névé and easy to get up on frontpoints. I tottered forward over the flat top, leaning like a drunk at forty five degrees into the wind, shielding my eyes from the freezing rip of icy particles. Finding Mal huddled in the shelter of a small circular crevasse, I collapsed besides him and he slapped me on the shoulder and grinned.

'You're enjoying this,' I shouted above the wind.

'Brings back old memories,' he yelled. 'Do we stop here or descend to the col and camp there?'

I looked down the north ridge and west face. There were steep icy slopes for the first couple of hundred feet and then the angle of the ridge lessened. A few seracs blocked the direct line down the ridge, and I could see that it would require an excursion on to the west face to get past them. There was nothing technically very difficult about the descent to the col 2,000 feet below.

'We'll get no rest here in this,' I shouted into Mal's ear. 'It'll be dark in less than an hour. We should get past those seracs by then. We can do the rest in the dark.'

'Right, let's go.'

He stood up and began carefully descending the hard steep

300

névé slope below the crevasse. I let him go down the full length of the rope, before I stood up to follow. The wind tugged insistently at the rope bowing it out in a huge arc that hung five feet clear of the snow. *We should really take it off and solo down,* I thought. *It's more of a danger than a help.* But I was tired and Mal was out of earshot, and anyway it was easy ground. We wouldn't fall on good ice like this.

I watched Mal cross a shallow angled ramp of névé leading to a steep drop away. The rope flew clear of the snow for the entire distance of 150 feet between us, arched out in a curve by the gale. *Should I suggest we take it off?* I saw Mal turn slightly and begin to step tentatively down on to the steep ice below. Already the face was in shadow and night was coming on apace. The temperature had plummeted with the loss of the sun. I could feel the wind stripping me of warmth. The wind chill factor must have been close to minus 70°F. This was no time to be messing around with the rope. We had to get down fast and into the shelter of the tent before the cold addled our minds.

There was a very steep ice slope between me and the spot where Mal had crossed the ramp. I felt the wind pull the rope at my waist and it hummed with a strangely ominous sound. As I stepped down, facing outwards, I saw Mal's body hunch over. It took perhaps a millisecond to register what was happening and in that endless pause I slipped suddenly out of time. He fell in a blur and was gone, yet I seemed to have all the time in the world to have noted every detail – the peculiar body position that warned me something was wrong, the desperately thrown arm and the axe waving in the air, futile and mute, the curve of the rope instantly straightening.

I hurled myself backwards, powering my ice axe into the névé as hard as I could. I saw the pick embed itself up to the shaft as I was moving to get myself over the head of the axe. My arm was still at full stretch when the impact whipped up the rope and ripped me backwards into the air. There was a curious sense of disappointment as I watched the pick fly free of the ice.

After completing a half somersault, I landed heavily on my

neck and left shoulder before accelerating, head first on my back, down the icefield. For a brief moment I watched the fall from my upside down position and saw coils of loose rope snaking past me. The accelerated jerk meant I was travelling faster than Mal. Frantically I swung myself round and up so that I was on my stomach, with my crampons held up free of the ice. I knew that if I caught them I would begin cartwheeling and somersaulting out of control. My mind seemed very calm, detached from the violence of the fall. By the time I was in a position to attempt an ice axe brake I had hit the ramp. I slowed momentarily and then plunged off the edge of the steep drop over which Mal had fallen. I couldn't use the axe while I was airborne, and it was then that I knew it was hopeless. On hard ice the brake would have to be made the instant I landed if there were to be any chance of it holding, and at the speed I was travelling I knew the axe would simply be ripped out of my hands.

Mal was hurtling down the ridge, flying over small seracs that humped out from the crest. I was falling more to the west, heading for the huge buttresses of the west face of the mountain, slanting diagonally away from Mal and overtaking him. I could feel the ice hammering under my bent elbows. *Wait for it. Wait for softer snow, then brake.* The thought came calmly, without fear. I waited and knew it was all over. There was mild sense of surprise at how fast one can fall in a shiny Goretex suit, and a small bleat of outrage at the injustice of it all which quickly faded. I had no time for anger, no time even for fear. *How far now?* A long way, I knew it was a long way.

I was overcome with a sense of déjà vu. It was exactly how I had always imagined falling to one's death would be. I saw it all in black and white; there was no colour, just a stark monochromatic slow motion film of the world passing me by. I hadn't expected the profound sense of resignation, almost tranquillity, despite the ferocity of the fall. It was almost a pleasant revelation. I had read *The White Spider* at the age of twelve; this was how I had imagined they had died. This was exactly the same. That sudden recollection made me certain that this fall was going to be my last.

So convinced was I that I felt my arms relax. *Why even bother? What's the point? You always said after Peru that you had used up all your luck.* And I spun off down into the shadows with a flare of anger that it had happened again, that I hadn't heeded the warnings, that I should have been so stupid, so arrogantly stupid. *Why me? For fuck's sake! Why me, again?*

While I died in anger, and my world ran away, Mal spun out over an ice cliff to thump heavily into stillness at its base. He saw the rope fizzing out into the shadows and grabbed it with one instinctive lunge. 'Silly sod,' he said as the impact twanged him out and down into the darkness, back into the crazy see-saw race down the mountainside.

I was still overtaking him in a rip-roaring Goretex hissing violence, with a resigned mind but the urgent thought that I must do something soon. I was curious about the speed at which I was moving . . . *like shit off a shiny shovel* I thought, and almost laughed. My stomach was empty and I was holding my breath. I tensed, expecting the explosive final impact, and lurched briefly airborne as I skimmed over a hump in the slope. It pulled at my guts as I crashed back on to the ice and careered on with my mind trying to catch up as it spun down through the shadows, seconds out of reach.

I have to do it. I have to do it. I hugged the axe tight against my shoulder ready to brake, though I knew it wouldn't work. Modern ice tools have a wickedly angled pick for vertical ice-climbing but this makes it impossible to use effectively for braking. *It'll pull my arms off,* I thought as I jammed the pick into the ice. My life stopped and there was blackness and the blessed peace of unconsciousness.

Mal had shot past me for the second time when once again he plunged over a fifteen-foot cliff. This time he dug the shaft of his axe in deep and lay on it, waiting for the wrenching impact of a five-hundred-foot fall. Then there was only the wind screaming across from the west and a glimpse of stars in a black sky and his chest heaving and the ominous desolate thrumming of the rope in the wind.

It seemed that in those few violent seconds of the fall the

night had rushed in like a hungry black predator and now the darkness crowded round expectantly as a man clung to an axe and listened, disbelieving, to the sound of the wind returning to his senses, to the sound of being alive. For Mal real time came rushing back and he felt suddenly scared. He had time to imagine what had almost happened, even though he still couldn't understand why he had fallen. Glancing at his foot, he saw the crampon hanging loosely by the strap round his ankle. The bail bar on the toe had gone. A spray of ice crystals lashed across his face and jacket with the sound of a heavy surf. There was no movement from the rope except for the high-frequency vibration of the wind, which made a low humming sound. Looking down into darkness, he tried in vain to see me, wondering whether I would be hurt, or dead, or slowly dying. And as the minutes passed the certainty grew that he had lost me. He prepared to tie the rope off to his axe and begin the careful descent to discover the truth.

Ten minutes passed and then the blackness in my head began to ease and I awoke to the fury of the wind. I lay against the ice with my face fastened to the mountainside in a frozen slick of blood. The wind tugged insistently at my body like an impatient child pulling at its mother's dress. *Come on, wake up, I want to play.* Confusing signals seemed to be jolting into my mind and I felt tired, very tired in the full grip of death's passiveness. I lifted my head and saw the rope cutting across the ice above me and vanishing into the night. I had no idea where I was. Rolling my head from side to side, I tried to shake the porridge free from my brain. The movement twisted my body and pain flared up from my leg. At once I was back in Peru, back to the nightmares and the dread that I had so neatly cupboarded away. *Not again, for pity's sake, not that again, please . . .*

I flicked on my headtorch, still miraculously attached to my helmet, and saw a crimson spray of blood on the ice. I saw thick globs on the sleeve of my jacket, hard and dark, already frozen. My face was also frozen, my left eye closed, and I couldn't breathe through my nose. I lifted my hand and touched my face but it felt hard and cold. There was blood on my mitt when I pulled it away.

I looked up the rope and shouted into the wind. The words whipped away across Nepal and there was no answer, not even the hopeful flash of a headtorch. *What was holding the rope?* The thought sent a sudden savage jolt of fear through me. *Mal couldn't possibly have stopped and held the fall. Perhaps he is hanging down the east side. Maybe it's just snagged on something. Get off it quick in case he falls again.*

I hacked my axe into the ice and tried to get to my feet. Bones grated in my left ankle and I screamed with shock. I lay back and tried to think it away. It subsided slowly. I knew without needing to look that the ankle was broken and, judging by its sensitivity, it was badly broken. I was all too accustomed to the feel of grating bone ends. I clenched my teeth in an old familiar grimace and kicked the front points of my uninjured foot into the ice. With both axes firmly picked into the ice above me, I executed a combined pull up and hop and felt the points bite in a foot higher up the slope. The sudden spasmodic effort caused another crunching flare of agony. I leaned my left knee on the ice, holding the boot safely out of harm's way, and made another hop, gritting my teeth against a sickening wave of pain as my foot spun in full circles on the end of my leg.

The slow painful climb seemed to last for ever. At first I screamed with every hop, and then, as I weakened, and the cold began to take me, I moaned. It all seemed so familiar. I slid easily into a world of pain and realised that it was Peru all over again, but this time I wasn't getting away with it. After about twenty feet my addled concussed mind recognised that the rope was being taken in. I felt it pulling at my waist. A surge of hope flushed through me. *Mal's okay. He's pulling the rope.* It wasn't the steady drag of a dead weight sliding down the other side of the mountain but the active feel of someone pulling. Like a child's string and a tin can, the rope was communicating every urgent desperate effort that Mal was making. For a while it gave me strength and I hopped with renewed vigour, clinging to the hope that we would make it.

I looked up into the darkness and thought I saw the faint

yellow flash of Mal's torch. The rope tugged insistently but I was exhausted. I seemed to be viewing events from a distance, feeling sickly and lethargic about what was happening. My thoughts seemed thick and muggy and I was unable to grasp hold of a train of thought for any length of time. I tried to create a rhythm, the old familiar patterns that had helped me in Peru, but I couldn't concentrate. I wanted to sleep.

I rested my head on the ice and felt the soothing cold on my wounds. When I raised it again, a moment later, I saw the dark blood stains left behind. *It must be bad,* I thought. *I'm still bleeding.* There was no pain from my face and, when I lay still against the slope, the heat in my ankle subsided. I tried climbing again but rested almost immediately. I knew what I must do but I couldn't make my body do it. I closed my eyes, listened to the wind rushing across my body, and shivered. The cold was taking me, sending me into a dreamless sleep, a dark place that I recognised and couldn't resist – a vacuum, pain free, lost in time, like death – and I wanted it.

I cannot remember precisely what happened during that long painful climb up to Mal. I know I was cold, and weary, and wanted to give up. I don't know why I kept going. It would have been so easy to die, almost pleasant. Perhaps I became angry. I often respond in anger when I am hurt. Maybe my concussed brain managed to hold on to one basic command – *climb, keep climbing, don't give up* – that long ago had become an instinct. But I can recall none of the details of that bewildered, confusing struggle.

I reached a shelf below the cliff where Mal had held my fall in a state of collapse. I slumped beside him, face down on the ice, and sobbed for air. When I lifted my face there was blood on the snow. I stared bleakly at Mal who tried to smile.

'I'm going to die, Mal,' I said, and at once felt ashamed at my weakness. I did think I was going to die. I knew I couldn't get lucky again. I curled up at his feet and shivered with pain and cold.

Mal was in a practical mood. 'Don't be stupid, lad. Pull yourself together.'

I lay there and all I could think of was *no more chances.*

Here I was at twenty thousand feet, smashed up, cold, concussed and bleeding, and I knew it wouldn't work for me again. I almost cried.

Mal moved away in the darkness. I hadn't seen his expression when he had caught sight of my face so I didn't know how bad I looked.

'I'm going to try to dig a platform for the tent,' he said, pressing a reassuring arm on my shoulder. 'We've lost the poles. Don't move. And don't worry. I'm coming back.'

But I *was* worried. I was scared that he would leave me alone in the wind and the dark. I had been left before, and I never wanted that loneliness again. He took one of my crampons and moved away into the darkness. I lay still and tried to rest, but the wind kept tugging me and I became colder and colder. Some time later I found myself being held by Mal. I can't recall what happened but he had found me crawling up the slope towards him, moaning and calling out for someone in the darkness. I seemed to be drifting through grey lost periods and moments of lucidity. It was unnerving to feel so bewildered and hazy. It made me feel weak and unable to fight. I wanted to be hard and stubborn and angry, but instead all I could muster was a feeble mushy submissiveness.

'I've dug a little ledge in the ice,' Mal said, and I looked at the pathetic two-inch-deep scoop he had hacked in the ice. The wind howled over the crest of the ridge. Beyond us in the darkness I knew was the 4,500-foot drop to the foot of the face, and behind me lay the same. It wasn't a good place for camping without poles or anchors.

'I'm dying, Mal.'

This time I knew I had nothing to be ashamed of; I was going into shock and hypothermia, bleeding copiously from my head wounds and freezing slowly in the wind. It brought on a familiar sensation – of somebody's cold fingers pulling at my innards and of a dark sleep beckoning. Mal looked at me and knew that death couldn't be far away.

'We'll be fine,' he lied convincingly, despite the sight of me with one foot turned backwards and the face all smashed. He saw one eye socket filled with blood, and it looked as if the

307

eye had gone. There was a frightful gaping wound where my axe had smashed into my left eye, exposing glistening bone and dragging the brow and lid down so that he could see only a bloody pulp. My nose had been partly ripped off my upper lip and the left nostril torn open so that the wind sprayed blood over the snow as I tried to breathe.

Once inside the thrashing, billowing tent and saved from the lethal wind, I began to revive. Mal asked me if I wanted a painkiller and then saw my face again in the torchlight. The obscene white glisten of bone and the dull concussed look in the one good eye made him suggest quietly that it might be safer to wait a while. He smiled and patted my arm. I was too tired and confused to care. I lay back and clutched at the tent and tried to hug it to my chest.

Somehow in the chaos Mal made a brew of lukewarm water and got me painfully into my sleeping bag. He kept talking to me and I was dully aware that he was using all his experience to keep me alive. When I muttered a brief thanks, he said nothing and looked away. The sight of me made him feel guilty. Already he was full of recriminations for falling in the first place. He had never fallen on snow or ice before, and he was proud of the fact. I didn't have the energy to explain that I understood. We could do it later, if there was a later.

We didn't sleep. All night we lay in a state of hollow dread as the wind fought to lift the tent and hurl it off the mountain. We lay side by side grasping the wrenching nylon, feeling the wind pushing us towards the east and trying to force buttocks, elbows and shoulders into the hard ice beneath us. The night was endless and full of fear, unlike the fall when there had been no time for fear. The wind never slackened. It harried us like a demented terrier, chaffing at the pole-less tent with terrifying ferocity, sometimes squeezing under us until we seemed to lift and hover uncertainly towards the long eastern abyss.

Dawn rose a bright sun and a lapis lazuli sky. The wind was still howling from the west but the darkness had gone, and with it the dread. The darkness had made the wind seem to be something other than an elemental force. It had crashed in from nowhere with the frenzied evil of the truly deranged, pulling and pushing and hitting hard, like a million demons besetting us. It seemed to have a mind. It was alive, and in the darkness this was frightening. So determined and deliberate was the onslaught that it was hard not to believe it would inevitably triumph and hurl us, screaming, into the depths. As the sun warmed the tent and I caught a glimpse of the mountains to the east my spirits rose. I looked west and could see where the wind came from. Nothing there but mountains. There was no evil.

While Mal prepared for lowering me I lay in the sun by the hastily stuffed rucksacks and tried to grasp what was happening. *I don't believe it. Not again, surely.* It seemed impossible that Peru could repeat itself. Stranded high on a mountain, badly injured and with no chance of rescue, here again was my partner preparing the ropes for lowerering me down to the col.

It's not the same. We're still together. I had broken my ankle and not my knee. I'd fallen over five hundred feet down an open mountainside rather than one hundred into a crevasse. The ice was hard, so we had good anchors for the lowers. *Don't worry. We'll pull through. You've been through worse.*

'Are you ready?' Mal asked, and immediately I was full of anxiety. I was about as ready as a condemned man being led to the gallows. I felt an empty aching stomach and knew there was nothing that could be done to avoid it. Mal saw the fear in my eyes and leant forward with a forced grin.

'It's going to be a doddle.' He clipped the rope to my harness and swung me gently round so that I hung between his legs. 'You know, there's one thing good about all this,' he said.

'No. What?' I asked.

'You're the most experienced person I know at this game.' He laughed, and I laughed too, until I looked down and saw the 1,200-foot fall to the Tesi Lapcha col.

'Just make sure you don't lower me off anything you can't see,' I said fervently.

'Don't worry, it's clear all the way . . .'

'And another thing,' I cut in, 'stop telling me not to worry. I'm worried stiff.'

'Aye, I know,' he said, sombre for a moment. 'Here take this.'

He handed me his Swiss army knife, and we laughed again. It wasn't the forced laughter of hysteria but genuine and heart-warming. *If we can laugh like this we're going to make it*, I thought. I stopped laughing as soon as Mal released the rope and I began to slide.

The lowers went smoothly. The angle of the slope was less steep and more consolidated than it had been in Peru, and the sunshine made it seem almost normal. I could keep my knee bent so that the ankle was held free from snagging, and when the first lower finished, I found good solid placements with my axes to hold me until Mal descended.

By midday we were approaching the level ground of the col. Mal was shouting and pointing to the east and waving his arms. Two tiny figures were approaching from the direction of our base camp. They waved back, seeing nothing amiss until Mal started dragging me over the easier angled ground where I couldn't slide, and then they hurried to meet us.

Tchwang, our Sirdar, had watched us climb the face the previous evening and had sent Pemba and Jetta up to the col to help us down with our gear. We had a plane to catch from Lukla in three days' time and speed was vital if we were going to make the flight. They hurried towards us, smiling broad happy smiles and shouting congratulations until they saw my face.

We spent several hours at the col. Mal brewed cups of tea and tenderly removed my boot to examine the grossly swollen ankle that was streaked with the tell-tale blood bruises of a severe fracture. A crude but effective splint was fashioned from a split cane marker wand and then they took it in turns to carry me piggy-back down the forty degree névé slopes above the camp. I clung to their backs, staring fixedly down the lethal slopes and watching their every step. They wore on their feet nothing more sturdy than smooth rubber-soled

Chinese baseball boots as they carried more than a triple load surefootedly down hard icy slopes, not once failing to smile and almost making me cry when they hurt me as I was lowered to the ground for a rest. Immediately they crowded round me, arms protectively embracing me so that I could loll my head against them. I felt overwhelmed by their courage and tenderness.

That night, at base camp, the wind increased in ferocity, and by the morning my tent had collapsed around me. Mal rescued me with a cup of tea and sat me against a rock in the warm sun so that I could watch while they fashioned a crude seat out of a porter's basket. It was a long painful carry to some yak pastures by a small hamlet called Zengbo. At last we had escaped the wind and I lay in my tent surfacing from the nightmare while we waited two days for the helicopter to come.

I borrowed Mal's shaving mirror and gingerly inspected my face. My first fear was for my eye. Poking aside the drooping brow and swollen lower cheek I was pleased to find it still in place. After a difficult session digging with my finger-nails I managed at last to get both contact lenses out despite the swelling. Squinting into the dappled orange light inside my tent, with my left eye open and a hand covering the right, I found that I couldn't see. An opaque milky view changed only marginally when I stared at the sun.

'Mal,' I said in a small voice, 'I think I'm blind.'

'You've still got the other eye,' he answered cheerfully. 'Don't worry, it's probably all the blood and the bruising.'

He dressed and bandaged the gash, gave me painkillers and antibiotics and told me to rest. I dozed through the sunny afternoon, listening to the chiming of yak bells in the pastures and wondering at how unperturbed I was about losing my sight. My nose throbbed with unimaginable pain, and this confused me since I thought that the ankle should have been the most painful injury. When at last I was forced by the pulsating waves of pain to inspect it in the mirror, I carefully cleaned away the thick blood clots and saw the ruptured nostril. As I pressed the tip of my nose tentatively with an exploratory finger I was horrified to see the dried blood slide aside slightly to reveal a diagonal gash across my upper lip and the whole of the nose moved up and to one side. I quickly squashed it back in place with a yelp more of alarm than pain.

I lay back and lit another cheap Yak cigarette. Putting the mirror aside, I dragged deeply on the smoke, retched a couple of times, and closed my eyes.

The tents were packed away and the rucksacks allotted to our assembled porters when we heard the distinctive *whop-whop-whop* of the helicopter. With a fearful clattering roar it swung low round the valley to settle near the dry stone wall of our field. The blades drooped low and whopped lazy spirals as the engine was cut and the whine of the jet turbine faded to silence. Mal helped me to hop towards the door. I turned to sit on the bare metal floor and stared at the brown scrubby hillside. Six panic-stricken yaks galloped across it, chased by a whistling, cursing herder. The crisp morning air echoed to the laughter of our porters delighting in another man's misfortune. It seemed to me then that this is all we ever laugh at. I shuffled painfully into the cabin and stared grimly at my reflection in the perspex window. I appeared to have lost half my face as well as all sense of humour.

In the Katmandu Ciweh Clinic I had my ankle X-rayed and it was pronounced badly smashed A young doctor spent two hours putting my face back together, with litres of hydrogen peroxide to burn away the thick blood clots. When she had finished she handed me a mirror, like a hairdresser, and I was amazed by her good work. The nose was a mess but the eye was neatly stitched and there would be little scarring. Although slightly blurred, my vision had returned.

It had been a long and painful day before we phoned home. Suddenly hearing Jacky's concerned voice, I felt shivery and knew what I had so nearly lost. Within a few hours the BMC insurance service had swung efficiently into action and a first class flight was booked to Delhi the following morning, connecting with British Airways to London and Manchester, where an ambulance would be waiting to take me to the hospital of my choice.

As Con Moriarty, a huge Irishman I had met in a drunken session in Harrogate, strode confidently into the foyer of our guest house with his equally huge friend, Mike O'Shea, my heart sank. Although buoyed up at the prospect of flying home so soon, I still felt weak and dreaded a night on the town with the Irish.

'Well, Joe. You've been in the wars again, I see.' Con clapped me on the shoulder and I winced. 'I think this calls for a little celebration, now. What do you think?'

'I don't think I'd be up to it, Con . . .'

'Don't worry yourself lad . . .'

'I wish people would stop telling me not to worry . . .'

' . . . we'll just go for a quick beer. Nothing grand, just a few beers to loosen up.'

I sighed and reached for my crutches. It was useless to argue.

'Just one then, Con. No shenanigans, okay?'

'You have my word,' Con declaimed, hand on heart.

At a quarter past three the following morning I found myself in a rickshaw race, clutching my crutches and a bottle of Iceberg lager as we rattled through a deserted Katmandu. The Americans kept jumping out and pushing their rickshaw.

'Now, what do we do about this then Joe?' Con asked, as he watched one of the Americans preparing to cheat again. At that moment the two rickshaws drifted perilously close to each other and the wheels span almost hub nut on hub nut.

'Well, I suppose they've been warned,' I said as I scythed one of my crutches through the air, catching the unbalanced American a clip above his right ear. There was an anguished howl, and their rickshaw bounced wildly as it ran over the unfortunate man who had been thrown to the ground. Then we were off howling with laughter and delight, watching one of the Americans standing over the supine figure of his companion in the middle of the road.

'Now why didn't I think of that?' Con said.

'Do you think I've hurt him?'

'Not at all,' Con said confidently. 'It'll give him something to remember us by.'

Con had got me over the first major obstacle to recovery. His happy-go-lucky attitude had washed away much of the introspective depression caused by the event of the previous week.

'Life goes on. Thing's happen and that's the end of it. Come on now it's your round.' It was a good philosophy.

After the hour flight to Delhi, I crutched slowly up the steps of the 747 to London nursing a ferocious hangover. The hostess, concerned at my plight, carefully conducted me to an enormous seat in the first class cabin, thrust a glass of champagne into my hand, and showed me how to adjust everything. I pressed a button and the seat lunged backwards. Another button sent a shelf shooting out to support my legs. She topped up the champagne I had spilt and wished me a pleasant flight. For the next eight hours I ignored my classy fellow passengers who looked in shocked horror at the stinking mess of bandages, caked blood, stitches and black eyes. The champagne kept flowing and I lay back, gazing out at a sea of downy clouds beneath the plane. Only five days earlier, I had been just as high in a vicious wind, crippled and blinded, beaten up and bleeding and telling Mal I was dying. It seemed absurd. I smiled and asked for more champagne.

I said goodbye to Mal when we landed at Heathrow. After a day in Edinburgh he was to fly on to Anchorage and Alaska. Eventually I reached Manchester's Ringway Airport – dazed, jet lagged and hungover – to meet an anxious Jacky. I can't remember which of us cried first when we embraced. It was a Sunday, and Jacky said there was a party at the Marquis of Granby near Bamford for Chris Bonington's retirement from his post as President of the British Mountaineering Council. We gave the ambulance the slip and headed for Derbyshire. I had been injured for six days, and another without medical attention would do no harm. I was damned if I was going to miss a good blow-out by spending the weekend in hospital.

19

HEART OF DARKNESS

MR KAY TURNED slowly towards me with a thoughtful expression on his face. He gave my hugely swollen leg a perfunctory prod with his forefinger and I winced. Then as he turned again to the X-ray glowing on the screen he bent forward and stared intently at the picture. The rest of his team dutifully leaned with him, those on the outside performing a twisting bend and cocking their heads to one side. Mr Kay straightened abruptly so that for a second they all seemed to be bowing to him.

'It's a terrible ankle, Joe,' he said at last, and my heart sank.

'How terrible?' I asked nervously.

'Well, it's a comminuted fracture of both tibia and fibula.'

'What does comminuted mean?'

'Exploded, might be a better description. Both sides have sheared off where the talus has driven up into the foot here,' he said, pointing at a vague white blur on the X-ray. The team nodded knowingly.

'What's a talus?'

'It's the square-shaped block of bone on the foot that forms the centre of the joint. Anyway, it would appear', he continued, 'that much of the bone below the shear point has been crushed. I'd say about fifty per cent of the ankle is mush.'

'Ah, I see,' I said, not really seeing anything. I had a brief vision of Neil Foster who had broken his ankle so badly while soloing a rock climb that the doctors he consulted had considered amputating his foot. 'Can you put it back together?' I asked Mr Kay doubtfully.

'Well, it's very, very bad.' He looked thoughtfully at the X-ray.

'I seem to have a knack when it comes to breaking bones. No half measures and all that nonsense,' I said with an attempt at cheerfulness.

'Quite. And this time I think it needs fusing.'

'Fusing? The old stiff leg treatment?' I felt that I was on comfortably familiar ground.

'It's not as bad as fusing a knee, I grant you. You won't have a limp, but you definitely won't climb again.'

'I've heard that before.' This was better.

'The problem is that there isn't enough bone to fuse it.' He turned to his team and had a brief mumbled debate before saying any more to me.

'Best thing we can do is to put a bolt through your heel and one through your shin bone, pull the foot back out of the joint where it has impacted, plaster it into position and then hope that the bone fragments all coalesce back into their former positions.'

'Ouch!' I winced, uncomfortable when orthopaedic surgeons go into gruesome details. 'Will that work then?'

'I can't tell you. As I said, it's a terrible ankle. We will have to wait and see.'

He started to walk away as the team made notes for the operation scheduled for the following morning.

'Mr Kay?' I called and he turned to me. 'I thought you might like to have this,' I said, holding out a copy of *Touching the Void*.

'Thank you,' he said, reading the inscription I had written and laughing. *'To Mr Kay – We must stop meeting like this! Joe.'*

I awoke the next morning to the foul smell of anaesthetic gas on my breath, an Omnipon injection in my thigh, and the sight of two long kebab skewers poking out of the plaster on my lower leg at shin and heel.

Two and a half months later I sat in Mr Kay's consulting room and waited for his prognosis.

'Bad,' he said, shaking his head. 'Very bad. It's very fragile here' – he pointed to what looked like a hole in the fibula – 'and appears to be splitting here.' He indicated some faint white cracks. 'See how you get on, but I suspect you'll need more work on this. We've got enough bone to fuse it now.'

'Whoa!' I held up my hand. 'Not just yet. You never know, it might work out, like the knee did.'

'I doubt it.'

'Well, before I go for a fusing I want to put it through its paces and see what it can tolerate. I'm due to go on an expedition to Nepal in two months' time. That should be a good test.'

'I don't suppose it's any good my telling you not to go,' Kay said with a resigned expression. 'No. Don't bother answering that one.'

During my months in plaster I worked on my novel, *The Water People*, and by the time I set out for Nepal in September it was nearly finished. One advantage of breaking my legs was that it made me sit down and work.

Before leaving, I showed the post-operative X-rays to my physiotherapist, Ted Morgan Jones. In his opinion, the fibula was still broken, and that was depressing news. He lent me a special air-filled ankle splint which I wore inside my boot to prevent me rolling the ankle and snapping whatever tenuous link was left. I joined Mal Duff and some incredulous clients in Katmandu and prepared for the long walk-in to Pumori – a beautiful pyramid-shaped 7,000-metre mountain at the head of the Khumbu valley, where our base camp was dominated by the huge cirque of Nuptse, Lhotse and Everest.

After flying in to the tiny airstrip at Lukla, we set off on the seven day walk, but within an hour I realised that the ankle was too unstable to cope with the rough ground. Any hope of climbing Pumori was dashed. Fortunately I had had the foresight to bring a pair of crutches with me, so I decided to see how far I could get on them. To my amazement, I not only reached base camp but climbed with Mal up to the site of camp two at 20,500 feet. After that I could barely take my weight on the ankle and decided enough was enough. The knee damaged in Peru, on what was now my good leg, was beginning to complain of the workload. Two days later I watched the tiny specs of Mal, his wife Liz and Mark Warham approaching the summit of Pumori and then turned and crutched my way back towards Lukla, reaching it in the astonishingly fast time of four days, much to the annoyance of many struggling trekkers.

I was seething with frustration and anger. Tom Richardson had arrived the day before I left camp and we planned to climb the mountain together, but it was impossible. I left in a rage of self-pity, crutching hard and fast in an effort to vent my anger. It was yet another cruel unfair blow. *Why hadn't it been Mal who had been hurt on Pachermo? Why couldn't I have done some lowering for a change? And why did the fracture have to be so bad?*

While I was storming through Nepal in a self-righteous tantrum, Tom watched Mal and the others return triumphantly to base. Ari Gunnerson, an Icelandic fisherman, who had joined the trip as a climbing client, set off the following day on a solo bid for the summit, despite Mal's warning not to go alone. Ari was a quiet man who I had come to like during the three weeks I had known him. He had shown us photographs of the mountains in Iceland, and there had been pictures of his ten-year-old son catching salmon in a fast-running icy stream. We were so enchanted by his enthusiasm and the beauty of Iceland that we promised to join him for a climbing holiday the following spring.

I arrived back at Katmandu airport five days after leaving Tom and the team. Having booked in at the hotel, I ordered a beer and telephoned Biman Air to change the date of my flight home. The phone rang as soon as I had replaced the receiver. A voice at the other end said that he was from Rover Treks, Mal's agents in Nepal, and what he had to tell me came as a dreadful shock. A runner had arrived at Lukla with the news that Ari was dead. I said thank you and put down the phone, feeling numb.

'Do you know why I want to climb Pumori?' Ari had asked me on the walk-in. 'Because two Icelandic climbers were killed attempting to climb it two years ago. I want to do it as a memorial for them, you see.'

I felt a superstitious chill run down my spine. 'Were they your friends?' I asked.

'I knew them, yes. There are not so many mountain climbers in Iceland. Mostly we are fishermen.'

'It's not a very good reason to climb a mountain, Ari,' I said.

'It is as good as any other reason,' he said confidently, and I couldn't argue with him. After Pachermo, I wasn't entirely sure why I was climbing. To say it felt right seemed altogether inadequate. Ari clearly thought the memory of his friends was important, and it felt right to him. I wanted to say that they were gone, that they would never know of his memorial – and don't, whatever he did, climb for the sake of the dead, but I kept silence.

Liz Duff and Mark Warham arrived in Katmandu two days after I received the news of Ari's death. Ari had successfully climbed the mountain in a very fast time, they told me, and was descending to camp two when the accident happened. For some strange reason, best known to himself, Ari had left his helmet and harness behind and had taken the wrist loop off his ice axe. Perhaps it was to save weight, but even so, it was the act of an inexperienced man.

A German climber saw Ari stop to take a drink of water less than a hundred feet from the safety of camp two. A single lump of ice detached itself from the cliffs on the ridge above and fell hundreds of feet down a mountain face thousands of feet wide and struck Ari a stunning blow on the head. He had fallen slowly at first, dropping his axe, which, without the wrist sling, rested forlornly on the easy-angle slope. Ari was seen to regain consciousness as the slope steepened but it was too late and, without the axe, he was unable to arrest his fall. He plunged thousands of feet down the couloirs below camp two. His body was never recovered. He has become a mute memorial to his two Icelandic friends. His name and the date of his death are carved into a granite slab of rock at base camp, with a backdrop of Mount Everest looming behind. It isn't much of a memorial.

Ari's death confused me more than any of the other deaths with which I'd had to come to terms. It seemed somehow so wrong. All the others had been talented and highly motivated mountaineers. They had known the risks and accepted them. Ari had had neither the time nor the good fortune to be able to do the same. Why that single lump of ice should have hit him is something that will always haunt me. That it should all come down to luck, chance, fate, whatever your ability, seemed so unfair, so unreasonable, so utterly to refute any notion of control.

Back in Sheffield Mr Kay confirmed that the ankle was, to all intents and purposes, still broken. I was booked in for a major operation during the Christmas period. In four hours of brilliant surgery he nailed, screwed, pinned and grafted the ankle together and saved it, at least temporarily, from fusing.

The Water People was finished, ready for publication the following spring and I cast around for something else to write. I had become morbidly obsessed with the number of friends I had lost over the fourteen years in which I had been climbing. Ari's death, and a heightened awareness of how many close calls I had experienced, caused me to doubt everything I had done. There was a remorseless attrition involved, and I couldn't square it with my own addiction to the sport, if sport it can be called. All my climbing friends acknowledged that they had experienced the same attrition yet, when pressed, they seemed strangely reluctant to comment upon it.

'It's just something you have to accept. It comes with the territory.'

'Everyone who died made some sort of mistake; the lesson is to learn from them and not make the same mistakes.'

'If the risk wasn't there, I wouldn't do it and nor would you.'

'They are our ghosts. They post warnings to us. We need them.'

Everyone had a glib phrase, a swift sound bite theory that scratched the surface but refused to delve very deeply. Tiring of climbers who cleverly side-stepped the truth and hid behind a well-constructed rationale that justified the slaughter, I thought that maybe I should write about what I had experienced and see if I could come to an honest conclusion.

It is not, as Christopher Isherwood once said of the search for the Northwest Passage, 'an adventure chosen because despite the appalling dangers and discomforts it is easier to face than the emotional trials of ordinary human life.'

Far from avoiding the trials of life, the danger enables 'ordinary life' to be seen in a true perspective, to be appreciated and cherished. And the addiction lies more in the setting off than it does in the arrival; it lies in deciding to go, to act, rather than in the achievement. It is hidden in the mournful horn of the ship, the roar of the aircraft jets, and the steam blasted whistle of the train racing across empty lands towards unknown futures.

I may know what I have looked for, what I wanted. I know quite a lot about fear and have some notion of death. I know my strengths and weaknesses. Sometimes I feel I know what it is that calls me back, and then I lose it again. I like the shift of perspective, days looking over the edge into the world where the ghosts have stepped, and returning with a fuller view of living.

I regret none of it. At times I didn't like the fear, and the pain, and sometimes the grief. If my earlier ambitions were cut short by injuries, well then, that is how it is. Other things were created in their place. I should have died in the avalanche on the Courtes, or during the disastrous bivouac on the Dru, in the crevasse in Peru and on the fall on Pachermo. I'm grateful to be alive but I can't understand why. I try not to think about the accidents and the questions they evoke. They were, on one level, terrible experiences, full of pain and despair and extremes of fear I never want to feel again. But I feel privileged to have enjoyed such moments in my life. I have seen things about myself and my friends that I would never otherwise have seen. I have discovered the scale of my strength and the depth of my frailty and have been forced to accept, however reluctantly, our fragile mortality.

It seems to me that I have lived my life like Billy Liar, and it sometimes becomes difficult to separate the dreams from the reality. So many of the things I once dreamed of doing I suddenly found myself doing. I have accumulated an impressive number of broken ribs and limbs, and hundreds of stitches and scars. When I'm tired on a damp winter day, I ache in places I didn't know I had, and now I have the luxury of being able to limp on whichever leg I like. But the abiding memories are of fun and laughter, never taking things too seriously, and once the pain of loss has eased, the laughing memories return.

Perhaps it is simply the doing of it that makes any sense. It was Andy Fanshawe who seemed to me to come closest to explaining what I sensed it was all about. After Andy retired as the National Officer of the BMC I had congratulated him on breaking the jinx. So many of the previous officers had been killed in the mountains that it had become a standard black joke to issue dire warnings to the present incumbent. Andy replied that all his predecessors had died after they had retired, and then he laughed uproariously at my alarmed expression, delighted that the joke had backfired on me. When next I met him at a symposium on adventure in the Plas-y-Brenin Outdoor Centre in Wales, where we were both giving slide lectures, I asked him about the attrition. What did he feel about all the deaths that seemed to make a mockery of what we did? He dismissed them.

'You can't dwell on them,' he said, 'it gets you nowhere. Listen, have you ever felt totally confident before a climb?'

'How do you mean?' I asked.

'It's a feeling,' he said, 'of absolute confidence. Sometimes you are standing beneath a big climb, a really serious climb, and you have weighed everything up, looked at the mountain and the difficulties, everything, and it's dark and quiet as you stand there, alone, beneath it, and suddenly you know you are going to succeed. You are absolutely sure, have no doubts. It's like nothing else you have ever known, and there's no reason for it, no logic, but you know, deep down you know, for certain. Have you ever had that?'

'Once, maybe twice,' I said, and he nodded.

'Do you think you'll ever have it again?'

'I don't know . . .' I hesitated, taken aback by the question. 'After Pachermo I don't know whether I can ever feel like that again. No, I suppose if I'm honest, I don't think I'll feel that way again.'

'In that case,' Andy said firmly, 'you should stop climbing.'

His words hit me like a slap across the face. I didn't know what to say, I could say nothing.

'That's a bit harsh, Andy,' Victor Saunders interjected. 'It's not as cut and dried as that.'

'Well, for me it is,' he replied, 'I have to know that the possibility is there, that I will feel like that again sometime. *I have to.*'

And he was right. Rather than ask questions why, and try to interpret the future by looking at the past, Andy looked forward to what the future could offer him. If, at any point, he believed that climbing could no longer offer him that sense of absolute confidence, a taste of immortality, then he would stop climbing and search elsewhere.

Four months after our conversation, while climbing Eagle Ridge on Lochnagar, Andy took a massive fall and died of his injuries. I'll remember him as someone brimming with enthusiasm and a zest for life, laughing, and full of confidence. Maybe on that day, on Eagle Ridge, his guard was down. It would be no surprise. I have felt that certainty only twice in all the years I have climbed, but the experience was enough to keep me coming back.

Armed with such certainty, I discovered the indescribable feeling that comes with stepping into a new perspective – as powerful on the first step as it is on the last, at the base or on the summit, the intensity only gradually fading on return to the valley. Taking heed of all I know and sensing the spectral figures from the past posting their simple warnings, I start the journey with a separate part of my mind that doesn't understand what I am doing but seems to whisper,

'*I'll go with you, then, since you must play this game of ghosts.*'

EPILOGUE

I HAVE A PIECE of Hemingway's prose glued to my word processor. It's a small extract from the epilogue to *Death in the afternoon*.

> The great thing is to last and get your work done and see and hear and learn and understand; and write when there is something that you know; and not too damned much after. The thing to do is work and learn to make it.

I thought it was done. I have written what I know, done my work and tried to learn and understand. I have come full circle. There is no more to write. I look at the words I have written and hope they will still be true in a year's time, and maybe a decade, but surely not a lifetime. There are many things that I will suddenly remember and wish I had put them into the book, but it will be too late. I decided it was done, printed it out, and sent it off to my publisher. Now I find that I must write too damned much after.

Towards the end of September 1992 I heard news of storms and floods in the Karakoram. Climbing friends returning from the area said the weather had been appalling. Mark Miller, Rob Spencer and Victor Radvils were climbing on Nanga Parbat; Jon Tinker had also been on the mountain. We all knew how serious and dangerous Nanga Parbat was as a mountaineering objective and in Sheffield were silently rooting for them, wishing them to come back safe. From a confused overheard conversation I had the gist of it. They were safely off the mountain. I knew that after the expedition Mark and

Victor were flying from Pakistan to Nepal to attempt Makalu II. Rob was flying home, and later I heard that Jon Tinker was safely off the mountain and planning to return to England shortly. The weight of anxiety was lifted after two months of worry.

Brendan Murphy and Kate Phillips were also safely returned from attempting Shani Peak in Pakistan. A metre of snow overnight, Brendan had written cheerfully on his postcard, and, although they had failed to climb Shani, I sensed an element of relief behind his words that they had come through safely. Paul Nunn had returned from his expedition to the north side of the Ogre, and earlier Stephen Venables had come home safely, though severely battered, with Chris Bonington and Victor Saunders after an epic accident and rescue on Panchuli V in the Kumaun Himalaya. Everyone I knew had come through with heads full of magic and stories to tell of places seen to inspire future visits. The merry-go-round of departing friends would temporarily cease until December, when friends would head off once more – to Patagonia, to Ecuador, and in the spring to the Himalayas. Then it would start all over again.

I returned in from a windy leaf-blown walk with Muttley, my hairy black and white mongrel, and flicked the kettle on for a cup of coffee. I switched on the television to catch the early evening news before going down to the Foundry climbing wall. There was a picture of a damp cloud-wrapped hillside and the instantly recognisable features of Nepalese porters picking their way gingerly through smouldering debris. An airplane's tail fin stuck up into the low cloud, with the green lettering of PIA clearly visible through the rain. I sat up and reached for the remote control to turn up the sound and hear the newsreader describe the scene of devastation after the Pakistan Airbus 300 had smashed into a hillside ten miles south of Katmandu. ' . . . *at least thirty-five Britons are feared to be among the 167 passengers and crew. It seems that there is no possibility of finding any survivors. Many of the passengers were Europeans destined for trekking and climbing holidays in Nepal . . .'*

The picture changed. A porter sifted through a pathetic heap of scattered belongings. A partly-burnt travel bag, a damp passport, and the alloy gleam of a karabiner lying in the trampled earth. Everything bar the tail fin had been shattered into pieces no bigger than a couple of square feet. I didn't need to be told that there were no survivors. It was brutally obvious. The massive destruction and total annihilation were so beyond my experience that it seemed unreal.

My first thought was of Tom. He was due to fly out to Nepal to lead a trek, but I couldn't remember the date of his departure. I rang his number and was dismayed to get his answering machine. I left a message, asking whether he was dead, and put down the phone, feeling foolish. At least the others were safe. I knew that, and the more I thought about it, the more certain I became that Tom wasn't leaving until the following week.

An hour later I met John Stevenson in the Foundry.

'Have you heard about that crash in Katmandu?' I asked him.

'Yes,' he said with a solemn face. 'I caught it on the news on the way here.'

'That's the second one in two months. I knew that Katmandu was dangerous but this is ridiculous.'

'And it *was* a PIA flight,' he added.

'I'm booking Royal Nepal when we go in the Spring,' I said, but John didn't hear me. He looked distracted.

'I'm worried about Victor and Mark,' he said quietly.

'Don't be silly. They are already in Nepal . . .

'No, they're not.'

'I thought Richard said Victor had telephoned from Katmandu?'

'No, he rang from Rawalpindi, said they were on their way to Karachi for the flight to Nepal.'

'You're joking?'

'I'm not. I reckon something has happened. I've had this feeling before. I think they were on that plane.'

'Come on, think about it,' I said uncertainly. 'Victor rang ages ago. They could have taken any number of flights. No, they'll be alright . . . ' And I had hardly finished speaking before Eileen appeared and said, 'They've gone. They were on the flight.' I looked up at John in disbelief.

'I knew it.' He turned away.

And that was it. Gone. Blown away, finished, all gone in one stupid air crash. *Bang*. Straight into a hillside with not a chance. There were four instructors I knew from Plas-y-Brenin with them.

It was madness. How many years of risk-taking had gone into the lives of those six people. Sixty, a hundred years of collective climbing experience between them, all those countless times they had stepped too close to the line and struggled back from the edge of things. The risks they had taken because they knew what they were doing, they had chosen to be there, and then gone in a moment of meaningless destruction on a cloud covered hillside.

If Mark and Victor had been swept away by an avalanche, they would be no less dead, and we no less sad. But that at least we could have understood. They would have been doing what they loved. If they had died in the mountains we could have learned something, analysed why it had happened and, comforted by the understanding, been able to accept the loss. They would have become the ghosts posting warnings when next we went to the hills. We could have celebrated their lives because we knew how and why they had died.

Instead they were stolen from us. I felt as if I had been mugged. It was so unexpected, violent and senseless, a mockery of any neat conclusions that I had tried to squeeze from the experience of my life.

Ghosts. Ghosts everywhere I look, all I see are ghosts – or perhaps I am the ghost, a spectre of my past, standing in the rubble of my present, anxiously awaiting the future. The one certainty is that I will be gone soon, and in going so will a legion of ghosts.

Maybe I am wrong, and there are no ghosts. Those spectral figures are simply a way of convincing oneself that there can be a reason for it all. And if the ghosts are gone, I wonder whether anything I have written, anything I have thought, is worth the time or paper it uses.

On a crisp sunny day at the end of October a memorial service was held in St Chad's church in Sheffield. I don't suppose it matters how we remember them or where they were at the time, or how they died. For me, different memories drift by unexpectedly, made funnier and the more poignant by the passing years. The fact that they've all gone seems unimportant now. We are still here, playing our silly game of life, forced eventually to forget the sadness and remember the brilliance and the good times and what they gave us. So much more, it sometimes seems, than we ever gave them. If there are any ghosts they are in my mind, in the haunting echoes of distant laughter, chuckling down from the past.

'That's three dead in six months,' I said to John in The Broadfield that night. 'I wonder who's next?'

'I know what you mean,' he said. 'Maybe we'll get two years off now. It's about one a year, I reckon, so we're in credit by two.'

'One a year. God, it's a mugs game. Where will it end?'

John looked at me over an empty pint glass with a bleak expression, then laughed, and said, 'Who knows? And who cares? It's your round.'

★

REMEMBER

Remember me when I am gone away,
Gone far away into the silent land:
When you can no more hold me by the hand,
Nor I half turn to go yet turning stay.
Remember me when no more day by day
You tell me of our future that you plann'd:
Only remember me; you understand
It will be late to counsel then or pray.
Yet if you should forget me for a while
And afterwards remember, do not grieve:
For if the darkness and corruption leave
A vestige of the thoughts that once I had,
Better by far you should forget and smile
Than that you should remember and be sad.

Christina Rossetti (1830–1894)

ACKNOWLEDGEMENTS

IN THIS BOOK I have looked back on my experiences and those of my friends and tried to make some sense of them, for myself as much as anyone else. It is not an attempt to explain why people climb. Mountaineering is a highly subjective experience, different for each individual. For the most part we were engaged in extreme standards of Alpine and Himalayan climbing, and so the risks were high.

Four of my friends died while I was writing the book and I was constantly forced to re-assess what I was trying to say, what I felt. I wanted to celebrate the good times, the brilliance, the life enhancing aspect of climbing – and sometimes it became extremely difficult.

My family, and especially my sister, Sarah, figure prominently in the first part of the book, and I feel that I may not have credited them with all the love and support they have always given me. Sarah was my closest companion for so much of my life that it is easy to take for granted the affection and love that bound us in the early years and forget how much I owe to her for such a wonderful childhood.

I would like to thank all the friends who listened to my questions, helped me to get my thoughts organised, and who were so helpful in providing photographs, and especially Pat Lewis for her help with assessing and scanning them.

Without the generous sponsorship of ˙Perpetual Independent Fund Management, and in particular Roger Cornick, the Ama Dablam expedition would not have succeeded. I cannot repay the debt I owe to Mal Duff who

THIS GAME OF GHOSTS

saved my life on Pachermo in 1991. I seem to have accumulated a lot of these debts in my mountaineering career. I must also thank John Stevenson, Eileen Cooper, Richard Hazsko, Geoff Birtles, Meg Stokes, and especially Jacqueline Newbold, for their unflagging enthusiasm and support.

Tony Colwell, my editor at Cape, gave me invaluable help and advice, as he has done on both my previous books, and without him I would be lost.